THE INNER CITADEL

THE INNER CITADEL

Essays on Individual Autonomy

Edited by
JOHN CHRISTMAN

New York   Oxford
OXFORD UNIVERSITY PRESS
1989

Oxford University Press

Oxford   New York   Toronto
Delhi   Bombay   Calcutta   Madras   Karachi
Petaling Jaya   Singapore   Hong Kong   Tokyo
Nairobi   Dar es Salaam   Cape Town
Melbourne   Auckland

and associated companies in
Berlin   Ibadan

Published by Oxford University Press, Inc.
200 Madison Avenue, New York, New York 10016

Oxford is a registered trademark of Oxford University Press

Library of Congress Cataloging-in-Publication Data
The Inner citadel : essays on individual autonomy
/ edited by John Christman.
p.   cm.
Some of the essays, which have been edited for this volume,
were originally presented at the annual spring conference
of the Philosophy Dept. of VPI in May 1987.
Bibliography: p.   Includes index.
ISBN 0-19-505861-5   ISBN 0-19-505862-3
1. Autonomy (Philosophy)   2. Individuality.
I. Christman, John Philip.
B808.67.I56   1989
126—dc 19   88-33280   CIP

2 4 6 8 9 7 5 3 1

Printed in the United States of America
on acid-free paper

To Mary Beth

Acknowledgments

The opportunity to begin this project was provided when the philosophy department at Virginia Polytechnic Institute decided on the topic of "Individual Autonomy" for its annual spring conference in May 1987. At that conference, earlier versions of the papers by Gerald Dworkin (Chapter 15), Russell Hardin, Thomas Hill, James Rachels and William Ruddick, David A. J. Richards (Chapter 16), and Susan Wolf were presented. I therefore am very grateful to VPI for the resources it provided for these meetings, as well as to the participants. Support for the conference was provided as well by a grant from the Franklin J. Matchette Foundation. Also, I would like to thank those who presented formal comments on the papers there, including Lawrence Becker of Hollins College and James Klagge and Eleonore Stump of VPI. I am especially grateful to my colleagues in the philosophy department at VPI for their help in developing the idea of both the conference and the ensuing anthology, in particular Harlin Miller (who was assistant director of the conference), Eleonore Stump, and Deborah Mayo for their advice and ideas.

The other papers (including the pieces by Dworkin and Wolf given at the conference) have appeared in print prior to this collection. Their sources are noted at the beginning of each article. I would like to thank the various journals and presses (as well as the authors) for their kind permission to reprint these excellent pieces.

During the academic year 1987–88 I was a visiting faculty member in the philosophy department at the University of California at San Diego, which with its resources and the encouragement of its members, generously supported those aspects of this project undertaken there. Richard Arneson and Nicholas Jolley were especially helpful with advice and encouragement. In addition, Thomas Christiano of the University of Chicago provided characteristically generous ideas and suggestions throughout the process of putting the volume together.

I have also benefited from those members of the staff of Oxford University Press who helped guide this project to fruition, especially Cynthia A. Read and Inger M. Forland. In addition, several referees, who must (alas) remain anonymous, offered valuable advice on the organization of the volume as well as the substance of my Introduction. I utilized many of their suggestions and wish I could thank them by name. I hope that they recognize their suggestions and think that I have done them justice.

September 1988 J. C.
Blacksburg, Virginia

Contents

THE INNER CITADEL

1

Introduction

John Christman

> I wish my life and decisions to depend on myself, not on external forces of whatever kind. I wish to be the instrument of my own, not other[s'] acts of will. I wish to be a subject, not an object. . . . I wish to be somebody, not nobody.
>
> It is as if I had performed a strategic retreat into an inner citadel—my reason, my soul, my 'noumenal' self—which, do what they may, neither external blind force, nor human malice, can touch. I have withdrawn into myself; there, and there alone, I am secure.
>
> Isaiah Berlin

Although in their original context[1] these phrases are used to describe the concept of positive liberty, they also eloquently evoke the essence of what, in an important sense, is that concept's identical twin, individual autonomy. Also, it is admittedly somewhat disingenuous to borrow the metaphor of an inner citadel to introduce a discussion of autonomy, since as students of Berlin will know, his use of the image is precisely to *attack* the plausibility of the notion of positive liberty or autonomy. But if the concept of autonomy—which refers to an authentic and independent self—is to be defended as a coherent idea as well as a value to be protected and sought, it will be suggestively captured, I think, by the metaphor of such a citadel. The walls of this structure may well be built with the bricks of those moral principles that all rational choosers are constrained to accept, or (at the other extreme) with the effects of social and individual conditioning that shape our personal histories. That all depends, of course, on the contours of what turns out to be the most plausible theory of individual autonomy. And indeed such a theory may well spurn the notion of a deeper "true" self altogether. But the internal complexity of the concept, as well as the deep disagreements over the meaning and importance of the term with which the history of Western thought is replete, calls for a sustained and focused treatment. Hence the present collection, which brings together both recently published work as well as new essays that, sometimes indirectly, illuminate this crucial notion.

Ideas and theories that make crucial use of the notion of autonomy, or what amount to close variations on that theme, are ubiquitous in the history of Western moral and political philosophy. Plato's view of the ruling part of the soul which represents the highest self—the purely intellectual part of the person poised to act on the basis of ideas alone—begins one strand in the concept. This was picked up and expanded by Augustine, in his insistence that the truly free person is guided only by the rational part of the soul. The Stoics, especially Epictetus, echo another major theme in their ideal of the truly free person as one moved only by rational desires, free of "lower" impulses and unfulfillable wishes. Rousseau takes up the mantle in his discussion of the general will as the collective expression of the self-legislating person involved in the cooperative business of a community. Here the guiding influence of the higher, rational self is replaced (or expanded) by the idea of the citizens' collective interests, considered reasonably in the light of the interests of every individual. It is this view, that self-government necessarily is the expression of one's rational will generalized across other human points of view, that was so influential to Kant, who makes autonomy such the centerpiece of his moral theory. Autonomy as self-legislation from the point of view of the impartial observer becomes, for Kant and later for John Rawls, the very expression of the free moral person. Kant is the one figure who looms so large in this history that his views are treated in a separate piece by Thomas Hill below. After Kant, John Stuart Mill also develops a version of the concept of individual autonomy in *On Liberty*, though this is not often emphasized, perhaps because of its seeming tension with his Utilitarianism. This is to say nothing of the use the notion is put to by Hegel and the Idealists, natural rights theorists up through Robert Nozick, and even Existentialists in their conception of the radically free self.

But this rich and multifarious history is glossed here only to provide a backdrop for the present collection, which, again except for Kant, is focused on the work of contemporary theorists. So many contemporary debates and queries turn crucially on the concept of autonomy—its nature and boundaries—that it is difficult to introduce the subject succinctly.[2] Often, of course, it is not the word 'autonomy' that is utilized in many of these contexts; writers prefer to speak about freedom, for example. And this leads many to resist the idea that there is any plausibly consistent use of the concept of autonomy. They consequently shy away from an idea that, outside of the Kantian tradition, is a comparatively *un*analyzed notion, compared especially to 'freedom' which has gotten so much more recent analytical attention. I think that this neglect of autonomy is a mistake, however, and for reasons I will presently suggest, see the need for more direct attention to this murky notion than it has traditionally received.

There are two basic reasons for organizing the following sustained and direct analysis of the concept of individual autonomy. First, while it is certainly true that the notion of autonomy is utilized in a variety of contexts in ways that suggest it names a cluster of disparate concepts, it is nevertheless useful to search for a specifiable and defensible conceptual core, which if it does not lie at the center of the various uses of the idea, does serve to connect those disparate uses. Second, it is on the very specification of this idea, described as the bare essentials of self-government to be suggested below, that so many crucial and seemingly intractable theoretical conundrums center, as the essays here will indicate. In addition, various other issues, ostensibly concerning quite different questions, turn back to the notion of autonomy for determination of their resolution: issues ranging from free will, to paternalism, to educational strategies, to the problem of exogenous preference formation in social theory. In this introduction my intention is first to discuss what the nature of that core notion might be and how a certain construal of it might be defended. I will then illustrate my second point—that autonomy, so conceptualized, is crucial in a wide variety of important theoretical debates—by giving a brief overview of the ways in which such debates revolve around the concept of autonomy as it is construed in each case. Now as I admitted, some of the writers included here avoid the use of the word 'autonomy' altogether in their papers, but I will suggest how the various and seemingly unrelated problems with which they are grappling are connected in the focus they all must make on this core notion.

One Idea or Many?

Joel Feinberg is explicit in his doubts that the idea that 'autonomy' has a single, coherent meaning. In his chapter he attempts to explicate the related notions that function to formulate the general conception of what he calls personal autonomy. He claims that "the word 'autonomy' has four closely related meanings," (p. 28) which refer either to the "capacity" to govern oneself, the "actual condition" of self-government, an ideal of virtue derived from that conception, and the "sovereign authority" to govern oneself. A full theory of autonomy, he suggests, would spell out the relations among these different meanings of the term and presumably would support the various implications of the notion of autonomy in its different guises. He then proceeds to illuminate those "virtues" that, he claims, exemplify the condition of autonomy.

However, nothing Feinberg says in his explication of the related manifestations of autonomy disturbs the claim that there is an important *core* upon which these related ideas rest (or grow out of). First, the four "meanings" of autonomy listed by Feinberg all center on just such a conceptual core: the actual *condition* of autonomy defined as a psychological ability to be self-governing. If I am trying to give an account of some property X, I will be looking for the major conditions of X actually obtaining. It is not inconsistent with seeing this as the core notion to point out, as Feinberg does, that there are related concepts corresponding to a *capacity* for X, seeing X as a *character ideal*, and the supposed *right* to X. These are ideas whose meaning must rest on the central account of X itself.

Feinberg is in some ways aware that the actual condition of autonomy is the key concept in the account of the property, but he explicates this notion again as a list of disjointed characteristics. These characteristics are intended to be exemplary of the various virtues that autonomy represents. While I will not go through the list here, one might contend that even these traits derive their meaning only in their relation to the more basic idea of self-government and can all be explained in terms of that notion. Feinberg may well not be averse to this contention in that the traits of "authenticity" and "self-determination" he discusses could straightforwardly be read as the core ideas of which the other characteristics in his list are extensions and variations.

This is of course not to deny that there is a wide variety of uses of the concept of individual autonomy that are extensions of, or related to, the idea of an actual psychological capacity for something that amounts to self-government. The latter notion is a descriptive property instantiated by some or most human beings. In many contexts, however, 'autonomy' is used to pick out, not the actual psychological condition of self-government ('PC-autonomy'), but rather a *right* not to be treated in certain ways. Specifically, autonomy as right ('R-autonomy') is a right against actions that attempt to disrupt or undercut one's PC-autonomy.[3] When a person brainwashes me they violate my R-autonomy by interfering with my ability to critically evaluate my desires and choices. Such is also the case with many threats, manipulations, and acts of violence. These acts interfere with my ability to control a certain area of my own life that should be left strictly up to me. My inner citadel is bombarded, as it were.

This still, however, may not capture all uses of R-autonomy. In some instances, my R-autonomy is violated when, although the capacity to critically evaluate my own choices has not *actually* been disrupted, I have nevertheless been treated *as if* I had no PC-autonomy or without sufficient *respect* for my PC-autonomy. For example, consider the way a person might violate the autonomy of, say, his spouse, by constantly preempting her important choices about her life (whether or not to have a child, say). The person violates the spouse's R-autonomy not because he prevents her from freely analyzing and identifying with her desires and tastes (i.e., blocking her PC-autonomy), but rather by treating her *as if* she could not do so herself adequately. In this way, it becomes clear why many writers view R-autonomy as the foundation for many rights to control our lives and possessions.[4]

An Account of the Core Idea

With this in mind, I will now return to the explication of the concept of autonomy as an actual characteristic of persons (PC-autonomy). The model of autonomy that can be seen to express the core idea of self-government grows out of the seminal work of Harry Frankfurt and Gerald Dworkin represented below.[5] The model rests on the notions of lower-order and higher-order desires (or first-order, second-order, etc.). The theory of the person worked out in Frankfurt's chapter and the explicit theory of autonomy put forth by Dworkin build on this distinction. Lower-order desires (LODs) have as their object actions of the agent: a desire to *do X* or *Y*; higher-order desires (HODs), however, have as their object other, lower-order desires: a desire to desire to do *X* or *Y*. It should be pointed out at this juncture, though, that the specification of lower- and higher-order desires is strictly *structural* and do not necessarily correspond to the metaphysical or ontological entities that make up the "real" self.[6]

Building on this distinction, Dworkin's "full formula for autonomy," then, is "authenticity [of lower-order desires with which the person identifies] and procedural independence [of this process of identification]" (p. 61). These notions—authenticity and procedural independence—are spelled out this way:

> A person is autonomous if he identifies with his desires, goals, and values, and such identification is not influenced in ways which make the process of identification in some way alien to the individual. Spelling out the conditions of procedural independence involves distinguishing those ways of influencing people's reflective and critical faculties which subvert them from those which promote and improve them. (p. 61)

Identification takes place when an agent reflects critically on a desire and, at the higher level, approves of having the desire. Whether or not such critical reflection must be *rational* is a question that divides many writers on the topic, and I will return to it below. For now, let us say merely that the authenticity condition is met when the agent accepts the desire, value, or preference as part of her larger set of desires, beliefs and principles, whether or not this is done for good reasons.

Similarly, in an attempt to spell out both the characteristics essential to persons as well as give an account of free will, Harry Frankfurt writes of the free person as one who has second-order "volitions," which are second-order desires to have one's first-order desires move one all the way to action. Frankfurt's account of freedom of the will can be quite easily said to also provide an account of individual autonomy, as we are explicating the notion here. For being free (autonomous) on this account means not only being in a position to do what one wants, but also being able to *want* what one wants (p. 67f). And he speaks also of "identifying" with the LODs that one wants to be one's will (to move one to action).

Some of the basic reservations concerning this model, as discussed by both Irving Thalberg and Gary Watson below, arise from skepticism concerning the vagueness of the notion of identification. As Watson reminds us, merely having a higher-order desire that one has another lower-order desire is not sufficient to pick out the special character of autonomous wants. In such a bare account, higher-order disapproval of a desire would amount to nothing more than a conflict of wants—one at one level and one at the other. What may help here is what, in a different context, Galen Strawson has called "integration." One could say (adapting Strawson's view) that an agent identifies with a desire when, from his own point of view, that desire's "being involved in the determination of the action (citable in true rational explanations of it) *just is* his being so involved."[7] This amounts to simply acknowledging the desire as *me*, without any corresponding endorsement of it.

This, however, highlights the deep ambiguity in the concept of identification. Either identification is simple *acknowledgment* of what desires I find myself with, or built into the notion is an *evaluation* of (the having of) that desire. On the former view, identification can appear to *conflict* with (an intuitive sense of) autonomy, for I can acknowledge a desire as my own, in a straightforward sense, even though it is not the result of autonomous processes of preference formation. (Say I was secretly given addicting amounts of heroin.) I'm stuck with my preference, so to speak, and I readily acknowledge the fact. But the judgment that this desire is (regrettably) part of *me* says nothing about my autonomy in relation to it. If, on the other hand, one strengthens the requirement of identification to include an *endorsement* of the desire, then this would (implausibly perhaps) rule out the possibility of having an autonomous desire I don't approve of. To be autonomous in this way, I would have to be, in a certain sense, perfect (in my own eyes). What must be done, in further work on this sort of model, is to specify the kinds of mental acts or behaviors that will count as accepting one's desires in light of considerations of one's own autonomy.

Another of the problems that Thalberg discusses is that the model actually gives counterintuitive results in the most important types of cases—coercion situations. Imagine the familiar bank robber accosting her victim. The teller, who has no wish to be heroic in such circumstances, gives over the money to the threatening robber. Note that the unheroic teller has no higher-order desire that is in conflict with her lower-order desire to fork over the cash: in fact if she did feel a sudden surge of unexpected bravado, she would try to repress this for the sake of her safety and well-being. So on this theory, she seems to have acted autonomously, a verdict that runs counter to our usual judgment in such cases (after all, coercion situations seem like paradigm cases of the loss of autonomy).

I think, however, we need not accept this evaluation in the end. If we look more closely at the case, there are actually two operative desires that the agent has, both with the same object: giving over the money. The first is the desire to not be heroic in threatening situations. The victim we are imagining formed or fostered such a character trait well before the robbery in question, and we can assume that she would identify with such a trait, given its origins. But the other relevant desire is to give over the money to the robber *in this particular case*. Although both these desires have the same object (in this particular case), they are importantly different because they have different origins: they were adopted for differing reasons and under different circumstances. On the account of autonomy I am discussing, the second desire—to give over *this* money—is not autonomous. The reason is that the agent does not identify with it fully in at least one relevant sense, for she does not accept the desire *given the conditions of its formation*. The victim does not, in this way, "approve" of the way in which the desire to hand over this money was formed, namely under duress. She knows that the only reason she is willing to give this person money in this case is that there is a gun at her head; she desires to do it only *begrudgingly*. The desire, in this particular case, is not her own, it is not one she approves of having, because she was forced to have it. But because of her other, autonomously formed desire to give in to dangerous threats, she hands over the money. So if one's account of autonomy requires that all the relevant desires causing an action be autonomously formed, then this person is not autonomous.

This reply, of course, is plausible only if the details of a theory of identification with one's desires can be worked out, a prospect I just cast doubt upon. What the reply *does* show at this juncture, I think, is that the notion of autonomy is essentially *historical*, in that the conditions of desires and values that must be met for them to be autonomous are properties of the *formation* of those desires. The discussion of these examples seems to lead to the conclusion that whether or not a person is autonomous (or whether her desires are) turns crucially on her *past*, on how and under what conditions her desires and values were formed. At any one time, it may be impossible to tell if the person is autonomous, no matter how closely her preferences cohere or are identified with. And while I do not, in this introduction, develop a new version of the DF model that avoids the difficulties discussed, I want to suggest that this historical approach, centering on the conditions of formation of preferences in the model of autonomy, will be an essential aspect of such a new version.

There is another set of criticisms of the account we are discussing, which both Susan Wolf and Irving Thalberg discuss in their papers, and which other writers elsewhere have discussed.[8] The thrust of the objection is this: We can imagine a person who lives a completely subservient and manipulated life, and who also identifies with the first-order desires that comprise such a life. Fierce socialization, education, and conditioning throughout the person's life lead her to see, let us say, the life of a subservient housewife as her only role. But on the hierarchical analysis, she passes the test of autonomy since her HODs are consistent with her LODs. She approves of the LODs and identifies with them. Obviously, however, she is a manipulated individual whose choice of lifestyle and values are not her own in a real sense. Her values, even at the second level, are the product of her Procrustean upbringing and conditioning.

The crux of the criticism from Wolf and Thalberg is that the requirement of Procedural Independence merely introduces an infinite regress, since the acts of identification must themselves be autonomous, requiring that another act of identification take place at a higher level. And since this act must also be carried out in a way that reflects procedural independence, then a fourth level must be postulated there, and so forth. Hence the regress.

One might be tempted to dodge this charge by dropping the requirement of independence, saying that as long as second-order approval has taken place, the person is autonomous. This effectively implies that a person can have autonomous first-order desires despite having nonautonomous higher-order desires. This introduces what could be labeled the "*ab initio* problem," in that it involves the claim that desires can be autonomous without foundations, a conclusion that renders this response implausible on its face. Certainly a person cannot be autonomous at a lower level of desire when those very desires are the result of manipulation further up the hierarchy of preferences.[9]

In some ways Frankfurt can be read below as providing a reply to this problem when he writes: "when a person identifies . . . *decisively* with [a] first-order [desire], this commitment 'resounds' throughout the potentially endless array of higher orders" (p. 71). In a recent article, he has attempted to expand on this suggestion and respond specifically to the regress argument. He there claims that there is no need for a higher-order endorsement of the initial act of identification (with an LOD) as long as that endorsement is made decisively. "[An endorsement] is decisive if and only if it is made without reservation . . . [that is, it is made] in the belief that no further accurate inquiry would require [the person] to change his mind."[10] Frankfurt goes on to explain and defend this view, but it nevertheless will not solve the problem. For no matter how decisive and final a person's identification with a desire is, that identification could still be the result of obviously heteronomous manipulations (hypnosis, say, which included the directive to maintain identification with the desire *even when informed of the hypnosis*). So either we declare the person to be lacking autonomy *despite* the decisive identification with the desire (in which case identification is no longer a crucial condition for autonomy) or we declare such obviously manipulated individuals autonomous (which renders the account subject to the *ab initio* problem). Now Frankfurt could mean that it must be *objectively reasonable* for the person to identify with the desire for her to be autonomous in regards to it. This would mean that it would be reasonable from an impartial (not the person's own) point of view. This brings up the complex claim that rationality is required for autonomy, an issue to which I will later turn where I will cast doubt on the acceptability of adding stringent "external" conditions of rationality as requirements for autonomy. What my response here does indicate, though, is how once again the "structural" aspects of the relation between a person and her preferences is incomplete as a theory of autonomy unless it is supplemented with an account of the ways that those preferences are formed. So again, the autonomy of a person vis-à-vis her preferences is a function of that person's history.

These various problems with the DF model can be sorted out this way: The regress problem concerns whether or not the acts of critical reflection, by which LODs are judged to be "one's own" or not, are themselves autonomous acts of reflection. If so, must they be autonomous in the same *way* that LODs are autonomous or in a different way. That is, either:

i. The acts of critical reflection that convey authenticity onto the person's desires are autonomous, in which case the account of autonomy simply goes back one step and the same question arises at this level (the regress problem).

Or:

ii. The acts of identification are not autonomous. (This, however, gives rise to the *ab initio* problem, that is, how can a desire be autonomous if it was formed or evaluated by a process that was not *itself* autonomous.)

If (i), then either

1a. These acts of identification are autonomous in the *same way* that LODs are autonomous, which gives rise to the regress problem;

or,

1b. These acts are autonomous in a different way, in which case we are owed an account of this new way.

Now these are the possibilities, but the DF model (at least Dworkin's version) pursues the line of disjunct (i), and thus avoids the *ab initio* problem. That view includes the condition of "procedural independence," so that the acts of identification (and critical reflection) must themselves be autonomous. But this is precisely how the regress problem arises. For we ask whether this process—conferring the status of authenticity on HODs—is autonomous in the same way that identification with LODs is. If it is the same way, then Dworkin's view faces the problem of autonomy arising again at this level.

But if the process is different, then there is the problem of *incompleteness*, because we have not been told what the mysterious conditions of *this* process are. This, I think, is the true locus of the problem with the DF model: not the threat of a regress, but the incompleteness of the conditions. In the kind of cases we have been discussing, the conditioning that has rendered a person nonautonomous has been so thorough that it extends to the acts of identification themselves by which a person approves of LODs. We could solve this problem, though, by adding an additional condition, one that is meant to fill out the requirement of procedural independence, but one that avoids the regress problem. What must be true of these acts of identification for them to be characterized as "autonomy-conferring" acts of an agent (vis-à-vis other desires)? One could define this condition negatively, by specifying what must be *absent* for these acts to convey autonomy. Dworkin in fact suggests such a characterization when he refers to "distinguishing those ways of influencing people's reflective and critical faculties which subvert them from those which promote and improve them." One could call these absent factors "illegitimate external influences." One suggestion for the specification of such illegitimate influences is that they are the sorts of factors that, as a matter of psychological fact, tend to inhibit the normal functions of individual self-reflection that is necessary for autonomy. While this may be a promising direction for a defense of this approach to go, a full account and defense of it must be pursued elsewhere.

An important question that should be addressed at this point is whether the critical evaluation of desires that is constitutive of autonomy must be a *rational* process or not. More broadly, must one be rational to be autonomous vis-à-vis a certain desire and action? In this vein, Richard Lindley has discussed the contrasts between minimal, Humean conditions for rationality and more stringent Kantian requirements. On his view, neither, as it stands, is a plausible requirement for autonomy. The kind of rationality that he has in mind, which he derives from Mill and labels "active theoretical rationality," requires that an agent take an active role in the investigation of the truth of her beliefs and the validity of her desires.[11]

What is at issue here is the demand that agents display some capacity for reasoning in order to be autonomous. The issue can only be glossed here, as it is complicated by the variations admissible in particular requirements for rationality. One approach is a minimal, "subjective," conception of rationality—where this might include mere consistency of beliefs and desires internal to the agent at a time. This, however, may seem to many to be insufficient to capture what is necessary in a rationality condition for autonomy. Following Aristotle's conception of voluntary action,[12] some may not want to count a person as autonomous who is ill informed or ignorant of relevant facts bearing on a decision, even if the agent's beliefs at the time are consistent and her desires are continuous and transitive.[13]

Susan Wolf, in her discussions of moral responsibility included here, argues for what amounts to an external condition of rationality ("sanity" of a special sort) as a requirement for free (morally responsible) actions. The criteria for sanity, which she urges are (for our purposes) necessary for autonomy, are the ability to know what one is doing and the ability to know that what one is doing is right (or wrong). Further, Wolf argues that the agent must be able to evaluate herself sensibly (rationally) and *accurately*, that is "to cognitively and normatively recognize and appreciate the world *for what it is*" (p. 145, emphasis added). And so, analogous to the external rationality requirement just mentioned, Wolf demands of free agents that they have accurate beliefs—both factual *and* moral—for them to be responsible for their actions.[14]

But adding objective or "external" conditions of rationality to the requirements for autonomy (conditions regarding optimal evidence gathering, for example)[15] may in fact conflict with the concept of self-government that autonomy is intended to express. (This is not to mention the indeterminacy of a demand like Wolf's—that an agent have the correct moral view—in light of the tremendous *lack* of general agreement over even fundamental questions of morals and value.) On the view that only rational, fully informed selves are autonomous, it follows that the most fierce and uncompromising interferences with a person's value judgments, desire formation, or thought patterns are not interferences with autonomy at all if those values, desires, or thoughts are irrational ones. As long as the interfering agent has beliefs that are better supported by the objective evidence, then no loss of autonomy is suffered from any form of manipulation for the sake of more reasonable beliefs and desires. Again Isaiah Berlin weighs in most forcefully here with effective irony: "The immature and untutored must be made to say to themselves: 'only the truth liberates, and the only way in which I can learn the truth is by doing blindly today, what you, who know it, order, or coerce, me, to do, in the certain knowledge that only thus will I arrive at your clear vision, and be free like you.'"[16] Theorists who include a requirement of rationality in the conception of autonomy they build on or presuppose must take into account considerations of this sort in spelling out and defending that requirement.

Autonomy and Freedom

As I pointed out above, much of the analytical work centering on issues having to do with human freedom and autonomy concentrate more on the former concept than on the latter, and avoid mentioning the relation between the two (indeed if any is recognized). But if the words 'freedom' and 'autonomy' are scrutinized closely, then there do appear to be important differences, particularly in the scope of the properties, and especially if the model of autonomy being pursued here has any plausibility.

What our discussion of autonomy so far has suggested, I think, is that, at its most basic level of application, autonomy is more properly seen as a property of preference or desire formation[17] than a property of whole persons or of persons' whole lives. One can see this by imagining how people vary, in different aspects of their lives, in the autonomy they manifest. A smoker might be perfectly autonomous in choosing whether to watch a baseball game or read a book, but is virtually powerless against the overwhelming urge for nicotine. (I myself do not smoke but am powerless when it comes to baseball.) Whether or not such a person is autonomous *tout court* hangs on the more basic characteristics of how each of her preferences were formed (or the degree of control she has over her choices). So it must be at the level of preferences, and indeed preference formation, that the question of autonomy arises first, and the idea that whole persons are autonomous is simply a function of this more basic property. Robert Young disagrees with this though and views autonomy as a property of a person insofar as her desires fit in with her overall life plan. But he then must view this "episodic" autonomy as partial autonomy, and the question then arises how this partial autonomy is autonomy at all and what else is needed for the "full" autonomy of the person. His essay here attempts to answer these questions.[18]

Freedom, on the other hand, is a property of human action—a characteristic of the relation among desires, bodily movements, and restraints that may be facing the agent,[19] although I would argue that a full spelling out of the idea of freedom must essentially include an account of autonomy (construed as a property of preference formation). This is so because no matter how rich a conception of a restraint one works out (that one must be "free from" to be free), it will always be a further question whether the desire a person is acting on is autonomous or not.[20] A person acting on the basis of a nonautonomous preference (placed into her brain through hypnosis, say) faces no restraint in the doing of the action that is the object of the preference. In fact, the language of restraints is wholly inappropriate here, because the person is not being stopped from doing the act, she is being *forced* to do it. What makes her unfree is that, vis-à-vis that desire, she is nonautonomous. A full formula for freedom (of action) then might be proposed: to be free (in a given context) means there is an absence of restraints (positive or negative, internal or external)[21] standing between a person and the carrying out of that person's *autonomous* desires.[22]

And it is this sense of autonomy that is so central to the issue of free will (though this issue is not the focus of the following essays).[23] For what is crucial there is whether the truth of determinism implies that desires cannot be formed in ways consistent with calling them a person's *own* in the relevant sense. The question of compatibilism, for example, hinges precisely on being able to work out a notion of autonomy that captures or entails responsibility for actions (in the relevant sense) but which is not inconsistent with determinism. Does the conjunction of forces that bear on the action of an individual, insofar as that act is determined by those forces, amount to the sort of "illegitimate external influence" of the sort I suggested was incompatible with autonomy? Seen in this way, the problem of free will simply *is* the problem of working out a plausible conception of autonomy.

Kantian Autonomy

The core concept of autonomy we are discussing here may in some ways seem an unacceptably abrupt departure from the traditional Kantian notion from which most modern construals of autonomy get their pedigree. A major difference between the model being discussed here and Kant's is at the level of metaphysics. For Kant, a person's autonomy—the self imposition of laws of reason—does not take place within space and time and is not amenable to empirical explanation.[24] Nothing in the theory suggested here presupposes such claims and indeed can be seen as neutral concerning the metaphysical status of the processes that constitute autonomy. The process of critical evaluation that makes up identification with one's desires need not avoid strictly causal descriptions in its specification (though doing so, of course, immediately brings up the question of the compatibility of autonomy with determinism).

Kant also makes a connection between autonomy and the Moral Law in that being autonomous, for him, involves commitment to principles of morality as expressed by the Categorical Imperative. But autonomy need not be "moralized" in this way. It is open to the theorist of autonomy to specify morally *neutral* conditions for the autonomous formation of preferences. (Though as we have seen, Susan Wolf's view is not morally neutral, though neither is it Kantian.) Moreover, the DF model we have discussed can be interpreted as being *content* neutral, in that nothing in the conditions described rules out any *particular* desires or values from passing the test of autonomy.

Despite these radical differences, there remain certain crucial aspects that our core idea of autonomy retains in common with its Kantian ancestor. For example, there is a close connection between autonomy as we have it here and Kant's view, as discussed by Thomas Hill in his essay below, that autonomy is an expression of negative freedom, which for Kant is "the property [the will] has of being able to work independently of *alien* causes" (p. 97). The purpose of the model of autonomy we are discussing here is to articulate just how the alien character of certain causes conflicts with autonomy, and how one's "true" desires are just those that are formed independently of such causes (at least I have argued that this is the crucial question). Hill takes us through more of the details of Kant's conception of autonomy in such a way that these contrasts and similarities are made more salient.

In a recent development of his famous theory of justice, John Rawls reflects the heavy influence of Kant in that he sees autonomy as one of the principal properties of persons that determines their ability to derive the principles of morality and justice. This amounts to construing autonomy as a kind of moral neutrality by which agents can be said to construct or derive moral principles from *their* point of view.[25] Hence, for Rawls, individuals in the original position display "Rational Autonomy" and are impartial in not being guided by prior conceptions of justice; and being ignorant of any personal characteristics (race, religion, talents, place in society, and their own conception of the good), they are not biased in their judgment concerning the correct principles of justice. In this way, agents achieve "Full Autonomy" when they go on to act (in a well ordered society out from behind the veil of ignorance) in accordance with principles that are "self-imposed" in the sense that they would have been chosen (by the agents) under conditions of fair and neutral choice.

Autonomy and Utility

If there is one area of moral theory where talk of autonomy has traditionally been *un*welcome, it is utilitarianism. Despite the fact that John Stuart Mill comes very close to assigning a direct and irreducible value to autonomy in *On Liberty*,[26] modern day utilitarians have shied away from so Kantian a notion. But if the concept of autonomy is shorn of its Kantian clothing, as we see it here, there may well be a place for it in the theoretical structure of utilitarianism. In their essays included here, both Jon Elster and Lawrence Haworth argue that without consideration for autonomy, utilitarianism is seriously incomplete. Though Elster suggests that there indeed may be no room in the utilitarian framework for the property of autonomy, Haworth argues that in fact utilitarianism is committed to it. On the other hand, Russell Hardin, in his piece below, resists suggestions such as these and argues that indeed there is much to be said *against* the inclusion of the property of autonomy in the value structure of utilitarianism. I wish to pursue this question now in some detail as it is directly relevant to the more general issue of the value of autonomy.

Utilitarianism is composed of three formal elements: *consequentialism*, whereby only future states of affairs are relevant to moral questions; *welfarism*, which is the value to be promoted; and the distributive principle of *aggregation*, which stipulates that states of affairs are ranked according to the total amount of welfare instantiated in the individuals in that state. (Some have suggested, of course, alternative distributive principles, like average utilitarianism.) Welfarism, which is our principal concern here, can be defined as follows: any state of affairs, X, can be evaluated exhaustively with no more information than that concerning the utility of each of the individuals who exist in X.[27] That is, the only thing of moral value is human welfare, where welfare refers to the subjective well being of individuals as measured by a utility function. If anything has value in the moral world, it must be describable in terms of utilities. (For the purposes of this discussion, the traditional dichotomy of "preference-satisfaction" and "psychological state" conceptions of utility will be ignored.) The serious question that faces any welfarist, then, is whether or not any version of welfarism can give us a fair rendering of something that some have considered to be a profound, if not basic, human value—personal autonomy.

Welfarists can try to take account of autonomy in a great number of ways, either directly or indirectly. Seen as a property of whole persons, the quality of being autonomous can be accounted for in a purely instrumental fashion by utilitarianism. One could argue that being left free to form one's own views and character, and being given the means to develop one's critical capacity for this, is the surest method to insure happiness for oneself. Much in the way that utilitarians deal with the value of freedom (of action), an account could be given of the value of autonomy so construed. It has been argued, however, that utilitarians cannot in this way take account of the *intrinsic* value of individual autonomy (or individuality) in a way that gives proper weight to the separate dignity of persons.[28]

But could the value of autonomy at the level of preference (the concept we are investigating presently) be accounted for by welfarism? There are several possibilities for how autonomy of preferences can fit into welfarism. The fact that the preferences to be satisfied (by some action or policy) are ones that pass the test for autonomy can be seen as having either instrumental or intrinsic value for the utilitarian (as was claimed at the level of autonomous persons). Unfortunately, to say that the autonomy of preferences is of *intrinsic* value seem to conflict with the exclusivity of welfarism as a conception of value. That is, all values are reducible to welfare and welfare is the *only* value. How can there be, then, a new and different value, namely the autonomy of individual desires, that can be fit into this picture? Haworth argues that in fact the narrowness of welfarism must consequently be rejected so that this consideration can be accounted for. He presents various ways in which the satisfaction of *non*autonomous desires simply lacks value, and hence ought not to be included in the value foundations of the theory. He further suggests that in fact utilitarians are *committed* to including autonomy within their conception of value, and this is so because utilitarians are committed to certain ideas (e.g., a principle of equality), which in turn imply the value of autonomy.

More might be said, however, to point out the need for an account of autonomy within the subjective welfarism defended, for example, by Russell Hardin. He, in fact, is quite skeptical about the proper role of autonomy in the value conception of utilitarianism, whether that role be one of intrinsic or instrumental value. However, an argument can be developed, along lines different from those of Haworth and Elster, for the necessity of including a place for autonomy—at the level of preferences—in the value structure of welfarism: Traditionally, the utility of an individual is seen as a function that maps preferences onto available goods. But imagine that not only are available goods put into the utility function, but also those aspects of a person that enable her to translate available goods into satisfaction. On this model we can have preferences over goods as well as over desires, natural skills, traits of character, and the like. So these latter aspects of ourselves will also be part of a function that measures our overall well-being. Whatever it is that explains differences in tastes among individuals (the fact that one person was brought up to like Mozart and thus does, and another to like reggae music, for example) can be an argument in the function that measures welfare. With this in mind, we could rank the various combinations of tastes and available goods in terms of comparable utility. In fact we can define a "fundamental preference" (or what Rawls calls "higher order common preference")[29] as that combination of, on the one hand, tastes, character traits, and skills and, on the other, available goods, which yields the highest ranking in the comparison.

Now recall that for a welfarist any state of affairs must be evaluated solely in terms of utility information available about the individuals who populate that state. Getting back to our example, it will be the case that any person whose subjective well-being can be measured with the kind of functions I've been describing, will prefer to change places with any other person who ranks above her in the utility rankings we are considering. Hence if a person has a set of preferences—even one that is intimately connected to her history, upbringing, and character—she would, on a welfarist account, be made *better off* were she to trade in her desires and character for any other that will yield a higher ranking function of subjective well-being.

The point here is that these comparisons, limited as they must be to considerations of subjective welfare, leave totally out of account the *special relation* that obtains between a person and that person's set of (autonomous) preferences. It indeed could well be claimed that this is the very relation described by the DF account of autonomy.[30] Examples such as this are the reason that Kenneth Arrow resisted the assumption of interpersonal utility comparisons. If they are allowed, and tastes, skills, and character can be admitted as arguments in the function, then something crucial concerning the individuality of character is lost in any evaluation of the state of affairs. He writes "the autonomy of individuals, an element of incommensurability among people, seems denied by the possibility of interpersonal comparisons."[31] Arrow saw the only alternative as purely ordinal utility comparisons and thus despaired of basing a theory of justice on utility. The other alternative, of course, is to give up on, or radically amend, a welfarist conception of value altogether.

One could respond to this by suggesting another possible connection between autonomy and utility that could be exploited by a welfarist. Hardin implies, for example, that the connection between autonomy and welfare with which he is most at home is one where the desire for autonomy is just that, a desire, and hence it should be counted as among the individual's set of preferences along with all the others. This view sees autonomy as the *object* of a preference and, thus, a component of welfare whenever the person in question has such a desire. Hence, he might reply here that to the extent that the relation between a person and her or his lower order preferences is an object of special value *for that person*, then the autonomy expressing that relation can be included in the elements of her or his well-being, and welfarism is none the worse for it. But this means that for anyone who, from lack of education, delusion, or simply existentialist dread, would be indifferent about the source and nature of her preferences, such a person is considered no worse off if none of her preferences were indeed "her own" in the way that autonomy guarantees. If she doesn't want her preferences to be autonomous, then their being so is simply not a value in her case. While this maintains the intuitional austerity of the value assumptions of utilitarian theory—sticking to the subjective guns—it is not clear that such a foundation will be sound enough to support the conceptual apparatus that could amount to a plausible guide to action.

The Value of Autonomy

The foregoing discussion of the relation between welfare and autonomy brought out in some detail one of the inroads into the more general question of the value of autonomy. When working outside of a utilitarian context, however, the question of how individual autonomy fits into a generally accepted conception of value is far less puzzling. To be autonomous in the way we are discussing is seen by many as the very core of a valuable human existence. As David A. J. Richards argues in "Rights and Autonomy," individual autonomy is the basis upon which moral rights are justified and, more particularly, the right to be treated as a free and equal moral person. Hence autonomy is foundational in the explanation and justification of these crucial moral values.

Richards also argues in "Autonomy in Law" that the basic value of individual autonomy was what the Framers of the U.S. Constitution utilized to replace the classical ideal of republican political virtue as the foundation for the basic liberties of the Bill of Rights. In particular, three, progressively more stringent, conceptions of autonomy are assumed by that constitutional framework in, respectively, the requirements for minimal criminal liability, the acceptability of the excuse of necessity, and the rights enumerated in the First Amendment. The sphere of individual control that self-government defines is what those rights and liberties are specifically designed to protect.[32] Though Richards's historical case for the Framers' shift from a classical conception of public virtue to the individualistic, secular notion of autonomy is convincing, one might puzzle over how a figure like Rousseau fits into this dichotomy. While he may well have had no influence on the Framers (his rough contemporaries), his views loom theoretically large since he develops a conception of self-government that precisely *combines* the ancient reverence for virtues manifested by citizens of autonomous states with the value of individual freedom prized by "modern" conceptions of liberty and rights. Participation in democratic institutions is, for Rousseau, the very expression (as well as the requirement) of individual self-government that must compliment the individual private rights defended, for example, by Locke, for the citizen to be considered truly self-governing.

But this claim—that autonomy is the foundation for other values—is only one approach to the problem of the value of autonomy more generally. Another is suggested by what James Rachels and William Ruddick say about the value of liberty. On their view, liberty should be seen not (merely) as instrumentally good nor (merely) as intrinsically good, but rather as valuable because of its constitutive role in the conditions for a person's even *having* a life. To live a life—to carry out a life plan and pursue projects as part of one's self-realization—one must enjoy a minimal degree of liberty. It might be pointed out that this account bears an important similarity with the views of Robert Young on autonomy.

It could be added here that the Rachels/Ruddick argument would apply in as compelling a way to the role that the property of being autonomous (as discussed in this introduction) has in the formation of values at all. As we have defined it here, the core notion of autonomy can be seen as constitutive of *any* component of a person's life activities that give value to that life. In the discussion of autonomy and welfare, I suggested how the "special relation" that obtains between a person and her "true" desires is fundamental to the status of those desires (as worthy of satisfaction). This perhaps could be generalized by arguing that autonomy is at the foundation of all personal values a person can call her own, since autonomy as we have it here is nothing but the specification of that which having desires of one's own turns out to mean.

Moreover, the political implications of placing a basic value on individual autonomy should not be overlooked. For many, one of the fundamental normative principles in the formation of political institutions is to value and respect personal autonomy *equally* among citizens. As we have it here, autonomy involves the ability to critically evaluate one's desires, choices, and opportunities. What needs to be stressed is how various resources, such as education, employment opportunities, medical services, and housing, are essential to the exercise and development of these abilities. And given that the distribution and production of these resources are within the purview of control of these political institutions, it follows that the *un*equal distribution of those resources essential to the development and maintenance of these capacities *violates* this basic regard for individual autonomy. At least it appears so at this juncture, and while more must be said to defend such a line of argument, the potential for such a claim is suggested by the model of autonomy we are considering.

Gerald Dworkin, in "Autonomy, Science, and Morality," returns to the notion of autonomy he suggests in his earlier essay to investigate the relation between "moral autonomy" (which he takes to be a special case of personal autonomy) and the "autonomy" with which we judge the truth of factual beliefs. He suggests that, contrary to the accepted dogma of modern empiricist philosophy, there is not so sharp a distinction between standards of justification in the realm of value judgments and that of factual claims. This is especially true in the relation of moral autonomy to accepted standards of authority and objectivity.

Autonomy and Other Issues

While the focus of this anthology is the role that autonomy plays in various *theoretical* debates, this is intended as a groundwork for the plethora of more particular or concrete issues, the resolution of which turns centrally on a theory of autonomy. The question of the justification of paternalism, for example, comes immediately to mind.[33] What many of the approaches to that question turn on is whether or not an interference with a person's liberty for her own good can be justified in a way that is consistent with respect for that person's autonomy. One aspect of the debate over the proper nature of autonomy we have touched upon applies directly to this question, and that is whether (and in what respect) a person must be rational to be autonomous. Hence, the various means by which some try to show that limited paternalism is not inconsistent with respect for autonomy will depend crucially on the resolution of that debate.

In the realm of medical ethics, it is often asked if certain treatment (or lack of treatment) will or will not infringe on the autonomy of the patient. Does a dying patient's request to be aided in the quickening of the process of death express the true autonomous choice of that person? This will depend of course on the details of the conditions for autonomy being presupposed in the case and whether or not its requirements are known to be met.[34] Also, questions about autonomy are central to issues in feminism, where the effects of living in a patriarchal society are examined in relation to the possibility of autonomy for women.[35] Another question for which autonomy is central is what economists call "exogenous preference change," which could be seen as directly involving a claim that traditional models of welfare economics are incomplete in their inability to differentiate preferences that are and that are not processed "internally" by the agent.[36] And finally, there is a protracted debate in the area of educational theory which surrounds the question of which pedagogical strategies effectively promote the development of autonomy in the student.[37]

What might all this attention to the notion of autonomy accomplish in the disparate realms of political, moral, and legal philosophy? First, it underscores the need for a coherent and defensible *concept* of individual autonomy, one which captures in one way or another the foundational role that the idea plays in theories of moral and political values. I have suggested here that there indeed exists a model for the conceptual core of the idea of individual autonomy, though, in response to the various criticisms of it discussed below, the theory needs to shift to the "historical" perspective I described and concentrate on conditions of preference formation. I have also tried to illustrate the breadth of topics in which this (or some related) idea of autonomy is the point of central debate and controversy. So insofar as the issues I have mentioned do in fact turn on the nature and value of individual autonomy, the focused attention that this concept receives in these pages will be fruitful work indeed.

It certainly would merit the effort, if only to rescue the "inner citadel" of human character and value formation from the thick walls of obscurity that neglect of this crucial notion may have constructed.

Notes

1. Isaiah Berlin, "Two Concepts of Liberty" in *Four Essays on Liberty* (Oxford: Oxford University Press, 1969), 118–172. The quotations are from pp. 131 and 135, respectively.

2. For a survey of recent work on the topic see John Christman "Constructing the Inner Citadel: Recent Work on Autonomy," *Ethics* Vol. 99, no. 1 (Oct., 1988), 109–24. I draw on that more detailed essay in the present introduction.

3. Cf. Thomas Hill "The Importance of Autonomy" in E. Feder Kittay and D. Meyers, eds. *Women and Moral Theory* (Totowa, NJ: Rowman and Littlefield, 1987), 129–38; cf. especially pp. 133ff.

4. For a further discussion of autonomy as right, cf. Michael J. Meyer, "Stoics, Rights and Autonomy," *American Philosophical Quarterly* Vol. 24 no. 3 (1987), 267–71.

5. More recently, book-length treatments of the concept have appeared: Robert Young, *Personal Autonomy: Beyond Negative and Positive Liberty* (New York: St. Martin's Press, 1986); Richard Lindley, *Autonomy* (London: Macmillan, 1986); and Lawrence Haworth, *Autonomy: An Essay in Philosophical Psychology and Ethics* (New Haven, Conn.: Yale University Press, 1987). I will begin here with a discussion of the Dworkin/Frankfurt model (the DF model), and indicate the refinements introduced by Young, Lindley, and Haworth.

Also, this introduction was written without the benefit of Gerald Dworkin's recent book of essays on autonomy: *The Theory and Practice of Autonomy* (Cambridge: Cambridge University Press, 1988); cf. especially ch. 1. Although Dworkin revises his earlier views (as represented, for example, in chapter 3 below), it is those earlier views that are considered here.

6. For a discussion of this issue, cf. Marylin Friedman, "Autonomy and the Split-Level Self," *Southern Journal of Philosophy* Vol. 24, no. 1 (1986), 19–35 and John Christman, "Autonomy: A Defense of the Split-Level Self," *Southern Journal of Philosophy* Vol. 25, no. 1 (1987), 281–93.

7. Galen Strawson, *Freedom and Belief* (Oxford: Oxford University Press, 1986), 45.

8. Cf., for example, Friedman, "Autonomy and the Split-Level Self."

9. For further discussion of this point, cf. Friedman *ibid*, 22–23, and Christman, "Autonomy: A Defense of the Split-Level Self."

10. Cf. "Identification and Wholeheartedness" in F. Schoeman ed., *Responsibility, Character and the Emotions* (Cambridge: Cambridge University Press, 1987), 27–45 (quote from p. 37).

11. Cf. Lindley *Autonomy*, 63–70.

12. *Nichomachean Ethics*, Bk. III.

13. To add that they must also be complete could make the requirement implausibly stringent, as few of us have a complete ranking of all the goods available to us at a given time.

14. For a comprehensive discussion of the inclusion of a rationality requirement for autonomy, cf. Young *Personal Autonomy*, 10–13.

15. John Benson, for example, argues that to be "intellectually" autonomous, one must be in the "best possible position vis-à-vis the truth of one's beliefs": cf. "Who is the Autonomous Man?" *Philosophy* Vol. 58 (1983), 5–17, especially p. 8.

16. Berlin "Two Concepts," 151–52.

17. Throughout this discussion, I use the word 'preference' very broadly to refer to any desire, value, or pro-attitude an agent might have.

18. For further development of Young's views, cf. *Personal Autonomy*.

19. For an explication of the "triadic" conception of freedom, cf. Gerald MacCallum "Negative and Positive Freedom," *Philosophical Review*, Vol. 76 (1967), 312–32 and Joel Feinberg, *Social Philosophy* (Englewood Cliffs, N.J.: Prentice-Hall, 1973), chapter 1.

20. For more on this point, cf. Wright Neely, "Freedom and Desire," *Philosophical Review* Vol. 83 (1974), 32–54.

21. These are the four types of restraints mentioned by Feinberg in his analysis of freedom; cf. Feinberg *Social Philosophy*, ch. 1.

22. In an excellent discussion of the concept of freedom, William Connolly argues along similar lines, that a full conception of freedom must include conditions of critical self-scrutiny and control in the formation of a person's wants: cf. *The Terms of Political Discourse* (Lexington, Mass.: D. C. Heath & Co., 1974), chapter 4.

23. For a new installment in that ongoing debate, and one which bears directly on the Frankfurt model discussed here, cf. the essays in John Martin Fischer, ed., *Moral Responsibility* (Ithaca, N.Y.: Cornell University Press, 1986). For an approach to the problem of free will that bears on the concept of autonomy, cf. Galen Strawson *Freedom and Belief.*

24. For illumination of this point, cf. Hill "Autonomy and Benevolent Lies."

25. Cf. Rawls, "Kantian Constructivism in Moral Theory," *Journal of Philosophy*, Vol. 77, 515–79. Cf. also, Thomas Hill "The Importance of Autonomy," 131–33 for a discussion of this construal of autonomy.

26. For a discussion of the relation to liberty and self development in Mill, cf. G. W. Smith, "J. S. Mill on Freedom" in Zbigniew Pelcynski and John Gray, eds., *Conceptions of Liberty in Political Philosophy* (New York: St. Martins, 1987), 182–216.

27. Cf. Amartya Sen, "Utilitarianism and Welfarism," *Journal of Philosophy* Vol. 76, no. 9 (1979), 463–89, especially p. 471, for a discussion of this.

28. Cf. Rawls's well-known argument to this effect in *A Theory of Justice* (Cambridge, Mass.: Harvard University Press, 1971), 22ff.

29. Cf. Rawls, "Social Unity and the Primary Goods" in A. Sen and B. Williams, eds., *Utilitarianism and Beyond* (Cambridge: Cambridge University Press, 1984), 159–86.

30. One might notice that this is a variation of Robert Nozick's "experience machine" example; cf. *Anarchy, State, and Utopia* (New York: Basic Books, 1974), 42ff.

31. Arrow, "Extended Sympathy and the Possibility of Social Choice," *American Economic Review*, Papers and Proceedings (Feb., 1977), 219–25.

32. For the relation between autonomy and the right to free speech, cf. Thomas M. Scanlon, "A Theory of Freedom of Expression," *Philosophy and Public Affairs* Vol. 1 (Winter, 1972), 204–226.

33. Cf. Rolf Sartorius ed., *Paternalism* (Minneapolis: University of Minnesota Press, 1983) for a recent installment in the literature on this question.

34. On this issue, cf. Bruce Miller, "Autonomy and the Refusal of Life-Saving Treatment," *Hastings Center Report* Vol. 11, no. 4 (Aug., 1981), 22–28; H. Tristram

Englehardt, Jr. *The Foundations of Bioethics* (New York: Oxford University Press, 1986); Tom Beauchamp and James Childress *Principles of Medical Ethics* (New York: Oxford University Press, 1979); and Jay Katz *The Silent World of Doctor and Patient* (New York: Free Press, 1984). Cf. especially Katz's discussion of whether autonomy refers only to "internal" capacities to reflect and make choices, or to external rights as well. Katz defends the former position (ch. 5) which keeps him in line with the general conception of autonomy discussed in this introduction.

35. Cf. Diana Meyers, "Personal Autonomy and the Paradox of Feminine Socialization," *Journal of Philosophy* Vol. 84, no. 11 (1987), 619–28, and "The Socialized Individual and Individual Autonomy: An Intersection Between Philosophy and Psychology" in E. Feder Kittay and D. Meyers, eds., *Women and Moral Theory* (Totowa, N.J.: Rowman and Littlefield, 1987), 139–53. Cf. also Carole Pateman and Elizabeth Gross eds., *Feminist Challenges* (Boston: Northeastern University Press, 1986), for examples of discussions of the importance of autonomy for feminism.

36. Cf. Jon Elster *Sour Grapes* (Cambridge: Cambridge University Press, 1983), David Braybrook, "From Economics to Aesthetics: The Rectification of Preferences," *Nous* Vol. 8 (1974), 13–24, and Menahem Yaari, "Endogenous Changes in Tastes: A Philosophical Discussion," *Erkenntnis* Vol. 11 (1977), 157–96.

37. Examples include: Steven Sanders, "Autonomy, Authority and Moral Education," *Journal of Social Philosophy* Vol. 13 (May, 1982), 18–24; R. F. Dearden, "Autonomy and Education" in R. F. Dearden et al. eds., *Education and the Developments of Reason* (London: Routledge and Kegan Paul, 1972), 451–2; and R. S. Downie and E. Telfer, "Autonomy," *Philosophy* Vol. 46 (1971), 296–301.

I

THE CONCEPT OF
AUTONOMY

2

Autonomy

Joel Feinberg

1. Conceptions of Personal Autonomy

Those who have experienced, or can experience hypothetically in their imaginations, irksome constraints justified wholly on paternalistic grounds, will testify that their resentment is not mere frustration or antipathy. Rather it has the full flavor of moral indignation and outrage. Their grievance is not simply that they have been unnecessarily inconvenienced or "irked," but rather that in some way they have been violated, invaded, belittled. They have experienced something analogous to the invasion of their property or the violation of their privacy. They want to protest in such terms as "*I'm* in charge *here*," "No one can tell me what I must do with *my own* time," and "What I do with *my own* life is no one else's business." The indignant feelings, in short, are those provoked by a sense of one's rightful prerogatives having been usurped. Moreover, the paternalistic "justifications" for the invasions rub salt in the wound by denying the very existence of the privacy, independence, and prerogatives asserted in the protests, and thereby are also belittling, degrading, and demeaning.

Philosophers have long had an expression to label the realm of inviolable sanctuary most of us sense in our own beings. That term is *personal autonomy*. The word "autonomy" is obviously derived from the Greek stems for "self" and "law" or "rule," and means literally "the having or making of one's own laws." Its sense therefore can be rendered at least approximately by such terms as "self-rule," "self-determination," "self-government," and "independence." These phrases are all familiar to us from their more frequent, and often more exact, application to states and institutions. Indeed it is plausible that the original applications and denials of these notions were to states and that their attribution to individuals is derivative, in which case "personal autonomy" is a political metaphor.[1]

This chapter was originally published as chapter 18 of *Harm to Self* by Joel Feinberg. Copyright © 1986 by Oxford University Press, Inc. Reprinted by permission.

Joel Feinberg is Professor of Philosophy at the University of Arizona.

When applied to individuals the word "autonomy" has four closely related meanings. It can refer either to the *capacity* to govern oneself, which of course is a matter of degree; or to the *actual condition* of self-government and its associated virtues; or to an *ideal of character* derived from that conception; or (on the analogy to a political state) to the *sovereign authority* to govern oneself, which is absolute within one's own moral boundaries (one's "territory," "realm," "sphere," or "domain"). Note that corresponding to these senses of "autonomous" there are parallel senses of the term "independent": The *capacity* to support oneself, direct one's own life, and be finally responsible for one's own decisions; the *de facto condition* of self-sufficiency, which consists in the exercise of the appropriate capacities when the circumstances permit; the ideal of self-sufficiency; and the sense, applied mainly to political states, of *de jure sovereignty* and the right of self-determination.[2]

2. Autonomy as Capacity

It is possible in theory, I suppose, to possess both the capacity and the condition without the right of self-government. It is clearly possible to possess the right and the capacity while falling short of the condition. But it does not seem possible either to achieve the condition or to possess the right while lacking (totally lacking) the capacity. Thus all those who have argued for a natural sovereign autonomy have agreed that persons have the right of self-government if and only if they have the capacity for self-government. That capacity in turn is determined by the ability to make rational choices, a qualification usually so interpreted as to exclude infants, insane persons, the severely retarded, the senile, and the comatose, and to include virtually everyone else. It is commonly said of those who qualify that they and only they are *competent* to govern themselves. As it is used in the law, the word "competence," referring to the possession of legal powers, expresses an all or nothing concept.[3] A being is "competent" (legally capable) of committing a crime, for example, only if it is a human being, of a certain age and mental condition. Unlike primitive systems, our law refuses to recognize that animals, plants, and inanimate objects, or human infants or lunatics can commit delicts, "no matter how hard they might try."

As Kelsen points out, the concept of "jurisdiction" is "nothing but the general concept of competence as applied to a special case. Jurisdiction properly so called is the competence of courts."[4] Similarly, one might add that "standing" is the competence to be a plaintiff or petitioner in certain forms of litigation. These concepts are also accurately rendered by the word "qualification." Not only is legal qualification all or nothing (not a matter of degree); it is relativized to contexts, applying or not applying to given persons depending on which legal role is at issue. Jones, a legislator, is competent to (help) make laws but lacks the legal power to make people married. The Reverend Mr. Smith is competent to conduct weddings but incompetent to legislate. Jones is neither more nor less competent than any other unqualified person to change people's marital status. In this sense of the word, "competence" is not a matter of degree permitting such comparisons; you are either competent or not, all or nothing. But some people exercise more kinds of legal competence than others. Judges are competent to create or alter more kinds of legal relationships than clergymen. Karen Quinlan in her incurable coma, was no longer competent to produce any legal changes whatever—not competent to consent, not even "competent" to commit a crime.

Daniel Wikler, in an important article,[5] has pointed out how these legal and legal-like concepts of competence differ from a more familiar commonsense notion of competence as natural ability. Wikler calls this ordinary notion "the relativist conception" to indicate that it applies to capabilities that people have in various degrees. Scales of intelligence, for example, employ such a notion, extending from the profoundly retarded, to the mildly retarded, the average, the bright, and the gifted. Those at the one end of the scale are less "competent" (capable), intellectually than those in the middle and at the other end. We also distinguish those who are intellectually competent in various degrees, on the one hand, from those who are simply incompetent, on the other, but where we draw that line is in part relative to the requirements of the tasks we are assigning. When we make the distinction in a general way with no specific tasks in mind, we do it in an unavoidably arbitrary fashion. "We draw it somewhere between the levels of capacity of normal adults and of the mildly retarded, but relative to the gifted, normal adults who are impaired or incompetent [in this sense]."[6] In contrast, Wikler's second notion of competence, which although it does not refer to the "power" to create status or alter legal relations, nevertheless resembles in one respect the legal conceptions described above, is a "threshold conception." Like Wikler's first sense, it refers to natural abilities rather than legal powers, but above a certain minimum (say of intelligence or age) competence in this sense is possessed in equal degree by all who have it, no matter how much they differ in degree of competence in the other sense; and below the threshold, everyone is equally incompetent despite other differences among them. In this "threshold sense of natural competence," the following remark of Wikler's is quite unexceptionable: "Though a person may have more intelligence than another, he will be no more *competent* at performing certain tasks; his added power is simply an unused surplus. Those lacking enough intelligence for the task will be incompetent to perform it; while those having sufficient intelligence will be equally competent however great the difference in their intellectual levels."[7]

It is the threshold conception of natural competence—minimal relevant capability for a task—that is used in stipulations of necessary and sufficient conditions for the sovereign right of self-government ascribed to individuals. Some competent persons are no doubt more richly endowed with intelligence, judgment, and other relevant capabilities than others, but above the appropriate threshold they are deemed no more competent (qualified) than the others at the "task" of living their own lives according to their own values as they choose. In respect to qualification for rightful self-government, their greater resources are "simply an unused surplus."

The actual condition of self-government, however, is differently related to competence. The person whose relevant capacities are just above the bare threshold of competence that qualifies him for *de jure* self-government may rightfully rule himself, but in fact he may rule himself badly, unwisely, only partially. He may in fact have relatively little personal autonomy in the sense of de facto condition, but like a badly governed nation, he may retain his sovereign independence nevertheless. A genuinely incompetent being, below the threshold, is incapable of making even foolish, unwise, reckless, or perverse choices. Jellyfish,[8] magnolia trees, rocks, newborn infants, lunatics, and irrevocably comatose former "persons," if granted the right to make their own decisions, would be incapable of making even "stupid" choices. Being stupid, no less than being wise, is the sole prerogative of the threshold-competent.

In summary, capacities relevant to self-government do differ in the degree to which they are possessed by various competent persons. Therefore, above a minimal threshold, the autonomy that is defined in terms of those capacities is also a property admitting of "more" and "less." The actual condition of self-government (and its associated virtues), which defines "autonomy" in the second sense, also is subject to differences in degree. Some people are "more in control of themselves" than others, have more prudence, sagacity, self-reliance, authenticity, or integrity than others. The explanation of these differences may in some cases be that the better governed (or more self-governed) people have more of the capacities that define autonomy in the first sense. But that is not the only possible explanation. Dispositions of character, feeling, or sensibility, and differences in life circumstances too, may be contributing factors. In any case, the fourth sense of autonomy—*de jure* independence—is not a matter of more or less. It belongs equally to the wise and the foolish, and is determined only by that competence which is itself not a matter of degree.

In the next section we shall examine the second family of senses of "autonomy," all derived from conceptions of the condition of self-government. That will be followed by a discussion, in Section 4, of the ways in which that conception requires modification if it is to serve as an attractive ideal for human character. Then throughout the remainder of this and subsequent chapters, when we speak of "autonomous persons," we shall refer, unless otherwise indicated, to persons who are autonomous in a quite different sense, those who have a right to self-determination analogous in certain ways to the right of nations to be politically independent, and it will be tacitly understood that the persons so designated are, of course, autonomous in the capacity sense as well. But it would take us too far afield to say more about the presupposed capacities here.[9]

3. Autonomy as Condition

A person with both the capacity for, and right to, self-government may in fact be an unwilling slave to another, with no opportunity to exercise his rights and capacities. Such a person falls short of autonomy in the sense that he does not actually govern himself, whatever his rights and capacities. What is it then to be in the actual condition of self-government? Whatever else we mean by autonomy in this sense, it must be a good and admirable thing to have, not only in itself but for its fruits—responsibility, self-esteem, and personal dignity. Autonomy so conceived is not merely a "condition," but a condition to which we aspire as an ideal.

We must mention first of all, however, that de facto self-government presupposes *luck*.[10] If a person's luck is bad, circumstances beyond his control can destroy his opportunities. I do not govern myself if you overpower me by brute force and wrongfully impose your will on mine, or if illness throws me into a febrile stupor, delirium, or coma, or if poverty reduces me to abject dependence on the assistance of others. (Similarly a nation may not be able to govern itself in time of famine, or when stripped of its natural resources.) So a certain amount of good luck, no less than capability, is a requisite condition of de facto autonomy. Sometimes, however, unlucky circumstances can actually contribute to autonomy, as when a person is so situated that he can depend only on himself. He stands alone with no one else to help; hence he is "thrown on his own resources," and develops firm habits of self-reliance.

For the most part when we think of a person as possessing or lacking de facto autonomy we think of him as neither enviable for his material good fortune nor pitiable for his bad luck (though these may be presupposed) as much as admirable for his excellence of character or blamable for his deficiencies. In normal circumstances, opportunity is more or less available for most people; the autonomous person is the one who makes the most of it. Autonomy, so understood, refers to a congeries of virtues all of which derive from a conception of self-determination, though sometimes by considerable extension of that idea. These virtues, in fact, are a remarkably miscellaneous lot, united only by a family resemblance, and a connection, however far removed, to the generating idea of self-government. The virtues, moreover, are causally and conceptually interconnected, and corresponding to each is a distinctive way of falling short of the composite ideal. Let us consider some of the chief items in this blend.

Self-possession

The autonomous person, as the saying goes, is "his own man" or "her own woman." He/she doesn't "belong" to anyone else, either as property or as possession. Anyone who would deal in her affairs must come to terms with *her*, or her agent. It will not do to negotiate only with her parents or her boss, and she has no "keeper."

Distinct Self-identity (Individuality)

The autonomous person is no mere reflection of another who doesn't have a sense of his own identity. He is not exhaustively defined by his relations to any particular other. For example, he may protest that he is not content to be known and described merely as the former husband of some movie star, as the newspapers might have it.

Authenticity; Self-selection

To the degree to which a person is autonomous he is not merely the mouthpiece of other persons or forces. Rather his tastes, opinions, ideals, goals, values, and preferences are all authentically *his*. (His moral principles are too, it goes without saying, but these will be considered below as a special case.) One way of being inauthentic, so understood, is to be a habitual and uncritical conformist who receives his signals from some group whose good opinion he needs, or from unknown tastemakers in the advertising agencies and public relations firms. The inauthentic person of this type is essentially the manipulated consumer. He has no taste in music or clothes except for what is fashionable this season. If blue flatters his complexion while green makes him appear sallow and sickly, yet green is "in," he will buy all green shirts, aesthetic considerations be damned. And if his temperament inclines him to a life style that is currently out of favor with his peers, he will adopt a different life style instead, even if it ill-fits and ill-becomes his temperament. Even his opinions and "convictions" will be chosen in the way he chooses his clothes, for their conformity to the public "image" he wishes to present for the approval of his peers. He can construct no rationale for his beliefs other than that they are the beliefs held by those to whom he responds (if he even knows who *they* are), and can give no reason for thinking that *their* beliefs (like those of some reasonably selected authority) might be correct.[11]

There is an equal and opposite way of failing to be authentic which was more common a century or two ago in the era of "rugged individualists." What David Riesman called "inner directedness" is no more a form of authenticity than the "other-directedness" (conformism) more common today. On the old pattern of inauthenticity, a set of "generalized but nonetheless inescapably destined goals"[12] and standards are implanted in the child by his parents, their authoritative source internalized, so that they become his forever more. He is no more capable of subjecting these governing ideals to rational criticism and then modifying them where necessary than the other-directed person is, for he has within him a kind of "psychological gyroscope" that keeps him steadily on his course on pain of powerful guilt feelings. This mechanism allows him "to appear far more independent than he really is: he is no less a conformist than the other-directed person, but the voices to which he listens are more distant, of an older generation, their cues internalized in his childhood."[13]

A person is authentic to the extent that, unlike both the inner-directed and the other-directed person, he can and does subject his opinions and tastes to rational scrutiny. He is authentic to the extent that he can and does alter his convictions for reasons of his own, and does this without guilt or anxiety. The authentic person will buy his clothes in part to match his purse, his physical characteristics, and his functions; he will select his life style to match his temperament, and his political attitudes to fit his ideals and interests. He cannot be loftily indifferent to the reactions of others, but he is willing to be moved by other considerations too.

Self-creation (Self-determination)

The autonomous person is often thought of as a "self-made man." He cannot, of course, be literally and wholly self-made without contradiction. Even his character as authentic cannot be entirely the product of his own doing. To suppose otherwise is to conceive of authenticity in such an exalted way that its criteria can never be satisfied, or else to promote the ideal of authenticity in a self-defeating way. To reflect rationally, in the manner of the autonomous-authentic person, is to apply some already accepted principles, in accordance with the rules of rational procedure, to the test of more tentative principles or candidates for principles, judgments, or decisions. Rational reflection thus presupposes some relatively settled convictions to reason from and with. If we take authenticity to require that *all* principles (beliefs, preferences, etc.) are together to be examined afresh in the light of reason on each occasion for decision, then nothing resembling rational reflection can ever get started.

The point is a modest one; but commonly overlooked by those whose conception of autonomy is unrealistically inflated. It is simply that a person must already possess at least a rudimentary character before he can hope to *choose* a new one. The other side of that point is that if a child needs to "learn to be authentic," it must be the case that he is not already authentic when he starts. There can be no magical *ex nihilo* creation of the habit of rational reflection.[14] Some principles, and especially the commitment to reasonable self-criticism itself, must be "implanted" in a child if she is to have a reasonable opportunity of playing a part in the direction of her own growth.

Yet we do speak of "self-made persons" and find warrant for such talk in philosophers as different as Aristotle[15] and Sartre.[16] What can we mean by it if we want both to make conceptual sense and to describe a plausible model of personal autonomy? A common-sense account of self-creation (the term "self-determination" has a less grating and paradoxical sound) can be given, provided we avoid the mistake of thinking that there can be no self-determination unless the self that does the determining is already fully formed. In the continuous development of the relative-adult out of the relative-child there is no point before which the child himself has no part in his own shaping, and after which he is the sole responsible maker of his own character and life plan. Such a radical discontinuity is simply not part of anyone's personal history. The extent of the child's role in his own shaping is, instead, a process of continuous growth already begun at birth. From the very beginning that process is given its own distinctive slant by the influences of heredity and early environment. At a time so early that the questions of how to socialize and educate the child have not even arisen yet, the twig will be bent in a certain definite direction. From then on, the parents in promoting the child's eventual autonomy will have to respect that initial bias. From the very beginning, then, the child must—inevitably *will*—have some input in his own shaping, the extent of which will grow continuously even as the child's character itself does. After that, the child can contribute towards the making of his own self and circumstances in ever increasing degree. These contributions are significant even though the child is in large part (especially in the earliest years) the product of external influences over which he has no control, and his original motivational structure is something he just finds himself with, not something he consciously creates. Always the self that contributes to the making of the newer self is the product both of outside influences *and* an earlier self that was not quite as fully formed. That earlier self, in turn, was the product both of outside influences and a still earlier self that was still less fully formed and fixed, and so on, all the way back to infancy. At every subsequent stage the immature child plays a greater role in the creation of his own life, until at the arbitrarily fixed point of full maturity, he is at last fully in charge of himself, his more or less finished character the product of a complicated interaction of external influences and ever-increasing contributions from his own earlier self. At least that is how growth proceeds when parents and other authorities raise a child with maximal regard for the autonomy of the adult he will one day be. That is the most sense that we can make of the ideal of the "self-made person," but it is an intelligible idea, I think, with no paradox in it.

Perhaps we are all self-made in the way just described, except those who have been severely manipulated, indoctrinated, or coerced throughout childhood. But the self we have created in this way for ourselves will not be an authentic self unless the habit of critical self-revision was implanted in us early by parents, educators, or peers, and strengthened by our own constant exercise of it. Self-creation in the authentic person must be a process of self-*re*-creation, rationally accommodating new experiences and old policies to make greater coherence and flexibility. Self-creation is possible but not *ex nihilo*. At the dawn of rational self-awareness, as Gerald Dworkin points out,

> We simply find ourselves motivated in certain ways, and the notion of choosing, from ground zero, makes no sense. Sooner or later, we find ourselves, as in Neurath's metaphor of the ship in mid-ocean, being reconstructed while sailing, in mid-history. But [insofar as we are autonomous] we always retain the possibility of stepping back and judging where we are and where we want to be.[17]

Self-legislation

No one took the ideal of autonomy in its literal sense, *auto* (self) *nomos* (law), more seriously than Immanuel Kant. His third formulation of the categorical imperative requires that we act so that our will "can regard itself at the same time as making universal law through its maxim."[18] The moral law exerts a compelling force on us, but only because our rational will is the very author (legislator) of the law to which it is subject. It is this state of being at once author and subject of the law that Kant calls "autonomy" and praises in his most glittering terms. Kant makes it abundantly clear that the authority of the moral law, the source of its binding obligation, is our own rational will. If we did not legislate the law ourselves through our own free wills it would not be binding on us."[19] "A man is only bound to act in conformity with his own will," he maintains, though he goes on to add immediately, "a will, however, which is designed by nature to give universal laws."[20] This qualification seems prima facie to be a giving with one hand and a taking away with the other, much as if Kant were to strike a blow for autonomy by maintaining that a person is bound by the laws of mathematics only insofar as he freely embraces them by an act of his rational will, and then add that our rational will, of course, is "designed by nature" to be attuned to mathematical truths, and the only source of those truths. The freedom to govern oneself in the realm of mathematical beliefs, in that case, is rather strained.

Nevertheless, there is a natural anarchistic interpretation of Kant which accords with one loose strand, at least, of our ordinary notions of autonomy, according to which the autonomous individual "lays down his own law" or even is "a law unto himself." Robert Paul Wolff, for example, draws from the Kantian premise the conclusion that an autonomous person cannot become "subject to the will of another. He may do what another tells him, but not because he has been told to do it. . . . For the autonomous man, there is no such thing, strictly speaking, as a command."[21] If laws bind only because they have been self-imposed, then no person is subject to the authority of any other person, and no one *must* ever do anything against his own will.

While Kant's anarchistic hand seems to grant Wolff this license, his rationalistic other hand seems quickly to take it away. At places in his book, *A Theory of Justice*, John Rawls seems to represent this second strand in the Kantian conception. The emphasis in Rawls's conception of autonomy is not so much on one's *free* will as on one's *rational* will. There are objectively correct moral principles to which all persons are subject whatever their actual choices, and these are the foundation principles that *would* be chosen by a group of hypothetical rational and impartial persons in position of equality. "Thus acting autonomously is acting from principles that we would consent to as free and equal rational beings, and that we are to understand in the way."[22] No matter that a person does not in fact consent to the rational principles; what is required is that hypothetical persons in certain circumstances *would* consent to them, and presumably he would too if only he were more rational. A rebellious outlaw or a conniving egoist might live by quite different principles, but on Rawls's view he would not be acting autonomously when he lies and cheats and steals. Autonomous persons, apparently, unlike autonomous nation-states, cannot at the same time be wicked, dishonorable, or selfish. For us to hold that an evil person does not truly govern himself, we must identify his "true self" with impersonal reason, rather than with his actual values and commitments.

One strand of Kantian autonomy (emphasizing "legislation") then seems to support anarchism in politics and unattractive moral isolation as a character trait ("*I* make *my own* laws"), while the other strand (emphasizing moral objectivity) supports moral rectitude at the expense of genuine independence. A conception of moral autonomy which avoids these extremes would be preferred.

Moral Authenticity

Intertwined with the notion of self-legislation and hypothetical rational consent in the Kantian philosophy, and perhaps underlying them, is a more familiar (and less confused) conception of moral autonomy which is but a special case of the concept of authenticity. The autonomous person is not only he whose tastes and opinions are authentically his own; he is also one whose moral convictions and principles (if he has any) are genuinely his own, rooted in his own character, and not merely inherited. It is possible in principle for an (otherwise) autonomous person—a person who genuinely governs himself—to have no moral convictions at all, and to base his conduct not on principle but only on prudential policies. But insofar as the autonomous person's life is shaped by moral beliefs, they are derived neither by mindless conformism nor unthinking obedience to authority, but rather from a committed process of continually reconstructing the value system he inherited.

Kant was surely right in attributing a compelling personal dignity to the man or woman who is morally authentic. No tenable conception of autonomy as an ideal would acknowledge the attainment of that ideal by a human parrot or automaton. The person whose moral beliefs are not rooted in her own system of reasons is an object of the contempt of bullies and demagogues. Her "convictions" are so shallow they can be lightly "washed" from her brain by seduction, indoctrination, or suggestion. The morally autonomous person, provided she is free of coercion, will change her own convictions only in response to argument; and she will not abandon her foundation beliefs (even if she is forced to act against them) even under intimidation.

Kant is misleading, however, when he makes legal statutes the model for moral convictions, even for our more general moral principles. Consider the great diversity of moral controversies that require us to take moral stands, however tentatively. What is our judgment about abortion? mercy killing? preferential treatment for the unjustly disadvantaged? sexual equality? contraception? "free love?" public school prayer sessions? capital punishment for murderers? redistribution of wealth through steeply graduated income taxes? painful experimentation on animals? Even the most thoroughly autonomous person will be constantly balancing and juggling his judgments on these questions, attempting to make them fit with his governing principles and cohere with one another, with no awkward tensions or disharmonies among them. If he simply borrows his views from an alleged moral authority whose word is "law" for him, not attempting to fit his reasons into a coherent scheme, or if he drifts along with the opinions characteristic of his class or station, he fails to be morally authentic. The rough untidy data of morality do not fit the statutory model very snugly, unless we think of "moral statutes" as containing voluminous complexes of exceptive clauses, qualifications, exemptions, and defenses. If we think of them as imposing clear duties of action and omission, directly apprehensible by all those who are subject to them, then we are left, in the difficult cases, with sizable blocs of "subjects" who interpret the duties differently or reject them altogether, and no "moral judiciary" to give authoritative guidance. In any event, the morally authentic person doesn't simply lay down his law; rather he reflects, and balances, and compromises.

A thorough treatment of moral authenticity would distinguish between relatively singular moral judgments and relatively general moral principles. A person's principles, in turn, can be divided into those that underlie and support his judgments (about such matters as equality, taxation, abortion, etc.) on the one hand, and those by which he tries to live his own life and regulate his own conduct, on the other. The latter, which can be called "personal moral principles," are at first sight more like the bills of legislation that were before Kant's mind. If a person *decides*, for reasons of his or her own, to forego all sex outside of marriage, he makes, as it were, a vow of chastity, and assumes a duty whose binding force (as he will see it) derives from his own will. He has bound himself, which is to say that he is subject to a "law" of his own making. There is a surprisingly small range, however, over which this model seems to have any plausible application. Again, when conflicts loom between self-imposed duties, the morally autonomous person must do more than lay down another law to himself. Now he must be his own moral court; he must weigh and balance interests, reconcile and distinguish cases, reason and decide, on his own.

Typically, the occasions for moral choice and decision are precisely when these duties conflict. At the more general level where principles are adopted (or discovered), there is relatively little choice even for the morally authentic person. Could the autonomous person, living in a social world with well-defined social practices and customs, genuinely adopt a principle that he should participate in such practices while breaking all the rules? Can he "decide," or "legislate for himself" that he should make and accept promises but violate his own? Can he adopt as his "principle" (in the United States) that he will always drive on the left side of the road? Where there are settled practices, defined by well-understood conventions, can the autonomous person invent his own alternative rules for playing the public game, and then adopt those rules as his "principle"? Gerald Dworkin hardly exaggerates when he writes: "It makes no more sense to suppose we invent the moral law for ourselves than to suppose that we invent the language we speak for ourselves."[23]

The morally authentic person, then, is severely limited in his choice of moral principles, and in respect to general rules that derive from social practices, it seems fair to say that he has scarcely any choice at all. Choosing and deciding come in at lower levels of generality when principles conflict. But we hardly ever select among rival moral principles at a general level. That is not to say that there cannot be autonomous persons who are wicked, cruel, and mean (see below, section 4), or even self-governed persons whose lives are regulated by evil policies. Immoral authenticity is as real as its moral counterpart. In theory we all have a choice between the moral life and its amoral and immoral alternatives. But if we opt to govern our lives by *moral* principle, then insofar as our subsequent moral convictions are authentically our own, certain life policies will no longer be eligible for our choice. We cannot even consider, for example, the Satanic life-principle that we should inflict as much pain as we can, or the principle that we should promote our interests at all costs to those who might get in our way. Persons who opt otherwise, to repeat, may be thoroughly self-governing (autonomous), but in order for moral principles to be authentically their own, they must have moral principles in the first place. Those who most conspicuously fall short of de facto autonomy are not those who are wicked, but rather those whose "morality" is a mindless reflex. To summarize, the morally authentic person *has* moral principles, and they are *his own* principles, but that does not imply that his will is their source or ground, or necessary for their objective validation.

Moral Independence

Wendell Wilkie, speaking of nation-states, once wrote that "sovereignty is something to be used, not hoarded." Much the same could be said of personal moral autonomy. Social rules define ongoing practices, many as old as human society, that were here when we were born and will long survive us. Many of these rules enable us to commit ourselves to others and/or be the recipients of others' commitments. In many cases we inherit our moral commitments, and in still others we have no control over the process. We are committed to the support of our parents, for example, even though we did not ask to be born, and war and famine, whose causes were altogether beyond our influence, or the chance discovery of an injured person, impose their own duties whether we like it or not. But with luck, if we so desire, we can minimize our commitments and thus achieve a greater amount of de facto moral independence. We may, if we wish, go through life unmarried, or forgo having children, or near neighbors. We may make as few promises as possible to others, incur no debts, join no partnerships. The picture that emerges from all of this is that of an uncommitted person, maximally independent[24] of the demands of others. Yet is is hard to imagine such a person with the moral virtues that thrive on involvement—compassion, loyalty, cooperativeness, engagement, trust. If we think of autonomy as de facto independence simply, then the uncommitted person is an autonomy-hoarder, who scores high on our scale. But if we think of autonomy as the name of a condition which is itself admirable, a kind of ideal condition, then the uncommitted person is subject to demerits on his score. He is clearly no paragon.

In fact, we should conceive of de facto autonomy in such a way that it is not diminished by voluntary commitments, at least below a reasonable threshold. The person who is harassed and dominated by a thousand peremptory moral creditors may be admirable, but he has bargained away much of the control of his own affairs. He too must get low marks for de facto independence. No matter how admirable he may be, he has not been lucky, and thus fails, perhaps through no fault of his own, to achieve autonomy (control over his own life). But short of such extremes, there should be no conflict between moral autonomy conceived as an ideal, and moral commitment. Consider the analogous case of nations. The United States is committed to the defense of Western Europe from attack, to the honoring of its trade agreements and formal treaties, to the care of its own helpless, and so on, but that hardly tempts anyone to speak of its degree of independent self-government as thereby dimininshed.

Integrity (Self-fidelity)

A person of integrity is faithful to his own principles. Integrity therefore presupposes moral authenticity, but the opposite is not true. One must *have* moral principles of one's own in order to act in fidelity to them, but one might very well fail to act as one's authentic principles dictate on a given occasion when one is "morally weak" in the presence of temptation of distracting passions. One would expect (with Plato and Aristotle) that the more authentic one's principles, and the more firmly and rationally they are held, the less likely one is to betray them. That may be true, but even complete moral authenticity is no guarantee of unfailing integrity. One reason for this (perhaps the only reason) is that other dispositions of character may sometimes have a greater motivating power than moral principle. (It would be obfuscatory to insist "by definition" that moral motivation is necessarily the most powerful kind.) When the motive that leads one away from one's principles is self-gain (as in bribery) or passionate pleasure (as in seduction) we are severely critical of the offender. A true person of integrity ("rock-like integrity" as we say) cannot be bought. Even a substantial amount of intimidation, if directed at the person of integrity, should be of no avail, since this virtue should be almost as resistant to fear as to the prospect of pleasure. When the motive that proves more powerful than principle is neither a self-regarding nor a malevolent one, when pity, mercy, sympathy, benevolence, or compassion erodes one's resolution, judgment is not as harsh. True integrity will not be displaced by tender feelings either, but that is not always to its credit.[25] Integrity is a virtue very intimately tied to our conception of autonomy, but even autonomy is not the whole of virtue, and may be made to look bad if it keeps bad company. (Imagine an inflexibly conscientious Robespierre.)

Self-control (Self-discipline)

In the case of nation states there are positive and negative aspects of self-government, and insofar as we take the analogy seriously, we should expect to find their counterparts in individual self-government. A person governs himself when he is *not* governed "from the outside" by someone else, and when he *does* govern from the inside—when he is "in control of himself."[26] It is possible, of course, both politically and personally, for one to be independent of outside control and yet to fall short of self-government because *no one* is in control. In politics this state is called anarchy, a condition which is neither heteronomy (government by another), nor autonomy (government by self), but no government at all.

Plato is the philosopher who has taken the positive aspect of the metaphor of self-government most seriously.[27] In his view, there is an "office" in the human mind that is properly occupied by that part of the soul that is meant to rule. When that office stands empty or is usurped by an alien or rebellious element, then the whole human organism is out of kilter, just as if the function of the heart or liver were left unfulfilled or hampered by disease. This political model of the human mind requires the conception of a larger and a narrower self. The inner core self is the "ruling part" with which we most intimately identify. The self outside the inner core is "internal" relative to the outside world, but external relative to the ruling part. This is the self "meant by nature" to be ruled. It includes the body, the passions, and particular desires, appetites, and emotions. The inner core is usually identified with "Reason," but if reason is to have any opportunity to do its job then (taking liberties with Plato) we must also attribute to it the materials it works with—one's most deeply entrenched first principles, ideals, goals, and values. Practical regulation by reason presupposes some relatively settled convictions to reason from and with, though as we have seen in the discussion of authenticity, even these convictions are subject to revision as internal coherence may require. The whole human economy of elements works smoothly when each does its proper job and does not usurp the function of another, and the one element that "plainly bears upon it the marks of authority over all the rest,"[28] that element whose job it is to rule, is the inner-core self, also called "reason" or "conscience," with its basic normative tools (principles, ideals, etc.).

If we democratize this picture somewhat we can reinterpret legitimate self-government as a constitutional monarchy, ruled by King Reason under the terms of a basic character of values, the two together—king and charter—forming that inner-core self which is the "real person." The model becomes even more democratic if we adopt David Hume's conception of reason as "the slave of the passions."[29] If Hume had spoken of a servant instead of a slave and endorsed a democratic conception of authorities as "public servants," his metaphor might not have been far from the mark, for then it would have permitted us to derive the authority of practical reason from the desires it regulates. So conceived, reason is like a traffic cop directing cars to stop and go in an orderly fashion so that they might get to their diverse destinations all the more efficiently, without traffic jams and collisions. The person whose desires obey no internal regulator will be torn this way and that, and fragmented hopelessly. Such a person fails to be autonomous not because of outside government but because of his failure to govern himself. He will also fail to be free from constraint insofar as his constituent desires thwart one another in internal jams and collisions. At its worst, where self-control has collapsed, such a condition approaches that which Emile Durkheim found to be a leading cause of suicide, for which he originally coined the term "anomie."[30]

Self-reliance

In one respect this traditional virtue is the reverse side of moral independence. The morally independent person does not bind himself to others any more than he can help. The self-reliant person does not rely on the commitments of others to him. In certain areas of his life, at least, he doesn't need others, and dispensable needs he doesn't want. Schemes of cooperation imposing two-way, commitments he will skirt warily. So construed, however, "the traditional virtue" is not much of a virtue at all. Perhaps more admirable is the trait of being *able* to rely on oneself if or when others fail. It is indeed a virtue, and not merely a self-regarding one, to have inner resources—strength, courage, ingenuity, toughness, resilience. Intellectual and moral resourcefulness are virtues of mind and character, but having economic and material resources is in large part a matter of luck; so like other elements in the oddly mixed ideal of autonomy, self-reliance is as much an ideal of circumstance as a virtue or ideal of character. Extreme moral resourcefulness, on the other hand, may be enough to permit a person to get along with hardly any physical resources at all, but it will not cure him of disease or prevent him from dying if hit by lightning. There are limits even to stoic self-reliance.

Ralph Waldo Emerson, in his celebrated essay on self-reliance, praises under that name authenticity, moral independence, integrity, and most of the other components of complex autonomy.[31] When he comes to speak of self-reliance proper, however, he makes a different and better case for it. In certain areas of life—the very most important ones—self-reliance consists not merely in having a self that one *can* rely on; it consists rather in having a self that one *must* rely on. A person's highest good in life is self-fulfillment, and by its very nature, fulfillment is not something that can be achieved for the self by someone else. Others can help and provide necessary means, but no one can simply make a gift to a person of his self-fulfillment. No one can make a gift of personal excellence. Insofar as these goods are produced by others for us, they are bogus goods made of plastic. "Nothing can bring you peace," Emerson writes, "but yourself. Nothing can bring you peace but the triumph of principles."[32] And even these, one might add, may not be sufficient if your luck is bad enough.

Initiative (Self-generation)

Not only are the autonomous person's tastes, opinions, and principles authentically his own; so are his projects and enterprises, designs and strategies. Autonomous persons might differ in their activity or passivity as collaborators, without being more or less autonomous as a result, and the responder to a proposal is as responsible for his reaction to it as the proposer is for his initiative.[33] But if a person, through his fixed habits, hardly ever initiates any undertakings on his own, if his activities fall into patterns determined by others' proposals, if his time between projects is spent "sitting by the telephone" waiting for someone to suggest something, then we should think him somewhat deficient, at the very least, in autonomy, even if his lifetime of responsive activity is full and meaningful, and such that he could take responsibility for. Such a person is not "governed" by those to whom he responds, but he is far more dependent on them than an authentic and self-reliant person would wish to be.

Responsibility for Self

"The root idea in autonomy," says Richard Arneson, "is that in making a voluntary choice a person takes on responsibility for all the foreseeable consequences to himself that flow from this voluntary choice."[34] At first sight it would seem that responsibility is derivative from de facto autonomy rather than its "basic idea." Those judgments of responsibility that are made after the fact (as opposed to those made prospectively in warnings and assignments) are a diverse lot, but most of them ascribe to their subjects past agency (identify them as the doer of some deed), causation of some state of affairs, credit or blame, answerability, accountability, liability to reward, punishment or some other responsive treatment, or simply liability to the judgment, if only "for the record," that certain propositions are true of them.[35] That is a lot of work for the one word "responsible" to do. If a person acts autonomously then he qualifies for many such retrospective responsibility judgments about what he did. He is properly subject to the judgment that he did the act, that its consequences are to be charged to him, perhaps that he gets credit or blame for the result, or that the costs of repairing the damage are to be charged to his account, or that he is the one who should be required to "answer," or to give an accounting of what happened. On the other hand, insofar as a person's act was not autonomous (or that the actor was not an autonomous person) the retrospective responsibility judgments must be revised or withdrawn. If, for example, he was out of control, when he "acted," then it is not even true, without severe qualification, that he acted at all. If he was governed by another in what he did (acting as a mere agent, servant, or pawn), then the consequences may not be chargeable to his account, but rather to that of his master. If his opinions and tastes are not authentically his own but simply reflect those of his manipulators or peer group, then he is not even subject, without severe qualification, to the judgment that they truly represent or belong to him.[36] De facto autonomy, it would seem, is a conceptually presupposed condition of most judgments of responsibility.

The connection between autonomy and responsibility, however, also works in the other direction: responsibility is a contributing cause of the development of autonomy. How does one promote in a child the development of self-possession, distinct identity, authenticity, self-discipline, self-reliance, and the other components of the autonomous ideal? Surely part of the required technique is to *assign* (prospectively) responsibilities, that is tasks that require initiative, judgment, and persistence, and after which the assignee must answer for his successes and failures. A corollary of prospective assignments, of course, are retrospective judgments of credit, blame, and the like.

"Responsibility" is itself the name of a specific set of virtues. We speak not only of people being responsible *for* actions and consequences, and responsible *to* others; we also speak of them as being responsible *tout court*. A responsible person is a fit subject of responsibility assignments, and a qualified subject of retrospective ascriptions, in virtue of his possession of the appropriate traits for the exercise of responsibility. The responsible person is contrasted both with irresponsible and nonresponsible (incompetent) persons. Unlike the irresponsible person, he is steady, trustworthy, and reliable; he has the virtues of good judgment, initiative, and self-reliance that make for the effective use of discretion in problem-solving; he can do things on his own. Insofar as this list of virtues overlaps the list that defines autonomy, then obviously, assumptions of responsibilities, practice at discharging them, and willingness to answer afterwards, are effective means of developing ever greater de facto autonomy. But the two lists only overlap; they do not coincide. Independent judgment, self-reliance, and initiative are on both lists, but trustworthiness, dependability, steadiness (as opposed to recklessness) and especially the willingness to take on new commitments are more firmly on the responsibility list than they are on the autonomy list, just as moral independence and self-legislation, sometimes assigned to the autonomy list, have no necessary place in the account of resopnsibility.

4. Autonomy as Ideal

The challenge to the philosopher who would characterize autonomy as an ideal complex of character traits is to fashion a conception sufficiently similar to that of the actual condition of self-government that the word "autonomy" remains a suitable designation for it, and yet which describes a character type genuinely worthy of admiration and emulation in the modern world. As we have seen, our conception of autonomy as actual condition is sufficiently vague and uncertain to allow us considerable flexibility. Not all of its components are equally central, and the pedigrees of some are so far removed from original models of political governance as to be stretched and dubious. So we can treat the twelve-part sketch in section 3 as a faithfully vague account of a concept, but one which must now be whittled down and reshaped if it is to make an attractive ideal.

It is important to emphasize at the outset that even a refined conception of autonomy will be at best only a partial ideal, for since it is consistent with some important failings it is insufficient for full moral excellence. No further analysis can be expected to rule out as impossible a selfish but autonomous person; a cold, mean, unloving but autonomous person; or a ruthless, or cruel autonomous person. After all, a self-governing person is no less self-governed if he governs himself badly, no less authentic for having evil principles, no less autonomous if he uses his autonomy to commit aggression against another autonomous person. The aggressor is morally deficient, but what he is deficient in is not necessarily autonomy. He may have more than enough of that.

We can only hope to refine a conception of ideal autonomy according to which *other things being equal*, it is better to be autonomous than not. If we are successful, it will follow that *insofar* as a person is autonomous, he is to that extent admirable. Indeed "autonomy," if we construct the ideal carefully, might even designate a necessary element in any full ideal of human character. But since it can coexist so comfortably with striking moral flaws, it cannot be the whole ideal.

As it stands, the ramshackle conception of actual autonomy set forth in section 3 will not do, without severe restriction, even as a partial ideal of character. Some of its components are doubtful virtues to begin with; others are virtues only within limits that are narrower than those customarily drawn; still others seem to be confused in their very conception. The Kantian notion of self-legislation, long associated with the concept of autonomy, seems to present us *either* with the picture of a proud anarchist who accepts no commitments he has not himself made, who can commit or uncommit himself at will to anyone or anything, and is in principle capable or "inventing" his own moral principles, *or*, if with Rawls we follow Kant's rationalistic and objectivist bent, a concept of a person who can act autonomously even when he acts against his will, if his compelled behavior would have been chosen by some hypothetical persons more "rational" than he. Moral independence is a less confusing concept, but no more attractive as an ideal. It is one thing to avoid the state of moral overcommitment which, like literal indebtedness, can lead to its own kind of bankruptcy, but quite another to arrange one's life deliberately to minimize involvement with, and therefore commitment to, other persons on the grounds that commitment per se dimininshes autonomy. It would take a misanthrope or egoist (though perhaps a principled one) even to aim at such an ideal.

Even integrity, when it is so rock-ribbed that it constricts spontaneous human feeling, can be overrated as a virtue, though when it begins to appear objectionable we probably would deny it its laudatory title, and call it "moral fanaticism." When it is a trait of an autonomous person self-governed by narrow or cruel principles, it is a "virtue" that makes him all the more rigid and repellant. Self-reliance, when extreme and "principled," can become not only an unsocial virtue but an anti-social one, inhibiting cooperative participation in group projects. When touched even lightly with pride or self-righteousness it inhibits helpfulness and charity. Self-control, to be rational and worthy of admiration, requires delicate accommodation among diverse elements within the self. It must be clear to the Humean traffic cop what the right-of-way rules are among conflicting desires and values, an he must apply those rules with gentle but firm consistency in the interest of inner harmony. When the self in control is a ruthless autocrat (King Reason) imposing order with an iron hand, then inner conflict is squelched only at great cost to elements of the self, and the presentation of rigid narrowness to the outside world. Self-control can be totalitarian repression, and self-discipline can become self-tyranny. The inner peace so secured is won only by driving dissident elements underground to plot subversion. Self-reliance, independence, and self-control can indeed be virtues, but they are not the sorts of virtues which are such that the more one has the better. They are virtues only when their elements exist in just the right degree, neither too little nor too much.

There is a danger in discussing, in the abstract, the ideal qualities of a human being. Our very way of posing the question can lead us to forget the most significant truth about ourselves, that we are social animals. No individual person selects "autonomously" his own genetic inheritance or early upbringing. No individual person selects his country, his language, his social community and traditions. No individual invents afresh his tools, his technology, his public institutions and procedures. And yet to *be* a human being is to be a part of a community, to speak a language, to take one's place in an already functioning group way of life. We come into awareness of ourselves as part of ongoing social processes. Their fruits and instruments, precedents and records, wisdom and follies accumulate through the centuries and leave indelible marks on all the individuals who are a part of them. And all individuals *are* a part of these social histories. We can no more select our historical epoch than we can select the country of our birth and our native tongue.

How do these truisms affect our thinking about personal autonomy? Very clearly they place *limits* on what the constituent virtues of autonomy can be. The human world does not and cannot consist of millions of separate sovereign "islands" each exercising his own autonomous choice about what, where, how, and when he shall be, each capable of surviving and flourishing, if he so chooses, in total independence of all the others, each free of any *need* for the others. The danger for the philosopher who forgets for a moment these truisms is to overreact to the human flaws we call unauthenticity, conformism, other-determination, lack of integrity, lack of self-control, overreliance on others, passive responsiveness, and the like, and assume that excellence consists in the states furthest from them on a common scale of measurement.

It is impossible to think of human beings except as part of ongoing communities, defined by reciprocal bonds of obligation, common traditions, and institutions. Any conception of ideal human virtue must be consistent with this presupposition. What liberals have always rightly deplored has been the effects on individual character of social manipulation, the condition in which individuality is swallowed up by the collective mass, and persons are interchangeable parts in a great organic machine. But philosophers are not forced to choose between totalitarian collectivism and atomic individualism. If they were so there would be no alternative to despair. Whatever their other ideological affinities, all social philosophers should attempt to describe the same ideal, that in which persons are integrated into communities rather than assimilated to social organisms or isolated in atomic units. The ideal of the autonomous person is that of an authentic individual whose self-determination is as complete as is consistent with the requirement that he is, of course, a member of a community.

5. Autonomy as Right

The final sense of "autonomy" [we will consider] is suggested by the language of international law in which autonomous nation-states are said to have the sovereign right of self-determination. It has become common in recent years, however, for "autonomy" and "sovereignty" to be distinguished in political discourse. Great Britain is a sovereign nation which under certain circumstances may be willing to grant more "local autonomy," but never full sovereignty, to its constituent parts, Wales and Scotland. Similarly, Egyptians and Israelis negotiate greater "autonomy" (or home rule) for the West Bank Palestinians. Sometimes the word used for the granting of limited "autonomy" is "devolution" in the sense of "the delegation of portions or details of duties to subordinate (local) officers or committees."[37] In any case, whatever the word used, the concept is sharply contrasted with that of full national sovereignty. If Scotland were to win sovereignty, it would become an entirely separate and independent nation.

Sovereignty and (mere) political autonomy seem to differ in at least two respects. First, autonomy is partial and limited, while sovereignty is whole and undivided. The autonomous region governs itself in some respects but not in others, whereas the sovereign state does not relinquish its right to govern entirely when it delegates autonomy. When the state grants home rule to a regional section, its own ultimate authority is not diminished, since in devolution sovereignty is not something given away in divisible parcels. (On the other hand, if the state intends to give away some of its sovereignty it has a sovereign right to do *that* too, as the United Kingdom did when it recognized the independence of India.)

A more important difference is that the authority of the sovereign state is a right, whereas the authority of the autonomous region is a revocable privilege. The sovereign grants autonomy freely at his pleasure and withdraws it at his will. Local autonomy is delegated; sovereignty is basic and underivative. Sovereignty is, in a sense, an ultimate source of authority.

If there is such a thing as "personal sovereignty," then presumably it belongs to all competent adults and to no newborn infants, but before the point of qualification for full sovereignty, children must be understood to have various degrees of "local autonomy." The analogy may be forced somewhat, though it does rest on some moral similarities. It becomes difficult, however, to think of the near-adult teenager as deriving *all* of his autonomy by parental delegation. A certain minimum, at least, he has by natural right, even if his privileges to use the family car, to stay out past midnight, and the like, are delegated and revocable. Because of the special sense assigned to the word "autonomy" in political discourse, I prefer to borrow the stronger term "sovereignty" for the fourth sense of "moral autonomy"; but where I do use the word "autonomy" in what follows I intend it simply to mean "personal sovereignty," not something analogous to the weaker kind of "local autonomy." Now we can proceed to examine carefully the analogy between sovereign nations and "sovereign persons."

Most theories of sovereignty are about the concept of sovereignty *in* the state rather than our concern, the sovereignty *of* the state. According to the theory deriving from Bodin and Hobbes and developed by Blackstone, Austin, and Dicey, there is (on some versions) or ought to be (on others) a determinate source of ultimate authority and/or power in every state—a monarch, council, legislature, or electorate. This sovereign person, or body of persons, is the "uncommanded commander" of society. It has become more and more difficult to apply this theory to modern states with their constitutional checks and balances, their universal electorates, and counterpoised social classes. But while the concept of the determinate internal sovereign has fallen out of favor, the concept of national sovereignty vis-à-vis external powers continues to be applied routinely in international forums. Sovereignty in this sense is what one nation "recognizes" in another when it acknowledges that the other is an independent nation, as opposed to an empty territory, or land occupied only by roving tribes without stable political institutions, or a regional segment or colony of another country.

Empty territory is not a state, but a political state is territory and more. The additional element is best expressed by the term "jurisdiction." A sovereign state is territory under a kind of unconditional and absolute jurisdiction. The assertion that "the state is sovereign," according to Bernard Crick, is "usually a tautology, just as the expression 'sovereign state' can be a pleonasm. For the concept of 'the state' came into use at about the same time as the concept of sovereignty, and it served the same purpose and had substantially the same meaning."[38] The state is the juridical entity that maintains sovereignty over a territory, no matter how its own internal lines of authority are organized, and sovereignty is the form of legal control a state exercises over its territory. Thus we mention "sovereignty" in the very definition of a state, and we mention "state" in the very definition of sovereignty.

Perhaps the concept of a "nation" can take us further toward an understanding of the conceptual complex "sovereign-state." Here we must proceed with caution for the word "nation" is treacherously vague. Sometimes it is still used interchangeably with "state"; "France" is the name of both a nation and a state. That is probably its original usage,[39] but it can now also be used to refer to the entity that can acquire its own state, and can be said to deserve to be a state even before it actually is one. We can refer to that second, and still obscure sense of "nation" as the "prepolitical" sense. In this sense a "nation" may exist before it acquires its own state, or after it loses it, or it may exist in numerous states, as talk of "the Arab nation" testifies. On the other hand, people of distinct ethnic, linguistic, and religious backgrounds can co-exist as citizens of the same nation because they use still other criteria to identify their fellow nationals. Such criteria include a common national self-image as the shared focus of their sentiment and loyalty, or an extended history of faithful support and collaboration.[40] Thus, "French, German, and Italian-speaking Swiss are simply three sorts of Swiss: their national image transcends or embraces linguistic differences, and it would be odd to make distinctions of nationality where they make none themselves."[41]

Where does a sovereign right of political independence come from: dispensations? contracts? conquests? There is no single obviously correct answer for a question this general. Suffice it to say, for our purposes, that apart from philosophical skeptics, nobody in practice seriously questions that Peru, for example, is a sovereign nation with the exclusive prerogative of governing its own territory, and the same is true of all the other established national states. That is just what a nation naturally is: a collection of individuals given a high degree of unity by common cultural elements who in fact occupy a territory over which they have established a system of law or authority. Nations need to become states if they are to survive and flourish as nations. And the phrase "sovereign state" is a redundancy.

If there is an analogous kind of personal sovereignty, where does *it* come from? One way of looking at individuals is to regard them, in a parallel way, as just naturally persons, so that the phrase "sovereign person" would also be a redundancy. In fact the word "person" has an ambiguity directly parallel to that of the word "nation." "Nation" can refer, as we have seen, either to a juridical entity, the state, or to a collection of individuals united by various kinds of cultural bonds into a cohesive group. Similarly, "person" can refer to the entity that is a proper subject of such moral predicates as "right" and "duty,"[42] or it can refer to the unity of a collection of diverse psychic elements—memories, loyalties, preferences, opinions—which puts on them all the stamp of a single self.[43] "One self" is the analogue of "one people"; it provides the sense of "person" analogous to the pre-political "nation." Indeed, most normal people have achieved a degree of personal integration far stronger than the social integration that unifies national groups. If anything, one would expect the case for a "natural" personal sovereignty to be even stronger than that for its political counterpart. The other sense of person ("an appropriate locus of rights and duties") is essentially juridical. It refers to a moral agent and possessor of rights, as "naturally sovereign" over itself as the state is over its territory; and just as some have argued that pre-political nations need to be (sovereign) states, so one might argue, do integrated individual selves *need* to be (juridical) persons. Whether the analogy can be fruitfully pursued further is the question to which we must now turn.

A word of caution, however, is required at this point. The system of nation-states has not always served the world well, as its sorry record of wars attests. The walls of national sovereignty may weaken and crumble as a sense of world community grows, nourished by increasing cultural homogeneity and spurred by common dread of nuclear holocaust. The case for individual sovereignty conceived on the national model, however, as we have seen, may well be stronger than the partial analogy between persons and nations suggests, for where that analogy fails, the differences tend to strengthen rather than weaken the attribution of individual sovereignty. There are cases, and not merely hypothetical ones, in which a sovereign state chooses to exterminate a part of its own population, just as a sovereign person might choose to have one of his own limbs or organs removed. But the morally crucial difference between these cases is obvious. The "parts" of persons are themselves nonpersons: desires, values, purposes, organs, limbs. The "parts" of nations, however, are themselves persons with their own sovereign rights. A state may intervene in a neighboring state's internal affairs to protect the lives of sovereign persons threatened with extermination, but a second party may not interfere, in a parallel way, in a sovereign person's "internal affairs" to protect the "rights" of desires, organs, and the like, for the latter, being nonpersons, have no rights of their own. This is another example of a difference between nations and persons that strengthens the concept of personal sovereignty even as it weakens the concept of national sovereignty that served as its model. What I have been proposing here simply is that the individual be thought of in the terms in which *for better or worse* we have thought of nations in the past, even if we cease thinking of nations in that way in the future.[44]

Notes

1. *The Oxford English Dictionary* lists three senses of "autonomy." The first and oldest is political; the other two are biological and social. The first is: "Of a state, institution, etc.: The right of self-government, of making its own laws and administering its own affairs." The earlier cited use of the word in English is in this sense (1623). Plato, when he refers to "the ruling part of the soul" in the *Republic* quite self-consciously creates a political metaphor. C. S. Lewis writes that the Greek *eleutheria* and the Latin *liberas*, which are usually translated as "freedom," were used in ancient times "chiefly, if not entirely, in reference to the freedom of a state. The contrast implied is sometimes between autonomy and subjection to a foreign power; sometimes between the freedom of [within] a republic and the rule of a despot." If Lewis is right, one of the oldest senses of "free," if not the original one, is "autonomous" as applied to a state, a sense which still survives. See his *Studies in Words* (Cambridge: Cambridge University Press, 1961), 124–25.

2. The word "free" is more complicated, but it too has has an ambiguity similar to that of "autonomous" and "independent," especially when applied to nations and states. When colonies achieve independence of an imperial power they are said to have won their freedom, though their citizens may not be any freer as individuals. When we speak of people as (generally) free or unfree, we can mean either that they are generally capable of acting or omitting to act as they please (the "optionality" discussed in vol. I, of *The Moral Limits of the Criminal Law* [Oxford: Oxford University Press, 1984] ch. 5, sec. 7), or that they are independent, "sovereign" beings, persons in actual and/or rightful control of their own choices. See the essay "The Idea of Free Man" in Joel Feinberg, *Rights, Justice, and the Bounds of Liberty* (Princeton, N.J.: Princeton University Press, 1980), 3–29.

3. See Hans Kelsen, *General Theory of Law and State*, trans. Anders Wedberg (Cambridge, Mass.: Harvard University Press, 1945), 90–92.

4. Kelsen, *General Theory*, 91.

5. Daniel Wikler, "Paternalism and the Mildly Retarded," *Philosophy and Public Affairs* 8 (1979), 377–92.

6. Dan Brock, "Paternalism and Promoting the Good," in *Paternalism*, ed. Rolf Sartorius (Minneapolis: University of Minnesota Press, 1983), 241.

7. Wikler, "Paternalism," 384. Emphasis added.

8. The point applies to higher animals too. Could a cow, for example, if given the choice of living on a ranch in Texas or Nebraska, decide *at all*, much less "wisely" or "foolishly"? There is a kind of minimal compliment in being called "foolish."

9. But see, *inter alia*, Timothy Duggan and Bernard Gert, "Voluntary Abilities," *American Philosophical Quarterly* 13 (1979); Harry Frankfurt, "Freedom of the Will and the Concept of a Person," *Journal of Philosophy* 68 (1971); Jonathan Glover, *Responsibility* (London: Routledge & Kegan Paul, 1970), chs. 3–7; and Hans Kelsen, *General Theory of Law and State* (Cambridge, Mass.: Harvard University Press, 1945), pt. 1, chs. 7–9.

10. This is a truth that the ancient Greeks, in their diverse ways, struggled to come to terms with. See Martha Nussbaum's engrossing account in *The Fragility of Goodness: Luck and Rational Self-sufficiency in Greek Ethical Thought* (Cambridge: Cambridge University Press, 1986).

11. Perhaps the most famous portrait in world literature of this sort of inauthenticity is Tolstoy's account of Stepan Arkadyevitch near the beginning of *Anna Karenina*, trans. Constance Garnett (New York: Dodd, Mead & Co., 1966), pt. 1, ch. 3, 7ff. "Stepan Arkadyevitch took in and read a liberal paper, not an extreme one, but one advocating the views held by the majority. And in spite of the fact that science, art, and politics had no special interest for him, he firmly held those views on all these subjects which were held by the majority and by his paper, and he only changed them when the majority changed them—or more strictly speaking, he did not change them but they imperceptibly changed of themselves within him.

Stepan Arkadyevitch had not chosen his political opinions or his views, these . . . opinions and views had come to him of themselves, just as he did not choose the shapes of his hat and coat. And for him, living in a certain society—owing to the need, ordinarily developed at years of discretion, for some degree of mental activity—to have views was just as indispensable as to have a hat." This passage is also quoted by Gerald Dworkin in his "Moral Autonomy" in *Morals, Science, and Sociality*, ed. H. Tristram Englehard, Jr., and Daniel Callahan (New York: Hastings Center, 1978), 160. Dworkin is probably our most sensitive writer about autonomy, and I am indebted to him at numerous places.

12. David Riesman et al., *The Lonely Crowd*, abridged paperbound ed. (New Haven: Yale University Press, 1961), 15.

13. Riesman, *Lonely Crowd*, 31.

14. Gerald Dworkin makes this point vividly both in his "Moral Autonomy" (see above, n. 11) and in his article "Autonomy and Behavior Control," *Hastings Center Report* 6 (February 1976). In the latter he writes (p. 24): "We all know that persons have a history. They develop socially and psychologically in a given environment with a given set of biological endowments. They mature slowly and are heavily influenced by their parents, siblings, peers, and culture. What sense does it make to speak of their convictions, motivations, principles, and so forth as "self-selected" [self-created]? This presupposes a notion of the self as isolated from the influences just enumerated, and, what is almost as foolish, that the self which chooses does so arbitrarily. For to the extent that the self uses canons of reason, principles of induction, judgments of probability, etc., these also have either been acquired from others or, what is no better from the standpoint of this position, are innate. We can no more choose *ab initio* than we can jump out of our skins. To insist on this position is to make autonomy impossible."

15. Aristotle, *Nicomachean Ethics*, Bk. III, ch. 5. "The man then must be a perfect fool who is unaware that people's characters take their bias from the steady direction of their activities. If a man, well aware of what he is doing, behaves in such a way that he is

bound to become unjust, we can only say that he is voluntarily unjust." In such a way do people "choose their own characters," and make themselves what they are.

16. Jean-Paul Sartre, "Existentialism is a Humanism" in *Existentialism* (New York: Philosophical Library, 1947), 18. "Man is nothing else but what he makes of himself."

17. G. Dworkin, "Autonomy and Behavior Control," in Englehard and Callahan, 25. (See n. 11.)

18. Immanuel Kant, *Fundamental Principles of the Metaphysic of Morals*, trans. H. J. Paton, in *The Categorical Imperative* (London: Hutchinson's University Library, 1947), 180.

19. As Paton puts it, "We make the law which we obey. The will is not merely subject to the law: it is so subject that it must also be regarded as making the law, and as subject to the law *only* because it makes the law." (*The Categorical Imperative*, emphasis added.)

20. Immanuel Kant, *Fundamental Principles of the Metaphysic of Morals*, trans. Thomas K. Abbott (Indianapolis: Bobbs-Merrill, 1949), 49.

21. Robert Paul Wolff, *In Defense of Anarchism* (New York: Harper & Row, 1979), 14.

22. John Rawls, *A Theory of Justice* (Cambridge, Mass.: Harvard University Press, 1971), 516. Rawls's later discussion of autonomy in his John Dewey Lectures is no longer subject to these objections. There he clearly distinguishes between "rational autonomy," a mere "device of representation" used to characterize the abstract individuals in the original position, and "full autonomy," a moral ideal which applies to "free and equal" moral agents in the real world. The latter corresponds closely to the conception of autonomy developed in this work. See John Rawls, "Kantian Construction in Moral Theory: Rational and Full Autonomy," *Journal of Philosophy* 77 (1980), 515–35.

23. Gerald Dworkin, "Moral Autonomy," in Englehard and Callahan (see n. 11), 158. One of Dworkin's more forceful arguments is from the social character of moral principles: "What my duties are as a parent, how close a relative must be to be owed respect, what duties of aid are owed to another, how one expresses regret or respect, are to some extent relative to the understandings of a given society. In addition moral rules often function to provide solutions to a coordination problem—a situation in which what one agent wishes to do depends upon his expectations of what other agents will do—agents whose choices are in turn dependent on what the first agent will do. Such conventions depend upon the mutual convergence of patterns of behavior . . . all of these preclude individual invention" p. 159.

24. Gerald Dworkin calls this "substantive" as opposed to "procedural" independence. Autonomy, as he and I both see it, more strongly requires the latter than the former.

25. Dworkin cites a famous example: "There is something admirable about the person who acts on principle, even if his principles are awful. But there is something to be said for Huck Finn, who 'knowing' that slavery was right, and believing that he was morally damned if he helped Jim to escape, was willing to sacrifice his integrity in favor of his humanitarian impulses." "Moral Autonomy," in Englehard and Callahan (see n. 11), 163.

26. As I put it elsewhere: "There are necessarily two aspects of autonomous self-government. The governing self must be neither a colony of some external self, or 'foreign power,' nor powerless to enforce its directives to its own interior subjects. If we appropriate William James's usage (modified for our own purposes) and call the 'inner core self' the I, and the rest of the comprehensive self over which it rules its Me, then we

can put the dual aspect of personal autonomy felicitously: *I am autonomous if I rule me, and no one else rules I.*" Feinberg, *Rights, Justice, and the Bounds of Liberty* (see n. 2), 20–21. The reference to William James is to his *Principles of Psychology* (New York: Henry Holt and Co., 1890), vol. I, ch. X.

27. Plato, *The Republic*, Bks. II–IV. The clearest modern statement of a similar "parapolitical conception of the self" may be that of Joseph Butler in his *Five Sermons Preached at the Rolls Chapel, and A Dissertation Upon the Nature of Virtue*, published in one volume (Indianapolis: Bobbs-Merrill, 1950). The sermons were originally published in 1726.

28. Butler, *Five Sermons*, preface, p. 11.

29. David Hume, *A Treatise of Human Nature* (London, 1739), Bk. II, pt. III, Ch. III. "Reason is, and ought only to be the slave of the passions, and can never pretend to any other office than to serve and obey them."

30. Emile Durkheim, *Suicide*, trans. John A. Spaulding and George Simpson (New York: Free Press, 1951), 241–76.

31. Ralph Waldo Emerson, "Self-Reliance," *Essays, First Series* (Boston, 1841).

32. Emerson, "Self-Reliance." The quoted passage consists of the final two sentences of the essay.

33. See my "Causing Voluntary Actions" in *Doing and Deserving* (Princeton, N.J.: Princeton University Press, 1970), 152–86.

34. Richard J. Arneson, "Mill versus Paternalism," *Ethics* 90, no. 4 (1980), 475.

35. For a detailed account of the variety of responsibility judgments, see Feinberg, *Doing and Deserving* (see n. 33), 119–251.

36. See my discussion of responsibility as "representational attributability" in Feinberg, *Doing and Deserving*, 250–51.

37. *Shorter Oxford English Dictionary*, 3d ed. (Oxford: Clarendon Press, 1933), 497.

38. Bernard Crick, "Sovereignty," *International Encyclopedia of the Social Sciences* (New York: Free Press, 1968), vol. 15, 77.

39. S. I. Benn and R. S. Peters, *Social Principles and the Democratic State* (London: George Allen & Unwin, 1959), 247. They write there:

> "The nation" is a relatively modern conception, just as nationalism is a modern political ideal. In the Middle Ages, men did not think of themselves as Englishmen, Frenchmen, or Germans, but as vassals of their overlord, subjects of their king, and ultimately members of a universal order of Christendom. Gradually the monarchs of Western Europe strengthened themselves against the Emperor and the Pope on the one side and their barons on the other, each building up an increasingly centralized structure of political authority, and becoming a more important focus for loyalty than any competitor. At this stage the idea of nationality [nationhood] was co-terminous with political allegiance.

40. "A nation's history is a sort of myth, holding up heroes for reverence and imitation, and thus setting standards and ideals." Benn and Peters, *Social Principles*, 251.

41. Benn and Peters, 251.

42. I discuss this sense of "person" under the rubric "normative personhood" and contrast it with "descriptive" or "commonsense personhood" in my "Abortion," in *Matters of Life and Death*, ed. Tom Regan (New York: Random House, 1978), pp. 186ff. and Feinberg, *Rights, Justice, and the Bounds of Liberty* (see n. 2), 191–93.

43. Cf. Ralph Barton Perry, *Realms of Value* (Cambridge, Mass.: Harvard University Press, 1954), 62–63. We are persons (in the nonjuridical sense), according to Perry, to the extent that our interests are integrated: "That which makes a man a person is the integration of his interests, both time-wise and space-wise. The person can look ahead, and plan accordingly; he can launch upon trains of purposive activities; he can relate his past to his future fortunes, and the distant to the near; he can keep his bearings; he can manage the household of his diverse interests; he can put first things first; he can hold in mind the wood, despite the trees; and all this he can do because of his cognitive capacities. . . . A man is a person insofar as there is a central clearinghouse where his interests . . . take account of one another, and are allowed to proceed only when the demands of other interests are consulted, and are wholly or partially met." Note how similar things might be said about the extent to which a group of persons is "a people," or a "community," or a "nation."

44. It has been pointed out to me by Alan Fuchs that the way nation-states actually behave towards one another today shows that the stringent traditional conception of political sovereignty has been much weakened, or at best only honored in the breach. Governments now openly acknowledge that they send "spy-satellites" over one another's territories, and one of the worst-kept secrets in the world is that governments monitor other nations' radio and telephone signals, plant listening devices in foreign embassies, and support similar clandestine activities. The counterpart of spying in the personal realm would be an outrageous violation of privacy, and hence of personal autonomy.

3

The Concept of Autonomy

Gerald Dworkin

In both theoretical and applied contexts the notion of autonomy has assumed increasing importance in recent philosophical discussion. Philosophers such as Rawls, Wolff, and Scanlon have used the concept to illuminate problems including the characterization of principles of justice, the limits on free speech, and the nature of legitimate authority. In the biomedical context the notion is used in discussions of the legitimacy of various forms of behavior control, and in clarifying the rationale behind the doctrine of informed consent. In contemporary discussion concerning the nature of education, and the possibility of moral education as part of the curriculum, notions of autonomy and self-direction are invoked. In the psychological literature we find claims by Skinner and others that an adequate explanatory scheme for understanding human behavior can and should dispense with ideas of autonomy. It is clear that the notion of autonomy deserves the same kind of careful and comprehensive philosophical examination that concepts such as liberty and equality have received.

It is also apparent that the term is used in very different ways by different authors. It is not at all clear that they are all referring to the same concept, nor that they should be given that they are dealing with very different issues.

It is apparent that while not used just as a synonym for qualities that are usually approved of, the term is used in an exceedingly broad fashion. It is used sometimes as an equivalent of liberty (positive or negative in Berlin's terminology), sometimes as equivalent to self-rule or sovereignty, sometimes as identical with freedom of the will. It is equated with dignity, integrity, individuality, independence, responsibility, and self-knowledge. It is identified with qualities of self-assertion, with critical reflection, with freedom from obligation, with absence of external causation, with knowledge of one's own interests. It is related to actions, to beliefs, to reasons for acting, to rules, to the will of other persons, to thoughts and to principles. About the only features held constant

This chapter was originally published in *Science and Ethics*, Rudolph Haller, ed. Copyright © 1981 by Rodopi Press. Reprinted by permission.

Gerald Dworkin is Professor of Philosophy at the University of Illinois at Chicago.

from one author to another are that autonomy is a feature of persons and that it is a desirable quality to have.

Given various problems which it is believed may be clarified or resolved with the aid of a concept of autonomy, how may we most usefully characterize the concept? I use the vague term "characterize" rather than "define" or "analyze" because I do not think it possible with any moderately complex philosophical concept to specify necessary and sufficient conditions without draining the concept of the very complexity which enables it to perform its theoretical role. Autonomy is a term of art introduced by a theorist in an attempt to make sense of a tangled net of intuitions, conceptual and empirical issues, and normative claims. What one needs, therefore, is a study of how the term is connected with other notions, what role it plays in justifying various normative claims, how the notion is supposed to ground ascriptions of value, and so on—in short a theory.

A theory, however, requires conditions of adequacy, constraints we impose antecedently on any satisfactory development of the concept. In the absence of some theoretical, empirical or normative limits we have no way of arguing for or against any proposed explication. To say this is not to deny the possibility we may end up some distance from our starting point. The difficulties we encounter may best be resolved by adding or dropping items from the initial set of constraints. But without some limits to run up against we are too free to make progress.

I propose the following criteria for a satisfactory theory of autonomy:

Logical Consistency

The concept should be neither internally inconsistent nor inconsistent (logically) with other concepts we know to be consistent. So, for example, if the idea of an uncaused cause were inconsistent and autonomy required the existence of such a cause it would fail to satisfy this criterion.

Empirical Possibility

There should be no empirically grounded or theoretically derived knowledge which makes it impossible or extremely unlikely that anybody ever has been, or could be, autonomous. Thus, a theory which required as a condition of autonomy that an individual's values not be influenced by his parents, peers, or culture would violate this condition. It is important to note that this condition is not designed to beg the question (in the long run) against those, such as Skinner, who deny the possibility of autonomy. I am attempting to construct a notion of autonomy which is empirically possible. I may fail. This might be due to my limitations. If enough people fail the best explanation may be that Skinner is correct. Or he may be correct about certain explications and not others. It would then be important to determine whether the ones that are not possible are the ones which are significant for moral and political questions.

We see here how the constraints operate as a system. It would not be legitimate to reject a proposed explication of autonomy on the grounds that we know that nobody is autonomous in that sense if *that* sense were the very one that people have appealed to when deriving normative claims.

Value Conditions

It should be explicable on the basis of the theory why, at the least, people have thought that being autonomous was a desirable state of affairs. A stronger constraint would require that the theory show why autonomy is not merely *thought* to be a good, but why it *is* a good. A still stronger constraint would require that the theory show why, as Kant claimed, autonomy is the supreme good. Since I do not intend my theory as an explication of Kant's views, and since it is plausible to suppose that there are competing values which may, on occasion, outweigh that of autonomy, I do not adopt the strongest constraint.

As an additional constraint I suggest that the theory not imply a logical incompatibility with other significant values, that is, that the autonomous person not be ruled out on conceptual grounds from manifesting other virtues or acting justly.

Ideological Neutrality

I intend by this a rather weak constraint. The concept should be one that has value for very different ideological outlooks. Thus, it should not be the case that only individualistic ideologies can value autonomy. This is compatible with the claim that various ideologies may differ greatly on the weight to be attached to the value of autonomy, the tradeoffs that are reasonable, whether the value be intrinsic or instrumental, and so forth.

Normative Relevance

The theory should make intelligible the philosophical uses of the concept. One should see why it is plausible to use the concept to ground a principle protecting freedom of speech, or why Rawls uses the idea of autonomous persons as part of a contractual argument for certain principles of distributive justice. One may also use the theory in a critical fashion to argue that a theory which argues from a notion of autonomy to the denial of legitimate authority has gone wrong because it uses too strong a notion of autonomy.

Judgmental Relevance

The final constraint is that the explication of the concept be in general accord with particular judgments we make about autonomy. These judgments may be conceptual, that is, one may believe that autonomy is not an all-or-nothing concept but a matter of more or less. The judgments may be normative, that is, that autonomy is that value against which paternalism offends. The judgments may be empirical, that is, that the only way to promote autonomy in adults is to allow them as children a considerable and increasing degree of autonomy.

I do not believe, however, that one can set out in advance a "privileged" set of judgments which must be preserved. If the judgments do not hang together, then any of them may have to be hanged separately.

These are the criteria. It is possible that no concept of autonomy satisfies them all. Just as Arrow discovered there was no social welfare function satisfying certain plausible constraints, we may find there is no concept satisfying ours. That itself would be an interesting discovery and would raise the question of whether we ought to drop or weaken some of the constraints or, perhaps, abandon the idea of autonomy.

What is more likely is that there is no single conception of autonomy but that we have one concept and many conceptions of autonomy—to make use of a distinction first introduced by Hart and developed by Rawls. The concept is an abstract notion which specifies in very general terms the role the concept plays. Thus, a certain idea of persons as self-determining is shared by very different philosophical positions. Royce speaks of a person as a life lead according to a plan. Marxists speak of man as the creature who makes himself; existentialists of a being whose being is always in question; Kantians of persons making law for themselves. At a very abstract level I believe they share the same concept of autonomy. But when it comes to specifying more concretely what principles justify interference with autonomy, what is the nature of the "self" which does the choosing, what the connections between autonomy and dependence on others are, then there will be different and conflicting views on these matters. This filling out of an abstract concept with different content is what is meant by different conceptions of the same concept.

What I believe is the central idea that underlies the concept of autonomy is indicated by the etymology of the term: *autos* (self) and *nomos* (rule or law). The term was first applied to the Greek city state. A city had *autonomia* when its citizens made their own laws, as opposed to being under the control of some conquering power.

There is then a natural extension to persons as being autonomous when their decisions and actions are their own; when they are self-determining. The impetus for this extension occurs first when questions of following one's conscience are raised by religious thinkers. Aquinas, Luther, and Calvin placed great stress on the individual acting in accordance with reason as shaped and perceived by the person. This idea is then taken up by the Renaissance humanists. Pico della Mirandola expresses the idea clearly in his Oration on the Dignity of Man. God says to Adam:

> We have given thee, Adam, no fixed seat, no form of thy very own, no gift peculiarly thine, that . . . thou mayest . . . possess as thine own the seat, the form, the gift which thou thyself shalt desire . . . thou wilt fix the limits of thy nature for thyself . . . thou . . . art the molder and the maker of thyself.[1]

Berlin says under the heading of "positive liberty":

> I wish to be an instrument of my own, not other men's acts of will. I wish to
> be a subject, not an object . . . deciding, not being decided for, self-directed
> and not acted upon by external nature or by other men as if I were a thing, or
> an animal, or a slave incapable of playing a human role, that is, of conceiving
> goals and policies of my own and realising them.[2]

But this abstract concept only can be understood as particular specifications are made of the notions of "self," "my own," "internal," and so forth. Is it
the noumenal self of Kant, or the historical self of Marx? Which mode of
determination (choice, decision, invention, consent) is singled out? At what
level is autonomy centered—individual decision, rule, values, motivation? Is
autonomy a global or a local concept? Is it predicated of relatively long
stretches of an individual's life or relatively brief ones?

While Marxists have been most vocal in raising the issues of "false consciousness," and "true versus false needs," it is important to see that the
question is one which a wide range of social theorists must address. For it is a
reasonable feature of any good society that it is self-sustaining in the sense that
people who grow up in such a society will acquire a respect for and commitment to the principles which justify and regulate its existence. It is very unlikely
that the development of such dispositions is something over which individuals
have much control or choice. Socialization into the norms and values of the
society will have taken place at a very young age. It looks, then, as if we can
only distinguish between institutions on the basis of what they convey, their
content, and not on the basis that they influence people at a stage when they
cannot be critical about such matters. It looks, therefore as if autonomy in the
acquisition of principles and values is impossible.

In the use of the concept in social philosophy we find that there is a notion
of the self which is to be respected, left unmanipulated, and which is, in certain
ways, independent and self-determining. But we also find certain tensions and
paradoxes. If the notion of self-determination is given a very strong definition—the unchosen chooser, the uninfluenced influencer—then it seems as if
autonomy is impossible. We know that all individuals have a history. They
develop socially and psychologically in a given environment with a set of
biological endowments. They mature slowly and are, therefore, heavily influenced by parents, peers, and culture. How, then, can we talk of self-determination?

Again there seems to be a conflict between self-determination and notions
of correctness and objectivity. If we are to make reasonable choices then we
must be governed by canons of reasoning, norms of conduct, standards of
excellence which are not themselves the products of our choices. We have
acquired them at least partly as the result of others' advice, example, teachings,
or perhaps, by some innate coding. In any case we cannot have determined
these for ourselves.

Finally, there is a tension between autonomy as a purely formal notion
(where what one decides for oneself can have any particular content) and

autonomy as a substantive notion (where only certain decisions count as retaining autonomy while others count as forfeiting it). So the person who decides to do what his community, or guru, or comrades tell him to do cannot on the latter view count as autonomous. Autonomy then seems in conflict with emotional ties to others, with commitments to causes, with authority, tradition, expertise, leadership, and so forth.

What I shall try to do now is introduce a conception of autonomy which satisfies the criteria set out at the beginning and which is (1) possible to achieve and (2) able to avoid the difficulties and problems just enumerated.

It is characteristic of persons that they are able to reflect on their decisions, motives, desires, and habits. In doing so they can form preferences concerning these. Thus a person may not simply desire to smoke but also desire that he not have that desire. He may not only be motivated by jealousy or anger. He can also desire that his motivations be different (or the same).

A person may want to break the habit of smoking and prefer to stop smoking because he recognizes its harmful character and because that recognition alone is causally effective in changing his behavior. But if he sees that causal path closed he may, all things considered, prefer to have a causal structure introduced which causes him to be nauseated by the taste or odor of tobacco. Even though his behavior is not then under his voluntary control, he may wish to be motivated in this way in order to stop smoking. When this is true he views the causal influences as "his." The part of him that wishes to stop smoking is recognized as his true self; the one whose wishes he wants to see carried out.

To give another example, a person might desire to learn to ski. He might believe there is no further motivation or he might believe that what causes the desire is the wish to test his courage in a mildly dangerous sport. Suppose he is now led to see (correctly) that he desires to ski because he is envious of his brother who has always excelled in sports. Having recognized the source of his desire he can now either wish he were not motivated in this way or reaffirm the desire. If the latter, then he is acting authentically in that he identifies himself as the kind of person who wants to be motivated by envy.

In an article written some years ago I made use of these considerations in an attempt to explain why certain ways of influencing people (threats) are regarded as interferences with a person's liberty and others (incentives) are not. I said:

> I suggest it is the attitude a man takes toward the reasons for which he acts, whether or not he identifies himself with these reasons, assimilates them to himself, which is crucial for determining whether or not he acts freely . . . . We only consider ourselves as being interfered with, as no longer acting of our own free will, when we find acting for certain reasons painful.[3]

I think now that the second-order preference theory, if correct at all, applies to a broader notion than acting freely. For it is clear that we resent other ways of being influenced besides coercion.

People mind being motivated by false beliefs, by manipulation, by being kept uninformed of relevant information. But not all these are considered interferences with a person's freedom. If a dying patient is deceived about his condition or if one person takes advantage of another's weakness to tempt him into some course of action desired by the first person, then we do not think of these as being interferences with freedom. Yet many of the same implications of depriving a person of freedom hold in these cases as well. For example, just as a deprivation of freedom may count as an excuse or (partially) relieve a person of responsibility so may these interventions. Just as duress may break the normal link between action and character so may manipulation and deception. Just as a person may feel used, may feel that he is an instrument of another's will, when his freedom is interfered with, so may he feel when he is deceived or manipulated or tempted. His actions while in one sense his, he did them, are in another sense attributable to another. It is his autonomy which is threatened.

We have seen cases in which a person's autonomy is interfered with but not his freedom. What about the other direction? Isn't it clear that when we do interfere with somebody's freedom we are limiting his autonomy? If we, for example, prevent someone from smoking for paternalistic reasons then it is clear we are limiting their liberty, but isn't this also a clear example of negating self-determination, and hence, autonomy?

I think that the answer is—not necessarily. If we only focus on cases where the person wishes to be free from interference, resents being made to do something for his own good, then indeed autonomy is violated. But that is because of his not wanting to act for these kinds of considerations and not just because his liberty has been infringed.

Suppose, for example, we consider the classical tale of Odysseus. Not wanting to be lured by the sirens onto the rocks, he commands his men to tie him to the mast and refuse his anticipated later order to be set free. He wants to have his freedom limited so that he can survive. Under these circumstances why should we regard his autonomy as violated?

Freedom is neither necessary nor sufficient for autonomy. Not only are they different concepts, their scope is different. Freedom is a local concept; autonomy a global one. The question of freedom is decided at specific points in time. He was free to do such and such at a particular time. At a later time he was not free to do that. Whereas the question of autonomy is one that can only be assessed over extended portions of a person's life. It is a dimension of assessment that evaluates a whole way of living one's life.

My suggestion is that it is the broader notion of autonomy that is linked with the identification of a person with his projects, values, aims, goals, desires, and so forth. It is only when a person identifies with the influences that motivate him, assimilates them to himself, views himself as the kind of person who wishes to be moved in particular ways, that these influences are to be identified as "his." If, on the contrary, a person resents being motivated in certain ways, is alienated from these influences, would prefer to be the kind of person who is motivated in different ways, then these influences, which may be causally effective are not viewed by him as "his."

Note that it does not follow that we can always change our behavior, or make certain desires effective in our actions. But that is another issue. To use

Frankfurt's example, the drug addict who desires to be an addict, who wants to be the kind of person who craves drugs, may not be able to change his behavior or his desires.[4] But his actions express his view of what kinds of influences he wants to motivate him. And he is, therefore, on my view, autonomous. And it is precisely because he is autonomous that he can be held responsible for being that kind of person.

I believe this way of looking at things is what underlies the distinction (which I have up to now found mysterious) that Aristotle makes between the involuntary and the nonvoluntary.

> Everything that is done by reasons of ignorance is *not* voluntary; it is only what produces pain and repentence that is *in*voluntary.[5]

Given two people who act in ignorance, suppose neither is to blame for what he did but one regrets what he did, does not wish to be that kind of person, whereas the other is indifferent or even welcomes what he did. For the latter the act is not only his in the sense that he performed it; it is his in the sense that he identifies with it.

The condition specified thus far cannot be the whole story of autonomy. For the second-order identifications a person makes, or the choice of the type of person he wants to be, may have itself been influenced by others in such a fashion that we do not view it as being his own. In this case his motivational structure is his, but not his own. I shall call this a failure of procedural independence.

The full formula for autonomy, then, is authenticity plus procedural independence. A person is autonomous if he identifies with his desires, goals, and values, and such identification is not itself influenced in ways which make the process of identification in some way alien to the individual. Spelling out the conditions of procedural independence involves distinguishing those ways of influencing people's reflective and critical faculties which subvert them from those which promote and improve them.

There are two important objections which have been raised to what Thalberg has called "heirarchy theories." The first is why go to the level of second-order reflection at all. If we have to make principled distinctions between different ways of influencing people's critical reflections on their first-order motivations, why not do this initially at the first-order.

The second objection is why should we stop at the "second" level. A person might have third-order desires, values, and so forth, about his second-order preferences. Will not this lead to infinite regress?

In reply to the first objection I believe that we cannot capture something important about human agents by making distinctions solely at the first level. In addition to distinguishing between the man who is coerced (acts because of threats) from the man who acts, say, to attain pleasure, we also need to distinguish the different agents, both of whom act because of coercion. One resents being motivated in this fashion, would not choose to be in situations in which threats are present. The other welcomes being motivated in this fashion, would choose to be threatened. Our normative and conceptual theories would be poorer if this distinction were not drawn.

In reply to the second objection, I believe there is something correct about it but there need be no infinite regress. Autonomy as defined here is a theory about the presence or absence of certain psychological states. As such it is subject to empirical constraints. I believe it is true that for some agents, and for some motivations, there is third-level reflection. If this is present then autonomy will be defined as the highest-order approval of one's lower-order motivations. But I also believe, as a matter of contingent fact, that human beings either do not, or perhaps cannot, carry on such iteration at very great length.

Let me conclude by pointing out that, on my view, there is no specific content to the decisions an autonomous person may take. An autonomous person may be a saint or sinner, a rugged individualist or a conformist, a leader or a follower. This raises the question why the development, preservation, and encouragement of autonomy is desirable. I leave these issues to another essay.

Notes

1. Quoted in P. O. Kristeller, "The Philosophy of Man in the Italian Renaissance" *Italica* 24 (1947): 100–101.

2. I. Berlin, *Four Essays on Liberty* (Oxford: Oxford University Press, 1969), 131.

3. G. Dworkin, "Acting Freely," *Nous* 4, no. 4 (1970), 377, 378–79.

4. H. Frankfurt, "Freedom of the Will and the Concept of a Person," *Journal of Philosophy* 68 (1971).

5. Aristotle, *Nichomachean Ethics*, Bk. III, ch. 1, ll. 18–19.

4

Freedom of the Will
and the Concept of a Person

Harry G. Frankfurt

What philosophers have lately come to accept as analysis of the concept of a person is not actually analysis of *that* concept at all. Strawson, whose usage represents the current standard, identifies the concept of a person as "the concept of a type of entity such that *both* predicates ascribing states of consciousness and predicates ascribing corporeal characteristics . . . are equally applicable to a single individual of that single type."[1] But there are many entities besides persons that have both mental and physical properties. As it happens— though it seems extraordinary that this should be so—there is no common English word for the type of entity Strawson has in mind, a type that includes not only human beings but animals of various lesser species as well. Still, this hardly justifies the misappropriation of a valuable philosophical term.

Whether the members of some animal species are persons is surely not to be settled merely by determining whether it is correct to apply to them, in addition to predicates ascribing corporeal characteristics, predicates that ascribe states of consciousness. It does violence to our language to endorse the application of the term 'person' to those numerous creatures which do have both psychological and material properties but which are manifestly not persons in any normal sense of the word. This misuse of language is doubtless innocent of any theoretical error. But although the offense is "merely verbal," it does significant harm. For it gratuitously diminishes our philosophical vocabulary, and it increases the likelihood that we will overlook the important areas of inquiry with which the term 'person' is most naturally associated. It might have been expected that no problem would be of more central and persistent concern to philosophers than that of understanding what we ourselves essentially are. Yet this problem is so generally neglected that it has been possible to make off with its very name almost without being noticed and, evidently, without evoking any widespread feeling of loss.

This chapter was originally published in the *Journal of Philosophy* 68 (1971). Copyright © 1971 by the *Journal of Philosophy*. Reprinted by permission.
Harry Frankfurt is Professor of Philosophy at Yale University.

There is a sense in which the word 'person' is merely the singular form of 'people' and in which both terms connote no more than membership in a certain biological species. In those senses of the word which are of greater philosophical interest, however, the criteria for being a person do not serve primarily to distinguish the members of our own species from the members of other species. Rather, they are designed to capture those attributes which are the subject of our most humane concern with ourselves and the source of what we regard as most important and most problematical in our lives. Now these attributes would be of equal significance to us even if they were not in fact peculiar and common to the members of our own species. What interests us most in the human condition would not interest us less if it were also a feature of the condition of other creatures as well.

Our concept of ourselves as persons is not to be understood, therefore, as a concept of attributes that are necessarily species-specific. It is conceptually possible that members of novel or even of familiar nonhuman species should be persons; and it is also conceptually possible that some members of the human species are not persons. We do in fact assume, on the other hand, that no member of another species is a person. Accordingly, there is a presumption that what is essential to persons is a set of characteristics that we generally suppose—whether rightly or wrongly—to be uniquely human.

It is my view that one essential difference between persons and other creatures is to be found in the structure of a person's will. Human beings are not alone in having desires and motives, or in making choices. They share these things with the members of certain other species, some of whom even appear to engage in deliberation and to make decisions based upon prior thought. It seems to be peculiarly characteristic of humans, however, that they are able to form what I shall call "second-order desires" or "desires of the second order."

Besides wanting and choosing and being moved *to do* this or that, men may also want to have (or not to have) certain desires and motives. They are capable of wanting to be different, in their preferences and purposes, from what they are. Many animals appear to have the capacity for what I shall call "first-order desires" or "desires of the first order," which are simply desires to do or not to do one thing or another. No animal other than man, however, appears to have the capacity for reflective self-evaluation that is manifested in the formation of second-order desires.[2]

I

The concept designated by the verb 'to want' is extraordinarily elusive. A statement of the form "*A* wants to *X*"—taken by itself, apart from a context that serves to amplify or to specify its meaning—conveys remarkably little information. Such a statement may be consistent, for example, with each of the following statements: (1) the prospect of doing *X* elicits no sensation or introspectible emotional response in *A*; (2) *A* is unaware that he wants to *X*; (3) *A* believes that he does not want to *X*; (4) *A* wants to refrain from *X*-ing;

(5) A wants to Y and believes that it is impossible for him both to Y and to X; (6) A does not "really" want to X; (7) A would rather die than X; and so on. It is therefore hardly sufficient to formulate the distinction between first-order and second-order desires, as I have done, by suggesting merely that someone has a first-order desire when he wants to do or not to do such-and-such, and that he has a second-order desire when he wants to have or not to have a certain desire of the first order.

As I shall understand them, statements of the form "A wants to X" cover a rather broad range of possibilities.[3] They may be true even when statements like (1) through (7) are true: when A is unaware of any feelings concerning X-ing, when he is unaware that he wants to X, when he deceives himself about what he wants and believes falsely that he does not want to X, when he also has other desires that conflict with his desire to X, or when he is ambivalent. The desires in question may be conscious or unconscious, they need not be univocal, and A may be mistaken about them. There is a further source of uncertainty with regard to statements that identify someone's desires, however, and here it is important for my purposes to be less permissive.

Consider first those statements of the form "A wants to X" which identify first-order desires—that is, statements in which the term 'to X' refers to an action. A statement of this kind does not, by itself, indicate the relative strength of A's desire to X. It does not make it clear whether this desire is at all likely to play a decisive role in what A actually does or tries to do. For it may correctly be said that A wants to X even when his desire to X is only one among his desires and when it is far from being paramount among them. Thus, it may be true that A wants to X when he strongly prefers to do something else instead; and it may be true that he wants to X despite the fact that, when he acts, it is not the desire to X that motivates him to do what he does. On the other hand, someone who states that A wants to X may mean to convey that it is this desire that is motivating or moving A to do what he is actually doing or that A will in fact be moved by this desire (unless he changes his mind) when he acts.

It is only when it is used in the second of these ways that, given the special usage of 'will' that I propose to adopt, the statement identifies A's will. To identify an agent's will is either to identify the desire (or desires) by which he is motivated in some action he performs or to identify the desire (or desires) by which he will or would be motivated when or if he acts. An agent's will, then, is identical with one or more of his first-order desires. But the notion of the will, as I am employing it, is not coextensive with the notion of first-order desires. It is not the notion of something that merely inclines an agent in some degree to act in a certain way. Rather, it is the notion of an *effective* desire—one that moves (or will or would move) a person all the way to action. Thus the notion of the will is not coextensive with the notion of what an agent intends to do. For even though someone may have a settled intention to do X, he may nonetheless do something else instead of doing X because, despite his intention, his desire to do X proves to be weaker or less effective than some conflicting desire.

Now consider those statements of the form "*A* wants to *X*" which identify second-order desires—that is, statements in which the term 'to *X*' refers to a desire of the first order. There are also two kinds of situation in which it may be true that *A* wants to want to *X*. In the first place, it might be true of *A* that he wants to have a desire to *X* despite the fact that he has a univocal desire, altogether free of conflict and ambivalence, to refrain from *X*-ing. Someone might want to have a certain desire, in other words, but univocally want that desire to be unsatisfied.

Suppose that a physician engaged in psychotherapy with narcotics addicts believes that his ability to help his patients would be enhanced if he understood better what it is like for them to desire the drug to which they are addicted. Suppose that he is led in this way to want to have a desire for the drug. If it is a genuine desire that he wants, then what he wants is not merely to feel the sensations that addicts characteristically feel when they are gripped by their desires for the drug. What the physician wants, insofar as he wants to have a desire, is to be inclined or moved to some extent to take the drug.

It is entirely possible, however, that, although he wants to be moved by a desire to take the drug, he does not want this desire to be effective. He may not want it to move him all the way to action. He need not be interested in finding out what it is like to take the drug. And insofar as he now wants only to *want* to take it, and not to *take* it, there is nothing in what he now wants that would be satisfied by the drug itself. He may now have, in fact, an altogether univocal desire *not* to take the drug; and he may prudently arrange to make it impossible for him to satisfy the desire he would have if his desire to want the drug should in time be satisfied.

It would thus be incorrect to infer, from the fact that the physician now wants to desire to take the drug, that he already does desire to take it. His second-order desire to be moved to take the drug does not entail that he has a first-order desire to take it. If the drug were now to be administered to him, this might satisfy no desire that is implicit in his desire to want to take it. While he wants to want to take the drug, he may have *no* desire to take it; it may be that *all* he wants is to taste the desire for it. That is, his desire to have a certain desire that he does not have may not be a desire that his will should be at all different than it is.

Someone who wants only in this truncated way to want to *X* stands at the margin of preciosity, and the fact that he wants to want to *X* is not pertinent to the identification of his will. There is, however, a second kind of situation that may be described by "*A* wants to want to *X*;" and when the statement is used to describe a situation of this second kind, then it does pertain to what *A* wants his will to be. In such cases the statement means that *A* wants the desire to *X* to be the desire that moves him effectively to act. It is not merely that he wants the desire to *X* to be among the desires by which, to one degree or another, he is moved or inclined to act. He wants this desire to be effective—that is, to provide the motive in what he actually does. Now when the statement that *A* wants to want to *X* is used in this way, it does entail that *A* already has a desire to *X*. It could not be true both that *A* wants the desire to *X* to move him into action and that he does not want to X. It is only if he does want to X that he can coherently want the desire to X not merely to be one of his desires but, more decisively, to be his will.[4]

Suppose a man wants to be motivated in what he does by the desire to concentrate on his work. It is necessarily true, if this supposition is correct, that he already wants to concentrate on his work. This desire is now among his desires. But the question of whether or not his second-order desire is fulfilled does not turn merely on whether the desire he wants is one of his desires. It turns on whether this desire is, as he wants it to be, his effective desire or will. If, when the chips are down, it is his desire to concentrate on his work that moves him to do what he does, then what he wants at that time is indeed (in the relevant sense) what he wants to want. If it is some other desire that actually moves him when he acts, on the other hand, then what he wants at that time is not (in the relevant sense) what he wants to want. This will be so despite the fact that the desire to concentrate on his work continues to be among his desires.

II

Someone has a desire of the second order either when he wants simply to have a certain desire or when he wants a certain desire to be his will. In situations of the latter kind, I shall call his second-order desires "second-order volitions" or "volitions of the second order." Now it is having second-order volitions, and not having second-order desires generally, that I regard as essential to being a person. It is logically possible, however unlikely, that there should be an agent with second-order desires but with no volitions of the second order. Such a creature, in my view, would not be a person. I shall use the term 'wanton' to refer to agents who have first-order desires but who are not persons because, whether or not they have desires of the second order, they have no second-order volitions.[5]

The essential characteristic of a wanton is that he does not care about his will. His desires move him to do certain things, without its being true of him either that he wants to be moved by those desires or that he prefers to be moved by other desires. The class of wantons includes all nonhuman animals that have desires and all very young children. Perhaps it also includes some adult human beings as well. In any case, adult humans may be more or less wanton; they may act wantonly, in response to first-order desires concerning which they have no volitions of the second order, more or less frequently.

The fact that a wanton has no second-order volitions does not mean that each of his first-order desires is translated heedlessly and at once into action. He may have no opportunity to act in accordance with some of his desires. Moreover, the translation of his desires into action may be delayed or precluded either by conflicting desires of the first order or by the intervention of deliberation. For a wanton may possess and employ rational faculties of a high order. Nothing in the concept of a wanton implies that he cannot reason or that he cannot deliberate concerning how to do what he wants to do. What distinguishes the rational wanton from other rational agents is that he is not concerned with the desirability of his desires themselves. He ignores the question of what his will is to be. Not only does he pursue whatever course of action he is most strongly inclined to pursue, but he does not care which of his inclinations is the strongest.

Thus a rational creature, who reflects upon the suitability to his desires of one course of action or another, may nonetheless be a wanton. In maintaining that the essence of being a person lies not in reason but in will, I am far from suggesting that a creature without reason may be a person. For it is only in virtue of his rational capacities that a person is capable of becoming critically aware of his own will and of forming volitions of the second order. The structure of a person's will presupposes, accordingly, that he is a rational being.

The distinction between a person and a wanton may be illustrated by the difference between two narcotics addicts. Let us suppose that the physiological condition accounting for the addiction is the same in both men, and that both succumb inevitably to their periodic desires for the drug to which they are addicted. One of the addicts hates his addiction and always struggles desperately, although to no avail, against its thrust. He tries everything that he thinks might enable him to overcome his desire for the drug. But these desires are too powerful for him to withstand, and invariably, in the end, they conquer him. He is an unwilling addict, helplessly violated by his own desires.

The unwilling addict has conflicting first-order desires: he wants to take the drug, and he also wants to refrain from taking it. In addition to these first-order desires, however, he has a volition of the second order. He is not a neutral with regard to the conflict between his desire to take the drug and his desire to refrain from taking it. It is the latter desire, and not the former, that he wants to constitute his will; it is the latter desire, rather than the former, that he wants to be effective and to provide the purpose that he will seek to realize in what he actually does.

The other addict is a wanton. His actions reflect the economy of his first-order desires, without his being concerned whether the desires that move him to act are desires by which he wants to be moved to act. If he encounters problems in obtaining the drug or in administering it to himself, his responses to his urges to take it may involve deliberation. But it never occurs to him to consider whether he wants the relations among his desires to result in his having the will he has. The wanton addict may be an animal, and thus incapable of being concerned about his will. In any event he is, in respect of his wanton lack of concern, no different from an animal.

The second of these addicts may suffer a first-order conflict similar to the first-order conflict suffered by the first. Whether he is human or not, the wanton may (perhaps due to conditioning) both want to take the drug and want to refrain from taking it. Unlike the unwilling addict, however, he does not prefer that one of his conflicting desires should be paramount over the other; he does not prefer that one first-order desire rather than the other should constitute his will. It would be misleading to say that he is neutral as to the conflict between his desires, since this would suggest that he regards them as equally acceptable. Since he has no identity apart from his first-order desires, it is true neither that he prefers one to the other nor that he prefers not to take sides.

It makes a difference to the unwilling addict, who is a person, which of his conflicting first-order desires wins out. Both desires are his, to be sure; and whether he finally takes the drug or finally succeeds in refraining from taking it, he acts to satisfy what is in a literal sense his own desire. In either case he does something he himself wants to do, and he does it not because of some external influence whose aim happens to coincide with his own but because of his desire to do it. The unwilling addict identifies himself, however, through the formation of a second-order volition, with one rather than with the other of his conflicting first-order desires. He makes one of them more truly his own and, in so doing, he withdraws himself from the other. It is in virtue of this identification and withdrawal, accomplished through the formation of a sec-ond-order volition, that the unwilling addict may meaningfully make the analytically puzzling statements that the force moving him to take the drug is a force other than his own, and that it is not of his own free will but rather against his will that this force moves him to take it.

The wanton addict cannot or does not care which of his conflicting first-order desires wins out. His lack of concern is not due to his inability to find a convincing basis for preference. It is due either to his lack of the capacity for reflection or to his mindless indifference to the enterprise of evaluating his own desires and motives.[6] There is only one issue in the struggle to which his first-order conflict may lead: whether the one or the other of his conflicting desires is the stronger. Since he is moved by both desires, he will not be altogether satisfied by what he does no matter which of them is effective. But it makes no difference *to him* whether his craving or his aversion gets the upper hand. He has no stake in the conflict between them and so, unlike the unwilling addict, he can neither win nor lose the struggle in which he is engaged. When a *person* acts, the desire by which he is moved is either the will he wants or a will he wants to be without. When a *wanton* acts, it is neither.

III

There is a very close relationship between the capacity for forming second-order volitions and another capacity that is essential to persons—one that has often been considered a distinguishing mark of the human condition. It is only because a person has volitions of the second order that he is capable both of enjoying and of lacking freedom of the will. The concept of a person is not only, then, the concept of a type of entity that has both first-order desires and volitions of the second order. It can also be construed as the concept of a type of entity for whom the freedom of its will may be a problem. This concept excludes all wantons, both infrahuman and human, since they fail to satisfy an essential condition for the enjoyment of freedom of the will. And it excludes those suprahuman beings, if any, whose wills are necesarily free.

Just what kind of freedom is the freedom of the will? This question calls for an identification of the special area of human experience to which the concept of freedom of the will, as distinct from the concepts of other sorts of freedom, is particularly germane. In dealing with it, my aim will be primarily to locate the problem with which a person is most immediately concerned when he is concerned with the freedom of his will.

According to one familiar philosophical tradition, being free is fundamentally a matter of doing what one wants to do. Now the notion of an agent who does what he wants to do is by no means an altogether clear one: both the doing and the wanting, and the appropriate relation between them as well, require elucidation. But although its focus needs to be sharpened and its formulation refined, I believe that this notion does capture at least part of what is implicit in the idea of an agent who *acts* freely. It misses entirely, however, the peculiar content of the quite different idea of an agent whose *will* is free.

We do not suppose that animals enjoy freedom of the will, although we recognize that an animal may be free to run in whatever direction it wants. Thus, having the freedom to do what one wants to do is not a sufficient condition of having a free will. It is not a necessary condition either. For to deprive someone of his freedom of action is not necessarily to undermine the freedom of his will. When an agent is aware that there are certain things he is not free to do, this doubtless affects his desires and limits the range of choices he can make. But suppose that someone, without being aware of it, has in fact lost or been deprived of his freedom of action. Even though he is no longer free to do what he wants to do, his will may remain as free as it was before. Despite the fact that he is not free to translate his desires into actions or to act according to the determinations of his will, he may still form those desires and make those determinations as freely as if his freedom of action had not been impaired.

When we ask whether a person's will is free we are not asking whether he is in a position to translate his first-order desires into actions. That is the question of whether he is free to do as he pleases. The question of the freedom of his will does not concern the relation between what he does and what he wants to do. Rather, it concerns his desires themselves. But what question about them is it?

It seems to me both natural and useful to construe the question of whether a person's will is free in close analogy to the question of whether an agent enjoys freedom of action. Now freedom of action is (roughly, at least) the freedom to do what one wants to do. Analogously, then, the statement that a person enjoys freedom of the will means (also roughly) that he is free to want what he wants to want. More precisely, it means that he is free to will what he wants to will, or to have the will he wants. Just as the question about the freedom of an agent's action has to do with whether it is the action he wants to perform, so the question about the freedom of his will has to do with whether it is the will he wants to have.

It is in securing the conformity of his will to his second-order volitions, then, that a person exercises freedom of the will. And it is in the discrepancy between his will and his second-order volitions, or in his awareness that their coincidence is not his own doing but only a happy chance, that a person who does not have this freedom feels its lack. The unwilling addict's will is not free. This is shown by the fact that it is not the will he wants. It is also true, though in a different way, that the will of the wanton addict is not free. The wanton addict neither has the will he wants nor has a will that differs from the will he wants. Since he has no volitions of the second order, the freedom of his will cannot be a problem for him. He lacks it, so to speak, by default.

People are generally far more complicated than my sketchy account of the structure of a person's will may suggest. There is as much opportunity for ambivalence, conflict, and self-deception with regard to desires of the second order, for example, as there is with regard to first-order desires. If there is an unresolved conflict among someone's second-order desires, then he is in danger of having no second-order volition; for unless this conflict is resolved, he has no preference concerning which of his first-order desires is to be his will. This condition, if it is so severe that it prevents him from identifying himself in a sufficiently decisive way with *any* of his conflicting first-order desires, destroys him as a person. For it either tends to paralyze his will and to keep him from acting at all, or it tends to remove him from his will so that his will operates without his participation. In both cases, he becomes, like the unwilling addict though in a different way, a helpless bystander to the forces that move him.

Another complexity is that a person may have, especially if his second-order desires are in conflict, desires and volitions of a higher order than the second. There is no theoretical limit to the length of the series of desires of higher and higher orders; nothing except common sense and, perhaps, a saving fatigue prevents an individual from obsessively refusing to identify himself with any of his desires until he forms a desire of the next higher order. The tendency to generate such a series of acts of forming desires, which would be a case of humanization run wild, also leads toward the destruction of a person.

It is possible, however, to terminate such a series of acts without cutting it off arbitrarily. When a person identifies himself *decisively* with one of his first-order desires, this commitment "resounds" throughout the potentially endless array of higher orders. Consider a person who, without reservation or conflict, wants to be motivated by the desire to concentrate on his work. The fact that his second-order volition to be moved by this desire is a decisive one means that there is no room for questions concerning the pertinence of desires or volitions of higher orders. Suppose the person is asked whether he wants to want to want to concentrate on his work. He can properly insist that this question concerning a third-order desire does not arise. It would be a mistake to claim that, because he has not considered whether he wants the second-order volition he has formed, he is indifferent to the question of whether it is with this volition or with some other that he wants his will to accord. The decisiveness of the commitment he has made means that he has decided that no further question about his second-order volition, at any higher order, remains to be asked. It is relatively unimportant whether we explain this by saying that this commitment implicitly generates an endless series of confirming desires of higher orders, or by saying that the commitment is tantamount to a dissolution of the pointedness of all questions concerning higher orders of desire.

Examples such as the one concerning the unwilling addict may suggest that volitions of the second order, or of higher orders, must be formed deliberately and that a person characteristically struggles to ensure that they are satisfied. But the conformity of a person's will to his higher-order volitions may be far more thoughtless and spontaneous than this. Some people are naturally moved by kindness when they want to be kind, and by nastiness when they want to be nasty, without any explicit forethought and without any need for energetic self-control. Others are moved by nastiness when they want to be kind and by kindness when they intend to be nasty, equally without forethought and without active resistance to these violations of their higher-order desires. The enjoyment of freedom comes easily to some. Others must struggle to achieve it.

IV

My theory concerning the freedom of the will accounts easily for our disinclination to allow that this freedom is enjoyed by the members of any species inferior to our own. It also satisfies another condition that must be met by any such theory, by making it apparent why the freedom of the will should be regarded as desirable. The enjoyment of a free will means the satisfaction of certain desires—desires of the second or of higher orders—whereas its absence means their frustration. The satisfactions at stake are those which accrue to a person of whom it may be said that his will is his own. The corresponding frustrations are those suffered by a person of whom it may be said that he is estranged from himself, or that he finds himself a helpless or a passive bystander to the forces that move him.

A person who is free to do what he wants to do may yet not be in a position to have the will he wants. Suppose, however, that he enjoys both freedom of action and freedom of the will. Then he is not only free to do what he wants to do; he is also free to want what he wants to want. It seems to me that he has, in that case, all the freedom it is possible to desire or to conceive. There are other good things in life, and he may not possess some of them. But there is nothing in the way of freedom that he lacks.

It is far from clear that certain other theories of the freedom of the will meet these elementary but essential conditions: that it be understandable why we desire this freedom and why we refuse to ascribe it to animals. Consider, for example, Roderick Chisholm's quaint version of the doctrine that human freedom entails an absence of causal determination.[7] Whenever a person performs a free action, according to Chisholm, it's a miracle. The motion of a person's hand, when the person moves it, is the outcome of a series of physical causes; but some event in this series, "and presumably one of those that took place within the brain, was caused by the agent and not by any other events" (p. 18). A free agent has, therefore, "a prerogative which some would attribute only to God: each of us, when we act, is a prime mover unmoved" (p. 23).

This account fails to provide any basis for doubting that animals of subhuman species enjoy the freedom it defines. Chisholm says nothing that makes it seem less likely that a rabbit performs a miracle when it moves its leg than that a man does so when he moves his hand. But why, in any case, should anyone *care* whether he can interrupt the natural order of causes in the way Chisholm describes? Chisholm offers no reason for believing that there is a discernible difference between the experience of a man who miraculously initiates a series of causes when he moves his hand and a man who moves his hand without any such breach of the normal causal sequence. There appears to be no concrete basis for preferring to be involved in the one state of affairs rather than in the other.[8]

It is generally supposed that, in addition to satisfying the two conditions I have mentioned, a satisfactory theory of the freedom of the will necessarily provides an analysis of one of the conditions of moral responsibility. The most common recent approach to the problem of understanding the freedom of the will has been, indeed, to inquire what is entailed by the assumption that someone is morally responsible for what he has done. In my view, however, the relation between moral responsibility and the freedom of the will has been very widely misunderstood. It is not true that a person is morally responsible for what he has done only if his will was free when he did it. He may be morally responsible for having done it even though his will was not free at all.

A person's will is free only if he is free to have the will he wants. This means that, with regard to any of his first-order desires, he is free either to make that desire his will or to make some other first-order desire his will instead. Whatever his will, then, the will of the person whose will is free could have been otherwise; he could have done otherwise than to constitute his will as he did. It is a vexed question just how "he could have done otherwise" is to be understood in contexts such as this one. But although this question is important to the theory of freedom, it has no bearing on the theory of moral responsibility. For the assumption that a person is morally responsible for what he has done does not entail that the person was in a position to have whatever will he wanted.

This assumption *does* entail that the person did what he did freely, or that he did it of his own free will. It is a mistake, however, to believe that someone acts freely only when he is free to do whatever he wants or that he acts of his own free will only if his will is free. Suppose that a person has done what he wanted to do, that he did it because he wanted to do it, and that the will by which he was moved when he did it was his will because it was the will he wanted. Then he did it freely and of his own free will. Even supposing that he could have done otherwise, he would not have done otherwise; and even supposing that he could have had a different will, he would not have wanted his will to differ from what it was. Moreover, since the will that moved him when he acted was his will because he wanted it to be, he cannot claim that his will was forced upon him or that he was a passive bystander to its constitution. Under these conditions, it is quite irrelevant to the evaluation of his moral responsibility to inquire whether the alternatives that he opted against were actually available to him.[9]

In illustration, consider a third kind of addict. Suppose that his addiction has the same physiological basis and the same irresistible thrust as the addictions of the unwilling and wanton addicts, but that he is altogether delighted with his condition. He is a willing addict, who would not have things any other way. If the grip of his addiction should somehow weaken, he would do whatever he could to reinstate it; if his desire for the drug should begin to fade, he would take steps to renew its intensity.

The willing addict's will is not free, for his desire to take the drug will be effective regardless of whether or not he wants this desire to constitute his will. But when he takes the drug, he takes it freely and of his own free will. I am inclined to understand his situation as involving the overdetermination of his first-order desire to take the drug. This desire is his effective desire because he is physiologically addicted. But it is his effective desire also because he wants it to be. His will is outside his control, but, by his second-order desire that his desire for the drug should be effective, he has made this will his own. Given that it is therefore not only because of his addiction that his desire for the drug is effective, he may be morally responsible for taking the drug.

My conception of the freedom of the will appears to be neutral with regard to the problem of determinism. It seems conceivable that it should be causally determined that a person is free to want what he wants to want. If this is conceivable, then it might be causally determined that a person enjoys a free will. There is no more than an innocuous appearance of paradox in the proposition that it is determined, ineluctably and by forces beyond their control, that certain people have free wills and that others do not. There is no incoherence in the proposition that some agency other than a person's own is responsible (even *morally* responsible) for the fact that he enjoys or fails to enjoy freedom of the will. It is possible that a person should be morally responsible for what he does of his own free will and that some other person should also be morally responsible for his having done it.[10]

On the other hand, it seems conceivable that it should come about by chance that a person is free to have the will he wants. If this is conceivable, then it might be a matter of chance that certain people enjoy freedom of the will and that certain others do not. Perhaps it is also conceivable, as a number of philosophers believe, for states of affairs to come about in a way other than by chance or as the outcome of a sequence of natural causes. If it is indeed conceivable for the relevant stats of affairs to come about in some third way, then it is also possible that a person should in that third way come to enjoy the freedom of the will.

Notes

1. P. F. Stawson, *Individuals* (London: Methuen, 1959), 101–2. Ayer's usage of 'person' is similar: "it is characteristic of persons in this sense that besides having various physical properties . . . they are also credited with various forms of consciousness" (A. J. Ayer, *The Concept of a Person* [New York: St. Martin's, 1963], 82). What

concerns Strawson and Ayer is the problem of understanding the relation between mind and body, rather than the quite different problem of understanding what it is to be a creature that not only has a mind and a body but is also a person.

2. For the sake of simplicity, I shall deal only with what someone wants or desires, neglecting related phenomena such as choices and decisions. I propose to use the verbs 'to want' and 'to desire' interchangeably, although they are by no means perfect synonyms. My motive in forsaking the established nuances of these words arises from the fact that the verb 'to want', which suits my purposes better so far as its meaning is concerned, does not lend itself so readily to the formation of nouns as does the verb 'to desire'. It is perhaps acceptable, albeit graceless, to speak in the plural of someone's "wants." But to speak in the singular of someone's "want" would be an abomination.

3. What I say in this paragraph applies not only to cases in which 'to X' refers to a possible action or inaction. It also applies to cases in which 'to X refers to a first-order desire and in which the statement that "A wants to X" is therefore a shortened version of a statement—"A wants to want to X"—that identifies a desire of the second order.

4. It is not so clear that the entailment relation described here holds in certain kinds of cases, which I think may fairly be regarded as nonstandard, where the essential difference between the standard and the nonstandard cases lies in the kind of description by which the first-order desire in question is identified. Thus, suppose that A admires B so fulsomely that, even though he does not know what B wants to do, he wants to be effectively moved by whatever desire effectively moves B; without knowing what B's will is, in other words, A wants his own will to be the same. It certainly does not follow that A already has, among his desires, a desire like the one that constitutes B's will. I shall not pursue here the questions of whether there are genuine counterexamples to the claim made in the text or of how, if there are, that claim should be altered.

5. Creatures with second-order desires but no second-order volitions differ significantly from brute animals, and, for some purposes, it would be desirable to regard them as persons. My usage, which withholds the designation 'person' from them, is thus somewhat arbitrary. I adopt it largely because it facilitates the formulation of some of the points I wish to make. Hereafter, whenever I consider statements of the form "A wants to want to X," I shall have in mind statements identifying second-order volitions and not statements identifying second-order desires that are not second-order volitions.

6. In speaking of the evaluation of his own desires and motives as being characteristic of a person, I do not mean to suggest that a person's second-order volitions necessarily manifest a *moral* stance on his part toward his first-order desires. It may not be from the point of view of morality that the person evaluates his first-order desires. Moreover, a person may be capricious and irresponsible in forming his second-order volitions and give no serious consideration to what is at stake. Second-order volitions express evaluations only in the sense that they are preferences. There is no essential restriction on the kind of basis, if any, upon which they are formed.

7. "Freedom and Action," in K. Lehrer, ed., *Freedom and Determinism* (New York: Random House, 1966), pp. 11–44.

8. I am not suggesting that the alleged difference between these two states of affairs is unverifiable. On the contrary, physiologists might well be able to show that Chisholm's conditions for a free action are not satisfied, by establishing that there is no relevant brain event for which a sufficient physical cause cannot be found.

9. For another discussion of the considerations that cast doubt on the principle that a person is morally responsible for what he has done only if he could have done otherwise, see my "Alternate Possibilities and Moral Responsibility," *Journal of Philosophy* 66, no. 23 (Dec. 4, 1969), 829–39.

10. There is a difference between being *fully* responsible and being *solely* responsible. Suppose that the willing addict has been made an addict by the deliberate and calculated work of another. Then it may be that both the addict and this other person are fully responsible for the addict's taking the drug, while neither of them is solely responsible for it. That there is a distinction between full moral responsibility and sole moral responsibility is apparent in the following example. A certain light can be turned on or off by flicking either of two switches, and each of these switches is simultaneously flicked to the "on" position by a different person, neither of whom is aware of the other. Neither person is solely responsible for the light's going on, nor do they share the responsibility in the sense that each is partially responsible; rather, each of them is fully responsible.

5

Autonomy and the "Inner Self"

Robert Young

Autonomy is commonly held to be a presupposition of moral agency and hence of responsibility, dignity, and self-esteem. In philosophical writings as diverse as those of Aristotle, of Kant and Kantians like Rawls, of libertarians like Nozick, and of existentialists like Sartre, autonomy is closely linked with the concept of a person as a moral being. In fiction the often tragic effects of its defeat has been a recurring theme, and in *Nineteen Eighty Four* and *Brave New World* Orwell and Huxley have given us glimpses of what it would be like to live in a world where autonomy has for the most part been systematically eliminated. In everyday life we acknowledge its importance in that we lament its lack among those who are oppressed or who are severely mentally or physically ill, in wanting our children to develop it and in the fact that our own self-images fluctuate according to the degree to which we can realistically think of ourselves as being autonomous.[1] Yet for all its importance and despite the frequency with which it is appealed to, the concept of autonomy generally operates at an intuitive level and rarely is seriously explored. In this paper I shall explore an aspect of autonomy which is fundamental to any adequate understanding of the concept but which has been given less consideration even than the concept itself.

I

One of the few points about autonomy which is clear is that it is connected with liberty or freedom (which despite its various nuances[2] will on this occasion have to be left largely unexplored). To unravel what it is to be free in the relevant sense would involve sorting out what it is not to be subject to the will of another, what it is not to be subject to defeating natural conditions, and what it is to possess the means or power to achieve a chosen objective. It is not

This chapter was originally published in the *American Philosophical Quarterly* 17, no. 1 (Jan. 1980). Copyright © 1980 by *American Philosophical Quarterly*. Reprinted by permission.
Robert Young is Reader in Philosophy at La Trobe University.

because I think this task to be easy or unimportant[3] that I shall not here be considering it but because I think there is a need to redress the balance a little and give some attention to what it is to exercise one's freedom in such a way as to order one's life according to a plan[4] or conception which fully expresses one's own choices since intuitively this is the heart of our notion of autonomy. To this extent autonomy clearly involves more than just being free (even where freedom is construed so as to include both freedom of action and of decision). One must be free to be autonomous, but one can be free and still lack autonomy because it is, for instance, possible freely but mindlessly to mimic the tastes, opinions, ideals, goals, principles, values, and preferences of others. So freedom is necessary for autonomy but not sufficient. At least this much more is needed: that a person's choices actually be expressive of his or her individual preferences, aspirations, and so on.

Some of those who would agree with me that the self-directing aspect of autonomy has been neglected would wish to emphasize this notion of self-directedness to the virtual exclusion of any consideration of the extent to which a person's life needs to be unified in the manner suggested in "ordering one's life according to a plan or conception." On the minimalist view autonomy is, if you like, being one's own man or woman and to be sure this fits well with our use of "autonomy" in an occurrent way. We recognize that people act autonomously in particular situations. But I want to suggest that we also employ the term "autonomy" when we wish to make a more global point about someone's life. In this latter image the unified ordering of the autonomous person's life is what exemplifies most fully its self-directedness. While some of what I have to say below transfers readily enough to the autonomous acts of agents my concern will be more directly with the patterned conception of autonomy.

To the extent that an individual is self-directed he (or she) brings the entire course of his life into a unified order. This suggests that a person who is free of external constraints and who has the capacity to pursue a particular pattern of living may fail to be autonomous not just because his principles of thought and action (his motivational structure) are secondhand, but also because he is not able to organize these principles in a unified way. To put it more popularly, he may fail to get it all together because his inner self is disordered, is lacking integration. In the subsequent course of trying to show how such disorder may be avoided or overcome these notions will have to be filled out but it will be helpful first to indicate the variety of factors which may from within, as it were, obstruct the achievement of autonomy.

These factors range through from those neuroses which may give rise to long term and even permanent incursions into a person's autonomy, to self-deception, to ambivalence, to the kind of anomie produced by an individual's having ill-defined principles of action and on to weakness of will where the effects on autonomy are generally more isolated both in duration and impact. It would be satisfying, not to say neat, if these and other conditions of the "inner self" that obstruct autonomy could be traced to a single failure in the agent (such as a failure of self-awareness). But this seems unlikely. Still, I shall be arguing among other things that until persons achieve awareness concerning their motivations to that extent autonomy remains out of their reach. Even if I am right about this, however, it remains true that for certain of the inner obstructions I have mentioned (e.g., ambivalence and weakness of will) the agent's failure will not typically be a lack of self-awareness. Though even here there is a sense in which the agent's self-knowledge may have a contribution to make to enhancing his autonomy; it may enable the agent to avoid situations where his weakness is apt to be his undoing or to determine which of the contrary values generating his ambivalence will best promote his autonomy (either in the short or the longer term).

There is an objection which may be raised at this point which threatens the whole idea of matching up an agent's effective motivation with a motivational structure that, had it been acted upon, would have exhibited the agent's self-directedness. Were it to succeed it would call into question the whole conspectus of autonomy that I have till now been working with. Moreover, in the process of reckoning with it an account of authenticity in motivation will emerge which will provide a foundation for what I have to say subsequently about the inner obstacles to autonomy to which I have referred.

Gerald Dworkin has argued[5] that autonomy cannot be located at the level of first-order motivations because we cannot choose *ab initio* our convictions, principles, desires, and so forth. But, as he sees it, even if the autonomous person cannot adopt his motivations *de novo* he can make them *his* by identifying with them in his reflective judgings so that he views himself as the kind of person who wishes to be thus motivated. In forming such second-order desires by means of reflective self-evaluation a person's motivational structure does come to have the stamp of authenticity. On this account it does not matter how one comes to have one's particular first-order desires, what matters is whether or not one desires to have such desires. Dworkin puts it as follows in "Autonomy and Behaviour Control:"

> It is the attitude a person takes toward the influences motivating him which determines whether or not they are to be considered "his." Does he identify with them, assimilate them to himself, view himself, as the kind of person who wishes to be motivated in these particular ways? If, on the contrary, a man resents his being motivated in certain ways, is alienated from those influences, resents acting in accordance with them, would prefer to be the kind of person who is motivated in different ways, then those influences, even though they may be causally effective, are not viewed as "his." (p. 25)

In addition to this quality of authenticity, autonomy, for Dworkin, requires that a person's motivational structure display what he terms "procedural independence" for otherwise a person's motivations may be *his* but not his *own* because the product of manipulation, deception, or other undue influence. On that score I am in agreement with Dworkin's remarks though I have argued in "Compatibilism and Conditioning" that they are in need of elaboration.

I accept, too, the general thrust of Dworkin's (and Frankfurt's) insistence on the need for authenticity in a person's motivations if a person is to be autonomous. There are, however, grounds for refusing to run together the reflective self-evaluation manifested in the formation of second-order desires and the notion of identifying with, and thus making one's own, those desires which move to action. There seems no question that one can identify with one's first-order desires. Furthermore where there is a clash between a lower-order and a higher-order desire it would seem possible to identify with the lower-order one. If so, the idea of identification with one's desires is independent of the notion of 'orders of desires'. Moreover, the formation of second-order desires is not sufficient for identification with such desires since one may, for example, be self-deceived about what one really wants or weak-willed to the point where one's claims about one's own desires come to lack conviction. I shall have more to say about such phenomena below but mention of them makes plain that both Frankfurt and Dworkin (at least in "Acting Freely") in their insistence on the role of reflection appear to take too narrowly cognitivist a view of the way in which a commitment to certain wantings may be clarified.[6]

The opinions about their own motivations which people form, even after the most careful introspection, are not always the most reliable indicator of their deepest preferences. Where, for instance, a person shows remorse over his failure to perform some action which he believed he ought to have done (given that he was not self-reflectively aware of any countervailing want or inclination), or where he shows genuine admiration for the behavior of others—an admiration which does not flag even when he regularly fails to measure up to the standard of those he admires—we are apt to give maximum credence to such conative considerations in determining his real desires. This is especially so where circumstances arise in a person's life which provide a literally unique opportunity to do some important action. Any failure to capitalize on the opportunity will be an irredeemable failure. In such a case a person's remorsefulness may prove the only serious evidence we have of his true desires. Remorse, unlike guilt feelings or feelings of regret, is a peculiarly appropriate response to a failure to act as one believed one ought, because it is linked with a *wish* that one hadn't done what one did. In the light of these various considerations my inclination is to think of the formation of second-order (and, though they are probably uncommon, even higher-order) desires as *indicators* of a person's deepest preferences and ultimately of what desires are to be identified with. At the same time it must not be forgotten that there are other indicators, too, which can satisfactorily be taken as supporting a claim that a particular individual does identify with certain of his desires.

There is one final issue I want to consider in this context. It concerns how we should react to the individual who *does* recognize that the desires he acts on are those he wishes to be motivated by but nonetheless conceals this from others for use as a moral egress. Such a falsehood is, as Terence Penelhum[7] has suggested, something we swallow both about ourselves and others, though we should know better. Only rarely are we able legitimately to plead that what we did was done in circumstances comparable to those which must prevail before the plea "crime of passion" gains admission. For present purposes what we need to point out is that the occurrence of such moral hoaxing ought not to promote skepticism about the authenticity of other responses. Indeed, the hoaxer will typically engage in special pleading once too often and thus blow his cover.

I want now to move on to a consideration of how the failure to identify with a motivational structure which exemplifies the conception one has of one's life is central to an understanding of the neurotic, the self-deceived and the anomic. In the process I shall argue that progress in overcoming these conditions depends on the achievement of self-awareness about motivation. I shall then take up the argument about weak-willedness and argue that there is a genuine phenomena to be dealt with and that it too can be illuminated by reference to the idea of the agent's failure to identify with a motivational structure that exemplifies his life plan.

II

The neurotic behaves in a self-defeating manner yet can neither account for, nor control, the way in which he or she behaves. In his later writings[8] it is Freud's view that the neurotic manages to avoid satisfying those instinctual demands or impulses which would generate anxiety by resort to defense mechanisms such as repression but is all the while unconscious of what is happening. Since such behavior has a point, indeed can be seen to have systematic sense (in staving off anxiety), the neurotic is often characterized as having unconscious intentions. Provided a suitably restrained reading of such a term is given it need not be misleading to speak like this.[9] There are fairly obvious connections between this influential account of the neurotic's attempt to cope with anxiety-producing impulses and what holds true of the self-deceived person. Mischel has put the connection neatly in "Understanding Neurotic Behaviour:"

> . . . the neurotic has avoided the conflict by deceiving himself: his lack of awareness is motivated, he has made himself unconscious of an incompatible impulse which he knows, in one sense of that term, to be his. And he can do that only insofar as he can also keep himself unconscious of the technique he is intentionally using to deceive himself. (p. 235)[10]

With both conditions the role of ignorance as to one's own motivations is of paramount importance. Indeed if x were to set out deliberately to deceive himself the successful achievement of his aim would be hidden from him. This is because the self-deceiver sustains himself in his self-deception by manipulating the evidence in accordance with the personal stake he has in clinging obstinately to a false belief or in giving up a true but displeasing belief for a false but attractive one. Sometimes to bring about such a condition in oneself serves a protective or defensive role as, for example, when a person clings to a belief about whether a loved one involved in an airplane crash overseas remains alive despite the fact that the evidence is best read to the contrary.[11]

Nevertheless, the self-deceived person believes what he believes to be true and wants what he believes to be true because of his placing a distorted construction on the total evidence. And this is the means to overcoming a conflict in his beliefs even though he is not aware that it is such a means.

Self-deception, like neurosis, is something which any person who aspires to autonomy would prefer to avoid. Those in such conditions lack both understanding and control of their own lives or of a part of their lives and, what is more, the normal means of coming to understand one's situation—reflecting as to the reasons for or against one's behavior—is typically ineffective. (This is not to say that the person may not know that something is seriously amiss and neurotics in particular may well seek help on just such a ground.) With the self-deceived person what is needed is that the evidence be represented (either by someone else or, eventually, perhaps by the agent) in such a way as to show that there can be no room for argument about it or that the complexion to be placed on the evidence can realistically be of only one sort. The toehold in the evidence which provided the person with enough support to distort and misconstrue it and thus reduce its impact on him has to be shown to be inadequate to the task. It is precisely because the distorting and misconstruing go on outside of the agent's conscious scrutiny that the overcoming of self-deception requires raising the agent's consciousness or, to put it another way, promoting self-awareness about his imposition of an unnatural interpretation on the total evidence.

With the neurotic person, the coming to awareness of his resort to unconscious defenses to avoid facing up to situations apt to produce anxiety rarely proves as straightforward a matter as overcoming self-deception. There probably are cases where a neurosis is in a sense just outgrown. For instance, a neurotic fear of not being liked might disappear upon involvement in a serious loving relationship. In such cases a coming to self-awareness would not be a prerequisite for overcoming the inner obstacle to autonomy. Generally, though the neurotic's self-deceptive defenses not only have more deep-seated origins but play a sufficiently critical role in the maintenance of some sort of personal stability, albeit a precarious one, to necessitate some struggle and effort to lay them bare. Even treatment promising successful overcoming of the neurosis may encounter resistance.[12] Such successes as there are with laying bare the foundations of neurotic behavior and enabling the victim to cope with the impulses which give rise to his anxiety, nevertheless, take a similar course to that involved in defeating self-deception.

Since autonomous action is founded on sophisticated self-awareness[13] the securing of a degree of autonomy in a person's pattern of living where previously neurotic forces held sway cannot occur without awareness of the operation of such forces. What has been hidden from the agent: his instinctual impulses, his unconscious defensive maneuverings to avoid facing these impulses, perhaps even his resistance to the uncovering of these aspects of his being, have to be so revealed that the agent can see the inappropriateness of the behavior all this produces. Various forms of psychotherapy have been developed to help the neurotic person see his situation for what it is. Now I am not for one minute suggesting that we take an uncritical attitude to such techniques but there can be no doubt that sometimes they work and that when they do it is partly because they develop self-awareness in the agent. What has been effective because unconscious must be brought to consciousness if its effectiveness is to be stopped. Where the agent actively participates in the redirecting of his cognitive and affective structures he can identify with the changed or renewed self as continuous with, though different from, his neurotic one.

It is, of course, not enough to get the neurotic to understand, to become aware of his own psychological processes for the neurotic does not merely fail to understand such processes, he also is not in control of them. As elsewhere, to get to know of a flaw is not to eliminate it. And the more bound up with a person's self-image the neurosis happens to be, the greater the effort of will that must be made to get beyond self-awareness to self-directedness. As with the seriously self-deceived person who cannot be brought to take the evidence (whatever it may be) at face value, it may be that in the long run autonomy is forsaken not because of the dynamics of the unconscious but for want of the courage, honesty, effort of will and so on to forge one's life into a life of one's own. This is a theme to which I shall return in section IV when I consider the connection between weakness of will and the lack of autonomy.[14]

III

While the effects on an individual's autonomy of his holding his values in a compliantly secondhand way are readily acknowledged the effects on autonomy of a lack in inner coherence among an individual's concerns are less often noted. Where there is no inner unity because the self is divided and torn over which projects to engage in or what order to engage in them there will be no unified life (even in the fairly weak sense which I insisted on as involved in autonomy). The impact may be on generalized orientations (ultimate beliefs, norms or goals) or relatively specific goals. Thus a person who is free to do some particular action may fail to do so if his wanting to do other less significant actions is allowed to interfere with and ultimately frustrate his pursuit of what he would acknowledge to be more significant and more authentically "him." Frequently such people, having failed to engage in those activities most expressive of their intrinsic concerns, prefer to be told how to live. The terminology used by Durkheim in a related but distinct context has come to be applied to such persons—they are *anomic*.

The account of authenticity in motivation which I earlier advanced once again proves helpful. In failing to break out of the internal disorder of his pattern of living the anomic individual fails to carve out a truly autonomous existence. How can such an individual hope to overcome his hang-ups and begin to lead a more ordered life?

One way, of course, would be to allow his life to be governed by others. But to choose this way is to take the line of least resistance and to forsake autonomy and the self-esteem and dignity that go with it. So, too, to fall back on techniques which involve bodily intrusions or drastic interventions, like psychosurgery and aversion therapy, *may* as Dworkin[15] has pointed out, be causally to produce a state which might be called increased self-esteem or dignity but in a way which violates such qualities or at least fails to support them as such. They ought to be resorted to, therefore, only where no means of achieving the same effect is otherwise available and the subject is in a position to give informed voluntary consent (and if Murphy is right this will never be so while the subject is an inmate of an institution). The better way, surely, would be to seek to understand the malaise by a means which accords due place to human dignity and that would only seem possible if the anomic person can be brought to recognize for himself what produces his frustrations, resentment, or resignation about the course of his life. Where this is not within his own province, the means for achieving this will range through from the sympathetic, trusted friend who acts as a "sounding board" to professional counseling. But whatever the means the aim will be the same: to enable the person to gain awareness of his inner conflicts and hopefully to go on to replace the disorder with a realistic hierarchical ordering that reflects the priorities with which he would prefer to identify. The test for determining how well this latter condition is satisfied will be the extent of relief from bitterness, frustration, and resentment. (It would seem foolish to require complete contentment since even given a high degree of autonomy one may nonetheless regret that certain projects are beyond one's capacity or demand as prerequisite things to which one is not entitled and so on. But relatively greater contentment there must be if anomie has been brought under control and the end-state thought to be one which preserves individual integrity.)

IV

An individual who fails intentionally to do an action which he believes he ought to do and which is psychologically and physically within his power need not thereby fail of autonomy (especially in the occurrent sense). But where such a failure has some bearing on the person's broad conception of his life's direction, or where the failure becomes persistent, there will almost certainly be a diminution in global autonomy. Such failures are matters of everyday observation and sadly of personal experience. Yet various philosophers of note[16] have argued that there can be no such hiatus between belief and action for a free agent. There is not space here fully to traverse the issue of weakness of will but at least enough must be done to dispel the suggestion that it is radically unlike the other inner impediments to autonomy we've been considering because it is either incoherent or incompatible with acting freely. What I shall first do is argue against two influential views of the relation between convictions, desires, and actions that have wide currency and a certain initial plausibility and would undermine the commonsense conception of weakness of will if they were correct. Then I shall treat of the possibility of distinguishing the weak-willed agent from the compulsive.

   It is sometimes contended that we do *as a matter* of fact think that in accepting certain judgment about what we or others ought to do we imply that we will act in accordance with those judgments where we are able. In order to assess the force of this contention we need to determine what criteria have to be satisfied before we are willing to say of someone that he believes he ought to perform some specified action. Were we able to state a set of criteria sufficient for the truth of the proposition that a person, *X*, believes he ought to do *A*, then the conjunction of the assertion that the criteria are actually satisfied with the denial that *X* believes he ought to do *A*, would involve something like self-contradiction.

Can a convincing set of such criteria be stated? According to the position set out above if we suppose *X* believes that he ought to do *A* and, moreover, has no wants or inclinations that run counter to his belief that he ought to do *A*, then we must assert that there is an analytic connection between a statement about his belief and one about his doing action *A*. Such a view is not without initial plausibility. We do discount the protestations of those who never get around to acting on their well-voiced "beliefs." Nevertheless, if the position were correct it would follow that facts other than those about the absence of countervailing wants or inclinations could not provide logically adequate grounds for ascribing the belief to the person, *X*. But there surely could be such facts, in particular facts about *X* himself. In section I above I drew on such facts in qualifying Dworkin and Frankfurt's appeal to an agent's identification with his expressed second-order desires and volitions to establish motivational authenticity. To reiterate: where a person shows remorse over his failure (or persistent failures) to live up to his beliefs or where he shows genuine admiration for the behavior of others and does not flag in his admiration even when he fails to measure up his own standards, we are generally prepared to ascribe the appropriate beliefs and desires to him.

Still, it might be rejoined that we couldn't even identify a person's reaction as one of remorse without our being satisfied that he puts forth genuine efforts to make amends and alter his future conduct. My reply is that while remorse is certainly often accompanied by the intention to mend one's ways (and subsequently by the accomplishment of this task) it doesn't seem that it must be. Remorse, as I suggested previously, is the appropriate response (as against feelings of guilt or regret) to a failure to act as one believed one ought, because it goes hand in hand with a wish that one hadn't done what one did. And where one's failure comes in response to a literally unique opportunity the evidence of remorse (in its attendance on the weak behavior) should be sufficient to justify the claim that the person *did* believe that he ought to have done what, in fact, he didn't.

The recognition of the irrevocability of the past is what occasions remorse since that emotion cannot adequately be characterized without reference to the seeming inability of the agent to restore the situation to what it was prior to acting. Accordingly, some writers like Nietzsche have concluded that remorse is futile; yet others have noted that the remorseful person may also succumb to feelings of utter hopelessness just because the opportunity to do otherwise has been irretrievably lost. Now I do not believe that remorse need be unhealthy and willingly conclude therefore that even supposing that a person believes he ought to do some act and that he has no countervailing wants or inclinations, there cannot be established an analytic connection between a statement about the agent's beliefs about what he ought to do and a statement about his doing it. Moreover, it won't do to weaken the alleged relation to an empirical or probabilistic sort (e.g., that he will do it nine times out of ten) because we are supposed to be looking for a set of criteria *sufficient* for the truth of the doxastic proposition.

Certain other philosophers, who would accept the preceding conclusion, have argued that one can nevertheless determine what people believe they ought to do by consideration of what they want, because "believing one ought to do *A*" implies (they claim) "wanting-to-do-*A*-in-preference-to-anything-else."

Neil Cooper argues that the central case of (moral) weakness is one in which a person occurrently wants to-do-*A*-in-preference-to-anything-else, *and* occurrently can do *A*, and yet fails to do it.[17]

Donald Davidson has argued that the following principle is self-evidently true:[18] "If an agent judges that it would be better to do *x*, than to do *y*, then he wants to do *x* more than he wants to do *y*." He also believes in the self-evident truth of a further principle: "If an agent wants to do *x* more than he wants to do *y*, and he believes himself to be free to do either *x* or *y*, then he will intentionally do *x* if he does either *x* or *y* intentionally." Now if these two principles are true, an agent could only be weak-willed if he or she erred in judgment. Thus, like Aristotle, Davidson holds that weak-willedness *in the sense of knowingly doing what one believes wrong*, is impossible. Yet, (also like Aristotle) Davidson acknowledges that there are genuine cases of incontinence (or weakness of will)—namely cases in which the agent does what is not best, while not being aware that it isn't, due to failure in practical reasoning. The weak agent does something intentionally but he does not intentionally do what he believes to be wrong. This would yield a very attenuated sense of "weakness of will."

It might seem rather surprising that Cooper and Davidson, despite sharing a common principle about the relation between judging something to be what ought to be done and wanting to do it in preference to other things, hold such opposed views on weakness of will. The reason is that Cooper does not accept Davidson's second principle. I shall here argue that the principle held in common by Davidson and Cooper is false. (For the sake of argument I am prepared to accept Davidson's second principle.)[19] Like Cooper I shall insist on the genuineness of the commonsense belief in weakness of will rather than on Davidson's attenuated sense, even though I believe that Cooper's formulation of the "central" case of moral weakness is vitiated by his mistaken idea that if a person believes he ought to do some action that he will want to do it in preference to other things.

Why is the principle, which Cooper and Davidson support, false? The principle comes to grief because it does not do justice to the nature of either moral principles or prudential principles. An agent may surely genuinely accept a *moral* principle and yet violate it on occasions because on those occasions he accedes to the pull of self-interest. If so, then an agent may judge that it would be better morally (rather than better all things considered) to do x rather than to do y and yet want to do y more than he wants to do x. Equally in the case of *prudential* principles there seems to be no ground for denying in a non-question-begging way that there can be conflicts of wants. It is, of course, true that we do discount the claims of those who never put their feet where their mouths are and it may be thought, therefore, that we should insist that only those who act in accordance with their wants genuinely accept some particular prudential principle. But this insistence is either question-begging or else depends on the claim that humans are never truly ambivalent about what they want. The experience of most of us is, however, that people are motivationally less of a piece than this claim would lead us to believe. My conclusion is that the principle held in common by Cooper and Davidson, so far from being self-evidently true as Davidson contends, is false.

As I indicated earlier it has sometimes been argued that weakness of will is not possible for a free agent. Gary Watson, in an illuminating paper,[20] has recently argued that if a sufficient condition of compulsive motivation is that the motivation be contrary to the agent's better practical judgment, then weakness of will is a species of compulsion. And if, as seems to be so, compulsive behavior is unfree, weak behavior is too. According to Watson the way out of this unhappy conclusion is to hold that the weak agent gives in to desires which the possession of the *normal* degree of self-control would enable him to resist whereas compulsive desires are such that the normal capacities of resistance are or would be insufficient to enable the agent to resist. We can thus avoid collapsing the distinction between weakness and compulsion by holding that those who are weak fall short of standards of "reasonable" and "normal" self-control, whereas compulsives are motivated by desires which they could not resist even if they met those standards. Watson goes on to argue that his account has the advantage over the commonsense view in that his can explain weakness (as culpable failure to develop or maintain the relevant capacities of self-control) but the commonsense one can't because it proves insufficient to appeal either to the agent's choice not to resist or to the agent's failure to put out enough effort. And, he continues, neither appeal to choice nor to a failure to put out sufficient effort can restore the fortunes of the commonsense view. Appeal to choice won't do because the capacity of self-control is special in involving the capacity to counteract and resist the strength of desires which are contrary to what one has judged best to do. Appeal to a failure in output of effort won't do either because given the weak agent's strong motive for making an effort, namely his considered practical judgment, then in the absence of a special explanation for his not making it (like not thinking the project worth the effort) we should conclude that the agent *couldn't* resist.

This latest attack on the commonsense view is an impressive one but I believe an adequate response can be offered. To begin with, weakness of will is not only manifested in failures to measure up to normal standards of self-control. An intensely moral person, for instance, may fail in some highly demanding situation to do what on previous occasions he has shown he has the capacity to do and which he believes he ought to do when others would see the self-imposed obligation as supererogatory and his failure as totally excusable. Perhaps Watson would object that such an agent's standards have been pitched unreasonably high and hence that the counterexample should be rejected. The difficulty with this response is that it is question-begging. At the other end of the scale, a person who cares very little for social mores may still care enough about his own integrity as regards certain matters (even as regards what others would view as idiosyncratic concerns) to be shamed or remorseful when he fails to live up to his own standards even though he could have done what he thought he ought to have done and, despite his having below normal capacities for resistance, be far more lenient than is normally the case in his society. Similar remarks would surely apply to those whose weakness remains their own secret since the standard to which they aspire will not be some social norm even if it is identical with such a norm.

Secondly, in several places in his argument Watson mounts his attack from a doctrine I have had cause to reject earlier in this section. He argues[21] rather behavioristically that it is from an agent's performance or nonperformance of an action that we should infer what are his real motivations and convictions. Previously I argued that there can be other indicators of a person's true motivations and convictions (such as his displaying remorse). On the basis of the arguments offered before I suggest that we are entitled to resist Watson's doctrine and the conclusion he uses it to reach.

The final point I want to offer in response concerns Watson's attack on the explanatory power of the commonsense view. Suppose that we have evidence from previous conduct in similar circumstances that a person has the capacity to perform a particular action. Suppose further that it would be implausible to account for his failure to perform the action on a particular occasion in terms of psychological failure (e.g., a seizing up under pressure). Suppose finally that he fails to do it and evinces deep remorse because he believed he ought to have done the action on the occasion in question. Given all these suppositions it seems to me that we might justifiably conclude that the best explanation of his failure was weakness of will for he could have done otherwise and it is the possession of this capacity which distinguishes him from the compulsive. The coherence of the commonsense view of weakness of will can, therefore, be held onto.

If the conclusion is warranted that weakness of will is a human phenomenon that we do have to reckon with, its impact on autonomy will likewise have to be reckoned with. The degree to which it interferes with a person's autonomy will depend on the seriousness of the actions it affects and on the range of such actions. In general, though, the weak-willed human surely has the advantage over, for example, the neurotic or anomic one whose autonomy may be extensively curtailed. Notwithstanding this, one victory over his "worst self" for an individual oppressed by any of these conditions may enable a breakthrough to greater self-directedness and personal integrity. The role which self-knowledge or self-awareness, particularly in this context as regards one's capacities and motivation, plays in paving the way for any such victory may sometimes prove significant by directing one out of harm's way. As with the conditions discussed earlier on, however, in order to go beyond mere theory and remove this inner obstacle to autonomy it is the will which holds the key.[22]

Notes

1. On this see Sharon Hill, "Self-Determination and Autonomy," in R. Wasserstrom, ed., *Today's Moral Problems* (New York, 1975), 171–86.

2. Joel Feinberg has aired these thoroughly in his careful treatment in ch. 1 of *Social Philosophy* (Englewood Cliffs, N.J., 1973).

3. It has indeed been a source of continuing fascination for me (as for many others) and one to which I have recently given further attention in my "Compatibilism and Conditioning," *Nous* 13 (1979).

4. The notion of a life-plan as I use it differs from the rather formal one employed by John Rawls in *A Theory of Justice* (Cambridge, Mass. 1971), which, as Robert Paul Wolff points out in *Understanding Rawls* (Princeton: Princeton University Press, 1977), 137ff, is not only culture bound but modeled too closely on that of the profit-maximizing behavior of a firm in microeconomic theory. I use the term more broadly to refer to whatever it is that a person wants to do in and with his or her life.

5. Cf. "Acting Freely," *Nous* 4 (1970), 367–83 and "Autonomy and Behaviour Control," *Hastings Center Report* 6 (1976), 23–28. Similar views have been advanced by Harry Frankfurt in Chapter 4, "Freedom of the Will and the Concept of a Person," and by Wright Neely, "Freedom and Desire," *Philosophical Review* 83 (1974), 32–54. Gary Watson has made some criticisms of Frankfurt's and Neely's views in Chapter 7 "Free Agency."

6. Neely, "Freedom and Desire," makes it a condition of an agent's having freely performed some action that had he been given what he took to be good and sufficient *reason* for not doing what he did, that he would not have done it. Quite apart from the epistemological difficulties which this resort to counterfactuals introduces, Neely's condition also suffers from too intellectualist an orientation because of this stress on the role of reasoning.

7. "The Importance of Self-Identity," *Journal of Philosophy* 68 (1971), 667–78 (esp. pp. 670f).

8. *Inhibitions, Symptoms and Anxiety* and *New Introductory Lectures in Psycho-Analysis*, vols. 20 and 22 respectively, of *The Standard Edition of the Complete Psychological Works of Sigmund Freud* (London, 1953).

9. For an interesting defense of the employment of such terminology see, e.g., Theodore Mischel, "Understanding Neurotic Behaviour: from 'Mechanism' to 'Intentionality'" in Mischel, ed., *Understanding Other Persons* (Oxford, 1970).

10. Cf. also Herbert Fingarette, *Self Deception* (London, 1969), and D. W. Hamlyn, "Self Deception," *Proceedings of the Aristotelian Society, Supplementary Volume* 45 (1971), 61–72.

11. Béla Szabados has argued convincingly that while self-deception is inextricably tied up with moral considerations that one cannot always charge the self-deceiver with selfishness (as Butler did in his tenth *Sermon*) or lack of courage as Fingarette has. See further, "The Morality of Self-Deception," *Dialogue* 13 (1974), 25–34 and "Self-Deception," *Canadian Journal of Philosophy* 4 (1974–75), 51–68.

12. See, e.g., Freud's famous case-history of an obsessional neurosis, that of Paul Lorenz (the "rat man"): *Notes Upon A Case of Obsessional Neurosis*, vol. X of *The Standard Edition*.

13. In *Freedom of the Individual* (London, 1965), ch. 2, Stuart Hampshire makes some useful points about the processes of gaining self-awareness.

14. Though my concern in this paper is chiefly with those who regret their lack of autonomy, we cannot entirely neglect the possibility alluded to by Frankfurt, "Freedom of the Will," 67f., that a person may not, or may even be unable to, reflect on or evaluate the desires that happen to be at the time dominant in his life except to determine how best to satisfy them. Such a person may even be aware that this is his state. But because autonomy is not a serious concern with him, the search for a self-awareness that would avoid his lack of direction will not begin.

15. Cf. "Autonomy and Behaviour Control," esp. pp. 26–28. See, too, an as yet unpublished paper by Jeffrie Murphy: "Total Institutions and the Possibility of Consent to Organic Therapies."

16. In particular Socrates, Aristotle, and R. M. Hare whose views are outlined and subjected to powerful criticisms in G. Mortimore, ed., *Weakness of Will* (London, 1971).

17. See his papers on the topic in Mortimore, ed., *Weakness of Will.*

18. See his "How is Weakness of the Will Possible?," in J. Feinberg, ed., *Moral Concepts* (Oxford, 1969).

19. Michael Stocker, in some unpublished work entitled "Badness, Goodness and Desire" has argued that the second principle is defective because other things than good ones attract us. If he is right then we need not accept Davidson's second principle.

20. "Scepticism About Weakness of Will," *Philosophical Review* 86 (1977), 316–39.

21. Watson, 327 and 336.

22. I would like to thank John Campbell, Alec Hyslop, and John Kleinig for helpful comments on a previous draft and Michael Stocker for discussions about some of the matters I have considered.

6

The Kantian Conception
of Autonomy

Thomas E. Hill, Jr.

Autonomy is a central concept in contemporary moral debates as well as in discussions of Kant; but the only thing that seems completely clear about autonomy in these contests is that it means different things to different writers. Though no one denies the importance of autonomy in Kant's moral theory, there is surprisingly little agreement even about how Kant conceived autonomy. This is not entirely the fault of the commentators, of course, for what Kant says about autonomy is not only deep and richly suggestive but also incomplete, ambiguous, and (at times) opaque. Even those who seem confident that they have grasped what Kant was getting at are deeply divided about the value of Kant's idea of autonomy. To some it is the most central and profound concept in moral philosophy, but to others it is an inapplicable relic of unduly optimistic age, a desperate metaphysical flight from the implications of science and critical philosophy. Our topic, then, lies in an area where one understandably hesitates to "rush in," even though the ground is not completely untrod by angels.

Nevertheless, I propose to sketch here what I think the main Kantian conception of autonomy is, and what it is not. My main focus is on Kant's *Groundwork of the Metaphysics of Morals*, but the view of autonomy there, I believe, is generally consistent with Kant's later ethical writings. In keeping with the broad perspective of the conference for which this paper was intended,[1] I do not offer detailed analyses of particular texts but rather summarize some main implications of Kantian autonomy, as I understand this, and then discuss briefly some objections to it. My main thesis is not that all Kant's claims about autonomy are correct but just that they have important implications concerning rational deliberation that are, to a large extent, independent of his most troublesome metaphysical ideas and his special understanding of the moral law.

More specifically, my plan is this: *First*, I will survey some familiar conceptions of autonomy in order to distinguish them from the Kantian conception.

Thomas Hill is Professor of Philosophy at the University of North Carolina at Chapel Hill.

Second, I describe some main features of Kantian autonomy, distinguishing these from the claims Kant makes about the connection between autonomy and morality. *Third*, I highlight some implications of the Kantian conception, especially its relevance to contemporary views about rational choice. *Finally*, I take up briefly the objections that Kantian autonomy is incompatible with physical determinism and with the explanation of human action by reference to the agent's beliefs and desires.

1. What Kantian Autonomy Is Not

The term 'autonomy' appears frequently in philosophical theories of quite different sorts, and recently it has become a favorite term in practical disputes about politics, education, developmental psychology, and feminism. To avoid confusion, then, it may be well to begin by separating our special subject matter, Kantian autonomy, from some familiar but distinct ideas of autonomy.[2] Kant's conception of autonomy may well have inspired some of these contemporary notions, but in important ways they have been cut loose from their Kantian roots.

First, autonomy is sometimes conceived as a sort of psychological maturity, which some people have and others do not and which we attribute to people in various degrees on the basis of empirical evidence. An autonomous person, in this sense, has a kind of independence of judgment which young children and unthinking conformists lack. One shows a deficiency of autonomy when one blindly follows parental wishes, peer pressures, traditional norms, church authorities, or local fads, fashions, or folk heroes. Impulsive rebellion against custom and authority, however, does not mark one as autonomous, for autonomy is typically associated with a high degree of rational self-control. Compulsive gamblers and drug addicts, for example, are common paradigms of the nonautonomous. Some apparently think of autonomous persons as being, in addition, emotionally independent of others, self-reliant, and secure in their self-esteem. Other common criteria of autonomy include a propensity to think abstractly, to listen to alternative viewpoints, and to weigh reasons for acting.

A particular version of this idea of autonomy as a variable psychological trait serves for some as both a descriptive category and a normative ideal for moral agents. For example, this seems to be the role of autonomy in Kohlberg's account of moral development, which Carol Gilligan has criticized as reflecting a masculine bias.[3] The ideal includes not only reflectiveness, self-control, and independence of judgment, but also commitment to general principles, apart from hope of reward or fear of punishment; and it requires making moral decisions from this loyalty to abstract principle rather than from compassion for particular persons. Autonomous agents, on this view, make moral decisions from an impartial perspective, detached from the special feelings that stem from their particular personal relationships.

Now, though we can easily recognize here several ideas Kant would have applauded, there are some crucial differences between these psychological conceptions of autonomy and Kantian autonomy. For one thing, autonomy in the psychological accounts is an empirically discernable trait, attributed in various degrees to people on the basis of what they are observed to say and do in various circumstances. Kant, on the other hand, treats autonomy as an "Idea" of reason, attributed on a priori grounds to all rational wills. Despite some appearances to the contrary, Kant typically treats autonomy as an all-or-nothing trait that grounds a basic respect due to all human beings, as opposed to a variable respect earned only by the most conscientious. Because they have autonomy of the will, Kant argues, all (minimally) rational human beings have basic moral obligations. Though special obligations vary with circumstances, being under moral obligation at all presupposes autonomy, not as the special achievement of the few but as a universal condition of moral agency.

Further, many of the particular features of the psychologically autonomous person are not essential for Kantian autonomy: for example, emotional independence from others, special propensity for abstract thinking, and exceptionally critical attitudes toward current social norms. Even acting from internalized moral principles, contrary to social norms and without concern for reward and punishment, would not guarantee the possession of Kantian autonomy for that autonomy requires acknowledging the principles not only as "self-imposed," in some sense, but also as unconditional requirements of *reason*. With an optimism less common today, Kant believed that virtually all adult human beings acknowledge basic moral laws in this way. Thus, on the Kantian view, even those who are knowingly immoral and those whose most effective loyalties are to individuals rather than to impartial principles still have wills with the property of autonomy, though of course they fail to express their autonomy by living up to the commitments it entails.

Another current conception of autonomy treats autonomy as a right rather than an empirical trait. To be an autonomous person, on this view, is to have a moral right to make certain decisions for oneself, to control certain aspects of one's life without interference. The working analogy here, apparently, is with autonomous states, which are such not because they are governed in a particularly effective or high-minded way but because they have a right that other nations not interfere in their internal affairs. This right-sense, I take it, is what is presupposed when people complain that blue laws, coercive threats, and even well-intended manipulative lies violate their autonomy as persons.

The nature of the right may be spelled out in different ways, but however this is done, the conception of autonomy as a right will be significantly different from Kant's conception. Kant believed, of course, in rights to a high degree of self-determination in practical matters, and he thought all rights are grounded in some way in the fact that human beings have autonomy. But autonomy itself is not a right but a property of all rational wills, a property implying the possessor's recognition of rational principles other than desire-satisfaction but not by itself implying the wrongness of the specific forms of coercion, manipulation, and control that modern appeals to autonomy typically condemn. The confessed murderer on the gallows, I take it, has forfeited most of his rights to determine his future, but he has not thereby lost his Kantian autonomy.

Philosophers sometimes attribute to us a kind of autonomy that, unlike rights, makes no moral claim on others and yet, unlike psychological maturity, is attributed to everyone independently of empirical evidence. I have in mind what I call, without scholarly pretensions, Sartrean autonomy. This consists in part of a denial that human choices are subject to causal determination: we choose free from determination by the sort of causal factors that work in the nonhuman realm. Further, it implies a denial that there are objective moral and rational constraints on our choices: that is, we choose free from any "authoritative" principles not of our own making. To deny this sort of autonomy to persons is not to deny their rights or underestimate their maturity but to pretend that they "have to" make certain choices either because of the laws of nature or because of laws of reason or morality.

Most obviously this Sartrean conception is not Kant's. Choosing for oneself, on the Sartrean view, is not listening to the voice of one's reason amidst the din of "alien" desires; it is turning a deaf ear to any claim that one's choices are objectively constrained by reason, moral obligation, desire, or physical forces. The Sartrean applauds Kant's critique of mindless acceptance of norms as given, by tradition, by divine command, or by human nature; and, like Kant, he does so in the name of "freedom." This freedom is attributed to all as something that can be denied and belied but not escaped; and whatever the grounds for believing in Sartean freedom, they are out of the ordinary empirical kind. But despite these Kantian overtones, the essential element of Kantian autonomy is missing: the agent's commitment to rational principles of a special sort.

Another similar, but distinct notion of autonomy should perhaps be mentioned: this is Rousseau's idea of "moral liberty."[4] This is what citizens would have in a state so ideal that all its laws were backed by the "general will" of the people, and to obtain it, Rousseau argues, it is necessary and rational to abandon "natural liberty" by joining others in a social contract. When there is a general will behind all the laws, then the laws are approved by at least the "public will" of each citizen, that is, by each public-spirited citizen setting aside factionalism and aiming for the common good. If a citizen's "private," or self-interested, will is reluctant to obey these laws, he may be justly coerced to obey but then, Rousseau tells us, he is only "forced to be free." The relevant sense of freedom here is "moral liberty," which is the condition of being constrained only by laws which you give to yourself.

This has an obvious Kantian ring, and Kant's debt to Rousseau has often been noted. But, importantly for our purposes, there is for Rousseau a political interpretation of "being constrained only by laws which you give to yourself": the constraining is by law backed by police, and one can give laws to oneself by participating in a political process in an informed and public-spirited way. The resultant laws, according to Rousseau, are necessarily just, but they are not necessarily acknowledged as rational independently of the citizens' (other-regarding) feelings and desires. Kantian autonomy may have been inspired by Rousseau, but Kant transforms Rousseau's 'moral liberty' for more general use in the controversies about reason and morals.

Finally, I need to distinguish Kantian autonomy as I understand this from a conception of autonomy often attributed to Kant by students and at times by professional commentators.[5] The background of the former is an interpretation of the *Groundwork* according to which there are just two mutually exclusive ways in which human beings can act. *First*, one can act from inclination; and, in this case, the act is nothing but a product of natural forces, unfree, causally "determined" by desire, and "heteronomous." Though we may speak of a "heteronomous will," strictly such acts are not willed at all because "will" is identical with "practical reason," which chooses only the rational and the good. *Second*, one can act from moral principle; and, in this case, the act is a product of causally undetermined choice, free, and perfectly rational. The will, on this picture, cannot freely choose between acting from inclination and acting from moral principle because the will, as practical reason, is directed exclusively toward what is rational and moral. Nature sometimes, inexplicably, takes over a person, who then "acts" unfreely; but sometimes, inexplicably, the will is in control and then the person is free in the sense "uncaused and yet following reason." Autonomy, on this view, is just the freedom we have in our better moments, when willing rationally, guided by moral principles. Some have autonomy, some do not; or, more likely, sometimes one has it, sometimes not. When it is operative, we act autonomously; when not, we act heteronomously; but, strictly speaking, we do not *will* to do the one rather than the other because the will, by definition, is always on the side of the angels.

This conception of autonomy has several striking consequences that should give pause to anyone tempted to attribute it to Kant. Most obviously, all "immoral" acts prove to be unfree and not even willed by the agent. The adulterer is almost literally "carried away" by his lust as is the thief by his greed; and even minor, relatively passionless crimes must be construed on the same model. Further, since autonomy is the ground of human dignity, dignity and so the respect owed to human beings must vary with one's level of moral achievement. Again, since Kant argues both that negative freedom is inseparable from autonomy and that it is a necessary condition of moral obligation, we would have to conclude that whenever one lacks autonomy one is not under moral obligation. Thus the apparently immoral thief, acting from greed, is not merely excused from responsibility; he was not even acting contrary to a moral obligation.

The interpretation in question must also treat Kant's later distinction between *Wille* and *Willkur* as a radical departure from the *Groundwork*. Within the *Groundwork* many passages will become baffling, for example, passages implying that reason sometimes fails to "determine the will." Admittedly, there are other passages in the *Groundwork* that suggest the dualistic picture that I am opposing here, but on balance the evidence weighs heavily against it.

2. Main Features of Kantian Autonomy

In the *Critique of Pure Reason* Kant attempts to prove that all empirically discernable events are governed by causal laws, and yet he says that we can "think" of another sort of causation in which causes are themselves uncaused. Causes of their alternative kind, he tells us, are possible but cannot be known or even "comprehended." Kant defends the compatibility of belief in such causes with the (allegedly) proven fact that all empirical events have causes by denying that uncaused causes are spatiotemporal events.

According to Kant's strictest statements about the merely negative role of the idea of *noumena*, these expansive remarks about nonempirical causes are not to be understood as metaphysical speculations but merely as reminders that all that we can understand and know about the world is dependent upon our conceptual and perceptual frameworks.[6] Kant allows himself to write dramatically of our world as a world of "appearance" as opposed to "things in themselves"; but, strictly speaking, by his own doctrine "reality" is a "category" for empirical understanding, and so any working distinction between what is "real" and what merely "appears" must be empirically based.[7] The urge to read Kant as proposing a metaphysical picture of two worlds is hard to resist, but despite his own lapses, Kant repeatedly insists that we can have neither an "intuition" nor a "concept" of anything beyond experience.

Notoriously, Kant *seems* to ignore these warnings in his works on ethics, for he often writes of "the intelligible world," God, and "freedom" as a nonempirical property of human "wills." At the same time Kant insists that such usage is only for "practical," not "theoretical," purposes, and that none of his earlier warnings about metaphysics have been abandoned or violated.

Some readers take Kant's disclaimer that he speaks only from a "practical" perspective, to be simply an admission that he has nothing but weak, pragmatic arguments for his metaphysical speculations about "the will," and so forth. Far from removing our worries about the intelligibility of the two-worlds view, this interpretation would compound the problem by casting doubt on the *grounds* for believing what is admitted to be impossible to *understand*. A more sympathetic and profitable interpretative strategy, I suggest, is to try to construe Kant's disclaimer not so much as a remark about the *grounds* for belief as a clue about *how* we are to read his claims about freedom, the will, and so on. That is that, so far as possible, the content of such claims should be understood as "practical," or normative, rather than as metaphysical. Perhaps the metaphysics cannot be entirely eliminated; the effort to construe the problematic concepts normatively has textual support and yields more interesting results.

These preliminary remarks lead to my first suggestion about the Kantian idea of autonomy, namely, that we take it not so much a metaphysical account of what we are like than as a normative idea about the task, attitudes, and commitments of *rational* agents when deliberating about what to do. It has more to do with what we should count as reasons for acting, and with what we should hold ourselves responsible for, than with how human action fits into a metaphysical picture of what there is in the world.

Second, autonomy is said to be a property of human *wills*; to have a will, Kant says, is to have "the power to act in accordance with [one's] idea of laws . . . [or] principles" or "a kind of causality belonging to living things so far as they are rational."[8] The basic idea, I take it, is that in saying we have *wills* we are saying that we can "make things happen" for reasons, or according to policies or principles. We cannot isolate a particular physical or introspectible "event" as the "act of will," but we make sense of practical talk of doing things for reasons as opposed, say, to twitching, sneezing, and sleepwalking. Autonomy, then, must have something to do with the reasons, or principles, for which we act.

Next, and more controversially, I contend that Kant viewed autonomy as a property of (the wills of) virtually all adult, sane human beings, not as a special feature of the most perfectly rational or morally conscientious persons. This follows, I would argue, from his contention that autonomy is inseparable from "negative freedom," which in turn is a necessary condition for being under moral obligation.[9] The error of all previous moral philosophers, Kant implies, is their failure to recognize that moral obligation is grounded on the fact that the human will has autonomy. They misidentified the supreme moral principle because they tried to derive moral obligations from the idea of a will with heteronomy, rather than autonomy.[10]

This point is lost, I think, when contemporary writers refer to conscientious action as "autonomous" and to desire-motivated action as "heteronomous." These are not Kant's expressions and they misleadingly suggest that those who act wrongly, or act to satisfy innocent desires, lack autonomy (at least at the moment). Kant's predominant view, I would argue, is rather that all have autonomy, that this implies commitment to certain rational constraints, and that some live up to these commitments while others do not. The former, unlike the latter, *express* their autonomy in action;[11] but the commitment implied by 'autonomy' is something anyone must have to be a moral agent.

The next point to note is that any will with autonomy is necessarily "free in a negative sense," which Kant defines as "the property [the will] has of being able to work independently of alien causes."[12] Construed as a practical idea, the point is that, in deliberating and choosing to act, a rational agent must take oneself to be deciding between outcomes that are still open, that is, are not fixed by causes operating *independently* of one's deliberation and choice. Moreover, whatever the agent's *beliefs* about metaphysical determinism, one must *when deliberating* take the attitude that the choice itself is still "up to oneself." If the agent knew of a particular prospective "choice" that it is already determined by prior conditions to be the outcome of one's current reflections, then the agent would not be deliberating, and the bare knowledge, or belief, that *something* will determine one's choice, whatever that may be, would be of no use in deciding what to do.

The previous point captures one sense in which agents see themselves as able to act "independently of desire": that is, they see their desires not as determining causes of what they will choose but rather as considerations about which a choice has to be made. But Kant implies, I think, that negatively free agents can "act independently of desire" in a further sense, not concerned with causes.

Suppose we distinguish between being caused to act by a desire and choosing to act for the sake of satisfying a desire. In the first case, the desire figures as a prior causal condition; in the second, the desire is mentioned in a description of the agent's objective or end in acting. One who denied that acts are *caused* by desires might still maintain that acts are always *motivated* by desire, in the sense that they have satisfaction of desire as their intended object. By attributing "negative freedom" to rational agents, Kant in effect denies both claims, for "practical" purposes. This means at least that, in rational deliberation, one must not only take oneself to be able to choose and act without the choice having been causally determined by desire (or anything else), one must also take oneself to be able to act for the sake of ends other than the satisfaction of desire. In rational deliberation one cannot assume that what one will or must do is among those things for which one feels an antecedent desire.

A few words of caution may be helpful here. First, to say that in deliberation one "takes oneself" to be free (in the senses above) does not strictly imply that one denies that causal determinism is true or even that one disbelieves it while deliberating. Though Kant at times seems to argue (on moral grounds) for a belief in metaphysical freedom, his point that we can *act* only "under the Idea of freedom" is more limited and less controversial.[13] This idea, which I have paraphrased as "taking oneself to be free," is less concerned with which propositions about the world one affirms or denies than with which working framework one must adopt in order to take seriously the question, "What should I do?" The practical import of conceiving ourselves as negatively free is at least that, in seeking answers to *this* question, we are not looking for a causal basis to predict what we will do and we do not count our current and anticipated desires as finally settling what our aims and options are to be.

Also we should note that negative freedom for Kant is not an experienced "feeling of freedom" found to accompany all deliberations; nor is it any other psychological trait inductively inferred from repeated observations. The claim that in deliberating we must take ourselves to be free, then, is not meant as an empirical report that we constantly feel that our options are open whenever we raise practical questions. The point is quite different from my observation that whenever I play the piano from memory I must feel confident that I know the notes (even fleeting doubts disrupt the effort), for I can imagine what it would be like to play despite doubts (some do). By contrast, Kant is attempting to make a deep a priori point about what it is to engage in rational deliberation and action: we cannot even "think" what it would be for one who did not presuppose negative freedom.

Autonomy is not only negative freedom, Kant says, but is also freedom "positively conceived." This is characterized as the property a will has of being "a law unto itself . . . independently of every property belonging to the objects of volition."[14] No single paraphrase, however, adequately captures the idea, which gets its sense from a variety of contexts. Without going into textual details, let me just summarize the main features I think are contained in the complex Kantian idea of positive freedom.

To conceive a person as having positive freedom is to think of the person as having, (1) in addition to negative freedom, (2) a deep rational commitment to some principle(s) of conduct as (rationally) binding but (3) not adopted for the sake of satisfying desires, (4) not just prescribing means to rationally contingent ends, and yet (5) in some sense necessarily imposed on oneself by oneself as a rational agent. Further, though one may not always live up to it, (6) the commitment is seen by the agent as rationally overriding other sorts of principles and aims, in case of conflict. Finally, setting aside cognitive requirements and formal principles such as "Take the means or abandon the end," the *only* action-guiding principles that are rationally "authoritative" for the agent with autonomy are principles that satisfy these condtions; and so (7) no principle to which one is committed because of contingent features of one's human or individual make-up has this sort of necessary reason-giving force.

The basic idea is that, despite all the negative claims about what does *not* necessarily move the agent or provide reasons, there is still some rational standard of conduct, commitment to which is inherent in the point of view of agents who try to deliberate and choose rationally. This is later identified with the (supposedly) formal expressions of the supreme principle of morality, but the claim that wills with autonomy must adopt the supreme moral principle is not part of the idea of autonomy but rather something Kant sees a need to argue. The sense in which the principles of autonomy are "imposed on oneself by oneself" is puzzling, but at least it is clear that Kant did not see this as an arbitrary, optional choice but as a commitment that clear thinking reveals, implicit in all efforts to will rationally, the way one may think that commitment to basic principles of logic are implicit in all efforts to think and understand. Rational principles of conduct do not "exist" independently of agents the way a Platonist might think of them; but neither are they "inventions" of God, as Ockham and Descartes thought, or "natural laws" discovered empirically, as some other philosophers seem to have believed.

3. Some Normative Implications

The most famous, and controversial, use Kant made of his idea of autonomy was his attempt to derive from it his special conception of the supreme moral principle. That is, Kant argues that the one and only principle that satisfies the conditions for being a necessary rational commitment of all agents with autonomy is the so-called Categorical Imperative, to act only on maxims that one can will as universal laws.[15] If true, this would imply that every minimally rational agent, in deliberating and acting, is actually committed to this principle, as an overriding rational constraint, and so can violate it only on pain of inconsistency. Like many others, I have doubts about this part of Kant's theory; but I think that such doubts should not prevent us from seeing some striking implications of the idea of autonomy that are independent of this strong claim about its connection with morality. Thus my focus in this section will be on the normative significance of Kantian autonomy aside from its alleged role in providing a basis for morality.

The first consequence to note is a broad negative thesis. In Kantian language, this is that *material* principles of conduct are never *necessary* principles of practical reason. In more familiar terms, this means that it is not a necessary rational requirement that we try to maximize desire-satisfaction, the balance of pleasure/pain, or any other substantive value that, as human beings or as individuals, we happen to care about. Power, fame, knowledge, and even Stoic peace of mind are at best contingently rational ends, rational to pursue only because chosen by rational agents and only when their pursuit satisfies more formal requirements of reason. The point, I take it, is not merely that rational principles are not "maximizing" principles; for it also implies that substantive values, such as desire and pleasure, do not *necessarily* provide even prima facie reasons for action. Their status as reasons depends upon their endorsement by the individual agent, subject to certain constraints; and there is nothing in our *rational* nature that prevents us from refusing to count any given desire or pleasure as a justifying reason for acting.

The idea is a radical one, which Hume and many modern preference theorists might applaud, but it should not be misunderstood. Of course, we normally count the fact that we desire something, especially after due reflection, as a good prima facie reason to pursue it, and there may be some values, such as avoidance of severe physical pain, that human beings, thinking clearly, will *always* endorse as ends. Kantian autonomy does not deny *this* but only certain philosophical accounts of *why* desires, pleasure, and so forth, give us reasons. In particular it denies accounts that give these values necessary and unconstrained reason-giving force. Consider, for example, the view, held by Moore and more recently by Thomas Nagel, that pain has the objective property of being "bad in itself."[16] In this view, the intrinsic badness of pain by itself explains the rationality of choosing to avoid it, other things being equal. In Kant's view, by contrast, the claim that pain is bad is explained by the fact that, seeing pain for what it is and reflecting rationally, we choose to avoid it. No doubt the very concept of "pain" implies a *disposition* to avoid it, just as the concept of "desire" implies a tendency to seek objects of desire. But in the Kantian view dispositions to act are not necessarily reasons to act; they are considerations for deliberative agents to endorse or reject upon rational reflection. Substantive values do not exist independently of rational willing but are, as it were, created by it.

Another point emerges when we consider the Kantian claim that wills with autonomy, though "free," cannot be "lawless."[17] This implies, I take it, that the idea of a Sartrean "radical choice," utterly unconstrained by rational principles, has no place in Kantian theory. Even when someone wills to do what is irrational, according to Kant, we can attribute the act to him or her as an agent only by understanding it as being done for a reason (in this case an insufficient reason) by someone committed to rational standards. Similar considerations lead Kant to reject the "libertarian" view, ridiculed by Hume, that free acts are random uncaused mental events ("acts of will"), not explicable in terms of the character and policies of the agent.[18] A will with autonomy is not to be pictured as "lawless" in this sense, even if the agent, in deliberating and acting, must ignore thoughts of the causal determinants of his or her choice. The "laws," however, that must be introduced to make sense of free choices are not causal laws but policies and rational commitments of the agent.

A further implication of Kantian autonomy is that, whether or not moral requirements prove to be always rational, there must be some necessary action-guiding constraints on rational choice beyond cognitive standards (regarding how to establish background beliefs and make valid inferences) and beyond the Hypothetical Imperative "to take the means or abandon the end." Kant argues this anti-Humean point, I think, quite independently of his efforts to prove the rationality of moral conduct. The idea is that in rational deliberation we presuppose at least some formal or procedural standards other than merely understanding what we are up to and adjusting our means to our ends.

Kant's own suggestions for what these could be, besides his famous (or notorious) "universal law" formula, include the idea that rational deliberative agents are committed to both a principle of self-respect and an extension of this that includes respect for other rational agents. The former requires that one's choices be justifiable to oneself not merely *at the moment*, but over *time*, and not merely as one reflects on the *products* of one's choices but also as one reflects on *the sort of person one makes of oneself* by these choices. The more controversial requirement to respect other rational agents (as such) would have us confine our deliberations to what we could in principle justify to others who were willing to accept similar constraints. These suggestions, I take it, are part of Kant's idea of "rational nature" as an "end in itself."[19] Though controversial, these proposals are significantly different from the "material" principles Kant so vigorously opposes. For, though they purport to constrain what we may rationally choose, they do so not by prescribing any particular value to promote, such as knowledge, peace of mind, pleasure or desire-satisfaction, but rather by insisting that we constrain our current self-interested deliberations by giving weight to whatever other reflective agents, and we ourselves later, would choose. Even if the idea of autonomy does not, by itself, require these particular principles, it sets limits to the sort of principles that moral theory of a Kantian sort should be looking for.

4. Objections: Is it Obvious that We Lack Kantian Autonomy?

My remarks so far have been sketchy and leave us with only a promissory note that they can be supported by detailed examination of Kant's texts. But before closing, I want to address briefly a few further questions that most of us are inclined to ask, in exasperation, long before scholarly investigations are done. That is, does all this have any point in the modern world? Does it really make sense?

More specifically, aren't there familiar objections that are obviously decisive against the thesis that we have Kantian autonomy, as presented here?
While I am not convinced that the difficulties can be satisfactorily resolved, the
matter seems far from obvious to me. Some objections, I suspect, rest on
misunderstanding, and in any case, it is so difficult to get a solid grasp on these
issues that confidence one way or the other seems premature. My brief comments on the objections, then, should be taken not so much as defense of
Kantian autonomy as preliminary remarks designed to keep the questions
open.

A. First, isn't autonomy incompatible with a belief in determinism in
physical science? Even if quantum mechanics leaves room for a degree of
indeterminism at the subatomic level, most seem to agree that this makes little
practical difference when we turn to the explanation and prediction of large-
scale objects, such as human bodies. So doesn't this rule out autonomy? Kant,
of course, *believed* that universal causation among phenomenal events was
compatible with reasonable ascription of autonomy to human agents, but he
seemed willing to pay a heroic price to sustain this belief when he referred to
the will as not in space and time and thereby admitted the "incomprehensibil-
ity" of human agency. If we are unwilling to pay that price, do we not need to
give up autonomy as an outmoded and useless concept?

Before we answer, we need to keep in mind the context in which the idea of
autonomy is meant to be used. The context is not that of scientific, or even
common sense, explanation but rather the context of practical deliberation.
This alone does not make autonomy immune from criticism, of course, for one
could not make the idea of ghosts respectable just by restricting one's thoughts
of ghosts to occasions of deliberation. But there may be a difference. In
deliberation the issue is "what should I do?"; and this, for Kant, amounts to
"what is rational to do?", "what is there reason to do?" Now some beliefs about
causes are highly relevant in this context, for example, the beliefs that smoking
causes cancer and cancer causes pain. But what of the belief that, whatever I
decide to do, there will have been some physical cause of my bodily movements
and all the phenomena of decision making and, moreover, causes of those
causes, and so forth? This is a disturbing thought to many, which no doubt
prompts the desire, which Kant shared, to insist that the true decision, or act of
will, cannot be explained in this way, that it cannot be "reduced" to physical or
even introspectible phenomena. But stopping short of this, we may still ask,
how is the belief that all the phenomena, and even the "decision," are caused
supposed to be relevant to the problem at hand, namely, finding the rational
thing to do? If the belief were true, it would not follow that the rational thing to
do is to sit still or to do as one pleases. Nor would it follow that there is no
solution, that there is nothing rational to do. Determinism raises questions
about how to understand rational deliberation, but it offers no guidelines to
those who attempt to deliberate rationally.

The point, of course, is not new: it is just that rational deliberation is the
sort of activity in which conjectural, or even confident, belief in physical
determinism is irrelevant. This is not because we are built to have some

inescapable "feeling of freedom" but because of the sort of question we are asking. Thus in its proper place there may still be a use for at least one aspect of the idea of autonomy, namely, the idea of rational agents as deliberating among options not causally determined independently of the agent's choice and as having a decision to make for which it is irrelevant whether or not one believes that the final decision will have had causes.

The idea of autonomy, however, includes more than this notion of independence of causes; in particular, it includes the idea that rational agents have reasons not based on their desires, that practical rationality is not exhausted by hypothetical imperatives. Is this further idea undermined by determinism in physical science? Again, it is hard to see how it could be. The determinism in question, remember, is not a particular psychological thesis that human beings can act only for the sake of satisfaction of desire; it is rather that there are some physical causes for all phenomena. This does not tell us, one way or the other, what sort of reasons have weight in rational deliberation about what to do. "Why will it occur, if or when it does?" and "Why should I try to bring it about?" are different sorts of questions, and it is far from obvious how a general thesis about the former is relevant to the latter.

B. But isn't autonomy incompatible with the explanation of human action in terms of beliefs and desires? The real problem, the critic might continue, does not come from determinism in physical science but rather from the way we explain human action in everyday life and in much of psychology. That is, what people do is seen as a function of their beliefs about their situation and their desires (broadly construed). The desires in question, it might be added, need not be selfish, urgently felt, or momentary so long as they are empirically discernable. We do not deny that people act from respect for moral principle, says the critic; we only insist that respect is an empirical motive, a sort of desire to be moral or (as Richard Brandt has suggested) an aversion to being immoral.[20] The problem with the idea of autonomy, then, is not that it is disproved by scientific evidence but that it pictures human beings as capable of acting without any understandable motivation. The charge is not that autonomy is falsified by physical science so much as that it is rendered incoherent by its supposition that human beings can act when stripped of the motivational features that make human acts, as opposed to mere bodily movements, understandable.

The Kantian might reply by noting, first, that Kant does not deny that all observable human acts, even acts from duty, can be understood and explained by reference to empirical feelings and dispositions. The claims about autonomy are somehow *supposed* to be compatible with this admission, but how? One move, of course, is to say that what we observe is mere appearance whereas "will" and "reason" are admittedly incomprehensible noumenal entities. But for most of us this will not do. Is there anything left to autonomy without this? Again, I think, we must return to the primary context in which the idea of autonomy is to be applied: the point of view of agents deliberating about what they have reason to do. Here, as I have suggested, to attribute autonomy to oneself amounts to at least two things: seeing oneself as causally undetermined in the process and acknowledging that one is committed to rational standards of choice other than desire-satisfaction. This does not imply that anyone, including the agent in deliberation, must cease to believe that the act he chooses will be understandable in terms of desires (in the broad sense). Agents ask, "What should I do?," and so long as they take this question seriously they will find that it is neither a help nor a hindrance to believe that the outcome will be understandable in terms of empirical dispositions. If agents conceive themselves, practically, as having autonomy, then they will not assume that every disposition they find themselves to have is a reason for acting, nor will they assume that failure to feel or observe a disposition means that they have no reason to act. Their search for reasons will not be just a survey of present and predicted future dispositions and the means to realize them. But, again, this is not to deny that when they act there will have been a disposition in terms of which their acts can be explained.

The point, it should be noted, is just that the mere fact that there are always explanatory empirical dispositions is not something that enters into the solution of a deliberative problem. This is not to say that the knowledge that one has particular empirical dispositions (e.g., those of a compulsive gambler) cannot render deliberation pointless. Compulsions, addictions, and the like can (perhaps contrary to Kant) render rational deliberation useless, and if the agent is aware of this, genuine deliberation becomes impossible. But to grant that certain desires render practical reasoning ineffective is not the same as granting that these desires determine the rational course of action. The idea of autonomy has its use, if at all, within practical deliberation, not as a general descriptive characterization of human powers.

C. Finally, I imagine our exasperated critic to object as follows: "Suppose I grant that the idea of Kantian autonomy, or some residue you have distilled, is not shown useless or incoherent in the ways I had first thought. But have you, or Kant, given me any reason to accept it? You *say* that rational agents deliberate with the idea of autonomy, which implies commitment to rational standards independent of desires. But have you shown me even one such principle? Or demonstrated that there is one? Isn't the bottom line simply the old *assumption* that morality is rational whether it serves one's desires or not?"

Here, as a beginning, the Kantian would do well to invite the critic to examine again Kant's argument for autonomy in the third chapter of the *Groundwork*. There, as I have argued elsewhere, we find Kant's most tortured effort to avoid *assuming* that morality is necessarily rational and to give independent considerations for the belief that all reasons are not based on desires.[21] His strategy is easy to miss because it is so indirect: rather than trying to exhibit an example of desire-independent rational standard and show its connection with the concept of rational choice, he tries to argue from claims about how we must see ourselves in deliberation to the conclusion that we must acknowledge that there are such desire-independent standards, whatever they turn out to be. But whether, after all, there is any merit in the argument, and indeed whether my view of these matters are really Kant's, I must leave as open questions, along with many others.

Notes

1. Earlier versions of this paper were presented at conferences at the University of South Carolina and at the University of Virginia. Thanks are due to the participants in those conferences and to colleagues at the University of North Carolina for their helpful comments.

2. Some of these distinctions are discussed in my paper "Autonomy and Benevolent Lies," *Journal of Value Inquiry* 18 (1984), 251–67.

3. See Carol Gilligan, *In A Different Voice* (Cambridge: Harvard University Press, 1982) and Lawrence Kohlberg, "Stage and Sequence: The Cognitive Development Approach to Socialization" in *The Handbook of Social Theory and Research*, ed. D. A. Goslin (Chicago: Rand McNally, 1969), 347–480.

4. Jean-Jacques Rousseau, *The Social Contract* (Baltimore: Penguin Books, 1968), especially Bk. I, chs. 7 and 8.

5. In many respects this seems to be the view of Robert Paul Wolff in *The Autonomy of Reason* (New York: Harper and Row, 1973).

6. Immanuel Kant, *The Critique of Pure Reason*, trans. Norman Kemp Smith (London: Macmillan, 1956), especially pp. 257ff.

7. Kant, *The Critique of Pure Reason*, 111–19.

8. Immanuel Kant, *Groundwork of the Metaphysics of Morals*, trans. H. J. Paton (New York: Harper and Row, 1964), 80, 114. In further citations I refer to this work simply as "G.")

9. G 114.

10. G 110–12.

11. This distinction between having and expressing autonomy I take from John Rawls.

12. G 114.

13. G 115.

14. G 108; see also G 114.

15. G 108 and 114.

16. G. E. Moore, *Principia Ethica* (Cambridge: Cambridge University Press, 1903), and Thomas Nagel, *The View from Nowhere* (Oxford: Oxford University Press, 1986).

17. G 114.

18. David Hume, *A Treatise of Human Nature*, Bk. II, section III.

19. G 95–103. I discuss some implications of this idea in "Humanity as an End in Itself," *Ethics* 91 (October 1980), 81–99.

20. As I recall, Brandt made this suggestion in conversation at Oxford in 1973.

21. My attempt to reconstruct Kant's argument is in "Kant's Argument for the Rationality of Moral Conduct," *Pacific Philosophical Quarterly* 66 (1985), 3–23.

II

CRITICAL VIEWS

7

Free Agency

Gary Watson

In this essay I discuss a distinction that is crucial to a correct account of free action and to an adequate conception of human motivation and responsibility.

I

According to one familiar conception of freedom, a person is free to the extent that he is able to do or get what he wants. To circumscribe a person's freedom is to contract the range of things he is able to do. I think that, suitably qualified, this account is correct, and that the chief and most interesting uses of the word 'free' can be explicated in its terms. But this general line has been resisted on a number of different grounds. One of the most important objections—and the one upon which I shall concentrate in this paper—is that this familiar view is too impoverished to handle talk of free actions and free will.

Frequently enough, we say, or are inclined to say, that a person is not in control of his own actions, that he is not a "free agent" with respect to them, even though his behavior is intentional. Possible examples of this sort of action include those which are explained by addictions, manias, and phobias of various sorts. But the concept of free action would seem to be pleonastic on the analysis of freedom in terms of the ability to get what one wants. For if a person does something intentionally, then surely he was able at that time to do it. Hence, on this analysis, he was free to do it. The familiar account would not seem to allow for any further questions, as far as freedom is concerned, about the action. Accordingly, this account would seem to embody a conflation of free action and intentional action.

I have profited from discussions with numerous friends, students, colleagues, and other audiences, on the material of this essay; I would like to thank them collectively. However, special thanks are due to Joel Feinberg, Harry Frankfurt, and Thomas Nagel.

This chapter was originally published in the *Journal of Philosophy* 72 (1975). Copyright © 1975 by the *Journal of Philosophy*. Reprinted by permission.

Gary Watson is Associate Professor of Philosophy at the University of California at Irvine.

   Philosophers who have defended some form of compatibilism have usually given this analysis of freedom, with the aim of showing that freedom and responsibility are not really incompatible with determinism. Some critics have rejected compatibilism precisely because of its association with this familiar account of freedom. For instance, Isaiah Berlin asks: if determination is true,

> what reasons can you, in principle, adduce for attributing responsibility or applying moral rules to [people] which you would not think it reasonable to apply in the case of compulsive choosers—kleptomaniacs, dipsomaniacs, and the like?[1]

The idea is that the sense in which actions would be free in a deterministic world allows the actions of "compulsive choosers" to be free. To avoid this consequence, it is often suggested, we must adopt some sort of "contracausal" view of freedom.

   Now, though compatibilists from Hobbes to J. J. C. Smart have given the relevant moral and psychological concepts an exceedingly crude treatment, this crudity is not inherent in compatibilism, nor does it result from the adoption of the conception of freedom in terms of the ability to get what one wants. For the difference between free and unfree actions—as we normally discern it—has nothing at all to do with the truth or falsity of determinism.

   In the subsequent pages, I want to develop a distinction between wanting and valuing which will enable the familiar view of freedom to make sense of the notion of an unfree action. The contention will be that, in the case of actions that are unfree, the agent is unable to get what he most wants, *or values,* and this inability is due to his own "motivational system." In this case the obstruction to the action that he most wants to do is his own will. It is in this respect that the action is unfree: the agent is obstructed in and by the very performance of the action.

   I do not conceive my remarks to be a defense of compatibilism. This point of view may be unacceptable for various reasons, some of which call into question the coherence of the concept of responsibility. But these reasons do not include the fact that compatibilism relies upon the conception of freedom in terms of the ability to get what one wants, nor must it conflate free action and intentional action. If compatibilism is to be shown to be wrong, its critics must go deeper.

II

What must be true of people if there is to be a significant notion of free action? Our talk of free action arises from the apparent fact that what a person most wants may not be what he is finally moved to get. It follows from this apparent fact that the extent to which one wants something is not determined solely by the *strength* of one's desires (or "motives") as measured by their effectiveness in action. One (perhaps trivial) measure of the strength of the desire or want is that the agent acts upon that desire or want (trivial, since it will be nonexplana-

tory to say that an agent acted upon that desire because it was the strongest).
But, if what one most wants may not be what one most strongly wants, by this
measure, then in what sense can it be true that one most wants it?[2]

To answer this question, one might begin by contrasting, at least in a crude
way, a Humean with a Platonic conception of practical reasoning. The ancients
distinguished between the rational and the irrational parts of the soul, between
Reason and Appetite. Hume employed a superficially similar distinction. It is
important to understand, however, that (for Plato at least) the rational part of
the soul is not to be identified with what Hume called "Reason" and contradis-
tinguished from the "Passions." On Hume's account, Reason is not a source of
motivation, but a faculty of determining what is true and what is false, a faculty
concerned solely with "matters of fact" and "relations among ideas." It is
completely dumb on the question of what to do. Perhaps Hume could allow
Reason this much practical voice: given an initial set of wants and beliefs about
what is or is likely to be the case, particular desires are generated in the process.
In other words, a Humean might allow Reason a crucial role in deliberation.
But its essential role would not be to supply motivation—Reason is not that
kind of thing—but rather to calculate, within a context of desires and ends,
how to fulfill those desires and serve those ends. For Plato, however, the
rational part of the soul is not some kind of inference mechanism. It is itself a
source of motivation. In general form, the desires of Reason are desires for "the
Good."

Perhaps the contrast can be illustrated by some elementary notions from
decision theory. On the Bayesian model of deliberation, a preference scale is
imposed upon various states of affairs contingent upon courses of action open
to the agent. Each state of affairs can be assigned a numerical value (initial
value) according to its place on the scale; given this assignment, and the
probabilities that those states of affairs will obtain if the actions are performed,
a final numerical value (expected desirability) can be assigned to the actions
themselves. The rational agent performs the action with the highest expected
desirability.

In these terms, on the Humean picture, Reason is the faculty that computes
probabilities and expected desirabilities. Reason is in this sense neutral with
respect to actions, for it can operate equally on any given assignment of initial
values and probabilities—it has nothing whatsoever to say about the assignment of initial values. On the Platonic picture, however, the rational part of the
soul itself determines what has *value* and how much, and thus is responsible for
the original ranking of alternative states of affairs.

It may appear that the difference between these conceptions is merely a
difference as to what is to be called "Reason" or "rational," and hence is not a
substantive difference. In speaking of Reason, Hume has in mind a sharp
contrast between what is wanted and what is thought to be the case. What
contrast is implicit in the Platonic view that the ranking of alternative states of
affairs is the task of the rational part of the soul?

The contrast here is not trivial; the difference in classificatory schemes
reflects different views of human psychology. For one thing, in saying this (or

what is tantamount to this) Plato was calling attention to the fact that it is one thing to think a state of affairs good, worthwhile, or worthy of promotion, and another simply to desire or want that state of affairs to obtain. Since the notion of value is tied to (cannot be understood independently of) those of the good and worthy, it is one thing to value (think good) a state of affairs and another to desire that it obtain. However, to think a thing good is at the same time to desire it (or its promotion). Reason is thus an original spring of action. It is because valuing is essentially related to thinking or *judging* good that it is appropriate to speak of the wants that are (or perhaps arise from) evaluations as belonging to, or originating in, the rational (that is, *judging*) part of the soul; values provide *reasons* for action. The contrast is with desires, whose objects may not be thought good and which are thus, in a natural sense, blind or irrational. Desires are mute on the question of what is good.[3]

Now it seems to me that—given the view of freedom as the ability to get what one wants—there can be a problem of free action only if the Platonic conception of the soul is (roughly) correct. The doctrine I shall defend is Platonic in the sense that it involves a distinction between valuing and desiring which depends upon there being independent sources of motivation. No doubt Plato means considerably more than this by his parts-of-the-soul doctrine, but he meant at least this. The Platonic conception provides an answer to the question I posed earlier (p. 111): in what sense can what one most wants differ from that which is the object of the strongest desire? The answer is that the phrase 'what one most wants' may mean either "the object of the strongest desire" or "what one most *values*." This phrase can be interpreted in terms of strength or in terms of ranking order or preference. The problem of free action arises because what one desires may not be what one values, and what one most values may not be what one is finally moved to get.[4]

The tacit identification of desiring or wanting with valuing is so common[5] that it is necessary to cite some examples of this distinction in order to illustrate how evaluation and desire may diverge. There seem to be two ways in which, in principle, a discrepancy may arise. First, it is possible that what one desires is not *to any degree* valued, held to be worthwhile, or thought good; one assigns *no* value whatever to the object of one's desire. Second, although one may indeed value what is desired, the strength of one's desire may not properly reflect the degree to which one values its object; that is, although the object of a desire is valuable, it may not be deemed the most valuable in the situation and yet one's desire for it may be stronger than the want for what is most valued.

The cases in which one in no way values what one desires are perhaps rare, but surely they exist. Consider the case of a woman who has a sudden urge to drown her bawling child in the bath; or the case of a squash player who, while suffering an ignominious defeat, desires to smash his opponent in the face with the racquet. It is just false that the mother values her child's being drowned or that the player values the injury and suffering of his opponent. But they desire these things nonetheless. They desire them in spite of themselves. It is not that they assign to these actions an initial value which is then outweighed by other considerations. These activities are not even represented by a positive entry, however small, on the initial "desirability matrix."

It may seem from these examples that this first and radical sort of divergence between desiring and valuing occurs only in the case of momentary and inexplicable urges or impulses. Yet I see no conclusive reason why a person could not be similarly estranged from a rather persistent and pervasive desire, and one that is explicable enough. Imagine a man who thinks his sexual inclinations are the work of the devil, that the very fact that he has sexual inclinations bespeaks his corrupt nature. This example is to be contrasted with that of the celibate who decides that the most fulfilling life for him will be one of abstinence. In this latter case, *one* of the things that receive consideration in the process of reaching his all-things-considered judgment is the value of sexual activity. There is something, from his point of view, to be said for sex, but there is more to be said in favor of celibacy. In contrast, the man who is estranged from his sexual inclinations does not acknowledge even a prima facie reason for sexual activity: that he is sexually inclined toward certain activities is not even *a* consideration. Another way of illustrating the difference is to say that, for the one man, forgoing sexual relationships constitutes a *loss*, even if negligible compared with the gains of celibacy, whereas from the standpoint of the other person, no loss is sustained at all.

Now, it must be admitted, any desire may provide the basis for a reason insofar as nonsatisfaction of the desire causes suffering and hinders the pursuit of ends of the agent. But it is important to notice that the reason generated in this way by a desire is a reason for *getting rid* of the desire, and one may get rid of a desire either by satisfying it or by eliminating it in some other manner (by tranquilizers, or cold showers). Hence this kind of reason differs importantly from the reasons based upon the evaluation of the activities or states of affairs in question. For, in the former case, attaining the object of desire is simply a means of eliminating discomfort or agitation, whereas in the latter case that attainment is the end itself. Normally, in the pursuit of the objects of our wants we are not attempting chiefly to relieve ourselves. We aim to satisfy, not just eliminate, desire.

Nevertheless, aside from transitory impulses, it may be that cases wherein nothing at all can be said in favor of the object of one's desire are rare. For it would seem that even the person who conceives his sexual desires to be essentially evil would have to admit that indulgence would be pleasurable, and surely that is something. (Perhaps not even this should be admitted. For indulgence may not yield pleasure at all in a context of anxiety. Furthermore, it is not obvious that pleasure is intrinsically good, independently of the worth of the pleasurable object.) In any case, the second sort of divergence between evaluation and desire remains: it is possible that, in a particular context, what one wants most strongly is not what one most values.

The distinction between valuing and desiring is not, it is crucial to see, a distinction among desires or wants according to their content. That is to say, there is nothing in the specification of the objects of an agent's desires that singles out some wants as based upon that agent's values. The distinction in question has rather to do with the *source* of the want or with its role in the total "system" of the agent's desires and ends. It has to do with why the agent wants what he does.

Obviously, to identify a desire or want simply in terms of its content is not to identify its source(s). It does not follow from my wanting to eat that I am hungry. I may want to eat because I want to be well-nourished, or because I am hungry, or because eating is a pleasant activity. This single desire may have three independent sources. (These sources may not be altogether independent. It may be that eating is pleasurable only because I have appetites for food.) Some specifications of wants or desires—for instance, as cravings—pick out (at least roughly) the source of the motivation.

It is an essential feature of the appetites and the passions that they engender (or consist in) desires whose existence and persistence are independent of the person's judgment of the good. The appetite of hunger involves a desire to eat which has a source in physical needs and physiological states of the hungry organism. And emotions such as anger and fear partly consist in spontaneous inclinations to do various things—to attack or to flee the object of one's emotion, for example. It is intrinsic to the appetites and passions that appetitive and passionate beings can be motivated in spite of themselves. It is because desires such as these arise independently of the person's judgment and values that the ancients located the emotions and passions in the irrational part of the soul;[6] and it is because of this sort of independence that a conflict between valuing and desiring is possible.[7]

These points may suggest an inordinately dualistic view according to which persons are split into inevitably alien, if not always antagonistic, halves. But this view does not follow from what has been said. As central as it is to human life, it is not often noted that some activities are valued only to the extent that they are objects of the appetites. This means that such activities would never be regarded as valuable constituents of one's life were it not for one's susceptibility to "blind" motivation—motivation independent of one's values. Sexual activity and eating are again examples. We may value the activity of eating to the degree that it provides nourishment. But we may also value it because it is an enjoyable activity, even though its having this status depends upon our appetites for food, our hunger. In the case of sex, in fact, if we were not erotic creatures, certain activities would not only lose their value to us, they might not even be physiologically possible.

These examples indicate, not that there is no distinction between desiring and valuing, but that the value placed upon certain activities depends upon their being the fulfillment of desires that arise and persist independently of what we value. So it is not that, when we value the activity of eating, we think there are reasons to eat no matter what other desires we have; rather, we value eating when food appeals to us; and, likewise, we value sexual relationships when we are aroused. Here an essential part of the *content* of our evaluation is that the activity in question be motivated by certain appetites. These activities may have value for us only insofar as they are appetitively motivated, even though to have these appetites is not *ipso facto* to value their objects.

Part of what it means to value some activities in this way is this: we judge that to cease to have such appetites is to lose something of worth. The judgement here is not merely that, if someone has these appetites, it is worthwhile (*ceteris paribus*) for him to indulge them. The judgment is rather that it is of value to have and (having them) to indulge these appetites. The former judgment does not account for the eunuch's loss or sorrow, whereas the latter does. And the latter judgment lies at the bottom of the discomfort one may feel when one envisages a situation in which, say, hunger is consistently eliminated and nourishment provided by insipid capsules.

It would be impossible for a nonerotic being or a person who lacked the appetite for food and drink fully to understand the value most of us attach to sex and to dining. Sexual activity must strike the nonerotic being as perfectly grotesque. (Perhaps that is why lust is sometimes said to be disgusting and sinful in the eyes of God.) Or consider an appetite that is in fact "unnatural" (i.e., acquired): the craving for tobacco. To a person who has never known the enticement of Lady Nicotine, what could be more incomprehensible than the filthy practice of consummating a fine meal by drawing into one's lungs the noxious fumes of a burning weed?

Thus, the relationship between evaluation and motivation is intricate. With respect to many of our activities, evaluation depends upon the possibility of our being moved to act independently of our judgment. So the distinction I have been pressing—that between desiring and valuing—does not commit one to an inevitable split between Reason and Appetite. Appetitively motivated activities may well constitute for a person the most worthwhile aspects of his life.[8] But the distinction does commit us to the possibility of such a split. If there are sources of motivation independent of the agent's values, then it is possible that sometimes he is motivated to do things he does not deem worth doing. This possibility is the basis for the principal problem of free action: a person may be obstructed by his own will.

A related possibility that presents considerable problems for the understanding of free agency is this: some desires, when they arise, may "color" or influence what appear to be the agent's evaluations, but only temporarily. That is, when and only when he has the desire, is he inclined to think or say that what is desired or wanted is worthwhile or good. This possibility is to be distinguished from another, according to which one thinks it worthwhile to eat when one is hungry or to engage in sexual activity when one is so inclined. For one may think this even on the occasions when the appetites are silent. The possibility I have in mind is rather that what one is disposed to say or judge is temporarily affected by the presence of the desire in such a way that, both before and after the "onslaught" of the desire, one judges that the desire's object is worth pursuing (in the circumstances) whether or not one has the desire. In this case one is likely, in a cool moment, to think it a matter for regret that one had been so influenced and to think that one should guard against desires that have this property. In other cases it may not be the desire itself that affects one's judgment, but the set of conditions in which those desires arise—for example, the conditions induced by drugs or alcohol. (It is noteworthy that we say: "under the influence of alcohol.") Perhaps judgments made in such circumstances are often in some sense self-deceptive. In any event, this phenomenon raises problems about the identification of a person's values.

Despite our examples, it would be mistaken to conclude that the only desires that exhibit an independence of evaluation are appetitive or passionate desires. In Freudian terms, one may be as dissociated from the demands of the superego as from those of the id. One may be disinclined to move away from one's family, the thought of doing so being accompanied by compunction; and yet this disinclination may rest solely upon acculturation rather than upon a current judgment of what one is to do, reflecting perhaps an assessment of one's "duties" and interests. Or, taking another example, one may have been habituated to think that divorce is to be avoided in all cases, so that the aversion to divorce persists even though one sees no justification for maintaining one's marriage. In both of these cases, the attitude has its basis solely in acculturation and exists independently of the agent's judgment. For this reason, acculturated desires are irrational (better: nonrational) in the same sense as appetitive and passionate desires. In fact, despite the inhibitions acquired in the course of a puritan upbringing, a person may deem the pursuit of sexual pleasure to be worthwhile, his judgment siding with the id rather than the superego. Acculturated attitudes may seem more akin to evaluation than to appetite in that they are often expressed in evaluative language ("divorce is wicked") and result in feelings of guilt when one's actions are not in conformity with them. But, since conflict is possible here, to want something as a result of acculturation is not thereby to value it, in the sense of 'to value' that we want to capture.

It is not easy to give a nontrivial account of the sense of 'to value' in question. In part, to value something is, in the appropriate circumstances, to want it, and to attribute a want for something to someone is to say that he is disposed to try to get it. So it will not be easy to draw this distinction in behavioral terms. Apparently the difference will have to do with the agent's attitude toward the various things he is disposed to try to get. We might say that an agent's values consist in those principles and ends which he—in a cool and non-self-deceptive moment—articulates as definitive of the good, fulfilling, and defensible life. That most people have articulate "conceptions of the good," coherent life-plans, *systems* of ends, and so on, is of course something of a fiction. Yet we all have more or less long-term aims and normative principles that we are willing to defend. It is such things as these that are to be identified with our values.

The valuational system of an agent is that set of considerations which, when combined with his factual beliefs (and probability estimates), yields judgments of the form: the thing for me to do in these circumstances, all things considered, is *a*. To ascribe free agency to a being presupposes it to be a being that makes judgments of this sort. To be this sort of being, one must assign values to alternative states of affairs, that is, rank them in terms of worth.

The motivational system of an agent is that set of considerations which move him to action. We identify his motivational system by identifying what motivates him. The possibility of unfree action consists in the fact that an agent's valuational system and motivational system may not completely coincide. Those systems harmonize to the extent that what determines the agent's all-things-considered judgments also determines his actions.

Now, to be sure, since to value is also to want, one's valuational and motivational systems must to a large extent overlap. If, in appropriate circumstances, one were never inclined to action by some alleged evaluation, the claim that that was indeed one's evaluation would be disconfirmed. Thus one's valuational system must have some (considerable) grip upon one's motivational systems. The problem is that there are motivational factors other than valuational ones. The free agent has the capacity to translate his values into action; his actions flow from his evaluational system.

One's evaluational system may be said to constitute one's standpoint, the point of view from which one judges the world. The important feature of one's evaluational system is that one cannot coherently dissociate oneself from it *in its entirety*. For to dissociate oneself from the ends and principles that constitute one's evaluational system is to disclaim or repudiate them, and any ends and principles so disclaimed (self-deception aside) cease to be constitutive of one's valuational system. One can dissociate oneself from one set of ends and principles only from the standpoint of another such set that one does not disclaim. In short, one cannot dissociate oneself from all normative judgments without forfeiting all standpoints and therewith one's identity as an agent.

Of course, it does not follow from the fact that one must assume some standpoint that one must have only one, nor that one's standpoint is completely determinate. There may be ultimate conflicts, irresolvable tensions, and things about which one simply does not know what to do or say. Some of these possibilities point to problems about the unity of the person. Here the extreme case is pathological. I am inclined to think that when the split is severe enough, to have more than one standpoint is to have none.

This distinction between wanting and valuing requires far fuller explication than it has received so far. Perhaps the foregoing remarks have at least shown *that* the distinction exists and is important, and have hinted at its nature. This distinction is important to the adherent of the familiar view—that talk about free action and free agency can be understood in terms of the idea of being able to get what one wants—because it gives sense to the claim that in unfree actions the agents do not get what they really or most want. This distinction gives sense to the contrast between free action and intentional action. Admittedly, further argument is required to show that such unfree agents are *unable* to get what they want, but the initial step toward this end has been taken.

At this point, it will be profitable to consider briefly a doctrine that is in many respects like that which I have been developing. The contrast will, I think, clarify the claims that have been advanced in the preceding pages.

III

In an important and provocative article,[9] Harry Frankfurt has offered a description of what he takes to be the essential feature of "the concept of a person," a feature which, he alleges, is also basic to an understanding of "freedom of the will." This feature is the possession of higher-order volitions as well as first-order desires. Frankfurt construes the notion of a person's will as "the notion of an *effective* desire—one that moves (or will or would move) a person all the way to action" (p. 8). Someone has a second-order volition, then, when he wants "a certain desire to be his will." (Frankfurt also considers the case of a second-order desire that is not a second-order volition, where one's desire is simply to have a certain desire and not to act upon it. For example, a man may be curious to know what it is like to be addicted to drugs; he thus desires to desire heroin, but he may not desire his desire for heroin to be effective, to be his will. In fact, Frankfurt's actual example is somewhat more special, for here the man's desire is not simply to have a desire for heroin: he wants to have a desire for heroin which has a certain source, that is, is addictive. He wants to know what it is like to *crave* heroin.) Someone is a *wanton* if he has no second-order volitions. Finally, "it is only because a person has volitions of the second order that he is capable both of enjoying and of lacking freedom of the will" (p. 14).

Frankfurt's thesis resembles the Platonic view we have been unfolding insofar as it focuses upon "the structure of a person's will" (p. 6). I want to make a simple point about Frankfurt's paper: namely that the "structural" feature to which Frankfurt appeals is not the fundamental feature for either free agency or personhood; it is simply insufficient to the task he wants it to perform.

One job that Frankfurt wishes to do with the distinction between lower and higher orders of desire is to give an account of the sense in which some wants may be said to be more truly the agent's own than others (though in an obvious sense all are wants of the agent) the sense in which the agent "identifies" with one desire rather than another and the sense in which an agent may be unfree with respect to his own "will." This enterprise is similar to our own. But we can see that the notion of "higher-order volition" is not really the fundamental notion for these purposes, by raising the question: Can't one be a wanton, so to speak, with respect to one's second-order desires and volitions?

In a case of conflict, Frankfurt would have us believe that what it is to identify with some desire rather than another is to have a volition concerning the former which is of higher order than any concerning the latter. That the first desire is given a special status over the second is due to its having an n-order volition concerning it, whereas the second desire has at most an $(n - 1)$-order volition concerning it. But why does one necessarily care about one's higher-order volitions? Since second-order volitions are themselves simply desires, to add them to the context of conflict is just to increase the number of contenders; it is not to give a special place to any of those in contention. The agent may not care which of the second-order desires wins out. The same possibility arises at each higher order.

Quite aware of this difficulty, Frankfurt writes:

> There is no theoretical limit to the length of the series of desires of higher and higher orders; nothing except common sense and, perhaps, a saving fatigue prevents an individual from obsessively refusing to identify himself with any of his desires until he forms a desire of the next higher order (p. 16).

But he insists that

> It is possible . . . to terminate such a series of acts [i.e., the formation of ever higher-order volitions] without cutting it off arbitrarily. When a person identifies himself *decisively* with one of his first-order desires, this commit-ment "resounds" throughout the potentially endless array of higher orders. . . . The fact that his second-order volition to be moved by this desire is a decisive one means that there is no room for questions concerning the pertinence of desires or volitions of higher orders. . . . The decisiveness of the commitment he has made means that he has decided that no further question about his second-order volition, at any higher order, remains to be asked (p. 16).

But either this reply is lame or it reveals that the notion of a higher-order volition is not the fundamental one. We wanted to know what prevents wan-tonness with regard to one's higher-order volitions. What gives these volitions any special relation to "oneself"? It is unhelpful to answer that one makes a "decisive commitment," where this just means that an interminable ascent to higher orders is not going to be permitted. This *is* arbitrary.

What this difficulty shows is that the notion of orders of desires or volitions does not do the work that Frankfurt wants it to do. It does not tell us why or how a particular want can have, among all of a person's "desires," the special property of being peculiarly his "own." There may be something to the notions of acts of identification and of decisive commitment, but these are in any case different notions from that of a second- (or *n*-) order desire. And if these are the crucial notions, it is unclear why these acts of identification cannot be themselves of the first order—that is, identification with or commitment to courses of action (rather than with or to desires)—in which case, no ascent is necessary, and the notion of higher-order volitions becomes superfluous or at least secondary.

In fact, I think that such acts of "identification and commitment" (if one goes for this way of speaking) are generally to courses of action, that is, are first-order. Frankfurt's picture of practical judgment seems to be that of an agent with a given set of (first-order) desires concerning which he then forms second-order volitions. But this picture seems to be distorted. As I see it, agents frequently formulate values concerning alternatives they had not hitherto desired. Initially, they do not (or need not usually) ask themselves which of their desires they want to be effective in action; they ask themselves which course of action is most worth pursuing. The initial practical question is about courses of action and not about themselves.

Indeed, practical judgments are connected with "second-order volitions." For the same considerations that constitute one's on-balance reasons for doing some action, *a*, are reasons for wanting the "desire" to do *a* to be effective in action, and for wanting contrary desires to be ineffective. But in general, evaluations are prior and of the first order. The first-order desires that result from practical judgments generate second-order volitions because they have this special status; they do not have the special status that Frankfurt wants them to have because there is a higher-order desire concerning them.

Therefore, Frankfurt's position resembles the Platonic conception in its focus upon the structure of the "soul."[10] But the two views draw their divisions differently; whereas Frankfurt divides the soul into higher and lower orders of desire, the distinction for Plato—and for my thesis—is among independent sources of motivation.[11]

IV

In conclusion, it can now be seen that one worry that blocks the acceptance of the traditional view of freedom—and in turn, of compatibilism—is unfounded. To return to Berlin's question (p. 110), it is false that determinism entails that all our actions and choices have the same status as those of "compulsive choosers" such as "kleptomaniacs, dipsomaniacs, and the like." What is distinctive about such compulsive behavior, I would argue, is that the desires and emotions in question are more or less radically independent of the evaluational systems of these agents. The compulsive character of a kleptomaniac's thievery has nothing at all to do with determinism. (His desires to steal may arise quite randomly.) Rather, it is because his desires express themselves independently of his evaluational judgments that we tend to think of his actions as unfree.

The truth, of course, is that God (traditionally conceived) is the only free agent, *sans phrase*. In the case of God, who is omnipotent and omniscient, there can be no disparity between valuational and motivational systems. The dependence of motivation upon evaluation is total, for there is but a single source of motivation: his presumably benign judgment.[12] In the case of the Brutes, as well, motivation has a single source: appetite and (perhaps) passion. The Brutes (or so we normally think) have no evaluational system. But human beings are only more or less free agents, typically less. They are free agents only in some respects. With regard to the appetites and passions, it is plain that in some situations the motivational systems of human beings exhibit an independence from their values which is inconsistent with free agency; that is to say, people are sometimes moved by their appetites and passions in conflict with their practical judgments.[13]

As Nietzsche said (probably with a rather different point in mind): "Man's belly is the reason why man does not easily take himself for a god."[14]

Notes

1. *Four Essays on Liberty* (New York: Oxford, 1969), xx–xxi.

2. I am going to use 'want' and 'desire' in the very inclusive sense now familiar in philosophy, whereby virtually any motivational factor that may figure in the explanation of intentional action is a want; 'desire' will be used mainly in connection with the appetites and passions.

3. To quote just one of many suggestive passages: "We must . . . observe that within each one of us there are two sorts of ruling or guiding principles that we follow. One is an innate desire for pleasure, the other an acquired judgment that aims at what is best. Sometimes these internal guides are in accord, sometimes at variance; now one gains the mastery, now the other. And when judgment guides us rationally toward what is best, and has the mastery, that mastery is called temperance, but when desire drags us irrationally toward pleasure, and has come to rule within us, the name given to that rule is wantonness" (*Phaedrus*, 237e–38e; Hackforth trans.).

For a fascinating discussion of Plato's parts-of-the-soul doctrine, see Terry Penner's "Thought and Desire in Plato," in Gregory Vlastos, ed., *Plato: A Collection of Critical Essays*, vol. II, (New York: Anchor, 1971). As I see it (and here I have been influenced by Penner's article), the distinction I have attributed to Plato was meant by him to be a solution to the socratic problem of *akrasia*.

I would argue that this distinction, though necessary, is insufficient for the task, because it does not mark the difference between ("mere") incontinence or weakness of will and psychological compulsion. This difference requires a careful examination of the various things that might be meant in speaking of the strength of a desire.

4. Here I shall not press the rational/nonrational contrast any further than this, though Plato would have wished to press it further. However, one important and anti-Humean implication of the minimal distinction is this: it is not the case that, if a person desires to do *X*, he therefore has (or even regards himself as having) a reason to do *X*.

5. For example, I take my remarks to be incompatible with the characterization of value R. B. Perry gives in *General Theory of Value* (Cambridge, Mass.: Harvard University Press, 1950). In ch. v, Perry writes: "This, then, we take to be the original source and constant feature of all value. That which is an object of interest is *eo ipso* invested with value." And 'interest' is characterized in the following way: "liking and disliking, desire and aversion, will and refusal, or seeking and avoiding. It is to this all-pervasive characteristic of the motor-affective life, this *state, act, attitude* or *disposition of favor* or disfavor, to which we propose to give the name of 'interest'."

6. Notice that most emotions differ from passions like lust in that they involve beliefs and some sort of valuation (cf., resentment). This may be the basis for Plato's positing a third part of the soul which is in a way partly rational—viz., *Thumos*.

7. To be sure, one may attempt to cultivate or eliminate certain appetites and passions, so that the desires that result may be in this way dependent upon one's evaluations. Even so, the resulting desires will be such that they can persist independently of one's values. It is rather like jumping from an airplane.

8. It is reported that H. G. Wells regarded the most important themes of his life to have been (1) the attainment of a World Society, and (2) sex.

9. "Freedom of the Will and the Concept of a Person," *Journal of Philosophy* 73, no. 1, see ch. 4 above.

10. Frankfurt's idea of a wanton, suitably construed, can be put to further illuminating uses in moral psychology. It proves valuable, I think, in discussing the problematic phenomenon of psychopathy or sociopathy.

11. Some very recent articles employ distinctions, for similar purposes, very like Frankfurt's and my own. See, for example, Richard C. Jeffrey, "Preferences among Preferences," *Journal of Philosophy* 71, no. 13 (July 18, 1974), 377–91. In "Freedom and Desire," *Philosophical Review*, 83, no. 1 (January 1974), 32–54, Wright Neely appeals to higher-order desires, apparently unaware of Frankfurt's development of this concept.

12. God could not act *akratically.* In this respect, Socrates thought people were distinguishable from such a being only by ignorance and limited power.

13. This possibility is a definitive feature of appetitive and passionate wants.

14. *Beyond Good and Evil*, sec. 141.

8

Hierarchical Analyses
of Unfree Action

Irving Thalberg

Metaphysicians, ethical theorists, and philosophers of law squabble endlessly about what it is for a person to act—or perhaps even to "will"—more or less freely. A vital issue in this controversy is how we should analyze two obvious but surprisingly problematical contrasts. The first antithesis is between things we do because we are forced, and deeds we perform because we want to— sometimes after having discovered preponderant reasons in their favor. The other polarity is more general. In most situations, if I act on my desire, I act more freely than if I had not had the desire. But what if my attitude is the product of childhood conditioning—or later brainwashing, brain surgery, hypnosis, behavior modification, alcoholism, narcotics addiction, neurosis, psychosis, or worse? Then isn't my autonomy diminished? What is it about these latter desires, or their origin, that differentiates them from their unthreatening congeners?

My plan is to outline briefly why standard articulations of these two overlapping contrasts fail. Then I shall assess some variants of an approach to both dichotomies which has become explicit only in philosophical writings of the 1970s. What distinguishes this pattern of analysis is that its champions mark off at least two "orders," or levels, of desire, or "volition" within the coerced individual and the person afflicted by alien impulses.

This essay is based to some extent upon my earlier attempt to understand how so-called mental illness may diminish a person's control over his behavior: "Motivational Disturbances and Free Will," in H. T. Engelhardt, Jr., and S. Spicker, eds., *Mental Health: Philosophical Perspectives* (Dordrecht, Holland: Reidel, 1978). I thank the editors and publishers of that volume for allowing me to use some of that material here. I am also grateful to several participants in the conference on mental health at the University of Texas Medical Branch, during May 1976, where I read the parent essay. My commentator, Professor Caroline Whitbeck, gave me numerous helpful criticisms.

This chapter is reprinted from the *Canadian Journal of Philosophy* Vol. VIII, No. 2 June 1978 with the permission of the editors of the journal and Ms. Pellow-Thalberg.

Before his death in August 1987, Irving Thalberg was Professor of Philosophy of the University of Illinois at Chicago.

First we should be clearer about coercion. Here are two sample accounts, by well-known philosophers:

> If a hurricane wind blows you twenty yards across a street, you cannot be said to have crossed the street voluntarily, since you were compelled to do it and given no choice.[1]

> We act under *compulsion* in the literal sense . . . *when we are literally being physically restrained from without in implementing the desires which we have upon reacting to the total stimulus situation in our environment and are physically made to perform a different act instead.*[2]

The "hurricane wind" fits both formulations. My understanding is that the gale is supposed to lift you off your feet, and deposit you on the far side of the road. Your "*desires*," however, were to remain on this side, and to continue your stroll without interruption.

There are two notable hitches in these characterizations of being forced to act. For one thing, if you are "*physically restrained*" in this manner, something happens to you: you are blown twenty yards. To be thus swept along is not to perform any action. Therefore in the circumstances it is false to assert that you are "compelled to do" anything, that you are "*made to perform a different act*" than you desired. Which act, precisely? No act has been reported. So these accounts seem to rule out, rather than elucidate, acting under compulsion.

The other hitch is more important, as far as hierarchical analyses are concerned. These characterizations wrongly omit "choice." Our common sense dichotomy, 'acting under compulsion versus doing what you want', is philosophically baffling because in the end we must deny that a coerced individual is "given no choice." In a strange sense you choose, you want to do, what you are forced to do. This seems irrefutable in standard cases. Consider the hostages of a terrorist, their agonized relatives, and the embarrassed authorities. They might simply be overcome by panic. Their behavior might resemble shivering, stuttering, or uncontrollable weeping. These are not forms of action, any more than being propelled by a hurricane wind is a form of action. So the hostages and the others would not be doing anything in compliance with the terrorist's demands. But insofar as they are acting, and cooperating—however reluctantly or fearfully—they are doing what they want, what they have chosen to do: namely to minimize death and suffering. Presumably compliance seems to them, in their justifiably agitated condition, to be the least of evils.

The second author I quoted above displays some awareness of the mismatch between such familiar examples of being forced to act and his "literal" definition. But he takes the heroic course of rejecting these paradigms. He explains that "when a bankteller [*sic*] hands over cash during a robbery upon feeling the revolver pressing against his ribs, he is *not acting under compulsion in my literal sense*. . . . [He] is doing what he genuinely wants to do *under the given conditions*.[3] I feel like asking: If this teller's behavior and circumstances do not exemplify coercion, what could? A diehard might appeal to the quoted definition again, and reply that a "literal" instance would occur if the money were "physically" torn from the resisting teller's clutches. But then we confront the first hitch once more: to have currency wrenched from one's grasp is to be acted upon, not to act—and consequently not to be "compelled to do" anything.

Besides elucidating the sense in which a constrained person both acts and chooses to do so, we must follow up our original antithesis and reveal how he also acts unwillingly. Our mission sounds paradoxical: to set out how he both wants and also more "intensely" wants *not* to be doing what he is forced to do.

The earliest explicitly hierarchical treatment of these difficulties about coercion which I have seen in print is Professor Gerald Dworkin's. His main example definitely qualifies as an action: the prey of a highwayman timorously surrenders his billfold. Dworkin's holdup victim also exercises choice. He gives up money because he wants thereby to save his skin. What about unwillingness? This comes into the picture when Dworkin postulates a second level of choice and desire. He declares: "What [the victim] doesn't want to do when faced with the highwayman is to hand money over in these circumstances, for these reasons."[4] The hierarchical ordering of conative attitudes here is semantical or logical. Our protagonist's aversion is directed toward, and a negative evaluation of, the prudential motive on which he acts—which is, of course, directed toward his behavior and its likely results. Speaking generally, Dworkin asserts that people

> resent acting for certain reasons; they would not choose to be motivated in certain ways. They mind acting simply in order . . . to avoid unpleasant consequences . . . .
>
> [P]art of the human personality . . . takes up an "attitude" toward the reasons, desires and motives which determine . . . conduct . . . .
>
> [We] consider ourselves compelled because we find it painful to act for these reasons."[5]

Dworkin goes on boldly to define "acting freely" in similar terms: "[The person] A does X freely if A does X for reasons which he doesn't mind acting from."[6] Although my present goal is not nearly so ambitious, I should remark in passing that Dworkin's proposal seems inadequate. What of the chattel slave, or the subservient wife, who may not "mind acting from" motives of servility and self-effacement? Only a Stoic moralist would infer from this 'not minding' that such people always act freely.[7] I shall ask momentarily if Dworkin's definition even excludes someone who wisely obeys the highwayman.

First we should appreciate some refinements that Professor Harry Frankfurt has added to the split-level analysis of compulsion—most of them subsequently adopted by Dworkin.[8] Frankfurt attributes great ontological significance to planes of conation within the agent. On his view, "one essential difference between persons and other creatures" is that persons "are able to form what I shall call 'second-order desires'."[9] Actually Frankfurt goes on to distinguish between our second-floor desire that we should merely *have*, or experience, a certain ground-floor desire to act, and our upper-story desire that the ground-level desire "be the desire that moves [us] effectively to act" (p. 66). The latter kind of stratospheric yearning Frankfurt dubs a "second-

order volition." Then he declares: "it is having second-order volitions, and not
having second-order desires generally, that I regard as essential to being a
person" (ibid.). Individuals whom he brands as "wantons" fall short of personhood on this criterion. These "agents . . . are not persons because whether or
not they have desires of the second order, they have no second-order volitions . . . . a wanton . . . does not care about his will. . . . [H]e does not care
which of his [first-order] inclinations is the strongest."

Now for constraint. Frankfurt holds that both offers and threats are sometimes coercive. His upstairs-downstairs account of them reads:

> an offer is coercive . . . when the person is moved into compliance by a
> desire . . . which he would overcome if he could . . . a desire by which he
> does not want to be driven. . . .
>
> [A] person's autonomy may be violated by a threat in the same way. . . .
>
> In submitting to a threat, a person invariably does something which he
> does not really want to do.[10]

Here the coerced individual's second-order volition is at odds with his operative desire. But in Frankfurt's latest account of these matters, he seems to
acknowledge two further possibilities. One would be if the person faced a "set"
of unappealing options "from which he did not want to have to choose," yet
"preferred without reservation the one he pursued"—in which case his ground-
floor motive, as well as his deed, are "in accordance with a second-order
volition."[11] This upper-deck volitionist seems to violate Frankfurt's requirement of being "moved into compliance by a desire . . . by which he does not
want to be driven." Similarly in the other new situation Frankfurt acknowledges, where the constrained individual "is moved to act *without* the concur-
rence of a second-order volition."[12]

Now we can pick up the hint I dropped four paragraphs ago. Are we sure
any examples like Dworkin's or Frankfurt's will meet their general stipulation
that level-conflict must occur? The only case I am able to invent is when we
carry prudence to cowardly extremes, find ourselves unable to face reasonable
risks—especially when we put others in jeopardy to protect ourselves from
lesser harm. But we do not always fall apart this way in coercive situations.
Take Dworkin's holdup story. Most victims would, at the time and later, give
second-order endorsement to their cautious motives. They are unlikely to
yearn, from their elevated tribune, for more defiant ground-floor urges.

Upon further reflection, I wonder if we ought to have meekly accepted all
this apparatus of first- and second-order conation. Do we need such machinery
to interpret even Dworkin's and Frankfurt's hand-picked cases? Sticking with
the holdup victim: what is likely to be the principal object of his aversion—that
his money is gone, or that it was "for these reasons" that he abandoned his
money? Surely he "minds" his action, and particularly its financial consequences, more than he "minds" his own motivational state? Surely the former
is more "painful"? Why, *pace* Frankfurt, should the victim want to "overcome"
his operative desire? A dilemma emerges: Either he stratospherically dislikes
merely having the desire, or he opposes it because it "moves him effectively to

act." Presumably the latter. But is he distressed merely because the inclination is on hand while he acts—or because of what results from its presence, namely his deed and its consequences? Apparently our putative second-order volitional antics are more concerned with our behavior, and its effect, than with the first-order desires that engendered it. Dworkin and Frankfurt are mistaken, or anyway guilty of exaggeration, when they suppose that what a constrained person "doesn't want" is for some desire or other to move him.

We can bolster this objection if we look at the contrasting example which both Dworkin and Frankfurt offer, with fairly similar details, to illustrate how an *unconstrained* agent's first- and second-order attitudes mesh. In place of the robber's prey, who "doesn't want . . . to hand money over . . . for these reasons," Dworkin conjures up someone who "might want to hand over some money . . . because he is asked by a relative, or because he is feeling charitable, or because he desires to rid himself of worldly things."[13] Now I would rephrase my criticism by asking: Does this person long only, or primarily, for a desire—either (1) the impulse to help his kin, (2) the urge to help all unfortunates, or (3) the inclination to divest himself of lucre and property? A more plausible diagnosis would be that he is transferring his approval of certain acts to these desires, (1), (2), or (3). If we underscore his wanting to be moved "effectively to act" by (1), (2), or (3), then the dilemma I propounded above ought to show that what the uncoerced, would-be moneygiver wants is to perform generous acts.

I feel similarly about a more elaborate fiction of Frankfurt's:

> [A] man . . . decides to . . . give the money in his pocket to the first person he meets. . . . The first person he meets points a pistol at his head and threatens to kill him unless he hands over his money. The man is terrified, he loses touch with his original intention . . . and . . . hands over his money in order to escape death.

> [Now if he had] handed over his money with his original benevolent intention . . . he would not have been coerced in doing so. His motive in acting would have been just the motive from which he wanted to act.[14]

We have already noticed that you can say equally of a constrained moneygiver, "His motive in acting . . . [was] just the motive from which he wanted to act"—namely self-preservation. My present suspicion is that we needn't furnish either coerced or uncoerced donors with an upper-story volition. Imagine that Frankfurt's budding philanthropist had carried out his "original benevolent intention." If we want to bring out contrasts between this situation and the alternative one, where he gave under threats, we can accomplish this with ground-floor desires alone. We can say that he desired to engage in the activity of giving-without-intimidation, and not to engage in the activity of giving-under-pressure. If we wish to delete hyphens, we can suppose he had a couple of grass roots desires: to give, and to be in unmenacing circumstances.

Our goal so far is to elucidate the fundamental antithesis between acting under compulsion and doing what you want. Hierarchical theories help us understand the sense in which a coerced individual wants to comply. But they break down when they equate his unwillingness with a second-order aversion to the desire by which he is "moved into compliance." My objection was that coerced people should for the most part approve of their prudential motives, if they ever busy themselves with second-order high jinks. Then I tried to demonstrate why none of the standard cases of compelled and uncompelled behavior, including those selected by Dworkin and Frankfurt, require a split-level analysis, I am hardly attempting to prove that nobody, or no constrained person, ever can be stirred by the upper-deck attitudes that Dworkin and Frankfurt describe. I simply find their own examples questionable, and I doubt that second-order goings on could possibly do the jobs they are assigned in the Dworkin-Frankfurt system.

I illustrated a one-level analysis of the attitudes of a willing philanthropist. Can I do the same for his coerced counterpart? Specifically, how will I convey the basic notion that the latter, as Frankfurt puts it, "invariably does something which he does not really want to do"? For a crude start, my nonhierarchical answer is that he "does not really want to" *be* in the coercive situation. That is confusing, however. The very reason we say he is constrained is that no action of escaping the situation is available to him. Any endeavour to flee would be defiance, which he has rejected in favour of submission. There is no alternative action, other than complying, which we might say he does "really want to" perform. But we can legitimately reformulate his attitude as aversion to his circumstances. My proposal is to say that his top preference would be for a situation in which he did not face irresistible threats or offers. Translated into pragmatic terms, this might mean: If he had been forewarned of this situation, and alerted to a less coercive and otherwise no more disadvantageous alternative situation, he would have circumnavigated this one. Now that he has blundered into it, however, if he were asked to rank compliance, resistance, magical return to the *status quo ante*, and magical escape *simpliciter*, he would opt for one or the other miracle.[15] My purpose is not to introduce anything occult, but to suggest that his coercive situation, rather than the constrained person's act or first-order desire, is the object of his aversion. This nonhierarchical view even gets across our preanalytic "really": Although there is no deed the coerced individual really wants to perform, as conditions stand, his really important attitude is his preference for different conditions. Why "really important"? Because if he had been, or were now, in a position to choose, he would no longer want to comply with his coercers; he would select another scene.

This nonhierarchical sketch is not meant to be an exhaustive analysis of constraint—of what is involved when people or "natural forces" compel someone to act. I have investigated only the desires and other conative attitudes of a coerced individual. My aim has been to restore parity between his attitudes and those of people who are simply doing what they want. The difference is that he would always, but they would usually not, prefer to be out of the present situation. Although this is hardly a specification of logically necessary or sufficient conditions for saying that an agent is coerced, it is all we need. It also yields a dividend: it does justice to the statements of Dworkin and Frankfurt that their coerced protagonists did not "want . . . to hand money over in these circumstances," and "did not want to have to choose" among disagreeable alternative actions.

Maybe a similar approach will help us with our other puzzling contrast, between the normal, uncoerced instance of doing what you want and cases where the unusual nature or ancestry of our operative desire leads us to suspect that it somehow overpowered you and diminished your control of your behavior. A random sampling of heterogeneous but typical cases will indicate what sort of contrast we might elucidate. As I noted earlier, philosophers worry that a person acts less freely if the motive he acts on resulted mainly from brutal or deprived upbringing, from various forms of conditioning—indoctrination, behavior modification, from hypnosis, from psychosurgery, from abuse of alcohol and drugs, or from neurotic and psychotic compulsions." Evidently there is no compulsion at the time someone acts on these motives, since no natural force or human coercer is on the scene to exercise compulsion.

Hierarchical theories may be appealing at this juncture, precisely because they supply us with analogues to a coercive setup. The wayward motives I listed will function like threatening and enticing individuals, or like violent winds and tides. The victim will be the second-order person, whose ethereal volitions suffer defeat. I am not preparing to flog a dead horse. This is a new race. When someone is literally constrained, by others or by inanimate things, it may seem implausible and gratuitous to suppose that he has a second-order aversion toward his first-order desires for compliance. But if we delete external coercers, and imagine that he is being pushed around by a first-order desire to steal or whatnot, it may be quite appropriate to supply him with a higher con-attitude against that street-level desire.

But isn't it his own desire? Frankfurt discusses two relevant cases. The easy one is where a fiendish brain surgeon "manipulates his subject on a continuous basis, like a marionette, so that each of the subject's mental and physical states is the outcome of [a] specific intervention."[16] Frankfurt has no need to invoke his double-decker theory in order to conclude that "the subject is not a person at all," and that the desires he is afflicted with are not "his own" (ibid.). In fact, this remains true even if the wretch's mental states "include second-order desires and volitions" (ibid.).

Frankfurt does deploy his split-level analysis when he confronts the tougher case of an "unwilling" drug addict. Frankfurt supposes that the addict has a ground-floor disinclination to use narcotics, as well as a craving for them. But from his second-order balcony the fellow "identifies himself . . . with one . . . of his conflicting desires [the desire not to take his anodyne] . . . makes [it] . . . more truly his own and . . . withdraws himself from the other"; consequently the "force moving him to take the drug" must be "a force other than his own."[17] Dworkin has a similar analysis of someone who wants to give up tobacco. He declares:

> we need characterizations of what it is for a [person's] motivation to be *his*,
> and what it is for it to be his *own*. . . .

[A] person may not only desire to smoke. He can also desire that he desire to smoke. . . . He can also desire that his motivations be different. . . .

[H]e may . . . prefer to have a causal structure introduced which brings him to be nauseated by the taste or odor of tobacco. Even though his behavior is not then under his voluntary control, he may wish to be motivated in this way in order to stop smoking. When this is true he views the causal influences as "his." The part of him that wishes to stop smoking is recognized as his true self, the one whose wishes he wants to see carried out.[18]

Dworkin also speaks of identification:

the attitude a person takes towards the influences motivating him . . . determines whether or not they are to be considered "his." Does he identify with them, assimilate them to himself, view himself as the kind of person who wishes to be motivated in these particular ways? If [not], . . . then those influences, even though they may be causally effective, are not viewed as "his."[19]

Why is the drug user's, and the smoker's, craving not really "his"? Frankfurt and Dworkin seem to be telling us that he does not really want to drug himself, or to smoke, because the real he—his "true self"—on its second-order pedestal, abhors these first-order longings. This picture is attractive, but is it cogent?

Both Frankfurt and Dworkin assume that when you ascend to the second level, you discover the real person and what she or he really wants. I shall pack my misgivings into a couple of challenges; Why not go on to third-story or higher desires and volitions? And if that is somehow impossible, why grant that a second-order attitude must always be more genuinely his, more representative of what he genuinely wants, than those you run into at ground level? Perhaps his higher attitude is only a cowardly second thought which gnaws at him.

Frankfurt anticipates the "regress" challenge, and has several retorts. The most definite one begins with a person forming some "decisive" second-order volition. According to Frankfurt,

he has decided that no further question about his second-order volition, at any higher-order, remains to be asked. It is relatively unimportant whether we explain this by saying that this commitment implicitly generates an endless series of confirming desires of higher orders, or . . . [that it] . . . is tantamount to dissolution of the pointedness [*sic*] of all questions concerning higher orders.[20]

I get the impression that Frankfurt has not so much answered the "regress" challenge as forbidden us to raise such "questions concerning higher orders." But I am unsure, because I fail to understand this and related passages.

My other challenge is an attempt to elicit more particulars about identification—at whatever level it occurs. Frankfurt anticipates this as the question: Why can't a person fail to identify himself with second-order phenomena occurring in himself, and remain "a passive bystander" to them? Frankfurt replies:

> As for a person's second-order volition . . . , it is impossible for him to be a passive bystander to them. They *constitute* his activity—i.e. his being active rather than passive—and the question of whether or not he identifies himself with them cannot arise. It makes no sense to ask whether someone identifies himself with his identification of himself, . . . [except to ask] whether his identification is wholehearted. . . .[21]

Dworkin does not take up these issues. At least he does not just declare that they "cannot arise." For his part, Frankfurt adds that his pivotal "notion of identification is admittedly a bit mystifying." So I think it will not be unfair to conclude that, despite the initial attractiveness of a hierarchical approach to cases of alien motivation, its proponents have not yet sufficiently clarified it.

Perhaps they should not bother, since there are quite straightforward nonhierarchical accounts of the problem cases Frankfurt and Dworkin deal with. I remarked already that Frankfurt's own discussion of the living "marionette" of a malicious brain surgeon brings in no levels. Frankfurt implies that first- as well as any "second-order desires and volitions" which come over the victim, are not "his own," because the mad doctor has inflicted them upon him. Aren't they the doctor's? At all events, this one-level analysis is transferable to another longtime philosophical favorite: the case of hypnotically implanted desires. Neither a surgeon's nor a mesmerist's victim would want uncontrollably to do such-and-such, but for presumably unsolicited and unnoticed intrusions. I am not concerned with the situation where a Dworkinesque smoker has begged a hypnotist or surgeon to give him an overpowering distaste for tobacco; then we would find nothing especially alien in the smoker's new motivation.

Regarding "hooked" smokers, and people with an irresistible desire for alcohol and narcotics, I would tentatively advocate two complementary explanations why such desires sometimes do not reflect what the individuals really want. Like Frankfurt and Dworkin, I am only theorizing about apparently "unwilling" smokers, drinkers, and drug takers, who sincerely express their aversion toward their habit. My first, very simplistic approach would be to assimilate these cases to that of the mad surgeon's or the hypnotist's victim. At least sometimes, perhaps the user of tobacco, alcohol, or narcotics had no idea that he would develop a craving. He may have been given drugs or liquor during childhood, or generally without knowing what they were. So it is as if the craving were surreptitiously implanted in him.

This analysis will cover few cases. But the remainder, as well as this subgroup, may yield to the criterion I used to distinguish people who act under coercion and those who just do what they want. Suppose an "unwilling" addict, alcoholic, or smoker ran into a *deus ex machina*, who offered him a choice between continuing to indulge his habit, trying to resist it, turning back the clock to an addiction-free period of his career, or somehow getting out of his present "give in or resist" dilemma. Of course we must discount the appeal of becoming younger. Granting that, on my criterion he would elect a form of escape from his psychological situation. A "willing" drug taker, or anyone whose effective desires seem to be "his own," and not alien, would prefer the current setup over such radical changes. If my account of the contrast sounds vaguely hierarchical, I should explain that an "unwilling" addict does not merely elect to be rid of his desire for narcotics. What does he care about the craving *per se*? He may dislike the bodily pains he undergoes when the craving comes over him, but I think that is a separable matter. My point is that he is mainly opposed to the actions he performs, and their long-term effects, when he succumbs to his craving. Willing addicts, and other people who act on "their own," nonalien motives, prefer to continue doing what they are doing.

With the remaining examples of "foreign" motivation on my list, I am unsure how to draw the necessary contrast. Brainwashing is somewhat akin to the situation of the fiendish brain surgeon's human "marionette"—except that afterwards a brainwashed individual pursues a relatively unmanipulated career, almost "his own" life. The person who was psychologically scarred, or brutally indoctrinated, during childhood is at two further removes from brainwashed adults. We are reasonably certain what someone's desires were like before they were altered, without his consent, by brainwashing. But we can only guess how a child might have developed if he had not been conditioned to have these desires. Also the notions of consent and unconsent are not applicable when we are discussing the indoctrination of quite young people. A final complication, with harshly conditioned adults and children, is that they show none of the reluctance to do what they desire to do, which we found among "unwilling" addicts, alcoholics, and smokers.

How about neurotic and psychotic "compulsions"? I shall round out this inquiry by examining two analyses which are hierarchical in a broader sense than Dworkin's and Frankfurt's, and which seem ideally suited to distinguish these wayward desires from what a person really wants. One scheme, recently put back into the freewill debate by Professor Wright Neely, equates what I really desire with what I desire when I am thinking rationally. The other scheme, Professor Gary Watson's, assimilates a person's "values" to "what he most wants."[22] Both analyses are intended to be general accounts of the difference between free and unfree action. However, I am interested to see whether they help us articulate the narrower contrast between acting on a neurotic or psychotic desire, and doing what you genuinely want to do. Neither theory is hierarchical in the sense of placing our real desires on a higher logical or semantical plane than a foreign impulse, and having them directed approvingly or disprovingly toward the intruder. On Neely's and Watson's analysis, our genuine desires, as well as strange inclinations that overpower us, are desires to act. Hence the hierarchy seems straightforwardly ontological: some of the conative attitudes we have are really ours; others are not.

I shall begin by asking whether Neely's "rationality" doctrine elucidates and justifies this sort of claim. Actually the doctrine was stated two decades ago by Professor Alasdair MacIntyre. MacIntyre's thesis was that we act freely when our behavior is rational. We can put aside the obvious counterexample of a coerced, hence unfree, person who quite rationally decides to knuckle under.

Perhaps the account will still distinguish between acting on our "own" and foreign desires. MacIntyre wrote as follows:

> Behavior is rational—in this arbitrarily defined sense—if, and only if, it can [in principle] be influenced or inhibited by the adducing of some logically relevant consideration. . . . What is logically relevant will necessarily vary from case to case. If Smith is about to give generously to someone who appears to be in need, the information that this man . . . has in fact ample means, will be relevant. . . . [A]n impulsive action can in this sense be rational . . . [and] behavior can be reflective without being . . . rational. For a man may spend a great deal of time thinking about what he should do, and yet refuse to entertain a great many logically relevant considerations.[23]

This would help us contrast acting on our own desires, and giving in to alien urges, if it turns out that we are disposed to be rational in the first case, but not the latter. Unfortunately MacIntyre omitted to specify whose standards for "logically relevant considerations" should prevail. Shall we rely on commonly accepted tests? On the majority's judgment? On the verdict of logicians and other experts? Neely has an answer. He opts for the person's own criteria of logical relevance. If a desire makes us impervious to considerations which we take seriously at other times, then it is "irresistible," not really ours; otherwise it is "more intimately related to the self."[24] Neely illustrates his distinction by reference to Socrates's desire to stay in prison and drink the hemlock, rather than let Crito arrange his escape. Neely admits that we

> might well feel that Crito presented Socrates with good and sufficient reasons to escape. Yet . . . Socrates' decision to remain . . . [is not] a clear case of an unfree decision. . . . This leads us . . . [to suggest]: a desire is irresistable if and only if it is the case that if the agent had been presented with what *he took to be* good and sufficient reasons for not acting on it, he would still have acted on it.[25]

Neely's subjectivism creates a minor difficulty. What if the agent consistently holds to an absurdly high standard of germaneness and conclusiveness when he assesses reasons for not acting on his desire? In MacIntyre's phraseology, he refuses to ponder at all carefully a vast range of reasons which people generally accept as grounds for altering their planned behavior. Then, no matter how bizarre, how self-destructive, some of his desires are, none will be "irresistible."

But a deeper objection would be the one I urged against Frankfurt's view of how someone "identifies himself with" his "second-order volitions," and hence with any "first-order desire" they endorse. Just as Frankfurt and Dworkin take it for granted that the second-order me is my "true self," and that my second-order volitions represent what I truly want, Neely appears to assume that the rational me is the real one. But why can't I be, by my own admission in my rare moments of rationality, a generally irrational person? Why should it never be the case that when I am unamenable to reasoning, my desires still express what I really want? Neely's identification of rationality with authenticity seems to rule this out a priori.

Why not? In commonsense terms, I do not think it is impossible for someone to be a fundamentally irrational person, and to really desire such-and-such while he is in one of his bull-headed moods. In psychoanalytical jargon, I believe Neely's mistake is to have equated the core person, or "self," with those aspects of a human personality which Freud tried to capture with various labels: "consciousness," "the conscious system of ideas," "the reality principle," "the ego." Perhaps misled by some careless statements of Freud and his followers, Neely has begged the question against Freud's basic hypothesis that other, darker, savage, and nonrational aspects are equally—if not more— important: what Freud labeled 'the unconscious,' 'the unconscious system of ideas and impulses,' 'libido,' 'the pleasure principle,' 'id,' 'eros,' 'the urge toward self-destruction'. Freud's overall tendency is to highlight the nonrational sides of a human being. He allows that the "repressed content" of my dreams comes from "an 'id' on which my ego is seated"; however, "this ego developed out of the id, . . . forms with it a single biological unit . . . , [and] obeys . . . the id."[26] Freud even says the "core of our being . . . is formed by the obscure id. . . ."[27] My concern here is not exegesis, but rather to suggest that Neely's assumption precludes, without argument, our acceptance of a Freudian view of the individual as a smoldering, tense mixture of rational and nonrational elements. Neely must demonstrate why I cannot be acting on my own desires, and freely to boot, at any time that nonrational factors prevail.

My response is similar toward Watson's equation of genuine desires and moral values. Watson holds the comprehensive doctrine that

> [when] actions . . . are unfree, the agent is unable to get what he most wants, *or values*, . . . due to his own "motivational system". . . .
>
> [T]he strength of one's desire may not properly reflect the degree to which one values its object . . . .
>
> [I]t is possible that sometimes [one] is motivated to do things [one] does not deem worth doing. This possibility is the basis for the principal problem of free action: a person may be obstructed by his own will.[28]

Why should we agree, in effect, that our conscience is our real self, and that our moral principles specify what we really, or "most" want? Watson himself seems braced for an obvious Freudian challenge: Has he disproven the psychoanalytical hypothesis that our moral standards are slyly imposed upon us by our elders and other guardians of our social group? He admits that "one may be as dissociated from the demands of the superego as from those of the id."[29] But the only issue he confronts is whether a person's moral outlook has "its basis solely in acculturation . . . independently of [his] judgment." So he proceeds to compare values deriving from socialization and the more genuine ones that we reason out

> in a cool and non-self-deceptive moment. . . . That most people have articulate "conceptions of the good," coherent life-plans, *systems* of ends . . . is of course something of a fiction. Yet we all have more or less long-term aims and normative principles that we are willing to defend. . . . [T]hese . . . are . . . our values.[30]

Even on this point, most Freudians and many non-Freudians would reject Watson's distinction between acculturation and reasoning out as illusory. But the fundamental objection is quite independent of that. Similarly to the way Neely equated us with our rational side, Watson arbitrarily narrows us down to a rationally valuing self. Like Dworkin, Frankfurt, and Neely, he begs the question against Freudian and kindred personality theories, which depict us as conflict-prone systems of libidinal, destructive, morbid, self-preserving, sociable, conscientious, guilt-ridden, and other "forces," "principles," or mini-"agencies." Perhaps we value our disposition toward "cool and non-self-deceptive" moral thinking and life-planning more than we value our primitive urges and fantasies. But that is too circular to prove that the real self is the valuing self, that we "most want" things we value. Even if our valuing self were our most priceless asset, nothing would follow about its ontological superiority, nor about the comparative reality of our values over workaday desires.

I conclude that the four hierarchical theories I scrutinized have failed, despite the ingenuity of their proponents, to make sense of the contrasts which befuddled us. However, we managed to devise regrettably crude but adequate nonhierarchical accounts of the antithesis between acting under compulsion and doing what you want. We were also able to differentiate many relevant cases falling under the second antithesis, between acting upon an irresistible "alien" desire, and doing what you really want. My guess is that the recalcitrant cases, of desires resulting from early indoctrination, later brainwashing, and from neuroses and psychoses which do not originate with a germ or injury, are going to bother "free will" debaters for awhile. At least they may be convinced not to try hierarchical solutions.

Notes

1. Joel Feinberg, *Doing and Deserving* (Princeton, N.J.: Princeton University Press, 1970), 274ff.

2. Adolf Grünbaum, "Free Will and Laws of Human Behavior," *American Philosophical Quarterly* Vol. 8 (1971), 303ff., italics in original.

3. Grünbaum, "Free Will," p. 304, first italics added.

4. Gerald Dworkin, "Acting Freely," *Nous* Vol. 4 (1970), 372.

5. Dworkin, "Acting Freely," pp. 377ff; cf. also Dworkin "Autonomy and Behavior Control," *Hastings Center Report* Vol. 6 (1976), 23–28, especially p. 25.

6. "Acting Freely," p. 381; cf. also "Autonomy and Behavior Control," pp. 24ff.

7. Cf. "Acting Freely," pp. 380ff, and "Autonomy and Behavior Control," 24–28.

8. "Autonomy and Behavior Control," pp. 24ff.

9. Cf. Chapter 4 above; quote is from p. 64.

10. "Coercion and Moral Responsibility," in Ted Hondrich, ed. *Essays on Freedom of Action* (London: Routledge, 1972), 8ff.

11. "Three Concepts of Free Action II," in John Martin Fischer, ed., *Moral Responsibility* (Ithaca, N.Y.: Cornell University Press, 1986), 114.

12. "Three Concepts," p. 116, my italics.

13. "Acting Freely," p. 371.

14. "Coercion and Moral Responsibility," p. 82.

15. Cf. Robert Nozick, "Coercion," in S. Morgenbesser et al., eds., *Philosophy, Science, and Method* (New York: St. Martin's Press, 1969), 440–72, especially pp. 461ff.

16. "Three Concepts," p. 120.

17. Chapter 4 above, p. 69.

18. "Autonomy and Behavior Control," p. 24.

19. "Autonomy and Behavior Control," p. 25.

20. Chapter 4 above, pp. 71ff.

21. "Three Concepts," p. 121.

22. Wright Neely, "Freedom and Desire," *Philosophical Review* Vol. 83 (1974), 32–54; Gary Watson, Chapter 7 above, p. 110.

23. Alisdair MacIntyre, "Determinism," in B. Berofsky, ed., *Freedom and Determinism* (New York: Harper and Row, 1957), 240–54; quote is from p. 248.

24. "Freedom and Desire," p. 43.

25. "Freedom and Desire," p. 47.

26. James Strachey, ed. *Standard Edition of the Complete Works of Sigmund Freud*, Vol. 19 (London: Hogarth Press, 1954–74), 133ff.

27. *Complete Works*, Vol. 22, p. 197.

28. "Free Agency," pp. 110, 112, 115 (above).

29. "Free Agency," p. 116 above.

30. "Free Agency," p. 116 above.

9

Sanity and the Metaphysics
of Responsibility

Susan Wolf

Philosophers who study the problems of free will and responsibility have an easier time than most in meeting challenges about the relevance of their work to ordinary, practical concerns. Indeed, philosophers who study these problems are rarely faced with such challenges at all, since questions concerning the conditions of responsibility come up so obviously and so frequently in everyday life. Under scrutiny, however, one might question whether the connections between philosophical and nonphilosophical concerns in this area are real.

In everyday contexts, when lawyers, judges, parents, and others are concerned with issues of responsibility, they know, or think they know, what in general the conditions of responsibility are. Their questions are questions of application: Does this or that particular person meet this or that particular condition? Is he mature enough, or informed enough, or sane enough to be responsible? Was he acting under posthypnotic suggestion or under the influence of a mind-impairing drug? It is assumed, in these contexts, that normal, fully developed adult human beings are responsible beings. The questions have to do with whether a given individual falls within the normal range.

By contrast, philosophers tend to be uncertain about the general conditions of responsibility, and they care less about dividing the responsible from the nonresponsible agents than about determining whether, and if so why, any of us are ever responsible for anything at all.

In the classroom, we might argue that the philosophical concerns grow out of the nonphilosophical ones, that they take off where the nonphilosophical questions stop. In this way, we might convince our students that even if they are not plagued by the philosophical worries, they ought to be. If they worry about whether a person is mature enough, informed enough, and sane enough

This chapter was originally published in *Responsibility, Character, and the Emotions*, Ferdinand Schoeman, ed. Copyright © 1988 by Cambridge University Press. Reprinted with the permission of Cambridge University Press.

Susan Wolf is Associate Professor of Philosophy at The Johns Hopkins University.

to be responsible, then they should worry about whether he is metaphysically free enough, too.

The argument I shall make in this essay, however, goes in the opposite direction. My aim is not to convince people who are interested in the apparently nonphilosophical conditions of responsibility that they should go on to worry about the philosophical conditions as well, but rather to urge those who already worry about the philosophical problems not to leave the more mundane, prephilosophical problems behind. In particular, I shall suggest that the mundane recognition that *sanity* is a condition of responsibility has more to do with the murky and apparently metaphysical problems that surround the issue of responsibility than at first meets the eye. Once the significance of the condition of sanity is fully appreciated, at least some of the apparently insuperable metaphysical aspects of the problem of responsibility will dissolve.

My strategy will be to examine a recent trend in philosophical discussions of responsibility, a trend that tries, but I think ultimately fails, to give an acceptable analysis of the conditions of responsibility and that fails due to what at first appear to be deep and irresolvable metaphysical problems. It is here that I shall suggest that the condition of sanity comes to the rescue. What at first appears to be an impossible requirement for responsibility—namely, the requirement that the responsible agent must have created himself—turns out to be the vastly more mundane and noncontroversial requirement that the responsible agent must, in a fairly standard sense, be sane.

1. Frankfurt, Watson, and Taylor

The trend I have in mind is exemplified by the writings of Harry Frankfurt, Gary Watson, and Charles Taylor. I shall briefly discuss each of their separate proposals, and then offer a composite view that, while lacking the subtlety of any of the separate accounts, will highlight some important insights and some important blindspots that they share.

In his seminal article, "Freedom of the Will and the Concept of a Person,"[1] Harry Frankfurt notes a distinction between freedom of action and freedom of the will. A person has freedom of action, he points out, if she has the freedom to do whatever she wills to do—the freedom to walk or sit, to vote liberal or conservative, to publish a book or open a store, in accordance with her strongest desires. Even a person who has freedom of action may fail to be responsible for her actions, however, if the wants or desires she has the freedom to convert into action are themselves not subject to her control. Thus, the person who acts under posthypnotic suggestion, the victim of brainwashing, the kleptomaniac might all possess freedom of action. In the standard contexts in which these examples are raised, it is assumed that none of the individuals are locked up or bound. Rather, these individuals are understood to act on what, at one level at least, must be called *their own desires*. Their exemption from responsibility stems from the fact that their own desires (or, at least the ones governing their actions) are not up to them. These cases may be described in Frankfurt's terms as cases of people who possess freedom of action but who fail to be responsible agents because they lack freedom of the will.

Philosophical problems about the conditions of responsibility naturally focus on an analysis of this latter kind of freedom: What *is* freedom of the will, and under what conditions can we reasonably be thought to possess it? Frankfurt's proposal is to understand freedom of the will by analogy to freedom of action. As freedom of action is the freedom to do whatever one wills to do, freedom of the will is the freedom to will whatever one wants to will. To make this point clearer, Frankfurt introduces a distinction between first-order and second-order desires. First-order desires are desires to do or to have various things, second-order desires are desires about what desires to have or what desires to make effective in action. In order for an agent to have both freedom of action and freedom of the will, she must be capable of governing her actions by her first-order desires *and* capable of governing her first-order desires by her second-order desires.

Gary Watson's view of free agency[2]—free and responsible agency, that is— is similar to Frankfurt's in holding that an agent is responsible for an action only if the desires expressed by that action are of a particular kind. While Frankfurt identifies the right kind of desires as desires that are supported by second-order desires, Watson draws a distinction between "mere" desires, so to speak, and desires that are *values*. According to Watson, the difference between free action and unfree action cannot be analyzed by reference to the logical form of the desires from which these various actions arise, but rather must relate to a difference in the quality of their source. Whereas some of my desires are just appetites or conditioned responses which I find myself "stuck with," others are expressions of judgments on my part that the objects I desire are good. Insofar as my actions can be governed by the latter type of desire— governed, that is, by my values or valuational system—they are actions that I perform freely and for which I am responsible.

Both Frankfurt's and Watson's accounts offer ways of cashing out the intuition that in order to be responsible for one's actions, one must be responsible for the self that performs these actions. Charles Taylor, in an article entitled "Responsibility for Self"[3] discusses the same intuition. While Taylor does not describe his view in terms of different levels or types of desire, his view is related, for he claims that our freedom and responsibility depends on our ability to reflect on, criticize, and revise ourselves. Like Frankfurt and Watson, Taylor seems to believe that if the characters from which our actions flowed were simply and permanently *given* to us, implanted by heredity, environment, or God, then we would be mere vehicles through which the causal forces of the world traveled—no more responsible than dumb animals or young children or machines. But like the others, he points out that, for most of us, our characters and desires are not so brutely implanted—or, at any rate, if they are, they are subject to revision by our own reflecting, valuing, or second-order desiring selves. We human beings—and as far as we know, only we human beings—

have the ability to step back from ourselves and decide whether we are the selves we want to be. Because of this, these philosophers think, we are responsible for ourselves and for the actions that we produce.

Although there are subtle and interesting differences among the accounts of Frankfurt, Watson, and Taylor, my concern is with features of their views that are common to them all. All share the idea that responsible agency involves something more than intentional agency. All agree that if we are responsible agents, it is not just because our actions are within the control of our wills, but because, in addition, our wills are not just psychological states *in* us, but expressions of characters that come *from* us, or that at any rate are acknowledged and affirmed *by* us. For Frankfurt, this means that our wills must be ruled by our second-order desires; for Watson, that our wills must be governable by our system of values; for Taylor, that our wills must issue from selves that are subject to self-assessment and redefinition in terms of a vocabulary of worth. In one way or another, all these philosophers seem to be saying that the key to responsibility lies in the fact that responsible agents are those for whom it is not just the case that their actions are within the control of their wills, but also the case that their wills are within the control of their *selves* in some deeper sense. Because, at one level, the differences among Frankfurt, Watson, and Taylor may be understood as differences in the analysis or interpretation of what it is for an action to be under the control of this deeper self, we may speak of their separate positions as variations of one basic view about responsibility, the Deep Self View.

2. The Deep Self View

Much more must be said about the notion of a deep self before a fully satisfactory account of this view can be given. Providing a careful, detailed analysis of that notion poses an interesting, important, and difficult task in its own right. The degree of understanding achieved by abstraction from the views of Frankfurt, Watson, and Taylor, however, should be sufficient to allow us to recognize some important virtues as well as some important drawbacks of the Deep Self View.

One virtue is that this view explains a good portion of our pretheoretical intuitions about responsibility. It explains why kleptomaniacs, victims of brainwashing, and people acting under posthypnotic suggestion may not be responsible for their actions, although most of us typically are. In the cases of people in these special categories, the connection between the agents' deep selves and their wills is dramatically severed—their wills are governed, not by their deep selves, but by forces external to and independent from them. A different intuition is that we adult human beings can be responsible for our actions in a way that dumb animals, infants, and machines cannot be. Here the explanation is not in terms of a split between these beings' deep selves and their wills—rather the point is that these beings *lack* deep selves altogether. Kleptomaniacs and victims of hypnosis exemplify individuals whose selves are *alien-*

ated from their actions; lower animals and machines, on the other hand, don't have the sorts of selves from which actions *can* be alienated, and so they don't have the sort of selves from which, in the happier cases, actions can responsibly flow.

At a more theoretical level, the Deep Self View has another virtue: It responds to at least one way in which the fear of determinism presents itself.

A naive reaction to the idea that everything we do is completely determined by a causal chain that extends backwards beyond the times of our births involves thinking that in that case we would have no control over our behavior whatsoever. If everything is determined, it is thought, then what happens, happens, whether we want it to or not. A common, and proper, response to this concern points out that determinism does not deny the causal efficacy an agent's desires might have on her behavior. On the contrary, determinism in its more plausible forms tends to affirm this connection, merely adding that as one's behavior is determined by one's desires, so one's desires are determined by something else.[4]

Those who were initially worried that determinism implied fatalism, however, are apt to find their fears merely transformed rather than erased. If our desires are governed by something else, they might say, they are not *really* ours after all—or, at any rate, they are ours in only a superficial sense.

The Deep Self View offers an answer to this transformed fear of determinism, for it allows us to distinguish cases in which desires are determined by forces foreign to oneself from desires which are determined *by* one's self—by one's "real," or second-order-desiring, or valuing, or deep self, that is. Admittedly, there are cases, like that of the kleptomaniac or the victim of hypnosis, in which the agent acts on desires that "belong to" her in only a superficial sense. But the proponent of the Deep Self View will point out that even if determinism is true, ordinary adult human action can be distinguished from this. Determinism implies that the desires that govern our actions are in turn governed by something else, but that something else will, in the fortunate cases, be our own deeper selves.

This account of responsibility thus offers a response to our fear of determinism. But it is a response with which many will remain unsatisfied. For, even if my actions are governed by my desires and my desires are governed by my own deeper self, there remains the question, who, or what, is responsible for this deeper self? The above response seems only to have pushed the problem further back.

Admittedly, some versions of the Deep Self View—namely, Frankfurt's and Taylor's, seem to anticipate this question by providing a place for the ideal that an agent's deep self may be governed by a still deeper self. Thus, for Frankfurt, second-order desires may themselves be governed by third-order desires, third-order desires by fourth-order desires, and so on. And Taylor points out that, as we can reflect and evaluate our prereflective selves, so we can reflect and evaluate the selves who are doing the first reflecting and evaluating, and so on. But this capacity to recursively create endless levels of depth ultimately misses the criticism's point.

First of all, even if there is no *logical* limit to the number of levels of reflection or depth a person may have, there is certainly a psychological limit—it is virtually impossible to imaginatively conceive a fourth-, much less an eighth-order desire. More importantly, no matter how many levels of self we posit, there will still, in any individual case, be a last level—a deepest self about whom the question, "What governs it?" will arise as problematic as ever. If determinism is true, it implies that even if my actions are governed by my desires, and my desires are governed by my deepest self, my deepest self will still be governed by something that must, logically, be external to myself altogether. Though I can step back from the values my parents and teachers have given me and ask whether these are the values I really want, the "I" that steps back will itself be a product of the parents and teachers I am questioning.

The problem seems even worse when one sees that one fares no better if determinism is false. For if my deepest self is not determined by something external to myself, it will still not be determined by *me*. Whether I am a product of carefully controlled forces or a result of random mutations, whether there is a complete explanation of my origin or no explanation at all, *I* am not, in any case, responsible for my existence. I am not in control of my deepest self.

Thus, though the claim that an agent is responsible for only those actions that are within the control of her deep self correctly identifies a necessary condition for responsibility—a condition that separates the hypnotized and the brainwashed, the immature and the lower animals from ourselves, for example—it fails to provide a sufficient condition of responsibility that puts all fears of determinism to rest. For one of the fears invoked by the thought of determinism seems to be connected to its implication that we are but intermediate links in a causal chain, rather than ultimate, self-initiating sources of movement and change. From the point of view of one who has this fear, the Deep Self View seems merely to add loops to the chain, complicating the picture but not really improving it. From the point of view of one who has this fear, responsibility seems to require being a prime mover unmoved, whose deepest self is itself neither random *nor* externally determined but is rather determined *by* itself—who is, in other words, self-created.

At this point, however, proponents of the Deep Self View may wonder whether this fear is legitimate. For although people evidently can be brought to the point where they feel that responsible agency requires them to be ultimate sources of power, to the point where it seems that nothing short of self-creation will do, a return to the internal standpoint of the agent whose responsibility is in question makes it hard to see what good this metaphysical status is supposed to provide or what evil its absence is supposed to impose.

From the external standpoint, which discussions of determinism and indeterminism encourage us to take up, it may appear that a special metaphysical status is required to distinguish us significantly from other members of the natural world. But proponents of the Deep Self View will suggest that this is an illusion that a return to the internal standpoint should dispel. The possession of a deep self that is effective in governing one's actions is a sufficient distinction, they will say. For while other members of the natural world are not in control of the selves that they are, we, possessors of effective deep selves, are in control. We can reflect on what sorts of beings we are, and on what sorts of marks we make on the world. We can change what we don't like about ourselves and keep what we do. Admittedly, we do not create ourselves from nothing. But as long as we can revise ourselves, they will suggest, it is hard to find reason to complain. Harry Frankfurt writes that a person who is free to do what he wants to do and also free to want what he wants to want has "all the freedom it is possible to desire or to conceive."[5] This suggests a rhetorical question: If you are free to control your actions by your desires, and free to control your desires by your deeper desires, and free to control those desires by still deeper desires, what further kind of freedom can you want?

3. The Condition of Sanity

Unfortunately, there is a further kind of freedom we can want, which it is reasonable to think necessary for responsible agency. The Deep Self View fails to be convincing when it is offered as a complete account of the conditions of responsibility. To see why, it will be helpful to consider another example of an agent whose responsibility is in question.

JoJo is the favorite son of Jo the First, an evil and sadistic dictator of a small undeveloped country. Because of his father's special feelings for the boy, JoJo is given a special education and is allowed to accompany his father often and observe his daily routine. In light of this treatment, it is not surprising that little JoJo takes his father as a role-model and develops values very much like his dad's. As an adult, he does many of the same sorts of things his father did, including sending people to prison or to death or to torture chambers on the basis of the slightest of his whims. He is not *coerced* to do these things, he acts according to his own desires. Moreover, these are desires that he wholly wants to have. When he steps back and asks, "Do I really want to be this sort of person?" his answer is resoundingly Yes, for this way of life expresses a crazy sort of power that forms part of his deepest ideal.

In light of JoJo's heritage and upbringing—both of which he was powerless to control—it is dubious at best that he should be regarded as responsible for what he does. For it is unclear whether anyone with a childhood such as his could have developed into anything but the twisted and perverse sort of person that he has become. But note that JoJo is someone whose actions are controlled by his desires and whose desires are the desires he wants to have. That is, his actions are governed by desires that are governed by and expressive of his deepest self.

The Frankfurt-Watson-Taylor strategy that allowed us to differentiate our normal selves from the victims of hypnosis and brainwashing will not allow us to differentiate ourselves from the son of Jo the First. In the case of these earlier victims, we were able to say that although the actions of these individuals were, at one level, in control of the individuals themselves, these individuals themselves, *qua* agents, were not the selves they more deeply wanted to be. In this respect, these people were unlike our happily more integrated selves. But we cannot say of JoJo that his self, *qua* agent, is not the self he wants it to be. It *is* the self he wants it to be. From the inside, he feels as integrated, free, and responsible as we do.

Our judgment that JoJo is not a responsible agent is one that we can only make from the outside—from reflecting on the fact, it seems, that his deepest self is not up to him. Looked at from the outside, however, our situation seems no different from his. For in the last analysis, it is not up to any of us to have the deepest selves we do. Once more, the problem seems metaphysical—and not just metaphysical, but insuperable. For, as I mentioned before, the problem is independent of the truth of determinism. Whether we are determined or undetermined, we cannot have created our deepest selves. Literal self-creation is not just empirically, but logically impossible.

If JoJo is not responsible because his deepest self is not up to him, then we are not responsible either. Indeed, in that case responsibility would be impossible for anyone ever to achieve. But I believe that the appearance that literal self-creation is required for freedom and responsibility is itself mistaken.

The Deep Self View was right in pointing out that freedom and responsibility requires us to have certain distinctive types of control over our behavior and ourselves. Specifically, our actions need to be under the control of ourselves, and our (superficial) selves need to be under the control of our deep selves. Having seen that these types of control are not enough to guarantee us the status of responsible agents, we are tempted to go on to suppose that we must have yet another kind of control to assure us that even our deepest selves are somehow up to us. But not all the things necessary for freedom and responsibility must be types of power and control. We may need simply to *be* a certain way, even though it is not within our power to determine whether we are that way or not.

Indeed, it becomes obvious that at least one condition of responsibility is of this form as soon as one remembers what, in everyday contexts, we have known all along—namely, that in order to be responsible, an agent must be *sane*. It is not ordinarily in our power to determine whether we are or are not sane. Most of us, it would seem, are lucky, but some of us are not. Moreover, being sane does not necessarily mean that one has any type of power or control that an insane person lacks. All to our distress, some insane people, like JoJo and some actual political leaders who resemble him, may have complete control of their actions, and even complete control of their acting selves. The desire to be sane is thus not a desire for another form of control. It is rather a desire that one's self be connected to the world in a certain way—we could even say it is a desire that one's self be *controlled by* the world in certain ways and not in others.

This becomes clear if we attend to the criteria for sanity that have historically been dominant in legal questions about responsibility. According to the M'Naughten Rule, a person is sane if (1) he knows what he's doing and (2) he knows that what he's doing is, as the case may be, right or wrong. Insofar as one's desire to be sane involves a desire to know what one's doing—or more generally, a desire to live in the Real World—it is a desire to be controlled—to have, in this case, one's *beliefs* controlled—by perceptions and sound reasoning that produce an accurate conception of the world rather than by blind or distorted forms of response. The same goes for the second constituent of sanity—only, in this case, one's hope is that one's *values* be controlled by processes that afford an accurate conception of the world.[6] Putting these two conditions together, we may understand sanity, then, as the minimally sufficient ability to cognitively and normatively recognize and appreciate the world for what it is.

There are problems with this definition of sanity, at least some of which will become obvious in what follows, that make it ultimately unacceptable either as a gloss on or an improvement of the meaning of the term in many of the contexts in which it is used. The definition offered does seem to bring out the interest sanity has for us in connection with issues of responsibility, however, and some pedagogical as well as stylistic purposes will be served if we use sanity hereafter in this admittedly specialized sense.

4. The Sane Deep Self View

So far I have argued that the conditions of responsible agency offered by the Deep Self View are necessary but not sufficient. Moreover, the gap left open by the Deep Self View seems to be one that can only be filled by a metaphysical, and as it happens, metaphysically impossible addition. I now wish to argue, however, that the condition of sanity, as characterized above, is sufficient to fill the gap. In other words, the Deep Self View, supplemented by the condition of sanity provides a satisfying conception of responsibility. The conception of responsibility I am proposing, then, agrees with the Deep Self View in requiring that a responsible agent be able to govern her actions by her desires and to govern her desires by her deep self. In addition, my conception insists that the agent's deep self be sane and claims that this is *all* that is needed for responsible agency. By contrast to the plain Deep Self View, let us call this new proposal the Sane Deep Self View.

It is worth noting, to begin with, that this new proposal deals with the case of JoJo and related cases of deprived childhood victims, in ways that better match our pretheoretical intuitions. Unlike the plain Deep Self View, the Sane Deep Self View offers a way of explaining why JoJo is not responsible for his actions without throwing our own responsibility into doubt. For, although like us, JoJo's actions flow from desires that flow from his deep self, unlike us, JoJo's deep self is itself insane. Sanity, remember, involves the ability to know the difference between right and wrong, and a person who, even on reflection, can't see that having someone tortured because he failed to salute you is wrong plainly lacks the requisite ability.

Less obviously, but quite analogously, this new proposal explains why we give less than full responsibility to persons who, though acting badly, act in

ways that are strongly encouraged by their societies—the slaveowners of the
1850s, the German Nazis of the 1930s, and many male chauvinists of our
fathers' generation, for example. These are people, we imagine, who falsely
believe that the ways they are acting are morally acceptable, and so, we may
assume, their behavior is expressive of or at least in accordance with these
agents' deep selves. But their false beliefs in the moral permissibility of their
actions and the false values from which these beliefs derived may have been
inevitable given the social circumstances in which they developed. If we think
that the agents could not help but be mistaken about their values, we do not
blame them for the actions which those values inspired.[7]

It would unduly distort ordinary linguistic practice to call the slave-
owner, the Nazi, or the male chauvinist even partially or locally insane.
Nonetheless the reason for withholding blame from them is at bottom the
same as the reason for withholding it from JoJo. Like JoJo, they are, at the
deepest level, unable to cognitively and normatively recognize and appreciate
the world for what it is. In our sense of the term, their deepest selves are not
fully sane.

The Sane Deep Self View thus offers an account of why victims of deprived
childhood as well as victims of misguided societies may not be responsible for
their actions without implying that we are not responsible for ours. The actions
of these others are governed by mistaken conceptions of value that the agents
in question cannot help but have. Since, as far as we know, our values are not,
like theirs, unavoidably mistaken, the fact that these others are not responsible
for their actions need not force us to conclude that we are not responsible for
ours.

But it may not yet be clear why sanity, in this special sense, should make
such a difference; why, in particular, the question of whether someone's values
are unavoidably *mistaken* should have any bearing on their status as responsible agents. The fact that the Sane Deep Self View implies judgments that
match our intuitions about the difference in status between characters like
JoJo and ourselves provides little support for it if it cannot also defend these
intuitions. So we must consider an objection that comes from the point of view
we earlier considered that rejects the intuition that a relevant difference can be
found.

Earlier, it seemed that the reason JoJo was not responsible for his actions
was that although his actions were governed by his deep self, his deep self was
not up to him. But this had nothing to do with his deep self's being mistaken or
not mistaken, evil or good, insane or sane. If JoJo's values are unavoidably
mistaken, our values, even if not mistaken appear to be just as unavoidable.
When it comes to freedom and responsibility, isn't it the unavoidability rather
than the mistakenness, that matters?

Before answering this question, it is useful to point out a way in which it is
ambiguous: the concepts of avoidability and mistakenness are not unequivo-
cally distinct. One may, to be sure, construe the notion of avoidability in a
purely metaphysical way. Whether an event or state of affairs is unavoidable

under this construal depends, as it were, on the tightness of the causal connections, so to speak, that bear on the event's or state of affairs' coming about. In this sense, our deep selves do seem as unavoidable for us as JoJo's and the others' are for them. For presumably we are just as influenced by our parents, our cultures, and our schooling as they are influenced by theirs. In another sense, however, our characters are not similarly unavoidable.

In particular, in the cases of JoJo and the others, there are certain features of their characters that they cannot avoid *even though these features are seriously mistaken, misguided, or bad.* This is so because, in our special sense of the term, these characters are less than fully sane. Since these characters lack the ability to know right from wrong, they are unable to revise their characters on the basis of right and wrong, and so their deep selves lack the resources and the reasons that might have served as a basis for self-correction. Since the deep selves *we* unavoidably have, however, are sane deep selves—deep selves, that is, that unavoidably *contain* the ability to know right from wrong, we unavoidably do have the resources and reasons on which to base self-correction. What this means is that though in one sense we are no more in control of our deepest selves than JoJo and others, it does not follow in our case, as it does in theirs, that we would be the way we are, even if it is a bad or wrong way to be. But, if this does not follow, it seems to me, our absence of control at the deepest level should not upset us.

Consider what the absence of control at the deepest level amounts to for us: Whereas JoJo is unable to control the fact that, at the deepest level, he is not fully sane, we are not responsible for the fact that, at the deepest level, we are. It is not up to us to *have* minimally sufficient abilities to cognitively and normatively recognize and appreciate the world for what it is. Also, presumably, it is not up to us to have lots of other properties, at least to begin with—a fondness for purple, perhaps, or an antipathy for beets. As the proponents of the plain Deep Self View have been at pains to point out, however, we do, if we are lucky, have the ability to revise ourselves in terms of the values that are held by or constitutive of our deep selves. If we are lucky enough both to have this ability and to have our deep selves be sane, it follows that although there is much in our characters that we did not choose to have, there is nothing irrational or objectionable in our characters that we are compelled to keep.

Being sane, we are able to understand and evaluate our characters in a reasonable way, to notice what there is reason to hold on to, what there is reason to eliminate, and what, from a rational and reasonable standpoint, we may retain or get rid of as we please. Being able as well to govern our superficial selves by our deep selves, then, we are able to change the things that we find there is reason to change. This being so, it seems that although we may not be *metaphysically* responsible for ourselves—for, after all, we did not create ourselves from nothing—we are *morally* responsible for ourselves, for we are able to understand and appreciate right and wrong, and to change our characters and our actions accordingly.

5. Self-Creation, Self-Revision,
and Self-Correction

At the beginning of this chapter, I claimed that recalling that sanity was a condition of responsibility would dissolve at least some of the appearance that responsibility was metaphysically impossible. To see how this is so, and to get a fuller sense of the Sane Deep Self View, it may be helpful to put that view into perspective by comparing it to the other views we have discussed along the way.

As Frankfurt, Watson, and Taylor showed us, in order to be free and responsible, we need not only to be able to control our actions in accordance with our desires, we need to be able to control our desires in accordance with our deepest selves. We need, in other words, to be able to *revise* ourselves—to get rid of some desires and traits, and perhaps replace them with others on the basis of our deeper desires or values or reflections. Consideration of the fact that the selves who are doing the revising might themselves be either brute products of external forces or arbitrary outputs of random generation made us wonder whether the capacity for self-revision was enough to assure us of responsibility, however, and the example of JoJo added force to the suspicion that it was not. If the ability to revise ourselves is not enough, however, the ability to create ourselves does not seem necessary either. Indeed, when you think of it, it is unclear why anyone should want self-creation. Why should anyone be disappointed at having to accept the idea that one has to get one's start somewhere? It is an idea that most of us have lived with quite contentedly all along. What we do have reason to want, then, is something more than the ability to revise ourselves but less than the ability to create ourselves. Implicit in the Sane Deep Self View is the idea that what is needed is the ability to *correct* (or approve) ourselves.

Recognizing that in order to be responsible for our actions, we have to be responsible for ourselves, the Sane Deep Self View analyzes what is necessary in order to be responsible for our selves as (1) the ability to evaluate ourselves sensibly and accurately and (2) the ability to transform ourselves insofar as our evaluation tells us to do so. We may understand the exercise of these abilities as a process whereby we *take* responsibility for the selves that we are but did not ultimately create. The condition of sanity is intrinsically connected to the first ability; the condition that we be able to control our superficial selves by our deep selves is intrinsically connected to the second.

The difference between the plain Deep Self View and the Sane Deep Self View, then, is the difference between the requirement of the capacity for self-revision and the requirement of the capacity for self-correction. Anyone with the first capacity can *try* to take responsibility for herself. Only someone with a sane deep self, however, a deep self that can see and appreciate the world for what it is, can evaluate herself sensibly and accurately. And so, although insane selves can try to take responsibility for themselves, only sane selves will properly be accorded responsibility.

6. Two Objections Considered

At least two problems with the Sane Deep Self View are so glaring as to have certainly struck many of my readers, and, in closing, I shall briefly address them. First, some will be wondering how, in light of my specialized use of the term "sanity," I can be so sure that "we" are any saner than the nonresponsible individuals I have discussed. What justifies my confidence that, unlike the slaveowners, Nazis, and male chauvinists, not to mention JoJo himself, we are able to understand and appreciate the world for what it is? The answer to this is that nothing justifies this except widespread intersubjective agreement and the considerable success we have in getting around in the world and satisfying our needs. These are not sufficient grounds for the smug assumption that we are in a position to see the truth about *all* aspects of ethical and social life. Indeed, it seems more reasonable to expect that time will reveal blindspots in our cognitive and normative outlook, just as it has revealed errors in the outlooks of those who have lived before. But our judgments of responsibility can only be made from here, on the basis of the understandings and values that we can develop by exercising the abilities we do possess as well and as fully as possible.

If some have been worried that my view implicitly expresses an overconfidence in the assumption that we are sane and therefore right about the world, others will be worried that my view too closely connects sanity with being right about the world and fear that my view implies that anyone who acts wrongly or has false beliefs about the world is therefore insane and so not responsible for his actions. This seems to me to be a more serious worry, which I am sure I cannot answer to everyone's satisfaction.

First, it must be admitted that the Sane Deep Self View embraces a conception of sanity that is explicitly normative. But this seems to me a strength of that view rather than a defect. Sanity *is* a normative concept, in its ordinary as well as in its specialized sense, and severely deviant behavior, such as that of a serial murderer or a sadistic dictator, does constitute evidence of a psychological defect in the agent. The suggestion that the most horrendous, stomach-turning crimes could only be committed by an insane person—an inverse of Catch-22, as it were—must be regarded as a serious possibility, despite the practical problems that would accompany general acceptance of that conclusion.

But, it will be objected, there is no justification, on the Sane Deep Self View, for regarding only horrendous and stomach-turning crimes as evidence of insanity in its specialized sense. If sanity is the ability to cognitively and normatively understand and appreciate the world for what it is, then *any* wrong action or false belief will count as evidence of the absence of that ability. This point may also be granted, but we must be careful about what conclusion to draw. To be sure, when someone acts in a way that is not in accordance with acceptable standards of rationality and reasonableness, it is always appropriate to look for an explanation of why she acted that way. The hypothesis that she was unable to understand and appreciate that her action fell outside acceptable bounds will always be a possible explanation. Bad performance on a math test always suggests the possibility that the test taker is stupid. Typically, however, other explanations will be possible, too—for example, that the agent was too lazy to consider whether her action was acceptable, or too greedy to care, or in the case of the math test taker, that she was too occupied with other interests to attend class or study. Other facts about the agent's history will help us decide among these hypotheses.

This brings out the need to emphasize that sanity, in the specialized sense, is defined as the *ability* to cognitively and normatively understand and appreciate the world for what it is. According to our commonsense understandings, having this ability is one thing and exercising it is another—at least some wrong-acting, responsible agents presumably fall within the gap. The notion of "ability" is notoriously problematic, however, and there is a long history of controversy about whether the truth of determinism would show our ordinary ways of thinking to be simply confused on this matter. At this point, then, metaphysical concerns may voice themselves again—but at least they will have been pushed into a narrower, and perhaps a more manageable corner.

The Sane Deep Self View does not, then, solve all the philosophical problems connected to the topics of free will and responsibility, and if anything, it highlights some of the practical and empirical problems rather than solves them. It may, however, resolve some of the philosophical, and particularly, some of the metaphysical problems, and reveal how intimate are the connections between the remaining philosophical problems and the practical ones.

Notes

1. Harry G. Frankfurt, "Freedom of the Will and the Concept of a Person," *Journal of Philosophy* 68 (1971), 5–20; see ch. 4 above.

2. Gary Watson, "Free Agency," *Journal of Philosophy* 72 (1975), 205–20; see ch. 7 above.

3. Charles Taylor, "Responsibility for Self," in A. E. Rorty, ed., *The Identities of Persons* (Berkeley: University of California Press, 1976), 281–99.

4. See, e.g., David Hume, *A Treatise of Human Nature*, (Oxford: Oxford University Press, 1967), 399–406, and R. E. Hobart, "Free Will as Involving Determination and Inconceivable Without It," *Mind* (1934).

5. Frankfurt, "Freedom of the Will," p. 72.

6. Strictly speaking, perception and sound reasoning may not be enough to ensure the ability to achieve an accurate conception of what one is doing and especially to achieve a reasonable normative assessment of one's situation. Sensitivity and exposure to certain realms of experience may also be necessary for these goals. For the purposes of this essay, I shall understand "sanity" to include whatever it takes to enable one to develop an adequate conception of one's world. In other contexts, however, this would be an implausibly broad construal of the term.

7. Admittedly, it is open to question whether these individuals were in fact unable to help having mistaken values, and indeed, whether recognizing the errors of their

society would even have required exceptional independence or strength of mind. This is presumably an empirical question, the answer to which is extraordinarily hard to determine. My point here is simply that *if* we believe that they are unable to recognize that their values are mistaken, we do not hold them responsible for the actions that flow from these values, and *if* we believe that their ability to recognize their normative errors is impaired, we hold them less than fully responsible for the relevant actions.

III

AUTONOMY AND UTILITARIANISM

10

Autonomy and Utility

Lawrence Haworth

Introduction

Does the value of the good which utilitarians would maximize depend on the autonomy of those who experience it? In pursuing this question, I shall take account of two versions of utilitarianism, mental-state utilitarianism and want utilitarianism. The first identifies intrinsic good with pleasure; the second, with preference satisfaction. Later in the chapter it will be important to distinguish between the two, but at the start the term "happiness" will refer to both indiscriminately.

The utilitarian holds that actions should be evaluated by looking to their likelihood of maximizing happiness. No feature of an action is relevant to its rightness unless it affects the action's capability of increasing happiness. In particular, the fact that an action expresses autonomy, or is likely to increase the autonomy of the agent or others, is in itself of no special moral interest. Since as a rule people capable of autonomy want opportunities to live autonomously and find satisfaction in living autonomously, there is on utilitarian grounds abundant reason for increasing people's opportunity to live in that way. But the final reason for doing so is that people will be happier, not that autonomous life is worth promoting for its own sake.

The bite in the utilitarian position is its exclusiveness. No one doubts that an action's effect of making people happy counts in its favor. But for many it is just perverse to suppose that happiness is the only proper final end of action.

The idea that there is something more to pursue than happiness can be understood in two ways.

1. One may sense that the value of happiness itself is affected by some other condition, which by being present either gives happiness its value or contributes to its being of value.

This chapter was originally published in *Ethics* 95 (Oct. 1984). Copyright © 1984 by the University of Chicago Press. Reprinted by permission.

Lawrence Haworth is Associate Professor of Philosophy at the University of Waterloo, Ontario.

2. One may sense that there are intrinsic values in addition to happiness that also contribute to an action's rightness; for example, truth, beauty, justice, or autonomy.

I shall attempt to lend support to two theses. (1) Nonautonomous pleasures simply count for less than do autonomous pleasures; also, an action's effect of satisfying nonautonomous preferences contributes less to its rightness than does its effect of satisfying autonomous preferences. Autonomy thus conditions the value of happiness. (2) An implication is that development of people's capacity for autonomy is an independent value which we should strive to realize as having a kind of priority to pursuit of happiness.[1]

The argument, however, is internal to utilitarianism. When we ask what the considerations are which motivate utilitarians to endorse their position, we note that anyone motivated by such considerations thereby commits himself to the indicated theses. The idea that autonomy conditions the value of happiness underlies the utilitarian's "first commitment" to autonomy. The derivation of the view that autonomy is independently valuable and that this value has a kind of priority to the value of happiness leads to the utilitarian's "second commitment" to autonomy. (Of course, a utilitarian who is not motivated by the considerations may not be committed to the theses. But in that case we may wonder what reasons he does have for the position he takes.)

The Intuitive Idea

Before the details of the argument are examined, some perspective may be gained by considering a point of view from which the claim that utilitarians have these commitments to autonomy appears highly intuitive. In *The Affluent Society* John Galbraith argues that in the market economies of developed countries there is a "dependence effect." This is the idea that consumption or demand is dependent on production or supply. What people want, he claims, results from what is produced; supply creates demand.[2] This reverses the more orthodox view, that in a free market there is consumer sovereignty and the producers give the consumers only what they want. For purposes of discussion, assume that Galbraith is substantially correct: by and large, producers independently decide what to put on the market and then create a demand for their product.

To keep the essential points in view, imagine a simplified economy. There is one product, hula hoops, one producer, and one consumer. The producer creates a demand for hula hoops by presenting the consumer with highly seductive appeals to his emotions. Consumer demand is thus nonautonomous. The consumer has the means of satisfying his desire for hula hoops, and the producer has an abundant supply. This economy, then, is exceptionally successful in satisfying people's preferences. According to the view which identifies the good with preference satisfaction, the economy should receive high marks. The consumer, because his preferences are being satisfied, is living the good life. The producer, because he is responsible for this result, is a public benefactor. And the society at large, because it has found an arrangement of economic affairs which secures welfare, is a virtual utopia.

One intuits that this cannot be right. A producer who creates a demand which he then satisfies (and who creates it in order that he might profit by satisfying it) is no benefactor. Consideration of further consequences, the creation of jobs, for example, may confuse our intuitions. But if we just focus on the producer's role of satisfying a demand he has created, then it is natural to think that a theory which implies that he is a benefactor has made a moral mistake.[3]

Galbraith, looking at the situation from a slightly different perspective, catches the intuition:

> Were it so that a man on arising each morning was assailed by demons which instilled in him a passion sometimes for silk shirts, sometimes for kitchenware, sometimes for chamber pots, and sometimes for orange squash, there would be every reason to applaud the effort to find the goods, however odd, that quenched this flame. But should it be that his passion was the result of first having cultivated the demons, and should it also be that his effort to allay it stirred the demons to ever greater and greater effort, there would be question as to how rational was his solution. . . . Consumer wants can have bizarre, frivolous, or even immoral origins, and an admirable case can still be made for a society that seeks to satisfy them. But the case cannot stand if it is the process of satisfying wants [production] that creates the wants. For then the individual who urges the importance of production to satisfy these wants is precisely in the position of the onlooker who applauds the efforts of the squirrel to keep abreast of the wheel that is propelled by his own efforts.[4]

The treadmill image suggests the intuitive base for the utilitarian's first commitment, autonomy. But the intuition is not decisive on its own; reasons for endorsing it are needed. Before going on to consider the reasons, however, a preliminary word concerning the second commitment is in order. The basic idea is this. The argument for the first commitment leads to the conclusion that utilitarians must hold that right action consists in action which maximizes not just happiness, but "autonomous happiness." This is the idea that what is wanted is maximum satisfaction of autonomous preferences (or maximum autonomous pleasure). But autonomous happiness is impossible to anyone incapable of autonomous preferences, and the degree to which one is capable of autonomous happiness is a function of the degree to which he is capable of autonomous preferences. Since people's being autonomous is a necessary condition for their being autonomously happy, any view which values the latter must value the former. Hence the second commitment to autonomy.

Some Definitions

Often, "autonomy" is used normatively, to refer to a certain kind of right people are imagined to have. (Sometimes the right referred to is simply a right to freedom, sometimes a right to autonomy in the descriptive sense identified below.) On other occasions, saying of a person that he is autonomous is a way of attributing to him the personal characteristic of being in charge of his own life. He is not overly dependent on others and not swamped by his own passions, and he has the ability to see through to completion those plans and projects which he sets for himself. He has, one may say, procedural independence, self-control, and competence.[5] On these occasions, autonomy is used as a descriptive term. It is an empirical question whether, in what respects, and to what degree a person is autonomous. This descriptive sense of "autonomy" is the one of interest here.

An autonomous preference, then, is marked by procedural independence and self-control. (The idea of competence comes into play when attention is focused on the action by which one attempts to satisfy the preference.) Procedural independence refers to one's relationship with others; self-control, to one's relationship with oneself, one's own passions and impulses. The hula hoop advertiser was imagined to have short-circuited the consumer's procedural independence: the latter's preference for hula hoops was induced by the advertiser. Speaking in this way assumes that there is an important distinction between two cases. In one, a communication directed at getting a person to want something is processed by that person in such a way that if after the fact the person is found wanting that thing we are able to say that he made a decision to want it and that he might have decided otherwise. In the other case, the communication is not processed in that way and, after the fact, we take the view that the explanation of the person's wanting the thing lies largely with the form of the communication.[6] The first is a case of procedural independence. The person is envisaged as a gatekeeper who let the preference in. The second is a case of procedural dependence. The gatekeeper was lulled asleep by the communication and the preference simply entered. One need not be entirely happy with the metaphor to see that some such distinction as this is wanted to account for our understanding of the difference between what goes on when one is brainwashed and when one's preference for something reflects an initiative of one's own.[7]

Self-control is explained by appeal to a similar distinction. Now one's own passions and impulses play the role which otherwise is played by the advertiser's persuasive message. To continue the metaphor, the problem put is whether the passions and impulses will storm the gate with sufficient force to overpower the gatekeeper, so that, in effect, the gate is not opened but forced open. (If we had in mind an anomic rather than a passionate person, the appropriate metaphor would be that of a gate which is simply untended and swings freely on its hinges.)

Next, pleasure. Following Brandt, I shall use "pleasure" to refer to any sensation which "makes its continuation more wanted."[8] Thus, the taste of some food is pleasant in case it (that taste) causes one to want more of the taste. In this understanding of "pleasure," to be pleased is to have a preference of a certain kind. The autonomy of the pleasure is a function of the autonomy of that preference. One who finds the taste of some food pleasant has an autonomous pleasure in case the preference for more of the taste which the food yields is itself autonomous. Does one's wanting more of the taste reflect lack of self-control or having been subjected to an extremely persuasive advertise-ment? Or can we say that it is a preference for which *he* is responsible?

Three comments. First, although we speak as if a person either is or is not autonomous, it is probably more realistic to think of this as a matter of degree. One may be more or less lacking in self-control (inner-impelled) and more or less heteronomous. Second, it is an open question whether, to exercise the "gatekeeper" function in a way which establishes autonomy, one needs to consider reasons for wanting or doing something and then to decide in light of the reasons. The present argument does not require the view that "deciding for reasons" is essential for autonomy, although I think that it is. Third, we can say of any action which a person performs that it is "his own," regardless of whether it is markedly autonomous. (Being autonomous does not reduce to being voluntary.) But to the degree that the person's action is autonomous it is "his own" in a deeper sense. That is, regardless of his degree of autonomy, his actions are just that, *his* actions. But with enhanced autonomy he becomes or makes himself more responsible for them. This feature of autonomy is sug-gested by the "gatekeeper" metaphor. Self-control and procedural indepen-dence imply that what the person prefers and does carries his stamp of approval, so that attribution of those preferences and actions to him conveys a sort-of involvement which goes beyond merely noting that he had the preferen-ces and performed the actions.[9]

Considerations and Commitments

The want utilitarian identifies the good with satisfaction of preferences; the mental-state utilitarian with pleasure. In neither version is the question, How did the individual come to have his preference?, relevant, except, perhaps, in an incidental way. The value of satisfying a preference will not be discounted if the individual was manipulated into having it (unless that fact has other conse-quences which the theory is committed to recognizing).

Why should the utilitarian regard the origin of a preference or pleasure as relevant? Bentham and Mill both held that no proof of the principle of utility is possible.[10] Nevertheless, Mill at least believed it possible to offer "considera-tions" capable of persuading a rational person to accept the principle.[11] The considerations by which one hopes to persuade another will be, presumably, the same as those which motivate oneself. We may imagine, for example, that when Mill offers, as a reason for accepting that pleasure is desirable, the consideration that it is universally desired and the only thing desired for its own sake, he is telling us what motivates him to accept this view.[12] But the considerations which motivate a person to believe something may well have implications beyond and even at variance with the belief they motivate. In that case, the motivated person has a problem. Being rational he is committed, so long as he allows the consideration to motivate him, both to broaden his belief to incorporate the further implications of the motivating consideration and to adapt it so that the variance is overcome.

These remarks suggest the following two principles:

1. The first is the principle of commitment. If what motivates one to believe something implies something else, then one is committed to believe that as well.

2. The second is the principle of consistency. If that which is implied is inconsistent with the original belief, one is committed to either of two responses: rethink the consideration that first motivated one, looking toward a modification which, while not carrying the offending implication, nonetheless gives equally good reason for holding the original belief; or, use discovery of the inconsistency as an occasion for improving one's belief set by recasting the original belief so that the inconsistency is eliminated.

Bentham's and Mill's view, that no proof of fundamental ethical principles is possible, implies only that belief in any such principle is nonrational, not that it is irrational. If the principles of commitment and consistency are violated, however, this innocuous condition of nonrationality is transformed. It is not clear how to describe the result. The nonrational belief remains just that. But one's belief set becomes irrational. If one violates the principle of commitment, the irrationality lies in not assenting to that which is implied by something one believes. If one violates the principle of consistency, it lies in the inconsistency between the (nonrational) belief the consideration motivates and further implications of the motivating consideration.

The commitments to autonomy discussed below result from these principles.

The First Commitment: Want Utilitarianism

What then does motivate people to endorse want utilitarianism? Certainly often the decisive consideration is that want utilitarianism gives a manageable decision procedure, many aspects of which are quantifiable, with such commendable consequences as that results can be cross-checked and errors publicly identified. When there is uncertainty it concerns facts: one can at least say what needs to be known in order to answer one's normative questions.

But this is not a principled consideration. It identifies concomitant virtues of a procedure that requires a more basic line of defense. The virtues associated with quantifiability and objectivity attach as well to the opposite of want utilitarianism, the view which enjoins one to maximize dissatisfaction of preferences. What is wanted is the consideration that motivates one to think that it is specifically satisfaction of preferences that should be maximized rather than other conditions that can equally readily be measured and counted.

The principled consideration most often at work has two parts. The first is a variety of skepticism. Ideals abound, and frequently their adherents think of them as enjoying a species of objectivity. Jazz is better than rock; used car salesmen are despicable. This attitude toward his ideals might tempt one to wish the world were organized so that his own preferred conception of the good would become the goal of state legislation. Consider, for example, the attraction of the idea of an Islamic state to many Moslems. But some conclude that the attribution of objectivity to such ideals is mistaken. No proof that one ideal is preferable to any other is possible: they are just so many different attitudes concerning how to live.

The second part of the principled consideration is this: given the impossibility of showing that one conception of the good is more "correct" than any other, one reflects, Who am I to represent my ideals as more entitled to be realized than theirs? And, *mutatis mutandis.* Who are they to represent their ideals as more entitled to be realized than mine? There being no finally compelling reason for preferring one of the competing conceptions of the good, and wanting not to impose one's own preferences on others in the absence of such a reason, one comes to the pluralistic view that all conceptions of the good, or, more generally, preferences, are equally deserving of being satisfied and that when priorities among preferences are to be assigned the assignment should follow the priority rankings adopted by the individuals themselves. Formulated as an account of "right action," the result is want utilitarianism.

Recall that this motivating consideration is not a proof but a reflection by which one may become a convinced want utilitarian. Viewed as a deductive argument it is obviously invalid: one could as well infer from value skepticism that no preferences are to be respected as that all are to be respected equally. And if, wanting to represent the reflection as a valid argument, one sought to improve matters by supplying the missing premises, the defect of invalidity would be replaced by that of unsupported premises.

In the complex consideration which motivates endorsement of want utilitarianism, then, the motivational work is done by the idea of equal respect for preferences, which gets its attraction from the skeptical reflection that no preference can be shown to be more "correct" than others. It is evident that what counts about a preference here is not its content but its bearer: the claim to being satisfied that a preference presents has nothing to do with what is preferred and everything to do with the fact that someone prefers it. The good envisaged by the consideration which motivates endorsement of want utilitarianism is one's being satisfied in respect of whatever it is one happens to prefer and regardless of what that specifically is. As a result, the idea of equal respect for preferences is as well that of equal respect for the bearers of those preferences, considered as bearers of preferences.[13]

To respect preferences is to try to satisfy them, and to respect the bearers of preferences is to try to satisfy them. One might suppose, therefore, that respecting the bearers of preferences is inevitably tied to respecting preferences; that is, that in the indicated sense whenever one respects preferences one respects their bearers. But there is a complication. If the reason for trying to satisfy a preference refers to what is preferred, rather than merely to the fact that it is preferred, then in effect the attempt to satisfy it (for that reason) shows respect for the preference and for its being the sort of preference it is. In these circumstances, respecting the preference is not the same as respecting the bearer of the preference. But if the reason for trying to satisfy the preference does not refer to what is preferred, but only to the fact that it is preferred, then respecting the preference (by trying to satisfy it) comes to the same thing as respecting its bearer. That is, trying to satisfy the preference, just because it is someone's preference, is indistinguishable from trying to satisfy the one who prefers it.

It is at this point that the idea of autonomy enters into the consideration which motivates endorsement of want utilitarianism. The preferences one has in mind must be imagined to be the individual's "own." As noted previously, however, this can be understood in either of two ways. In one sense there is no alternative. If someone says, truthfully, that he prefers something, then that is "his own" preference: inescapably, every preference of his is "his own." But in another sense it is not his unless he is in some special way responsible for the fact that he has it. In this latter sense a subliminally induced preference for Coke is not, while the preference for Coke shown by a thirsty person who has knowingly arrived at the preference is, his own. When we notice that the underlying idea in the consideration which motivates endorsement of want utilitarianism is that of equal respect for every individual's preferences, it is the individual's own preferences in this deeper sense of his autonomous preferences that we must understand to be meant. Respecting a person's preference serves as a way of showing respect for the person whose preference it is only insofar as the preference genuinely is his. But the effect of ensuring that one's preferences are autonomous is precisely to ensure that they genuinely are one's own.

Perhaps the quickest way to confirm this view of the matter is to go back to the point where, in deciding in favor of want utilitarianism, one asks the rhetorical question, Who am I to represent my preferences as more entitled to be satisfied than another's? (That is, to wish to replace his preferences by my own.) Asking the question is a way of asserting that his preferences are just as entitled to be satisfied as one's own are. But insofar as his preferences are, say, heteronomous, so that although he has them (he really does want whatever it is he wants), he has not made them his own, no recognition of him, no respect for him, as the preferences' bearer, is shown by the attempt to ensure that they are satisfied.

To be sure, wanting can (but need not) be like an itch, in which case satisfying the want can serve to relieve the person. In that case (if the underlying idea were "satisfy the want in order to give the person relief"), the degree of autonomy of the want would be irrelevant. It would matter only that the want is the person's own in the thin sense of his having it; this would be sufficient to ensure that there is someone there to be relieved. But the consideration which motivates endorsement of want utilitarianism does not invoke the idea that we are to satisfy wants in order to give people relief. And rightly so. That idea functions, rather, as a second-order principle for the mental-state utilitarian. If the good is identified with pleasure and the absence of pain, then satisfying those wants which are like itches is a way of maximizing the good. The relief one experiences counts either as a positive state of pleasure or as the removal of a (possibly mild) pain. Once the idea that satisfying a want brings relief is dropped from consideration, it is unclear why one would attach value to satisfying wants, unless it were seen as necessary in order to show respect for the persons who autonomously framed them. That is, without the assumption that the wants which want utilitarians would satisfy must be autonomous, it would be incomprehensible how a person could be motivated by the indicated consideration to endorse the position. If the consideration were advanced as an argument for a version of want utilitarianism which does not incorporate the first commitment, that argument would be nothing more than a non sequitur.

Suppose, for example, that a person has been brainwashed, perhaps in the carefully engineered manner said to be practiced by such cults as the Moonies. Who now is the "other" referred to if, thinking of that brainwashed person, we ask, Who am I to represent my preferences as more entitled to be satisfied than another's? Evidently, it will be either that brainwashed person or the individual who has come to dominate him (the Reverend Mr. Moon). But if we really do take seriously the (contentious) claim that the former has been brainwashed, then we are bound to suppose that failure to respect his preferences—those preferences he merely bears, but which *ex hypothesi* are not his in the deeper sense—would not show lack of respect for him. Unless, that is, we are shifting to the view mentioned in the preceding paragraph but unavailable here, that respecting a person stretches to encompass the sort of compassion which is expressed in trying to relieve people's itches. The important point is not that in some sense we would be "respecting" another (here, the Reverend Mr. Moon). It is that, since the bearer of the preference has not exercised what I earlier referred to as the "gatekeeper" function, he has not put himself in that relation with "his" preference which would make it the case that by neglecting to respect it we fail to respect him.

The brainwashing example focuses on an induced preference. There are three other sorts of nonautonomous preferences to which the same line of argument applies: (1) anomic preferences, (2) preferences which are "inner-impelled," and (3) preferences resulting from pervasive acculturation or social-ization processes which are not directly manipulative in the ways brainwashing and subliminal advertising are. All three sorts resemble induced preferences in not being the individual's own in the relevant sense. In each case, the individual who has the preference fails to make himself responsible for the fact that he has it. The difference among them lies in the mechanism leading to this failure. The anomic preferrer is simply careless. The inner-impelled preferrer is bowled over by an impulse. The merely conventional preferrer passes on an attitude ab-sorbed from others or from his milieu. In all of these cases, the preference has just shown up. By contrast, when a preference is autonomous it may express what another, one's milieu, or passion recommends, but it has not become one's preference merely because of that recommendation.[14]

The conclusion is that, when belief in want utilitarianism is arrived at in the indicated, rather natural, way, it motivates endorsement of the view that the good to be maximized is satisfaction of, specifically, autonomous preferences. This view can accommodate the intuition that in many instances nonautono-mous preferences are also deserving of satisfaction. For one thing, on many occasions respecting preferences, even nonautonomous preferences, serves to nurture people's capacity for autonomy. For another, as I shall indicate later, some preferences are so deeply felt that their not being satisfied brings pain and suffering. The case for satisfying them rests on the principle that we are to alleviate pain and suffering.

The First Commitment: Mental-State Utilitarianism

The consideration which naturally gives rise to belief in mental-state utilitarianism is that suggested by the first paragraph of Bentham's *Introduction to the Principles of Morals and Legislation*. In stating that "nature has placed mankind under the governance of two sovereign masters, *pain* and *pleasure*" Bentham is claiming that we desire (and pursue) pleasure and avoidance of pain. When he goes on to say that "the *principle of utility* recognizes this subjection and assumes if for the foundation of that system"[15] he is announcing that the rationale for the view that pleasure and avoidance of pain are desirable is that they are universally (and, finally, solely) desired. The same view is stated more explicitly in Mill's *Utilitarianism*: "The utilitarian doctrine is that happiness is desirable,and the only thing desirable, as an end. . . . No reason can be given why the general happiness is desirable, except that each person, so far as he believes it to be attainable, desires his own happiness. This, however, being a fact, we have not only all the proof which the case admits of, but all which it is possible to require, that happiness is good: that each person's happiness is a good to that person, and the general happiness, therefore, a good to the aggregate of all persons."[16] Bentham thus assumes what Mill states, that there must be a close connection between what is desired and what is desirable.

I am not interested in exegesis but only with the sense of what Mill says, viewed as a consideration which motivates endorsement of mental-state utilitarianism. One arrives at the belief that pleasure and only pleasure is intrinsically good by reflecting that it alone is desired for its own sake. The consideration which motivates belief in mental-state utilitarianism, then, splits into two claims:

1. The preference principle: Whatever and only that which is wanted for its own sake is intrinsically good; and

2. The pleasure principle: Pleasure alone is wanted for its own sake.

A word first about the pleasure principle. Given the definition of pleasure adopted above, it is true by definition that pleasure is wanted for its own sake. For a person to find some sensation pleasant is for it to lead him to want its continuation. That continuation is not wanted in order that something else might happen; it is wanted "for itself." Any sensation which leads one to want more of the same, just to have it, is by definition "pleasant." Nevertheless, the pleasure principle is not a tautology, since it claims that pleasure is the only thing wanted for itself. (The definition of "pleasure" implies that anything properly called pleasure is wanted for itself, but not that anything wanted for itself is an instance of pleasure.) Possibly there are some things which we want for themselves which do not cause us to want them. In that case they are not pleasures. But if as a matter of fact there are such things the pleasure principle is false.

The first commitment to autonomy enters here by way of the preference principle. This enjoins us to decide what is good as such by asking what it is that people want as such. Should we be interested in the origin of that want? Intuitively it seems that we should. Suppose, for example, that above all people want to rub pet rocks, just to have that experience, and that everything else they want is wanted as a means to a pet-rock-rubbing experience. One may say that if they enjoy doing this then it should not matter that they have been brought to enjoy it by a clever advertising campaign mounted by the people who profit from the sale of pet rocks. But if the motivating consideration is that what people want as such should control our understanding of what is good as such, then that response may not be available. We need to decide how to interpret the reference to what is wanted as such. In particular, in terms of the two senses in which I can be said to want something—I want it in the sense that the want is mine and not another's, and I want it in the deeper sense that it is an autonomous want—which should be meant? The answer must be regulated by reflecting on a prior question, Why derive the account of "intrinsic good" from a view concerning what people want as such? What is there sbout the fact that something is wanted which gives us reason to conclude that, being wanted (for itself) it should be accepted as being good (for itself)?

The answer is similar to that given to a parallel question in considering want utilitarianism above, and the remarks made there apply here as well. We take the view that it is for the individual himself to determine what is to count as good for him. We suppose that ideal values, which society or some (religious or intellectual) elite within society for whatever reason think to be best regardless of the individual's own view of the matter, have no privileged place but just represent other people's conceptions of the good. But in looking at the matter in this way we are supposing that the individual has determined what is to count as good for him, that the preference he holds really is his, rather than one which has merely shown up. A subliminally induced desire for Coke and a brainwashed cult member's desire to devote eighteen hours a day to selling poppies are not among the preferences one is enjoined to respect by the principle that we are to get our view of what is good as such by asking what people want as such.

The Second Commitment

The utilitarian's second commitment to autonomy results from the first commitment. Because the considerations which motivate acceptance of the theory require endorsement of the idea that it is not preference satisfaction (or pleasure) as such which is intrinsically good, but satisfaction of autonomous preferences (or autonomous pleasures), they also require endorsement of the further idea that people's capacity for choosing autonomously should be nurtured and developed, and that social practices and institutions should exist which permit maximal expression of people's capacity for autonomy.

Consider the alternative. We would have the view that, in deciding on social policies, only those who have autonomous preferences should be consulted but that there is no reason for concern regarding how many of them there are or for the number of (nonautonomous) dissatisfied people there are. This elitist view would be unacceptable. Failings in autonomy may be congenital; or they may result from deprivation, from some deficiency, say, in one's early environment. But surely the situation of people so dealt with by fortune or so disadvantaged by social institutions should not be simply ignored. If it matters to the value of a preference whether it is autonomous, then personal autonomy itself must matter.[17] Or so an egalitarian would argue. But why is a utilitarian committed to this conclusion?

Mental-state and want utilitarianism share two logically independent and distinguishing features. They are maximizing theories; this characterizes their accounts of right action. And they reject ideal values; this characterizes their accounts of intrinsic good. Ideal values are replaced by an account of the good which incorporates the idea that by "good" we should understand the individual's own good, that which he can recognize as such. Focusing on the individual's preferences is one way of carrying out this replacement; focusing on his enjoyments is another. I have argued that in either case the project cannot succeed unless it is understood that the preferences (or enjoyments) referred to are autonomous. To the extent a person's preference or enjoyment is nonautonomous, satisfying or experiencing it does not count as "his own good" in the required sense. The maximizing feature of the two theories rests, one may say, on the idea that you cannot have too much of a good thing. Although this feature translates into talk about maximizing (autonomous) preference satisfaction or pleasurable experience, the generic idea is that of maximizing whatever should be taken as each person's own good; that is, whatever each autonomously decides is good for him.

Imagine now two societies. In the first, people generally hold autonomously formed conceptions of their own good and pursue these more or less competently. In the second, people generally lack autonomously formed conceptions of their own good but derive their opinions in these matters from marketers. Suppose that people generally are more satisfied in the second society.

It is evident that the injunction to maximize satisfaction of autonomous preferences (or autonomous pleasures) bestows prima facie validity on two policies. The first is that of seeking to improve the ratio of satisfied autonomous preferences to the total number of autonomous preferences.[18] Insofar as the extent to which people are autonomous is not a problem (as in the first society described above), the injunction to maximize translates directly into this first policy. The second policy is that of seeking to enhance the autonomy of the populace. Insofar as autonomy is lacking, so that generally speaking people's preferences are not autonomous (as in the second society described above), improving the ratio of satisfied to extant autonomous preferences (by ensuring that more of the extant autonomous preferences are satisfied) cannot buy much improvement to the society's overall welfare—all the more so on the indicated assumption that people generally are more satisfied in the second society than in the first. Significant improvement can come only from increasing the proportion of preferences which are autonomous or, more generally, from enhancing the autonomy of the populace. This second policy expresses the second commitment to autonomy.

If our goal is to maximize satisfaction of autonomous preferences or pleasures (the first commitment), then prima facie we should also strive to enhance the autonomy of people generally (the second commitment). In circumstances such as those imagined to obtain in the second society, the second commitment has priority over the first. In circumstances such as those imagined to obtain in the first society, the first commitment has priority.

Notes

1. Up to a point, the structure of the argument parallels that found in an essay by Robert Goodin ("The Political Theories of Choice and Dignity," *American Philosophical Quarterly* 18 [1981], 91–100). Goodin argues that not just utilitarians but also contractarians assume that "we should respect people's choices" and then claims that this rests on a more fundamental assumption (a "logical primitive") to the effect that "we should respect people." Consideration of how this should be understood leads to the conclusion that respecting people consists in respecting people's dignity. After rejecting the idea that people's dignity is founded on their autonomy, Goodin argues that dignity is tied to having an idea of "I" and thus to "possessing a self-image and self-respect." I follow Goodin in attributing to utilitarians an assumption that we should respect people's choices and in seeing this as founded on a more fundamental assumption that we should respect people, although here the idea of respecting people is less broadly construed. In opposition to Goodin, however, I argue that respect for people (and for their dignity) is founded on their capacity for autonomy—i.e., that this is the view to which utilitarians are committed by the considerations which motivate them to be utilitarians. Reconciliation of the differences between us should probably start with an exploration of the dependency of "having an idea of 'I'" (or, as I would prefer, "having an 'I'") on being autonomous. The critical point would be recognition that an additional source of self-respect (additional to the one Goodin stresses, the respect accorded to one by others) is the individual's own sense of competence. See also Jon Elster, Ch. 11 this book, who in a different manner pursues a question similar to that which this essay addresses: "Why should individual want satisfaction be the criterion of justice and social choice when individual wants themselves may be shaped by a process which preempts the choice?" (p. 109).

2. John Kenneth Galbraith, *The Affluent Society* (Boston: Houghton Mifflin Co., 1958), 152–60.

3. One's intuitions may, indeed, suggest that there are three mistakes here. First, the putative benefaction is self-serving. Second, by creating new wants, the benefactor initially makes the consumers worse off. Third, the wants, satisfaction of which is claimed to enhance welfare, are heteronomous. I am concerned only with the third.

4. Galbraith, *Affluent Society*, 153–54.

5. This account is drawn from my "Autonomy: An Essay in Philosophical Psychol-

ogy and Ethics" (Waterloo: University of Waterloo, 1984, typescript), in which the three characteristics mentioned are discussed at some length. The main complexity omitted here is that when autonomy is viewed psychogenetically it seems necessary to identify two distinct levels, the autonomy one enjoys before having developed ability to form second-order desires (in Frankfurt's sense), and the fuller autonomy available to one after that ability has been developed.

6. For a very good account of this distinction, embedded in a discussion of what distinguishes persuasive influences which are inconsistent with autonomy from those which are consistent with autonomy, see S. I. Benn, "Freedom and Persuasion," *Australasian Journal of Philosophy* 45 (1967), 259–75.

7. The metaphor has the advantage of blocking the mistaken view that autonomous desires are those which originate with the person who has them, as opposed to (heteronomous) desires, which are learned. Galbraith commits this mistake, thus leaving himself open to F. A. Hayek's reply: "Most needs which make us act are needs for things which only civilization teaches us to exist at all, and these things are wanted by us because they produce feelings and emotions which we would not know if it were not for our cultural inheritance. Are not in this sense probably all of our esthetic feelings 'acquired tastes'?" ("The *Non Sequitur* of the 'Dependence Effect,'" *Southern Economic Journal* 27 [1961], 346–48, 346). The question of autonomy is not whether one's desires originated with or in oneself. It is a question of the manner in which the person came to have the desires. Autonomous desires may originate with or in oneself, but they may also be acquired by "learning."

8. Richard Brandt, *A Theory of the Good and the Right* (Oxford: Oxford University Press, 1979), 40.

9. Elaboration of these remarks would require discussing the relevance of the distinction between first- and second-order desires to the concept of autonomy. See Harry Frankfurt, "Freedom of the Will and the Concept of a Person," *Journal of Philosophy* 68 (1971), 5–20. See also, for the distinction between substantive and procedural independence, Gerald Dworkin, "Autonomy and Behavior Control," *Hastings Center Report* 6 (1976), 100–122.

10. *The Works of Jeremy Bentham*, ed. John Bowring (Edinburgh: Tait, 1838-43), vol 1, p. 2; John Stuart Mill, Collected Works, ed. J. M. Robson (Toronto: University of Toronto Press, 1969), vol. 10, *Essays on Ethics, Religion and Society*, 207.

11. Mill, *Collected Works*, 208.

12. Mill, *Collected Works*, 234–35.

13. Adding "considered as bearers of preferences" serves to distinguish the intended sense of "equal respect for the bearers of preferences" from a more powerful principle, that of equal respect for people. According to this more powerful principle, respect may well require modes of treatment which go beyond ensuring that preferences are satisfied, and it may dictate ignoring preferences altogether when trying to satisfy them would be incompatible with those required modes of treatment (see Goodin). In referring to "respect for preferences" I have in mind the attitude that the mere fact a person prefers something constitutes a reason for supposing that it would be good if his preference were satisfied. In referring to "equal respect for preferences" I have in mind the attitude that if *A* prefers *X* and *B* prefers *Y*, it is no more and no less good for *A*'s preference to be satisfied than it is for *B*'s preference to be satisfied and that the preferences of each are to be respected. In referring to "equal respect for the bearers of preferences as bearers of preferences" I have in mind the attitude that *A* has as much and no more claim to have his preferences satisfied as *B* has and that the preferences of each are to be respected.

14. Two different images of the "merely conventional" preferrer are possible. According to one, he more or less mindlessly reflects the attitudes of his time and place. According to the other, those attitudes are deeply held convictions which serve to define the sort of person he is. If we think of the merely conventional preferrer in the latter way, it may seem wrong to hold that his preferences are not deserving of respect or that by not respecting them we do not fail to show respect for him in the relevant sense. But I suspect that, when we convince ourselves that a merely conventional preferrer is deserving of respect, we are thinking of him as being autonomous after all and not merely conventional. It is important to keep in mind that the "independence" on which autonomy depends is procedural not substantive: to value autonomy is not to value being different from others.

15. Bentham, *Works*, vol. 1, p. 1.

16. Mill, *Collected Works*, vol. 10, p. 234.

17. Elitism is not the only objection which might be brought against a theory which proposes that nonautonomous preferences should be discounted. Three additional ones are these. (1) Some nonautonomous preferences are so deeply felt that people experience pain or extreme discomfort when they are not satisfied. (2) It would be extremely difficult to enact a policy of discounting nonautonomous preferences, since it is seldom possible to know with any certainty how autonomous a preference is. (3) Such a policy would be unusually susceptible to corrupt administration. The appropriate response to the first objection would be to attempt to satisfy the preferences but from compassion and in response to the injunction to minimize suffering rather than from respect for preferences per se. The appropriate response to the second and third would be simply to ignore the first commitment, on the basis that it cannot be reliably acted on (second objection) and that acting on it would be too risky (third objection). Then (to the extent that these practical considerations suggested the desirability of not acting on the first commitment), its primary role would be that of serving as a premise in the argument for the second commitment, as suggested below.

18. And, we may add, having in mind the second commitment, *not* by reducing the dividend, i.e., the total number of autonomous preferences.

11

Sour Grapes—Utilitarianism and the Genesis of Wants[1]

Jon Elster

I want to discuss a problem that is thrown up by all varieties of utilitarianism: act and rule utilitarianism, average and aggregate, cardinal and ordinal.[2] It is this: why should individual want satisfaction be the criterion of justice and social choice when individual wants themselves may be shaped by a process that preempts the choice? And, in particular, why should the choice between feasible options only take account of individual preferences if people tend to adjust their aspirations to their possibilities? For the utilitarian, there would be no welfare loss if the fox were excluded from consumption of the grapes, since he thought them sour anyway. But of course the cause of his holding the grapes to be sour was his conviction that he would be excluded from consumption of them, and then it is difficult to justify the allocation by reference to his preferences.

I shall refer to the phenomenon of sour grapes as *adaptive preference formation* (or adaptive preference change, as the case may be). Preferences shaped by this process I shall call adaptive preferences.[3] The analysis of this mechanism and of its relevance for ethics will proceed in three steps. Section I is an attempt to circumscribe the phenomenon from the outside, by comparing it with some other mechanisms to which it is closely related and with which it is easily confused. Section II is an analysis of the fine grain of adaptive preferences, and proposes some criteria by which they may be distinguished from other preferences. And section III is a discussion of the substantive and methodological implications of adaptive preference formation for utilitarianism, ethics, and justice.

This chapter was originally published in *Utilitarianism and Beyond*, A. Sen and B. Williams, eds. Copyright © 1982 by Cambridge University Press. Reprinted with the permission of Cambridge University Press.

Jon Elster is Professor of Political Science at the University of Chicago and Research Director at the Institute for Social Research, Oslo.

I

I shall compare adaptive preference formation to one mechanism that in a sense is its direct opposite; and then to five mechanisms that either have similar causes or bring about similar effects. The purpose of this conceptual mapping is to prepare for the discussion in section III of the exact relevance of adaptive preferences for ethics.

The opposite phenomenon of sour grapes is clearly that of "forbidden fruit is sweet," which I shall call counteradaptive preference formation.[4] If when I live in Paris I prefer living in London over living in Paris, but prefer Paris over London when in London, then my wants are shaped by my feasible set, as in adaptive preference formation, but in exactly the opposite way. The question then is whether, in the theory of social choice, we should discount wants that have been shaped by counteradaptive preference formation. If someone wants to taste the forbidden fruit simply because it is forbidden, should we count it as a welfare loss that he is excluded from it? And would it be a welfare gain to give him access, if this would make him lose his taste for it? An ordinal-utilitarian theory of social choice offers no answers to these questions. This indeterminacy in itself points to an inadequacy in that theory, although we shall see in section III that counteradaptive preferences are less troublesome for ethics than adaptive ones, because they do not generate any conflict between autonomy and welfare.

Adaptive preference formation is now to be distinguished, firstly, from preference change through learning and experience. Consider the example of job preferences. Imperfect regional mobility sometimes leads to dual labor markets, for example, to income in agriculture being systematically lower than in industry. Such income gaps may reflect the agricultural laborer's preference for being his own master, or for certain commodities that are cheaper in the countryside than in the city. The laborer may prefer to stay in the countryside rather than move to the city, even if the demand for agricultural goods is too small to enable him to earn the same monetary income as a factory worker. What are the welfare implications of this state of affairs? The standard answer is that a transfer of the laborer to the city implies a loss in welfare for him and, *ceteris paribus*, for society. Consider, however, an argument proposed by Amartya Sen:

> Preferences about one's way of life and location are typically the result of one's past experience and an initial reluctance to move does not imply a perpetual dislike. The distinction has some bearing on the welfare aspects of employment policy, since the importance that one wishes to attach to the wage gap as a reflection of the labourer's preferences would tend to depend on the extent to which tastes are expected to vary as a consequence of the movement itself.[5]

On a natural reading of this passage, it seems to sanction the transfer if the *ex post* evaluation of city life makes it preferable to the countryside life that was more highly valued *ex ante*. We then need to ask, however, about the exact nature of the induced change in preferences. Two possibilities come to mind. One is that the transfer would imply learning and experience, another that it is due to habituation and resignation (adaptive preference change). On the first explanation the process is irreversible, or at least it cannot be reversed simply by a reverse transfer to the countryside. (It may, of course, be reversed by learning even more about the alternatives.) The second explanation does, however, permit a reversal of the preference change. I do not imply that irreversibility is a sufficient reason for concluding that preference change is due to learning more about the alternatives: preference change due to addiction also is irreversible in some cases. Nor is it exactly a necessary condition, for it is easy to think of ways in which preference change due to learning may be reversed, and not only through more learning. But, in the present context, irreversibility is the salient feature that permits us to distinguish between these two mechanisms of induced preference change: the reversal to the initial situation does not by itself bring about a reversal of the preferences.

Explanations in terms of learning can be fitted into an extended utilitarian framework, in which situations are evaluated according to *informed* preferences rather than just the given preferences. One should attach more weight to the preferences of someone who knows both sides of the question than to someone who has only experienced one of the alternatives. These informed preferences are, of course, those of the individuals concerned, not of some superior body. They are informed in the sense of being grounded in experience, not in the sense (briefly mentioned in section III) of being grounded in meta-preferences. They differ from given preferences at most in their stability and irreversibility. Informed preferences could be implemented in social choice by a systematic policy of experimentation that gave individuals an opportunity to learn about new alternatives without definite commitment. This no doubt would leave the persons involved with more information, but also with less character.[6] If individuals were reared every second year in the countryside, their eventual choice would be better informed, but they would have less substance as persons.

Be this as it may, it is clear that explanations in terms of habituation and resignation cannot even be fitted into this extended utilitarianism. If preferences are reversibly linked *to* situations, then preferences *over* pairs of situations appear in a very different light. If an initial preference for city life could be reversed by extended exposure to the countryside and vice versa, then Sen's argument (in my reading of it) implies that we do not have to bother with preferences at all. And this is not an extension of utilitarianism, but its breakdown. At least this holds for ordinal utilitarianism.[7] Cardinal utilitarianism, in its classical version, is perfectly capable of handling the problem, by comparing the total want satisfaction of countryside life with countryside preferences to city life with city preferences. But, as further argued in section III, cardinal utilitarianism then has to face other and even more serious problems.

Adaptive preference formation can be distinguished, secondly, from precommitment, by which I mean the deliberate restriction of the feasible set.[8] If my preferred alternative in the feasible set coincides with my preferred alternative in a larger set of possible alternatives, this may indeed be due to adaptive preference change, but it may also happen because I have deliberately shaped the feasible set so as to exclude certain possible choices. Some people marry for this reason, that is, they want to create a barrier to prevent them from leaving each other for whimsical reasons. Other people abstain from marriage because they want to be certain that their love for each other is not due to adaptive preference formation. It does not seem possible to ensure both that people stay together for the right reasons, and that they do not leave each other for the wrong reasons. If one deliberately restricts the feasible set, one also runs the risk that the preferences that initially were the reason for the restriction ultimately come to be shaped by it, in the sense that they would have changed had they not been so restricted.

Another example that shows the need for this distinction is the desire for submission to authority. As brilliantly argued by Paul Veynes[9] in his study of authority relations in Classical Antiquity, the mechanism of sour grapes may easily lead the subjects to glorify their rulers, but this is then an ideology induced by and posterior to the actual submission, not a masochistic desire that generates and justifies it. As in the preceding example, we need to distinguish between preferences being the cause of a restricted feasible set, and their being an effect of the set. The oppressed may spontaneously invent an ideology justifying their oppression, but this is not to say that they have invented the oppression itself.

Adaptive preferences, thirdly, differ from the deliberate manipulation of wants by other people. If one only wants what little one can get, one's preferences are perhaps induced by other people in whose interests it is to keep one content with little:

> *A* may exercise power over *B* by getting him to do what he does not want to do, but he also exercises power over him by influencing, shaping or determining his very wants. Indeed, is it not the supreme exercise of power to get another or others to have the desires you want them to have—that is, to ensure their compliance by controlling their thoughts and desires? One does not have to go to the lengths of talking about *Brave New World*, or the world of B. F. Skinner, to see this: thought control takes many less total and more mundane forms, through the control of information, through the mass media and through the processes of socialisation.[10]

There is an ambiguity in this passage, for does it propose a purposive or a functional explanation of wants? Do the rulers really have the power to induce deliberately certain beliefs and desires in their subjects? Or does the passage only mean that certain desires and beliefs have consequences that are good for the rulers? And if the latter, do these consequences explain their causes? As argued by Veyne, the purposive explanation is implausible.[11] The rulers no doubt by their behavior are able to induce in their subjects certain beliefs and values that serve the rulers' interest, but only on the condition that they do not deliberately try to achieve this goal. From the rulers' point of view, the inner states of the subjects belong to the category of *states that are essentially byproducts*.[12] The functional explanation hinted at in the reference to "processes of socialization" is no more plausible. True, adaptive preference formation may have consequences that are beneficial to the rulers, but these do not explain how the preferences came to be held. On the contrary, the very idea of adaptation points to a different explanation. It is good for the rulers that the subjects be content with little, but what explains it is that it is good for the subjects. Frustration with the actual state of affairs would be dangerous for the rulers, but also psychologically intolerable to the ruled, and the latter fact is what explains the adaptive preferences. How it explains them is brought out by the next distinction.

Adaptive preference formation, fourthly, differs from deliberate character planning. It is a causal process taking place "behind my back," not the intentional shaping of desires advocated by the Stoic, buddhist, or spinozistic philosophers, by psychological theories of self-control or the economic theory of "egonomics."[13] The psychological state of wanting to do a great many things that you cannot possibily achieve is very hard to live wtih. If the escape from this tension takes place by some causal mechanism, such as Festinger's "reduction of cognitive dissonance,"[14] we may speak of adaptive preference change. The process then is regulated by something like a drive, not by a conscious want or desire. If, by contrast, I perceive that I am frustrated and understand why, I may deliberately set out to change my wants so as to be able to fulfil a larger part of them. I then act on a second-order desire, not on a drive. To bring home the reality of the distinction between drives and second-order wants, consider counteradaptive preferences. No one could choose to have such preferences, and so they can only be explained by some kind of perverse drive of which it can be said, metaphorically speaking, that it has the person rather than the other way around.

The difference between adaptive preference formation and deliberate character planning may show up not only in the process, but in the end result as well. One difference is that I may, in principle at least, intentionally shape my wants so as to coincide exactly with (or differ optimally from) my possibilities, whereas adaptive preference formation tends to overshoot, resulting in excessive rather than in proper meekness.[15] Another is that adaptive preference change usually takes the form of downgrading the inaccessible options ("sour grapes"), whereas deliberate character planning has the goal of upgrading the accessible ones.[16] In a less than perfect marriage, I may adapt either by stressing the defects of the wise and beautiful women who rejected me, or by cultivating the good points of the one who finally accepted me. But in the general case adaptive preferences and character planning can be distinguished only by looking into the actual process of want formation.

Lastly, adaptive preference formation should be distinguished from wishful thinking and rationalization, which are mechanisms that reduce frustration and dissonance by shaping the perception of the situation rather than the evaluation of it. The two may sometimes be hard to tell from each other. In the French version of the fable of the sour grapes, the fox is deluded in his perception of the grapes: they are too green. (And similarly for counteradaptive preferences, as in "The grass is always greener on the other side of the fence.") But in many cases the phenomena are clearly distinct. If I do not get the promotion I have coveted, then I may rationalize defeat either by saying that my superiors fear my ability (misperception of the situation) or the top job is not worth having anyway (misformation of preferences). Or again I may change my life style so as to benefit from the leisure permitted by the less prestigious job (character planning).

Just as one cannot tell from the preferences alone whether they have been shaped by adaptation, so one cannot always tell from the beliefs alone whether they arise from wishful thinking. A belief may stem from wishful thinking, and yet be not only coherent, but true and even well-founded, if the good reason I have for holding it is not what makes me hold it. I may believe myself about to be promoted, and have good reasons for that belief, and yet the belief may stem from wishful thinking so that I would have held it even had I not had those reasons. This shows that wishful thinking, like adaptive preference formation, is a causal rather than an intentional phenomenon. Self-deception, if there is such a thing, has an intentional component in that I know the truth of what I am trying to hide from sight. But if what I believe out of wishful thinking is also what I have reason to believe, there can be no such duality. Wishful thinking, it seems to me, is best defined as a drive towards what I want to believe, not as a flight from what I do not want to believe.[17]

In the short run the result of wishful thinking and of adaptive preference change is the same, namely, reduction of dissonance and frustration. In the long run, however, the two mechanisms may work in opposite directions, as in the following important case. This is the classical finding from *The American Soldier* that there was a positive correlation between possibilities of promotion and level of frustration over the promotion system.[18] In the services in which the promotion chances were good, there was also more frustration over promotion chances. In Robert Merton's words, this paradoxical finding had its explanation in that a "generally high rate of mobility induced excessive hopes and expectations among members of the group so that each is more likely to experience a sense of frustration in his present position and disaffection with the chances for promotion,"[19] Other explanations have also been proposed that make the frustration depend on rational rather than excessive expectations.[20] We might also envisage, however, a quite different explanation in terms of sour grapes: frustration occurs when promotion becomes sufficiently frequent, and is decided on sufficiently universalistic grounds, that there occurs what we may call a release from adaptive preferences. On either hypothesis, increased objective possibilities for well-being bring about decreased subjective well-being, be it through the creation of excessive expectations or by the inducement of a new level of wants. The relevant difference between the two mechanisms for ethics is the following. Giving the utilitarian the best possible case, one may argue that frustration due to wishful thinking should be dismissed as irrational and irrelevant. But on the standard utilitarian argument, it is hardly possible to dismiss in the same manner frustration due to more ambitious wants. If we are to do so, we must somehow be able to evaluate wants, but this brings us outside the standard theory.

To recapitulate, then, adaptive preference formation has five distinctive features that enable us to locate it on the map of the mind. It differs from learning in that it is reversible; from precommitment in that it is an effect and not a cause of a restricted feasible set; from manipulation in that it is endogenous; from character planning in that it is causal; and from wishful thinking in that it concerns the evaluation rather than the perception of the situation. These phenomena are all related to adaptive preference formation, through their causes (reduction of dissonance) or their effects (adjustment of wants to possibilities). They also differ importantly from adaptive preferences, notably in their relevance for ethics. Some of these differences have been briefly noted in the course of the discussion; they form a main topic of section III below.

II

From the external characterization of adaptive preferences, I now turn to the internal structure of that phenomenon. I shall take an oblique route to the goal, beginning with a discussion of the relation between adaptive preference formation and freedom. In fact, both welfare and freedom, as well as power, have been defined in terms of getting or doing what one most prefers. It is well known, but not particularly relevant in the present context, that the attempt to define power in terms of getting what you want comes up against the problem of adaptive preferences.[21] It is equally well known, and more to the point, that adaptive preferences also create problems for the attempt to define freedom as the freedom to do what you want.

We need to assume that we have acquired some notion of what it means to be *free to do* something. This is not a simple question. It raises problems about the relation between formal freedom and real ability; between the distributive and the collective senses of mass freedom; between internal and external, positive and negative, man-made and natural, deliberate and accidental obstacles to freedom. I cannot even begin to discuss these issues here, and so I shall have to take for granted a rough notion of what freedom to act in a certain way means. But not all freedom is freedom to do something; there is also freedom *tout court*, being a free man. Freedom in this sense clearly in some way turns upon the things one is free to do—but how?

We may distinguish two extreme answers to this question. One is that freedom consists in being free to do what one wants to do. This view is sometimes imputed to the Stoics and to Spinoza, with dubious justification. In a well-known passage Isaiah Berlin argues against this notion of freedom: "If degrees of freedom were a function of the satisfaction of desires, I could increase freedom as effectively by eliminating desires as by satisfying them; I could render men (including myself) free by conditioning them into losing the original desire which I have decided not to satisfy."[22] And this, in his view, is unacceptable. Berlin is not led by this consideration into the opposite extreme, which is that freedom is simply a function of the number and importance of the things one is free to do, but his view is fairly close to this extreme.[23] The possibility of adaptive preferences leads him into downgrading the importance of actual wants, and to stress the freedom to do things that I might come to want even if I do not actually desire them now.

There is, however, an ambiguity in Berlin's argument. "Conditioning men" into losing the desires that cannot be satisfied is a form of manipulation, which means that the ensuing want structure is not a fully *autonomous* one. And I completely agree that full (or optimal) satisfaction of a nonautonomous set of wants is not a good criterion of freedom. And the same holds for the adjustment of aspirations to possibilities that takes place behind my back, through adaptive preference formation. But there is a third possibility, that of autonomous character formation. If I consciously shape myself so as only to want what I can get, I can attain full satisfaction of an autonomous want structure, and this can with more justification be called freedom, in the Stoic or spinozistic sense. Being a free man is to be free to do all the things that one autonomously wants to do. This definition is less restrictive than Berlin's (and certainly less restrictive than the extreme view to which he is closest), but more restrictive than the extreme Berlin is attacking, that being free is to be free to do the things one wants, regardless of the genesis of the wants.

If this definition of freedom is to be of real value, we need a definition or a criterion for autonomous wants. This I cannot provide. I can enumerate a large number of mechanisms that shape our wants in a nonautonomous way, but I cannot say with any confidence whatsoever that the wants that are not shaped in any of these ways are *ipso facto* autonomous. And so it seems that for practical purposes we must fall back on a definition similar to Berlin's. But I think we can do better than this. We can exclude operationally at least one kind of nonautonomous wants, namely, adaptive preferences, by requiring freedom to do otherwise. If I want to do x, and am free to do x, and free not to do x, then my want cannot be shaped by necessity. (At least this holds for the sense of "being free to do x" in which it implies "knowing that one is free to do x." If this implication is rejected, knowledge of the freedom must be added as an extra premise.) The want may be shaped by all other kinds of disreputable psychic mechanisms, but at least it is not the result of adaptive preference formation. And so we may conclude that, other things being equal, one's freedom is a function of the number and the importance of the things that one (1) wants to do, (2) is free to do and (3) is free not to do.

An alternative proof that my want to do x is not shaped by the lack of alternatives would be that I am not free to do x. It would be absurd to say that my freedom increases with the number of things that I want to do, but am not free to do, but there is a core of truth in this paradoxical statement. If there are many things that I want to do, but am unfree to do, then this indicates that my want structure is not in general shaped by adaptive preference formation, and this would also include the things that I want to do and am free to do, but not free not to do. And this in turn implies that the things I want to do and am free to do, but not free not to do, should after all count in my total freedom, since there is a reason for believing the want to be an autonomous or at least nonadaptive one. The reason is weaker than the one provided by the freedom to do otherwise, but it still is a reason of a sort. Given two persons with exactly the same things which they both want to do and are free to do, then (*ceteris paribus*) the one is freer (or more likely to be free) who is free not to do them; also (*ceteris paribus*) the one is freer (or more likely to be free) who wants to do more things that he is not free to do.

These two criteria do not immediately carry over from freedom to welfare. The objects of welfare differ from the objects of freedom in that, for some of them at least, it makes little sense to speak of not being free to abstain from them. It makes good sense to say that freedom of worship is enhanced by the freedom not to worship, but hardly to say that the welfare derived from a certain consumption bundle is enhanced by the option of not consuming that bundle, since one always has that option. Nevertheless it remains true that (1) the larger the feasible set and (2) the more your wants go beyond it, the smaller the probability that your wants are shaped by it. Or to put it the other way around: a small feasible set more easily leads to adaptive preferences, and even with a large feasible set one may suspect adaptive preferences if the best element in the feasible set is also the globally best element.

On the other hand, even if the best element in the feasible set is also globally best, preferences may be autonomous, namely, if they are shaped by deliberate character formation. The question then becomes whether we can have evidence about this beyond the (usually unavailable) direct evidence about the actual process of want formation. Quite tentatively, I suggest the following *condition of autonomy for preferences*:

> If S_1 and S_2 are two feasible sets, with induced preference structures R_1 and R_2, then for no x or y (in the global set) should it be the case that xP_1y and yP_2x.

This condition allows preferences to collapse into indifference, and indifference to expand into preference, but excludes a complete reversal of preferences. Graphically, when the fox turns away from the grapes, his preference for raspberry over strawberry should not be reversed. The condition permits changes both in intra-set and inter-set rankings. Assume x,y in S_1 and u, v in S_2. Then xP_1u and xI_2u could be explained as a deliberate upgrading of the elements in the new feasible set. Similarly xP_1y and xI_1y could be explained by the fact that there is no need to make fine distinctions among the alternatives that are now inaccessible. And uI_1v and uP_2v could be explained by the need to make such distinctions among the elements that now have become available. By contrast, xP_1u and uP_1x would indicate an upgrading of the new elements (or a downgrading of the old) beyond what is called for. (Recall here the observation that adaptive preferences tend to overshoot.) Similarly, xP_1y and yP_2x (or uP_1v and vP_2u) are blatantly irrational phenomena, for there is no reason why adjustment to the new set should reverse the internal ranking in the old.

For a conjectural example of preference change violating this autonomy condition, I might prefer (in my state as a free civilian) to be a free civilian rather than a concentration camp prisoner, and to be a camp prisoner rather than a camp guard. Once inside the camp, however, I might come to prefer being a guard over being a free civilian, with life as a prisoner ranked bottom. In other words, when the feasible set is (x,y,z), I prefer x over y and y over z, but when the feasible set is (y,z) I prefer z over x and x over y. In both cases the best element in the feasible set is also globally best, not in itself a sign of nonautonomy. But in addition the restriction of the feasible set brings about a reversal of strong preferences, violating the condition. If the restricted set had induced indifference between x and y, both being preferred to z, this would have been evidence of a truly Stoic mastery of self. For another example, consider the laborer who after a transfer to the city comes to reverse his ranking of the various modes of farming, preferring now the more mechanized forms that he previously ranked bottom. Thirdly, observe that modernization does not merely imply that new occupations are interpolated at various places in the prestige hierarchy, but that a permutation of the old occupations takes place as well.

When a person with adaptive preferences experiences a change in the feasible set, one of two things may happen: readaptation to the new set, or release from adaptation altogether. Proof of the latter would be if the globally best element were no longer found in the feasible set. And even if the feasible best remained the global best, release from adaptation might be conjectured if on reversal of strong preferences took place. Readaptation was illustrated in the city–countryside example, whereas release from adaptation is exemplified below in the example of the Industrial Revolution. In this example the release is diagnosed through the first criterion, that the global best is outside the feasible set. The second criterion (no strong reversal of preferences) presumably would not find widespread application, because of the relative rarity of conscious character planning.

A final remark may be in order. It is perhaps more common, or more natural, to think of preferences as induced by the actual state than by the feasible set. I believe, however, that the distinction is only a conceptual one. Consider again the city–countryside example. To live in the city may be considered globally as a state which (when in the city) I prefer over the countryside, considered as another global state. With a more fine-grained description of the states, however, it is clear that there are many modes of farming, all accessible to me when in the countryside, and many modes of city life that I can choose when I live in the city. Adaptive preferences then imply that according to my city preferences my globally best alternative is some variety of city life, but there may well be some varieties of countryside life that I prefer to some city lives. But in a useful shorthand we may disregard this and simply speak of states as inducing preferences, as will be done in the example developed below.

III

To discuss the relevance of adaptive preferences for utilitarian theory, I shall take up the question whether the Industrial Revolution in Britain was a good

or a bad thing. In the debate among historians over this question,[24] two issues
have been raised and sometimes confused. First, what happened to the welfare
level of the British population between 1750 and 1850? Secondly, could industrialization have taken place in a less harsh way than it actually did? Focusing
here on the first issue, what kind of evidence would be relevant? Clearly the
historians are justified in singling out the real wage, mortality, morbidity, and
employment as main variables: their average values, dispersion across the
population, and fluctuations over time. But if we are really concerned with the
question of welfare, then we should also ask about the level of wants and
aspirations. If the Industrial Revolution made wants rise faster than the capacity for satisfying them, should we then say that the Pessimist interpretation was
correct and that there was a fall in the standard of living? Or, following the
non-Pessimist[25] interpretation, should we say that an increased capacity for
want satisfaction implies a rise in the standard of living? Or, following Engels,[26]
should we say that, even if there was a fall in the material standard of living, the
Industrial Revolution should be welcomed because it brought the masses out of
their apathetic vegetation and so raised their dignity?

The problem is analogous to the one of *The American Soldier*, and as in
that example there is also the possibility that frustration (if such there was)
stemmed from excessive expectations and not from rising aspirations. If that
proved to be the case, the utilitarian might not want to condemn the Industrial
Revolution. He could say, perhaps, that insatisfaction derived from irrational
beliefs should not count when we add up the sum total of utility. If we require
preferences to be informed, then surely it is reasonable also to require beliefs to
be well grounded? But I do not think the utilitarian could say the same about
frustration derived from more ambitious wants, and if this proved to be the
main source of insatisfaction he could be led into a wholesale rejection of the
Industrial Revolution. I assume in the immediate sequel that there was indeed
some frustration due to a new level of wants, and try to spell out what this
implies for utilitarianism. Later on I return to the problem of excessive
expectations.

Imagine that we are initially in preindustrial state x, with induced utility
functions $u_1 \ldots u_n$. We may think of these as either ordinal and noncomparable (i.e., as shorthand for continuous preferences) or as fully comparable in the
classical cardinal sense. I shall refer to the two cases as the ordinal and the
cardinal ones, but the reader should keep in mind that the crucial difference is
that the latter permit one, as the former do not, to speak unambiguously of the
sum total of utility. Assume now that industrialization takes place, so that we
move to state y, with induced utility functions $v_1 \ldots v_n$. In addition there is a
possible state z, representing a society in which more people enjoy the benefits
of industrialization, or all people enjoy more benefits. Given the utility functions, we assume some kind of utilitarian device for arriving at the social
choice. In the ordinal case, this must be some kind of social choice function; in
the cardinal case we say that one should choose that state which realizes the
greatest sum total of utility. We then make the following assumptions about
the utilty functions $u_1 \ldots u_n$:

Ordinal case: According to the preindustrial utilty functions, x should be the social choice in (x,y,z).

Cardinal case: According to the preindustrial utility functions, the sum total of utility is larger in x than it would be in either y or z.

We then stipulate the following for the utility functions $v_1 \ldots v_n$:

Ordinal case: According to the industrial utility functions, the social choice mechanism ranks z over y over x.

Cardinal case: According to the industrial utilty functions, there is a larger sum of utility in z than in y, and a larger sum in y than in x.

And finally I add for the

Cardinal case: The sum total of utility in x under the preindustrial utility functions is greater than the sum total of utility in y under the industrial utility functions.

This means that before industrialization, in both the ordinal and the cardinal case, the individuals live in the best of all possible worlds. After industrialization, this is no longer true, as the social choice would now be an even more industrialized world. Nevertheless the industrialized state is socially preferred over the preindustrial one, even though (assuming the cardinal case) people are in fact worse off than they used to be. The intuitive meaning is that for everybody z is better than y on some objective dimension (actual or expected income) and y better than x; indeed y is sufficiently much better than x to create a new level of desires, and z sufficiently much better than y to engender a level of frustration that actually makes people (cardinally) worse off in y than they were in x, although, to repeat, the social choice in y is y rather than x. "We were happier before we got these fancy new things, although now we would be miserable without them." Clearly the story is not an implausible one.

What in this case should the utilitarian recommend? The ordinal utilitarian has, I believe, no grounds for any recommendation at all. State x is socially better than y according to the x-preferences, and y better than x according to the y-preferences, and no more can be said. The cardinal utilitarian, however, would unambiguously have to recommend x over y on the stated assumptions. But this, I submit, is unacceptable. It cannot be true that the smallest loss in welfare always counts for more than the largest increase in autonomy. There must be cases in which the autonomy of wants overrides the satisfaction of wants. And the release from adaptive preferences has exactly these consequences in the case that we have described; inducement of frustration and creation of autonomous persons. We do not want to solve social problems by issuing vast doses of tranquilizers, nor do we want people to tranquilize themselves through adaptive preference change. Engels may have overestimated the mindless bliss of preindustrial society and underrated the mindless misery, but this does not detract from his observation that "this existence, cosily romantic as it was, was nevertheless not worthy of human beings."[27]

I am not basing my argument on the idea that frustration in itself may be a good thing. I believe this to be true, in that happiness requires an element of consummation and an element of expectation that reinforce each other in some complicated way. "To be without some of the things you want is an indispensable part of happiness."[28] But a utilitarian would then be happy to plan for optimal frustration. I am saying that even more-than-optimal frustration may be a good thing if it is an indispensable part of autonomy. Nor am I arguing that the search for ever larger amounts of material goods is the best life for man. There certainly comes a point beyond which the frustrating search for material welfare no longer represents a liberation from adaptive preferences, but rather an enslavement to addictive preferences. But I do argue that this point is not reached in the early stages of industrialization. Only the falsely sophisticated would argue that to strive for increased welfare was nonautonomous from its very inception.

I should now explain exactly how this example provides an objection to utilitarian theory. Generally speaking, a theory of justice or of social choice should satisfy two criteria (among others). Firstly, it should be a guide to action, in the sense that it should enable us to make effective choices in most important situations. If in a given case the theory tells us that two or more alternatives are equally and maximally good, then this should have a substantive meaning and not simply be an artifact of the theory. The latter is true, for example, of the Pareto principle that x is socially better than y if and only if one person strictly prefers x and y and no one strictly prefers y over x, whereas society is "indifferent" between x and y if some person strictly prefers x over y and some other person strictly prefers y over x. Even though this principle formally establishes a ranking, it is hopelessly inadequate as a guide to action. A theory should not tell us that some alternatives are noncomparable, nor try to overcome this problem by stipulating that society is indifferent between all noncomparable alternatives.

Secondly, we must require of a theory of justice that it does not strongly violate our ethical intuitions in particular cases. If a theory suggests that people should take tranquilizers when the Coase theorem requires them to,[29] then we *know* that it is a bad theory. True, the proper role of such intuitions is not well understood. If they are culturally relative, one hardly sees why they should be relevant for a nonrelative theory of justice. And if they are culturally invariant, one suspects that they might have a biological foundation,[30] which would if anything make them even less relevant for ethics. Perhaps one could hope that persons starting from different intuitions might converge towards a unique reflective equilibrium,[31] which would then represent man as a rational rather than a culturally or biologically determined being. Such problems notwithstanding, I do not see how a theory of justice can dispense with intuitions altogether.

My argument against utilitarianism then is that it fails on both counts. Ordinal utilitarianism in some cases fails to produce a decision, and cardinal utilitarianism sometimes generates bad decisions. The indecisiveness of ordinal utilitarianism is due, as in other cases, to the paucity of information about the preferences. Cardinal utilitarianism allows for more information, and therefore ensures solutions to the decision problem. But even cardinalism allows too little information. Satisfaction induced by resignation may be indistinguishable on the hedonometer from satisfaction of autonomous wants, but I have argued that we should distinguish between them on other grounds.

The distinctions elaborated in section I may now be brought to bear on these issues. The reason why counteradaptive preferences are less problematic for ethics than adaptive ones is that release from counteradaptive preferences simultaneously improves autonomy and welfare. When I no longer possess (or no longer am possessed by) the perverse drive for novelty and change, the nonsatisfaction of nonautonomous wants may turn into the satisfaction of autonomous ones. The destructive character of counteradaptive preferences is well illustrated in an example due to von Weiszäcker.[32] Here a person obsessed by the quest for novelty is bled to death by a series of stepwise changes, each of which is perceived as an improvement in terms of the preferences induced by the preceding step. Clearly, to be released from this obsession is both a good thing in itself and has good consequences for welfare. Release from adaptive preferences, however, may be good on the autonomy dimension while bad on the welfare dimension.

Similar remarks apply to character planning, which may improve welfare without loss of autonomy. I am not arguing that character planning is *ipso facto* autonomous, for surely there are nonautonomous second-order wants, for example, being addicted to will power.[33] But I do not believe these cases to be centrally important, and in any case I am here talking about *changes* in the degree of autonomy. Character planning may improve welfare compared both to the initial problematic situation and to the alternative solution, which is adaptive preference change. First, recall that character planning tends to upgrade the possible, which cardinally speaking is better than a downgrading of the impossible. Both solutions reduce frustration, but character planning leaves one cardinally better off. Secondly, observe that the strategy of character planning is fully compatible with the idea that for happiness we need to have wants somewhat (but not too much) beyond our means. True, this notion is incompatible with the Buddhist version of character planning that sees in frustration *only* a source of misery.[34] But I believe that this is bad psychology, and that Leibniz was right in that "l'inquiétude est essentielle à la félicité des créatures."[35] And this means that character planning should go for optimal frustration, which makes you better off than in the initial state (with more-than-optimal frustration) and also better off than with adaptive preferences, which tend to limit aspirations to, or even below, the level of possibilities, resulting in a less-than-optimal level of frustration.

Endogenous preference change by learning not only creates no problems for ethics, but is positively required by it. If trying out something you believed you would not like makes you decide that you like it after all, then the latter preferences should be made into the basis for social choice, and social choice would not be adequate without such a basis. This is, of course, subject to the qualifications mentioned above: the new preferences should not be reversible simply by making the preferred object inaccessible, and the need for knowledge may be overidden by the need for substance of character. Nor does precommitment create any difficulties. If the wants are prior to and actually shape the feasible set, then the coincidence of aspirations and possibilities is in no way disturbing. As to the deliberate (exogenous) manipulation of wants, it can be condemned out of hand on grounds of autonomy, and possibly on grounds of welfare as well.

Hard problems remain, however, concerning the relation between misperception of the situation and misformation of the preferences. Consider again the alternative interpretation of the Industrial Revolution, in terms of excessive anticipations rather than of rising aspirations. From the work of Tocqueville, Merton, and Veyne, it would appear that below a certain threshold of actual mobility, expected mobility is irrationally low, in fact zero. Above this threshold, expected mobility becomes irrationally high, close to unity. And so, in society with little actual mobility, preferences may adapt to the perceived rather than to the actual situation, a contributing factor to what I have called overshooting or overadaptation. Similarly, once a society has passed the mobility threshold, irrational expectations are generated, with a corresponding high level of wants. The intensity of the desire for improvement grows with the belief in its probability, and the belief in turn through wishful thinking feeds on the desire.

This view, if correct, implies that one cannot sort out in any simple way the frustration due to irrational expectations from the one due to a new level of aspirations. Let us imagine, however, that there was no tendency to wishful thinking. Then the actual and the expected rates of mobility would coincide (or at least not differ systematically), and the rational expectation would then generate a specific intensity of desire or aspiration level, with a corresponding level of frustration. The utilitarian might then want to argue that in this counterfactual state with rational expectations there would not be generated so much frustration as to make people actually worse off after the improvement in their objective situation. I am not certain that this is a relevant counterargument, for should one's acceptance of utilitarian theory turn upon empirical issues of this kind? And in any case I am not sure that the counterfactual statement is in fact true. Even when one knows that there is only a modest probability that one will get ahead, it may be sufficient to induce a state of acute dissatisfaction. But I have less than perfect confidence in both of these replies to the utilitarian counterargument, and so there is a gap in my argument. I leave it to the reader to assess for himself the importance of the difficulty.

The criticism I have directed against utilitarian theory is, essentially, that it takes account of wants only as they are *given*, subject at most to a clause about the need for learning about the alternatives. My objection has been what one might call "backward-looking," arguing the need for an analysis of the *genesis* of wants. Before I spell out some methodological implications of this objection, I would like to point out that the assumption of given wants may also be questioned from two other directions, which for mnemonic purposes I shall call "upward-looking" and "forward-looking" respectively.

The language of directions suggests that preferences may be viewed along two dimensions. One is the temporal dimension: the formation and change of preferences. The other is a hierarchical dimension: the ranking of preferences according to higher-order preferences. If, in addition to information about the first-order preferences of individuals, we have information about their higher-order preferences, we may be able to get out of some of the paradoxes of social choice theory. This approach has been pioneered by Amartya Sen.[36] For some purposes this "upward-looking" correction of preferences may be useful, but it can hardly serve as a general panacea.

Preferences, however, may also be corrected in a more substantial manner. Instead of looking at politics as the *aggregation* of given preferences, one may argue that the essence of politics is the *transformation* of preferences through public and rational discussion. This "forward-looking" approach has been pioneered by Jürgen Habermas in numerous recent works. On his view, the multifarious individual preferences are not a final authority, but only idiosyncratic wants that must be shaped and purged in public discussion about the public good. In principle this debate is to go on until unanimity has been achieved, which implies that in a rationally organized society there will be no problem of social choice as currently conceived. Not optimal compromise, but unanimous agreement is the goal of politics. The obvious objection is that unanimity may take a long time to achieve, and in the meantime decisions must be made—and how can we then avoid some kind of aggregation procedure? In addition the unanimity, even if sincere, could easily be spurious in the sense of deriving from conformity rather than from rational conviction. There is no need to assume force or manipulation as the source of conformity, for there is good psychological evidence that a discordant minority will fall into line simply to reduce dissonance.[37] Habermas assumes crucially that in the absence of force rationality will prevail, but this is hardly borne out by the facts. I have argued that the containment of wants within the limits of the possible should make us suspicious about their autonomy, and similarly I believe that unanimity of preferences warrants some doubts about their authenticity. This implies, at the very least, that the forward-looking approach must be supplemented by the backward-looking scrutiny. The end result of unanimity does not in itself ensure rationality, for we must also ascertain that agreement is reached in an acceptable way.

The backward-looking approach in all cases involves an inquiry into the history of the actual preferences. One should note, however, that there are other ways of taking historical information into account. Thus we may make present decisions a function of present and past preferences, rather than of present preferences together with their past history. The rationale for using sequences of preferences as input to the social choice process could only be that they would somehow capture the relevant historical aspects of present preferences, and this they might well do. Persons tending to have adaptive preferences might be detected if they exhibit systematic variation of preferences with changing feasible sets. But the correlation would at best be a crude one, since the tendency towards adaptive preferences need not be a constant feature of a person's character.

The backward-looking principle is one of "*moral hysteresis.*"[38] Since information about the present may be insufficient to guide moral and political choice in the present, we may have to acquire information about the past as well. In Robert Nozick's terminology, I have been engaged in a polemic against end-state principles in ethical theory.[39] In Nozick's own substantive theory of justice, we need information about the historical sequence of transfers in order to determine what is a just distribution in the present. In Marxist theories of justice we also need to go beyond present ownership of capital goods, in order to determine whether it is justified by past labor.[40] And Aristotle argued that in order to blame or condone actions in the present, it is not enough to know whether the person was free to do otherwise in the present: we also need to know whether there was freedom of choice at some earlier stage.[41] In the present article, I have raised a more elusive problem, the historical dimension of wants and preferences. Adaptive preference formation is relevant for ethics, and it is not always reflected in the preferences themselves, and so it follows that ethics needs history.[42]

Notes

1. Earlier drafts of this paper were read at the universities of Oslo, Oxford, and East Anglia, resulting in major improvement and changes. I am also grateful for valuable and invaluable comments by G. A. Cohen, Robert Goodin, Martin Hollis, John Roemer, Amartya Sen, Arthur Stinchcombe, and Bernard Williams.

2. In fact, the problem is relevant for all want-regarding theories of ethics and justice. John Rawls's theory might seem to escape the difficulty, because it relies on primary goods rather than on utility or preferences. But in fact even his theory needs preference in order to compare undominated bundles of primary goods, and then the problem of sour grapes could easily arise.

3. The term 'adaptive utility' is used by R. M. Cyert and M. H. DeGroot: Cf. "Adaptive Utility" in R. H. Day and T. Groves, eds., *Adaptive Economic Models* (New York: Academic Press, 1975; but it is used in a sense more related to what I here call endogenous preference change due to learning. These authors also use the term to refer to what should rather be called 'strategic utility', which is the phenomenon that expected future changes in utility due to learning can be incorporated in, and make a difference for, present decisions. I do not know of any discussions in the economic literature of adaptive preferences in the sense of the term used here, but some insight can be drawn from the economic analysis of Buddhist character planning in S. C. Kolm "La philosophie bouddhiste et les 'hommes economique'," *Social Science Information*, Vol. 18 (1979), 489–588.

4. For the record, it may well be adaptive in some larger sense to have counteradaptive preferences, because of the incentive effects created by a moving target.

5. Amartya Sen, *Employment, Technology and Development* (Oxford: Oxford University Press, 1975), 43–54.

6. This observation owes much to Bernard Williams, "Persons, Character and Morality," in Amelie Rorty ed., *The Identities of Persons* (Berkeley: University of California Press, 1976), 197–216.

7. I am grateful to G. A. Cohen for pointing out to me the crucial difference between ordinal and cardinal utilitarianism in this respect.

8. Jon Elster, *Ulysses and the Sirens* (Cambridge: Cambridge University Press, 1979); ch. II has an extended analysis of this notion, with many examples.

9. P. Veyne, *Le Pain et le Cirque* (Paris: Seuil, 1976). For an exposition and interpretation of Veyne's view, see Jon Elster, "Un historien devant l'irrationel; Lecture de Paul Veyne," *Social Science Information* Vol. 19 (1980), 773–803.

10. Steven Lukes, *Power. A Radical View* (London: Macmillan, 1974), 23.

11. Veyne *Le Pain*, passim.

12. Farber has a brief discussion of a similar notion, "willing what cannot be willed." He restricts the idea, however, to the inducement of certain states (belief, sleep, happiness) in oneself, whereas it can also be applied to paradoxical attempts to induce by command certain states (love, spontaneity, disobedience) in others. Cf. L. Farber, *Lying, Despair, Jealousy, Envy, Sex, Suicide, Drugs, and the Good Life* (New York: Basic Books, 1976). For the latter, see the works of the Palo Alto psychiatrists, e.g., P. Watzlawick, *The Language of Change* (New York: Basic Books, 1978).

13. Thomas Schelling, "Economics or the Art of Self-Management," *American Economic Review*, Vol. 68, Papers and Proceedings, (1978), 290–94.

14. Leon Festinger, *A Theory of Cognitive Dissonance* (Stanford: Stanford University Press, 1957), and *Conflict, Decision and Dissonance* (Stanford: Stanford University Press, 1964).

15. Veyne 1976, 312–13.

16. Kolm "La philosophie bouddhiste."

17. I elaborate on these slightly cryptic remarks in Elster ("Belief, Bias and Ideology," in M. Hollis and S. Lukes, eds. *Rationality and Relativism* (Cambridge, Mass.: MIT Press, 1984), pp. 123–49.

18. S. Stouffer et al., *The American Soldier* (Princeton: Princeton University Press, 1949).

19. R. K. Merton, *Social Theory and Social Structure* (Glencoe, Ill.: Free Press, 1957); ch. VIII.

20. R. Boudon, *Effets Pervers et Ordre Social* (Paris: Presses Universitaires de France, 1977); ch. V.

21. Goldman, following Robert Dahl, calls this the problem of the *chameleon*. Cf. Alvin Goldman, "Toward a Theory of Social Power," *Philosophical Studies*, Vol. 23 (1972), 221–68. Observe that adaptive preferences do not detract from power, as they do from welfare and freedom. If you have the power to bring about what you want, it is irrelevant whether your wants are shaped by the anticipation of what would have been brought about anyway. There is nothing shadowy or insubstantial about preemptive power.

22. Isaiah Berlin, *Four Essays on Liberty* (Oxford: Oxford University Press, 1969); xxxviii–xl.

23. See Berlin *Four Essays*, 130n for an exposition of his view.

24. Jon Elster, *Logic and Society* (London: Wiley, 1978); 196ff. has further references to this debate.

25. As argued in Elster, *Logic and Society* the terms "optimism" versus "pessimism" are misleading. The issue of pessimism versus non-pessimism is the factual one discussed here, and the question of optimism versus non-optimism the counterfactual one of alternative and better ways of industrialization.

26. Frederick Engels, *The Condition of the Working Class in England* in Karl Marx and Frederick Engels, *Collected Works*, Vol. 4 (London: Lawrence and Wishart, 1975), 308–9.

27. Engels *Condition*, 309.

28. Bertrand Russell, quoted after A. Kenny, "Happiness," *Proceedings of the Aristotelian Society*, Vol. 66 (1965/6), 93–102.

29. As suggested by Robert Nozick, *Anarchy State and Utopia* (New York: Basic Books, 1974), 76n.

30. As suggested by John Rawls, *A Theory of Justice* (Cambridge, Mass.: Harvard University Press, 1971), 503.

31. Rawls *A Theory* is at the origin of this notion.

32. C. C. von Weiszäcker, "Notes on Endogenous Changes of Taste," *Journal of Economic Theory*, Vol. 3 (1971), 345–72; also Elster *Logic and Society*, 78, who gives as an illustration the sequence $(1/2,3/2)$, $(3/4,1/2)$, $(1/4,3/4)$, $(3/8,1/4)$ . . . , in which each bundle is seen as an improvement over the preceding one because it implies an increase in the smallest component. A very conservative person, conversely, might reject each change in the opposite direction because it implies a reduction in the largest component. Such conservatism is akin to adaptive preference change, since it implies that you systematically upgrade what is most abundantly available (or downgrade the relatively unavailable).

33. Elster *Ulysses*, 40.

34. See "La philosophie bouddhiste."

35. G. W. F. Leibniz, *Die Philosophische Schriften*, C. I. Gerhardt, ed. (Berlin: Weidmannsche, 1875–90), vol. V, 175.

36. Amartya Sen, "Choice, Orderings and Morality," in S. Korner, ed., *Practical Reason* (Oxford: Blackwell, 1974); and "Rational Fools: A Critique of the Behavioral Foundations of Economic Theory," *Philosophy and Public Affairs* Vol. 6, no. 1 (1977), 317–44.

37. S. Asch, "Studies of Independence and Conformity I. A Minority of One Against a Unanimous Majority," *Psychological Monographs: General and Applied* Vol. 70, no. 9 (1956).

38. Jon Elster, "A Note on Hysteresis in the Social Sciences," *Synthese* Vol. 33 (1976), 371–91 has a discussion of the more well-known notion of causal hysteresis.

39. Nozick *Anarchy*, 153ff.

40. Jon Elster, "Exploring Exploitation," *Journal of Peace Research* Vol. 15 (1978), 3–17; and "The Labour Theory of Value," *Marxist Perspectives* Vol. 1, no. 3 (1978), 70–101.

41. *Nicomachean Ethics*, 1114a.

42. This conclusion parallels the conclusion of my essay on "Belief, bias and ideology": "Since epistemology deals with the rationality of beliefs, and since the rationality of a belief can neither be read off it straight away nor be assessed by comparing the belief with the evidence, we must conclude that epistemology needs history."

12

Autonomy, Identity, and Welfare

Russell Hardin

Autonomy is a notion that is honored in some form in all major moral theories. It is related to or implicit in many other commonplace notions: liberty, respect for persons, endogeneity of values or preferences, life plans, paternalism, and even rationality. Despite this pervasiveness, however, some theories are defended against others on the claim that they are more firmly grounded in autonomy or that they more clearly support autonomy. In general, no constructive theory can be grounded in any far-reaching notion of autonomy because, at base, autonomy is an empty notion: a fully autonomous person would be no person at all. The idea of such a person recalls the derisive joke that you can tell a self-made man from the quality of the product.

In essence, the problem with autonomy is its starting point. This is typical of such other notions central to moral theories as concepts of value and of personal identity. At a relatively flaccid level of discussion, autonomy, personal identity, and welfare are all appealing and seemingly important. When pushed back to their subjectivist bases, however, they tend to lose their appeal as they are emptied of content. Their subjectivity, their basis in a strong concern with the individual person, leaves us with a hollow, abstract notion of the person.

My chief concern here is with autonomy and its value in moral theory. I will relate its problems to parallel problems in subjectivist value theory and personal identity. Autonomy in its down-to-earth guises is generally used as a descriptive notion. I am autonomous if the values that guide my actions are my own values in some crude sense. The difficult issues with such a notion are in how I come to have my "own" values, finally even in what my "own" could mean. These are the issues that I wish to discuss. After first surveying the origins of extreme subjectivity in the value theory of economics and in moral theory, I will then discuss the relationship of autonomy to the notion of a person and to welfarist moral theory.

Russell Hardin is Professor of Philosophy and Political Science at the University of Chicago.

Subjectivity in Economic Value Theory

Adam Smith explained the emergence of the market as a function of specialization in production. By concentrating on the production of potatoes or candles, I become much more efficient than if I tried to produce everything I need to live. Hence, I can get more of what I need by trading my excess potatoes or candles with others who have specialized in producing other things. Smith, like Rousseau and many others of his time, generally assumed that we are all more or less equal in our innate capacities, that the differences in our talents are largely socially produced. Hence, in French revolutionary rhetoric the point of *liberté* was to produce economic *égalité*. It was widely supposed that inequalities of the time were the result of legal preference so that the abolition of feudal laws would automatically lead to equality.[1] Another extreme view that was commonly held is that, as Burke put it, "the standard both of reason and Taste is the same in all human creatures."[2] These views are strikingly different from widespread views today that we are characterized by quite diverse abilities and that our preferences are exceedingly varied.

Perhaps the chief intellectual force in changing our views was the rise of evolutionary thought, particularly social evolutionary thought as in the work of Herbert Spencer, who supposed that evolution must produce certain especially fit individuals and others much less fit.[3] Leslie Stephen criticized utilitarianism because, he wrote, "it considers society to be formed of an aggregate of similar human beings. The character of each molecule is regarded as constant. [Utilitarianism] does not allow for the variation of character and of social relations."[4] Stephen thought evolutionary theory gave a firm rebuttal to such a view.

Another important force has been the effort of economists to understand value theory in economics. Economic value theory, or utility theory, became increasingly subjective and abstract, in part in order to make it more general and perhaps in part to fit it better to certain strands in utilitarianism, especially to Mill's and others' concern with liberty and paternalism. In the work of Pareto, value theory is almost entirely subjective and in the work of Edgeworth it is extremely abstract. Since their work, the general tendency is to assign a utility function to each actor and to let that function have values that vary as abstract inputs to it vary. With such a function, as Pareto wrote, "The individual can disappear, provided he leaves us this photograph [his indifference curves] of his tastes."[5] Along with the individual, actually valued objects have also largely disappeared and with them have gone any constraints on what different individuals may value. An extreme instance of this abstraction and lack of constraint is Kenneth Arrow's condition of "Universal Domain," under which any possible ordering of all states of affairs must be permitted a priori.[6] For example, if all possible states include that in which we set off a major nuclear war just for the hell of it, we must be able in our theories of social choice to deal with individual and social rankings that put that outcome above all other feasible states of affairs. That is to say, we must not restrict out of the range of our social choice that it select that awful state. In this theory rationality has lost all substantive content, it is reduced to a purely formal principle of consistency.

In partial defense of the extremity of this subjectivism, Arrow has written that "In a way that I cannot articulate and am not too sure about defending, the autonomy of individuals, an element of mutual incommensurability among people seems denied by the possibility of interpersonal comparisons. No doubt it is some such feeling as this that has made me so reluctant to shift from pure ordinalism, despite my desire to seek a basis for a theory of justice."[7] Contrary to Arrow's coupling of autonomy and extreme subjectivism, I think extreme subjectivism undercuts any notion of autonomy. In keeping with his views, Arrow generally does not use interpersonally comparable utilities in his work. One might nevertheless think it reasonable to suppose that we all or almost all share certain kinds of preference orders.

Even in the face of these developments in value theory and against Arrow's position, much of actual economic reasoning is based on the assumption that actors are rational in the sense of being self-interested. Here there is often substantive content, even though it may not be explicitly spelled out. For example, it is generally, if only implicitly, presumed that one will not deliberately waste one's own resources merely for the sake of wasting them. Indeed, many prescriptive claims in economics would make little sense without this and other background presumptions. Accounts of the efficiency of production, the accumulation of wealth, the tendency to specialization, and so forth, require substantive value assumptions. In general we may therefore suppose that 'self-interest' is a specifically substantive and not a purely abstract value term. It is substantive to the extent we agree with earlier writers that we are (almost) all more or less alike in some important respects and we build our explanations and judgments from this assumption. Hobbes, Rawls, and many other moral and political philosophers base their arguments in part on strong, universal substantive value assumptions.

Subjectivity in Moral Philosophy

Subjectivity enters moral theories in at least two quite different ways. First, it potentially enters moral theories at any point at which they rely on intuition for their grounding of principles; second, it enters when theories depend to any extent on welfare considerations, as utilitarianism does, because these may be supposed to be based in the individual.

Traditional intuitionists, who called themselves rationalists, supposed that certain moral ideas were as clear to our minds as are certain logical and mathematical ideas. Richard Price, a contemporary of Hume, sounds like H. A. Prichard and W. D. Ross of our own century. He writes, "It is on this power of intuition, essential in some degree or other, to all rational minds, that the whole possibility of all reasoning is founded."[8] Suppose, as evidently happens, that we do not agree on our direct intuitions. Then you and I must act from different moral principles. Nevertheless, each may be judged to act from moral motivations. Not merely the welfare value of various objects and experiences but rather the very content of morality is therefore subjective because your morality depends on your intuitions and my morality on mine. Sidgwick supposed that every moral theory turns on at least one or more intuitions. For example, commitment to utilitarianism depends on a basic intuition that human welfare is the good.[9] Utilitarianism is then built up from this basic intuition through deductions from substantive understandings of what makes for welfare and from understandings of causal relations. Intuitionism, as a so-called method, might more pervasively be used to reach each and every moral conclusion about how to act, as in Price's account.

Let us dwell on intuitions in moral theory for a moment. One of the compelling characteristics of intuitions about general principles is that they are invoked in so many different contexts that we think them through frequently and at length. They are made to withstand a lot of trials of what Rawls calls reflective equilibrium (this term has a falsely persuasive ring—there may be no equilibrium in our time). Intuitions at the level of cases simply cannot count as trumps to end an argument for us as Price supposed they can. We should always want to unpack and think further about our intuitions. Yet it is a commonplace to assert that one is more sure of some of one's specific intuitions than one could be of any general criterion or abstract principle. A characteristic example is that the wrongness of murdering an innocent person for the sake of producing greater happiness for a thousand other people is more compelling than, say, the rightness of a principle of maximizing welfare. The first and most obvious thing to say about most such cases is that they are examples of no intuition anyone has at all. If one tries to unpack such an example to set it up as an actual, plausible decision one might face, it becomes increasingly surreal the more one tries to make it actual.

There are direct intuitions that most of us seem to have that fit real and plausible cases. For example, it would seemingly be wrong for me to ignore the floundering child in the shallow pond I walk past on the way home. The chief problems with this direct intuition are that it does not differentiate any credible moral theory and that it may not be genuinely direct at all. On the first point, this conclusion is, if the example is adequately spelled out, an implication of every theory we would want to discuss. Is this the chief kind of reason we hold to these theories? Surely not. For one thing, we cannot sensibly suppose our theories flow backward from such intuitions. We hold to our theories in part because they fit lots of cases, including many about which our intuitions are so far from being trumps that they are actually reinforced by their fit with our theories. We also hold to them because they have certain abstract properties, such as coherence and completeness. Because our minds are not perfect in thinking through our theories, we should hesitate to count a failure to meet any of these "tests" as a trump, although a direct contradiction that seems transparent to virtually all of us probably is the nearest thing to a trump that we could ever invoke. It is certainly more compelling than any intuitions about supposed examples in the literature.

That last sentence may rankle in the light of the example of the child drowning in my pond. But note that the intuition in this case (as in all cases) is inherently abstracted from what might be the whole story. We have to pack contingent other considerations into the story before we finally get to the unimpeachable claim that it would be wrong to let the child drown. Those other considerations are, for a utilitarian, the overall welfare effects of my actions in saving or not saving the child. I may choose not to save the child because I can actually rescue two at once in a nearby pond—one may insert whatever additional facts one likes here. Now what is my basic, direct intuition about the case? It sounds suspiciously like a very abstract intuition about welfare enhancement as applied to the facts in this case. I think this conclusion is likely to follow for any supposedly compelling case one can give. Although linguistic roots can be as misleading as blind intuitions, here it is not surprising that 'case' and 'casuistry' are cognate. Efforts to reach correct understandings of cases push us via casuistry to principles.

What does this say for the use of intuitions about specific cases to test a particular moral theory? It says that at most our intuitions are evidence. But evidence can be circumstantial and utterly misleading. The actual intuitions philosophers often use are relatively unusual. There is not a long history of discussion of them, of trying to push them to their extreme implications, of trying to understand *how one might have come to have them independently of their rightness*. One of the beauties of our intuitions about many general principles is that they have been put through a wonderfully critical history of discussion, testing, and investigation. Some of these principles have lost their appeal along the way. For example, virtually no competent philosopher now takes seriously any notion of 'natural rights' in the sense in which these once held general sway. I also think that no one can seriously reject the intuitions that human welfare and fairness count for a great deal in any credible moral theory that is not essentially a theological or otherwise authoritatively dictated moral theory. If anyone finds a case that seems to provoke an intuition that welfare should be ignored, even those who are not utilitarian should want to unpack the case very carefully; if anyone finds a case that seems to provoke an intuition that fairness should be grossly overridden, even utilitarians should want to unpack it very carefully before they use it. The instantaneous counter-proofs by intuition from cute cases that are regularly offered in short journal articles mostly deserve ridicule. Intuitions seem to be most compelling when they are of general principles.

Turn now to the subjective bases of values, as in the value of welfare in economic theory and in utilitarianism. Here there seem to be fewer general principles. What general principles there are seem to be of values that are interpersonally comparable in some sense. Arrow's defense of the refusal to allow interpersonal comparisons of welfare is evidently driven by a moral theoretic concern with autonomy. His concern recalls that of Mill, who argued forcefully against the imposition of our notions of welfare on others and hence against paternalism. Moral theorists such as utilitarians generally have less difficulty with assuming that there are some values that we hold almost universally and that justify at least partial interpersonal comparisons. The very notion of welfare in utilitarianism and economics seems like a reasonable, if ill-defined, candidate for a value that is universally well regarded. Indeed almost no moral theorist would deny welfare as a moral value.[10]

Where do our welfare values originate? In part, of course, they seem to be innate in ways that do not seem to be what Price had in mind. His view was that they are rationally embedded. They seem in part to be physiological, instinctual, and perhaps neurological. It is extremely difficult to extinguish some of our desires, although parents, psychiatrists, and Buddhists often try to extinguish many of them. But many others seem not at all to be innate in such a strong sense. They seem, as Hume said, to be so varied from place to place and time to time that it is hard to imagine they are anything but socially determined to a large extent. It may be that a serious moral philosopher could rationally criticize all our values and give rational justifications for extinguishing our commitments to some and boosting our commitments to others.[11] But very many of the values that any one of us in a diverse society has seem eminently worthy of satisfaction and even cultivation despite the presumption that they are to some extent socially influenced and therefore are not fully our "own."

What are we to make of those of my values that are somehow the product or influence of my society? For some of them, there is no serious difficulty because they can sensibly be seen as mere tastes that select one or a few items from a large menu of possible consumptions, any of which would be pleasing if it were my taste. These are the one-person analog of coordination problems. In a coordination problem we could beneficially act in any one of many ways. The only reason for preferring one way to another is that it is the way we have chosen or happened onto. Similarly with my tastes. If I had grown up in India instead of the United States, I might have very different tastes for food, music, and art. However, the extent to which my tastes have been developed by the circumstances of my life need not detract from the pleasure I derive from following them. For example, I once lived in central Italy for a while. While there, from opportunity to see it and to think about it critically and comparatively, I came to love Renaissance painting of mostly religious themes even by relatively minor artists. Despite the subject matter of the paintings of Signorelli, Perugino, Pinturicchio, and their many peers, I now find great pleasure in seeing their work and in noting minute details in it. Fulfilling that pleasure is surely a good despite its dependence on accidental cultivation rather than exclusively on its intrinsic qualities.

Many of one's moral views, that some philosophers might suppose were basic intuitions, may similarly be the product of one's society. For example, we tend to moralize the social practices of marriage even though different societies have different practices. Such practices may genuinely have the structure of multiperson coordination problems: we are all or almost all better off if one practice prevails than if none prevails. Just as personal discipline in many ways enables us to accomplish things we could not accomplish without discipline, so too our possibilities may be beneficially affected by social constraints. If this is true of a particular practice that has become moralized in a norm, then on a utilitarian account it may be genuinely wrong to violate the norm. But this is far from saying that the norm is a basic intuition of what is somehow more generally, even necessarily, right. Certain rationalist moral theories notwithstanding, our morals are in part rightly determined by contingent facts.[12]

To the extent that our moral norms are socially determined in this fashion, reliance on them as though they were fundamental intuitions is little more than a kind of conservative functionalism. Our only defense for such reliance is that the norms have evolved or survived. But this defense can also be invoked on behalf of some appallingly bad social norms that are as deeply and morally felt as any norms. The self-evidence to many people of the truth of racist views, of social hierarchical views, and of nationalist views must finally be an argument for most moral theorists against the force of self-evidence in such matters. Of such views we may agree with Price that "Notions the most stupid may, through the influence (of custom, education and example) come to be rooted in the mind beyond the possibility of being eradicated, antipathies given to objects naturally the most agreeable, and sensation itself perverted."[13] If our beliefs and especially our values come from sources for which we cannot account and for which we cannot fully be held accountable, then concern for our autonomy is muddled by the muddiness of our autonomy.

Personal Identity and Autonomy

Strong views of descriptive autonomy and antipaternalism turn on the presumption that the individual can be self-created in important respects. One might say this is not true, that all that matters is that, in a given moment, the individual should be able to act from whatever motivations the individual has. But this would mean, among other things, that manipulation of views and values would be fair game so long as it would only affect future actions. A serious notion of autonomy must be more demanding than this. But if our notion is much more demanding than this, then it must presuppose a great deal about the nature of personal identity.

Let us consider possible views on personal identity and their relationship to a notion of autonomy.[14] Briefly stated, a first consideration in establishing the bounds of personal identity for a moral theory—certainly at least for a welfarist moral theory—is that we must be concerned with the relationship between identity and motivation. If I am not motivated by my distant future prospects, then I do not strongly identify with that future self. We may then say that my subjective sense of identification is weak in the long run. Indeed, it may even be weak in the short run. Certain issues in *akrasia* or weakness of will may readily be comprehended by a notion of weak subjective identification over time. In the contemporary literature on personal identity, the more common concern is with the consistency of one's various attributes over time. If my preferences today are very similar to my preferences ten years from now it is said that my identity is "strong." One of these preferences may be about my future self. To the extent that this latter preference is very strong, that is, that it heavily motivates present actions, I may be said to have strong subjective identification; to the extent it does not heavily motivate present actions, I have weak subjective identification.

When applied to 'identity', the predicates 'weak' and 'strong' are measures of consistency. When applied to subjective identification, they are, rather, measures of the strength of the identification or commitment over time, not of the consistency of this strength of commitment. One might have a weak commitment to one's distant future selves at age seventeen and a strong commitment at age forty, and there might be good theoretical explanations of such a shift. With respect to one's commitments to future selves, then, one would have a weak identity over time.

Another important issue, distinct from the strength of subjective identification over time, is the coherence of the person in any given moment. My actual identity may rightly be seen as a motley collection of urges, desires, understandings, and so forth, some of which may be inconsistent with others. If I am a distinctively inconsistent motley, I may suffer what seems to be weakness of will even over the very short run of this afternoon. Now autonomy begins to seem hollow in a perverse sense. I am autonomous but out of control. I am like Walt Whitman, contradicting myself and maybe pleased with that fact. If much of moral theory or autonomous choice more generally is to make sense, I cannot be too grievous a motley.

Suppose I suffer from (or enjoy) relatively weak subjective identification over time. I weigh the present very heavily and discount the distant future to virtually nothing. Or perhaps I value the distant future of that person who will be my future self as little different from the present or future of other persons who are not ever to be confused with my self. I cannot now be considered, by my own account, to be very autonomous except in the relatively unappealing sense that I simply act from my desires, values, and so forth of this moment. But those desires, values, and so forth must come to me largely by accident as far as I am concerned in this moment. I cannot plausibly be seen to have created them in this moment. I merely inherit most of them from former selves. Most of my character, preferences, and circumstances are simply what I find myself with—my present self cannot be responsible for them. On this view of the person, autonomy is not a notion that can carry much moral weight. Autonomy must reduce to a notion of acting from the character and preferences that one already has, that is to say, without immediate coercion. One might be capable of being very moral on certain moral theories but one cannot be very autonomous. To suppose that one is autonomous is inherently to insist that one has a relatively long-term identification with oneself.

Note how these considerations affect the view of Gerald Dworkin and others that autonomy is a "higher level" concept. Dworkin supposes that one must have a self-conception at a higher level than the level of one's immediate preferences. One may then assess the autonomy of one's actions at the lower level from their fit with the higher level self-conception.[15] This makes sense if one has a long-term commitment to one's future selves, hence, by implication, a long-term past commitment to one's present self. Otherwise it will be hard to define the second-order commitments as distinguishable from merely first-order present commitments. It is their grounding in a long-term view of the self that must give second-order commitments a coherent meaning.

Discussions of personal identity often seem to presuppose there is some core of the person that is identical over time. Discussions of autonomy often seem rather to suppose that there is something over and above the individual's momentary wants, pleasures, and so forth that regulates these. This extra something, the will or the higher-level desiring to desire certain things, might functionally resemble Freud's superego. Rather than being the core of the self, however, this regulator seems to be responsible for creating and monitoring the self. If the self is being constantly created, its identity is at best a tendency and therefore weak. A self that willfully regulates its first-order desires and that also displays *strong* identity suggests Gogol's tinsmith Schiller: "Schiller was a real German in the full sense of the word. From the age of twenty, that happy time when the Russian lives without a single thought of the next day, Schiller had already mapped out his whole life and did not deviate from his plan under any circumstances."[16] Gogol's caricature of Schiller's plan of life goes on in minute detail, including how often he kissed his wife and when he got drunk. A will as resolute as Schiller's must finally violate any appeal that a notion of autonomy might have been supposed to have. It could certainly not define autonomy for a compelling moral theory.

Conclusion

Briefly stated, the problem with autonomy is that, as many have concluded, the notion is substantively empty. This fact, Dworkin notes, "raises the question why the development, preservation and encouragement of autonomy is desirable."[17] To move from being a vacuously autonomous person to being a person of any moral concern, one must generate ideas and values spontaneously or one must largely absorb these from the larger society. The former is surely not a possibility of any interest.

A similar conclusion follows for the most abstract contemporary economic value theory, which is reduced to ordinal preferences that are substantively unrestricted. John Harsanyi defines 'preference autonomy' as "the principle that, in deciding what is good and what is bad for a given individual, the ultimate criterion can only be his own wants and his own preferences."[18] One may reasonably suppose that a concern to satisfy preferences *tout court* lacks grounding unless either we can give justifiable content to the preferences or we can justify the way in which they come to be held. If they are accidentally formed and could as well have been radically different, it will be hard to justify them. We may raise an analog of Dworkin's question, the question why the fulfillment of preferences is morally desirable.

One must be as skeptical of arguments from autonomy as of arguments from pure preference satisfaction. The value of autonomy must be contingent:

we value it in *our* circumstances. In a moral theory we may honor it largely as a proxy for something else. Or we may value it as a means of achieving something else, such as welfare. But we cannot sensibly view it as the core value of our moral theory unless we are content with a hollow core.

Notes

This paper has benefited from extensive commentary by John Christman.

1. R. H. Tawney, *Equality*, 1964 reissue of 4th ed. (London: George Allen and Unwin, 1952, 1st ed., 1931), 91–100.

2. Edmund Burke, *A Philosophical Enquiry into the Origin of Our Ideas of the Sublime and the Beautiful* ed. James T. Boulton 2d ed. (London: Routledge and Kegan Paul, 1958; 1st ed., 1757), opening sentence, p. 11.

3. In some respects, it was odd for evolutionary theory to lead to the view that *individuals* would be especially selected to be talented. For a long while, evolutionary biologists assumed that within species morphological variation was less than morphological variation between the means of two closely related species. This view has only recently been rejected in favor of the view that within group variation may be substantially greater.

4. Quoted in William Ritchies Sorley, *The Ethics of Naturalism*, 1904 ed. (reprint, Freeport, N.Y.: Books for Libraries Press, 1969; 1st ed., 1885), 199. This seems like an odd criticism of a theory whose best known proponent was the author of *On Liberty*. Compare it to a seemingly contrary criticism more in vogue today. Rawls says that "The classical [utilitarian] view results in . . . impersonality, in the conflation of all desires into one system of desire." (John Rawls, *A Theory of Justice* [Cambridge, Mass.: Harvard University Press, 1971], 188.)

5. Vilfredo Pareto, *Manual of Political Economy*, trans. Ann S. Schwier (New York: Kelley, 1971), sec. 57.

6. In the variant version of his theorem in his second edition, Arrow's condition is that "All logically possible orderings of the alternative social states are possible." (Kenneth J. Arrow, *Social Choice and Individual Values*, 2d ed. [New Haven, Conn.: Yale University Press, 1963, 1st ed., 1951], 96.)

7. Kenneth J. Arrow, "Extended Sympathy and the Possibility of Social Choice," *American Economic Review* 67 (1977), 219–25, quote on p. 225.

8. Richard Price, *A Review of the Principle Questions in Morals* (3rd ed. 1787; first published 1758), paras. 655–762 in D. D. Raphael, *British Moralists 1650–1800* (Oxford: Clarendon Press, 1969) 2 vols., para. 704.

9. Henry Sidgwick, *The Methods of Ethics*, 7th ed. (London: Macmillan, 1907), 386–87 and 406–7.

10. Perhaps one cannot be too sure of Kant. In some of his more flamboyant statements, Kant seems to rule it out as something that we should desire. He supposes that the principle of moral action "is free of all influences from contingent grounds" and that "the universal wish of every rational being must be . . . to be wholly free from [the inclinations]." (Immanuel Kant, *Grounding for the Metaphysics of Morals*, in Kant, *Ethical Philosophy*, trans. James W. Ellington [Indianapolis, Ind.: Hackett, 1983; originally published in German in 1785], 34, 35.)

11. Brandt's project of "cognitive psychotherapy" has this purpose. (Richard B.

Brandt, *A Theory of the Good and the Right* (Oxford: Clarendon Press, 1979), ch. 6, especially p. 113.)

12. Russell Hardin, "Does Might Make Right?," in J. Roland Pennock and John W. Chapman, eds., *Nomos 29: Authority Revisited* (New York: New York University Press, 1987), 201–17.

13. Richard Price, *A Review of the Principle Questions in Morals*, ed. D. D. Raphael (Oxford: Clarendon, 1974), 173.

14. I discuss the issues of personal identity more fully in Russell Hardin, *Morality within the Limits of Reason* (Chicago: University of Chicago Press, 1988), 191–201.

15. Gerald Dworkin, ch. 3 above, especially p. 61.

16. Nikolai Gogol, "Nevsky Prospekt," in Leonard J. Kent, ed., *The Complete Tales of Nicolai Gogol*, vol. 1 (Chicago: University of Chicago Press, 1985), 207–38, quote from p. 234.

17. Dworkin, "The Concept of Autonomy," 62.

18. John C. Harsanyi, "Morality and the Theory of Rational Behaviour," in Amartya Sen and Bernard Williams, eds., *Utilitarianism and Beyond* (Cambridge: Cambridge University Press, 1982), 39–62, quote from p. 55.

IV

AUTONOMY AND VALUES

13

Rights and Autonomy

David A. J. Richards

H. L. A. Hart has recently taken note of and applauded a discernible paradigm shift in political and legal theory from the "widely accepted old faith that some form of utilitarianism . . . *must* capture the essence of political morality" to one of "basic human rights . . . , if only we could find some sufficiently firm foundations for such rights."[1] Hart argues that recent exponents of this paradigm shift, whether associated with libertarian conservatism (Nozick) or the liberal welfare state (Dworkin), powerfully make their negative point against utilitarianism, but fail to lay adequate foundations for their constructive alternatives.[2] Such theorists are, in the terms of Hart's paper, "between utility and rights": they have begun to develop the long overdue transition from one paradigm to another, but they are too much in thrall to the utilitarianism they reject clearly to justify a constructive alternative.

In this essay, I take Hart's argument as both premise of challenge to my own inquiry; his arguments, with characteristic brilliance and incision, reveal our needs for fundamental conceptual work in the concept of human rights in a spirit which puts behind it the obsession with the inadequacies of utilitarianism and freshly faces the task of clarifying the deontological alternative. In order to do so, we must, in the spirit of the recent works of John Rawls[3] and Alan Gewirth,[4] articulate in defensibly contemporary terms the perspective on human rights of its greatest classical philosophers, in particular, Rousseau and Kant. The idea of human rights represents a major departure in civilized moral thought. When Rousseau and Kant gave the idea its first articulate and profound theoretical statements, they defined a way of thinking about the moral attitude to personality that was, in ways I must explain, radically new. The practical political implications of this way of thinking are a matter of history. The idea of human rights was one among the central moral concepts in terms of which a number of great political revolutions conceived and justified their demands.[5] Once introduced, the idea of human rights could not be

This chapter was originally published in *Ethics* 92 (Oct. 1981). Copyright © 1981 by The University of Chicago Press. Reprinted by permission.

David A. J. Richards is Professor of Law at New York University School of Law.

cabined. In American institutional history, the idea of human rights lay behind the American innovation of judicial review: since human rights are not the just subject of political bargaining and compromise, countermajoritarian courts with the American power of judicial review are a natural institutional way to secure such rights from the incursions of the institutions based on majority rule.[6] In our own time, the language and thought of human rights has been elaborated to articulate a number of social and economic rights (anticipated, strikingly, by Tom Paine),[7] and has, in the international sphere, been the central moral idea in terms of which colonial independence and postcolonial interdependence have been conceived and discussed.[8] An adequate theory of human rights would cast light on why the notion of human rights has naturally been put to such uses in the history of human institutions and how it should continue to be elaborated and extended.

My aim in this essay is to clarify the human rights perspective (i.e., the underlying structure of the language and thought of human rights). I take this structure to include certain fundamental attitudes to human personality which find expression in the weight which considerations of human rights have in practical reasoning; often claims of such rights override other considerations, and sometimes they justify revolution, rebellion, and ultimate resistance. I characterize and explicate this structure in terms of the autonomy-based interpretation of treating persons as equals.

1. Treating Persons as Equals

The notion of treating persons in the way one would oneself want to be treated is a conception of the nature of ethics or morality familiar to many moral traditions. Ethical conduct, on this view, treats persons as equals, for the ultimate moral imperative to treat others in the way one would oneself want to be treated presupposes that we are, in some sense, equals. However, the notion of treating persons as equals is ambiguous. A fundamental way to distinguish among moral theories is in terms of how they resolve this ambiguity. For example, John Stuart Mill, following Bentham, argued that utilitarianism treated people as equals in the important sense that everyone's pleasures and pains were impartially registered by the utilitarian calculus; thus, utilitarianism satisfies, Mill argued,[9] the moral imperative of treating persons as equals, where the criterion of equality is pleasure and pain. The great attraction of utilitarianism to humane and liberal reformers like Mill was, I believe, this: its capacity to interpret the basic moral imperative of treating people as equals in a way that enabled reformers concretely to assess institutions in the world in terms of human interests.[10] Any alternative moral theory must provide a coherent interpretation of the notion of treating people as equals which also enables critical moral intelligence concretely to assess and humanely criticize institutions in terms of relevant consequences.

From the perspective of neo-Kantian moral theory, utilitarianism fails to treat persons as equals in the morally relevant sense. To treat persons in the way required by utilitarianism is to focus obsessionally on pleasure alone as the *only* ethically significant fact and to aggregate it as such.[11] Pleasure is treated as a kind of impersonal and elemental fact, and no weight is given to its location in the separate creatures who experience it. This flatly ignores that the only *ethically* crucial fact can be that *persons* experience pleasure, and that pleasure has moral significance only in the context of the life that a person chooses to lead[12] and the evaluative weight, if any, that a person gives to it. Utilitarianism, thus, fails to treat persons as equals in that it literally dissolves moral personality into utilitarian aggregates.

But what is this alternative conception of human personality in terms of which the moral imperative of treating persons as equals should be interpreted? Why has it been supposed from Kant to Rawls and Gewirth to justify human rights that are not merely nonutilitarian but antiutilitarian? Certainly, theorists otherwise sympathetic to Kant's analysis of ethics have not consistently drawn antiutilitarian conclusions; R. M. Hare, for example, whose universalistic prescriptivism clearly is rooted in Kant, has recently defended utiltarianism as a substantive normative conception.[13] In order to explicate the form of Kantian theory which is antiutilitarian and fundamental to the idea of human rights, we must investigate the autonomy-based interpretation of treating persons as equals.

2. Autonomy

Autonomy, in the sense fundamental to the idea of human rights, is a complex assumption about the capacities, developed or undeveloped, of persons, which enable them to develop, want to act on, and act on higher-order plans of action which take as their self-critical object one's life and the way it is lived.[14] As Frankfurt put it, persons "are capable of wanting to be different, in their preferences and purposes, from what they are. Many animals appear to have the capacity for . . . 'first-order desires' or 'desires of the first order,' which are simple desires to do or not to do one thing or another. No animal other than man, however, appears to have the capacity for reflective self-evaluation that is manifested in the formation of second-order desires."[15] These capacities enable persons to establish various kinds of priorities and schedules for the satisfaction of first-order desires. The satisfaction of some desires (hunger) is regularized; the satisfaction of others is sometimes postponed. Indeed, persons sometimes gradually eliminate certain self-criticized desires (smoking) or over time encourage the development of others (cultivating one's still undeveloped capacities for love and tender mutual response).[16] Such capacities of self-criticism explain the personal emotions (regret or shame or guilt, or, on the other hand, self-respect or pride or a sense of integrity).

One way to bring out the nature of these complex capacities is to consider forms of their absence. I once described such cases in terms of our being prepared to say or think that a person is not in or not fully in her or his body.[17] Stanley Benn has recently categorized them as defects of practical rationality, or epistemic rationality, or of psychic continuity whether as believer or agent.[18] Defects in practical rationality occur, for example, in young children who cannot act now on the basis of future probable desires (conserving water for later thirst); or in a psychosis like kleptomania, in which a present compulsion (to steal) cannot be resisted though it conflicts with other desires of the agent, both now and in the future, which the agent deems more important. Paranoid fantasy exemplifies defects in epistemic rationality: the person's beliefs are systematically immune to argument or evidence, so that the person's experience is one of devouring fantasy with no external check of reality. Forms of schizophrenic disassociation evince defects of psychic continuity: the person is a kind of impassive observer of the body which may not be regarded as hers or his, or the person cannot identify the self as the same person over time.

Among the complex capacities, constitutive of autonomy, are language and self-consciousness, memory, logical relations, empirical reasoning about beliefs, and their validity (intelligence), and the capacity to use normative principles in terms of which plans of action can be assessed, including principles of rational choice in terms of which ends may be more effectively and coherently realized. Such capacities enable persons to call their life their own, self-critically reflecting on and revising, in terms of arguments and evidence to which rational assent is given, which desires will be pursued and which disowned, which capacities cultivated and which left unexplored, with what or whom in one's history one will identify, or in what theory of ends or aspirations one will center one's self-esteem, one's integrity, in a life well lived. The development of these capacities for individual self-definition is, from the earliest life of the infant, the central developmental task of the becoming of a person.[19]

Autonomy, as a theory of the person, was, I believe, historically a relatively late development. We may distinguish two stages in its development: first, the emergence of certain forms of language and the self-consciousness this made possible, brilliantly suggested in Julian Jaynes's *The Origin of Consciousness in the Breakdown of the Bicameral Mind*,[20] second, the further elaboration of the idea of autonomy as a capacity of all persons. This latter conception, probably first suggested in the late Middle Ages[21] and emerging into secular political practice in the English Civil War,[22] flowered into a self-consciously powerful political and social ideal in the works of Milton[23] and Locke[24] and was given its deepest philosophical expression in the works of Rousseau[25] and Kant.[26] The thinkers and artists of ancient Greece, or at least the ones whose works remain extant, apparently lacked the concept at least in the form of a conception of the capacities of all persons.[27] Correlatively, the Greeks lacked the idea that people, in view of their capacity for autonomy, are entitled to equal concern and respect as persons. As a corollary, Greek political theory does not invoke the language and thought of human rights.[28]

Of course, the artists and philosophers of ancient Greece cultivate with genius human capacities of critical self-consciousness[29] and thus lay the foundations for later moral ideals which build on these foundations. For example, one of Plato's seminal contributions to philosophical psychology was to formulate and explicate in *The Republic* a conception of the capacity of the philosophical soul for rational self-rule which is the first philosophical investigation anywhere of what I have called autonomy.

However, it was, I believe, the common sense of ancient Greece, which Plato and Aristotle understandably shared, that humans do not, in general, have what contemporary ego psychology denominates a developed ego (i.e., the executive capacity to formulate an integrated plan of life and pursue it as an independent person).[30] The general view of personal competence of the ancient Greeks suggests the fragmented ego, the "divided self"[31]—generally passive, with appetites, emotions, and intellect isolated as independent agencies on the battleground of the body, unintegrated by any coherent higher-order planner within the self. Rather than integration from within, the Greeks supposed that each person, internally divided and vulnerable, depended for the order of his life on his *agathos*, the noble man, on whom the *kakos* depended to provide the order of his life that the *kakos* was constitutionally unable to afford from internal resources of the self.[32] Certain exceptional people might achieve something close to the contemporary concept of developed ego strength (i.e., Plato's philosophical souls), but they were rare, exceptional, godlike—the natural rulers of society. Correlatively, Greek political theory understandably focuses on rule by the best.[33] The fundamental Greek vision is that of Plato's *Republic*: the ruler, a benevolent physician who alone understands the health of the balanced human organism, has unlimited power to realize the desirable health which humans cannot realize on their own. Such a benevolent physician may quite completely control the life of the disabled patient, as in chattel slavery and the institutionalized subjection of woman, both of which Aristotle justifies,[34] for such intrusive control is the indispensible means to the health desired.

In contrast, when the notions of equal concern and respect for autonomy appear as powerful political and social ideals in Rousseau and Kant,[35] they radically repudiate the vision of the Platonic therapeutic state on the basis of emerging conceptions of human rights whereby persons are now conceived as having final authority to control their own lives. The scope of legitimate paternalistic concern among mature adults, even for putatively benevolent motives, is subject now to moral constraints which were, for Plato and Aristotle, unthinkable. The idea of human rights expresses a normative attitude of respect for the capacity of ordinary persons for rational autonomy—to be, in Kant's memorable phrase, free and rational sovereigns in the kingdom of ends,[36] that is, to take ultimate, self-critical responsibility for one's ends and the way they cohere in a life. Kant characterized this ultimate respect for the choice of ends as the dignity of autonomy,[37] in contrast to the heteronomous, lower-order ends (pleasure, talent) among which the person may choose. Kant thus expressed the liberal imperative of moral neutrality among many disparate visions of the good life:[38] the concern is not with maximizing the agent's pursuit of any particular lower-order end, but rather with respecting the higher-order capacity of the agent to choose her or his ends, whatever they are.

Understandably, Rousseau's and Kant's articulation of the notion of autonomy is limited by the undeveloped state of the psychology and social theory of the period, and is confused by even so profound a thinker as Kant with certain ideas from which that of autonomy is in fact quite distinct. The consequence is a view of autonomy which in some ways underestimates its depth and in others overestimates its force. In order to clarify the sense of autonomy, it is useful to distinguish the idea from a number of theses with which it has been and continues, sometimes disastrously, to be confused. I shall discuss these points seriatim as (1) changes in psychological theory which deepen, and do not contradict, the idea of autonomy; (2) autonomy not a thesis of causal indeterminism and thus broadly consistent with many social theories; (3) autonomy not willfulness; and (4) autonomy not egoism.

Psychological Theory and Autonomy

The concept of autonomy, being in part a view of psychological capacities of persons, obviously may be deepened as psychological theory expands our understanding of these capacities. The most striking development, which differentiates the modern conception of autonomy from that found in Rousseau and Kant, is the profounder understanding of the self achieved by Freud's theory of the defenses and subsequent developments in ego psychology.[39] The idea of autonomy has, I believe, been deepened in the precise way that Freud, in his best moments, argued that knowledge of the unconscious mind and its processes increased the range and strength of the ego in controlling id and superego impulses: "Where id was, there shall ego be."[40] Through our self-conscious retrieval and investigation of the fantasy data of the unconscious (dreams, free association, slips, and the like), we may achieve a remarkable capacity to deepen and control our understanding of mental processes which are otherwise inexplicable and often stupidly, rigidly, and self-destructively repetitive. Surely such insights enable us to increase autonomy; through our knowledge of the unconscious defenses and their form in our lives, we are able to assess consciously the work of the unconscious, deciding whether desires disowned by the unconscious (repression) should be reclaimed or desires promoted by the unconscious (sublimation and projection)[41] should be cut back. We may, in addition, thus render ourselves self-conscious and independent of our earliest, most intense emotional identifications, achieving an understanding of our life history so that we may see our lives and what we want from them individually as our own and not as the unconscious and unexamined derivative of the wishes of significant others; with this kind of understanding, we strengthen our autonomy to decide with what or with whom in our life history we will or will not identify or continue to identify.[42]

In contrast, Rousseau, the greatest introspective thinker among early proponents of autonomy and the theory of rights, is notoriously superficial about the depth-psychological influences on his thought. Such unconscious influences on his thought may explain the totalitarian strains in Rousseau which are foreign to the spirit of his theory of autonomy and rights.[43] In any event, it is a mistake to suppose that autonomy, as an ingredient of the concept of human rights, is frozen in the psychology of the period of its intellectual birth.

Autonomy Not Causal Indeterminism, But Consistent with Social Theory

A salient confusion in the tradition of autonomy, found from Kant[44] to Sartre,[45] is the idea that autonomy *requires* the truth of causal indeterminism. The idea appears to be that in exercising capacities of rational choice and deliberation regarding the form of our lives, we exercise a spontaneous freedom from causal determination in any form. But this conception may overestimate the force of autonomy, investing it with connotations which confuse and distort the *moral* import which the idea does properly have.

The relevant sense of independence, on which the use of the term "autonomy" here used depends, is twofold. First, the evaluations of one's life that autonomy makes possible enable persons not to be bound to immediate present desires, but to give weight to their desires and projects over time. Second, the standards of self-critical evaluation are determined not by the will of others but by arguments and evidence which one has oneself rationally examined and assented to. I cannot, of course, deal here with all the complex issues of free will and determinism.[46] Rather, a more limited point seems in order: neither form of independence establishes that the exercise of autonomy is inconsistent with causal explanation in general. It seems possible that a human life may be autonomous in both senses (desires over time are given weight, and the standards of evaluation are personally assented to), and yet forms of causal explanation thereof may be true. Perhaps some forms of causal explanation are clearly incompatible with autonomy;[47] perhaps there is some general argument which shows them to be inconsistent in general. But nothing in the analysis of autonomy so far supports this view.

Let me assume, briefly, what I have not shown, that causal explanation and the exercise of autonomy are consistent. On this view, autonomy is a cluster of capacities which a society, depending on its normative purposes, may foster or stunt. The idea of human rights embodies a normative perspective of respect for such capacities. Accordingly, the putative consistency of our moral concern for autonomy and causal explanation enables us lucidly to address what should, on this conception, be a central undertaking of social justice: how causally we may promote, in ourselves and others, the development and exercise of autonomy. In this way, we may fruitfully integrate moral theory with the insights of social theory. Autonomy may be perceived, not as asocial isolation, but in terms of a supportive social environment of critical dialogue and reciprocity. Society may accept responsibility for defects in autonomy which it has unjustly fostered and to which, in the balance of considerations of justice (for example, in punishment),[48] it must give appropriate weight. And larger decisions of alternative forms of basic institutions (e.g., democratic socialism vs. democratic capitalism)[49] may be assessed in terms of which institutions better foster moral aims of autonomy.

Autonomy Not Willfulness

From Kant to Hare, moral theorists have interpreted autonomy as a kind of continual willing or willfulness. To be autonomous is construed as the willing of rules to which one consistently adheres. In Hare, for example, the idea of morality is analyzed as a kind of consistency in one's willing of rules of conduct no matter what the substantive content of the rules willed.[50] There is, I believe, no good reason to accept this interpretation of autonomy; and there is enough to be said against it to suffice for repudiating it.

Autonomy, as here described, is a capacity for second-order, rationally self-critical evaluations and wants and plans. This is, in part, a description of the human will and its force in our lives. But the exercise of autonomy is not the same thing as the consistent willing of something, no matter what it is. To so construe autonomy as a definitional matter invites tendentious confusion of all exercises of autonomy with willfullness. But, surely, persons often exercise their autonomy in invoking self-critical evaluations which subject forms of consistent willing to various forms of criticism; we think, for example, that such actions are unreasonable because they are inhumanely rigid and inflexible, or stupidly masochistic, or simply arbitrarily willful. Autonomy includes the will, but it also includes a substantive component of rational goods which persons reasonably want whatever else they want. Our self-critical evalutions often assess our lives in terms of these goods and cannot be sensibly interpreted without reference to them.

Indeed, by forcing autonomy into the Procrustean model of willfulness, we blind ourselves to those rational goods which we cannot willfully compel, but which we must receptively develop and foster—for example, the imagination, emotional spontaneity and depth of feeling, creativity, insight, and the like. If we take seriously the rational goods in terms of which we self-critically reflect on our lives, we must take seriously those forms of self-criticism and change, surely not uncommon, which invoke our emotional and imaginative failures and which call for deeper insight into what emotionally we are and want to become. We must, in this connection, note Leslie Farber's cautionary warnings,[51] garnered from years of perceptive therapeutic practice, about the psychopathology of the will, which destructively makes the will, in Yeats's phrase, do the work of the imagination.[52] Such willfullness is evidently a familiar form of contemporary neurotic distortion, one which has, I submit, not uncommonly been indulged by moral philosophers, who are as prone to the Faustian myth as anyone. Thus, autonomy is construed as a form of willful exertion *simpliciter*, when it invokes other kinds of consideration as well.

Autonomy Not Egoism

The classical opposition of autonomy-based conceptions of ethics to the morality of love and benevolence, utilitarianism, has sometimes been misinterpreted in the form of the claim that autonomy is a kind of unobstructed egoism. In fact, the confusion of autonomy and egoism derives not from the natural rights tradition of Rousseau and Kant but from the traditions of utilitarian economics (i.e., Adam Smith and Hume)[53] who interpret autonomy as egoistic consumer sovereignty. The liberalism of civil and political rights is thus analogized to classical economic liberalism; equal voting allows people to establish and foster their ends, as sovereigns in the kingdom of ends, in the same way, allegedly, that consumer sovereignty in economic markets allows individuals to make choices as they please.[54] Accordingly, the ideal of autonomy underlying both is alleged (e.g., by Nozick and others)[55] to be a form of egoistic consumer sovereignty. But the liberal conception of autonomy, including the idea of neutrality about individual ends, is not the same idea as egoism. Such an assimilation invites natural attack from the left, familiar from Marx[56] to Unger,[57] to the effect that the liberal tradition of rights rests on a shrunken and decrepit view of Hobbesian egoistic human nature. If autonomy were egoism, these critics would be correct. But it is not.

The idea of autonomy, as we have discussed it and as classically articulated in Rousseau and Kant, has nothing to do with egoism or with an egoistic view of human nature.[58] It identifies capacities of persons to entertain and act on second-order desires and plans self-critically to have and revise a form of life. The conception is neutral regarding the particular ends, egoistic or altruistic, that the person adopts. Presumably, the exercise of autonomy will at least sometimes result in repudiation of the egoistic meanness and narcissim of one's previous life, acting on the higher-order want that one's wants be more generously and abundantly human.

It *is* true that the tradition of autonomy, from its beginnings in the works of Kant, insisted that autonomy, the root of ethics and human rights, has nothing to do with benevolence or love (or Love).[59] But the contrast Kant has in mind is not between egoism and altruism, but between mutual respect and sympathetic benevolence. Kant perceived the malign failure of utilitarianism to take seriously the separateness of persons as at one with its being the morality of love.[60] Utilitarianism's absorption in the aggregate of pleasure derives from its focus on the loving benevolence of the ideal observer who sympathetically conflates the pleasures or pains experienced by other persons into a net aggregate of pleasure over pain in himself. In contrast, Kant insisted that the separateness of autonomy is the root of ethics and defined ethical principles as expressive of this separateness—as expressing, not love, but respect. This conception has nothing whatsoever to do with egoism, which, in fact, it sharply constrains.

The idea that Kantian autonomy is meanly antagonistic to the proper claims of love has been argued by Bernard Williams in criticism of my own and others' attempts to develop a Kantian theory of personal relationships.[61] Williams argues that the Kantian approach cannot be the whole truth, for it conflicts with our judgment that the claims of lovers override moral claims of a more universalistic, autonomy-based kind and requires, *pro tanto*, that we deracinate that part of the concept of the self which turns on the freedom to develop personal relationships. Neither claim can be sustained. As for the former, Kantian moral theory makes only the modest claim that obligations to friends and lovers arise in a moral context: we are, only within limits, bound to advance the interests of our lovers over others. Williams suggests there are no such limits, but in this he accedes, I believe, to the narcissistic romance that personal love releases us from moral relations to others. This form of personal love, however, is only one among others,[62] and is often circumscribed and regulated in the process of developing capacities for mature reciprocal love that is not isolable from the rest of our ordinary moral nature. On the other hand, Williams's suggestion that Kantian morality causes us to deracinate interests fundamental to the concept of ourselves is equally illegitimate. The accusation would only be plausible if Kantian principles required us to forgo altogether the pursuit of personal love. So far from this being true, Kantian principles can be shown to justify a fundamental right to autonomy in deciding whom and how to love in order to preserve underlying values of personal emotional integrity and self-expression in intimate relations.[63] In short, such arguments precisely justify a moral right to love on the grounds of personal integrity that Williams, mistakenly, believes Kantian theory would sacrifice. In short, the claims of personal love and autonomy-based morality are congruent and indeed mutually supporting over a wide range.

In summary, the idea of autonomy has been confused with a number of distinguishable ideas and theses, so that putative attacks on autonomy have often been attacks, not on the idea itself, but on preverse and sometimes disastrous misinterpretations of it. The truth in the concept is in Kant's moral ideal that persons are free and rational sovereigns in the kingdom of ends. The contemporary neo-Kantians Rawls and Gewirth formulate this idea in different though related ways. Rawls deploys the idea of the veil of ignorance[64] which has the consequence that the rational choices of persons, by which Rawls defines the concept of morality, cannot take account of their particular ends, but must ask what things enable rational persons to choose their ends, whatever they are. Gewirth follows Kant more literally in arguing that the central normative concept is human action in general,[65] versus any particular ends of human actions, which, on analysis, turns out to be rational autonomy. Rawls and Gewirth articulate the same Kantian intuition. The central mark of ethics is not respect for what people currently are or for particular ends. Rather, respect is expressed for an idealized capacity which, if appropriately treated, people can realize, namely, the capacity to take responsibility as a free and rational agent for one's system of ends.

If Rawls and Gewirth in these ways correctly give expression to the fundamental idea of moral personality, Nozick clearly does not. For Nozick, the interpretation of autonomy is not in terms of higher-order, self-critical capacities, but a kind of capitalistic reductio thereof, namely, natural property in one's body, sentiments, and labor.[66] This account confuses, as earlier suggested, moral personality with privatized egoism. Basic ethical theory must explicate the most general features of moral personality, which is correctly supplied by Kant, Rawls, and Gewirth in terms of an idealized description of capacities for self-critical choice of one's ends, as a free and rational being.

Nozick, in contrast, identifies the person with certain inalienable assets, which are neither necessarily nor naturally associated with the morally fundamental idea of free and rational choice of one's ends.

3. The Autonomy-Based Interpretation
of Treating Persons as Equals

We must now connect these investigations into the nature of autonomy with what I earlier called the autonomy-based interpretation of treating persons as equals, a conception alleged to yield strongly antiutilitarian ideas of human rights. Let us contrast the utilitarian with the deontological interpretation of treating persons as equals.

Utilitarianism, we noted, interprets equality in terms of pleasure or pain: all such experiences are equal before the utilitarian calculus. The consequence of this perspective is to treat pleasure as a kind of impersonal fact, and no weight is given to the separateness of the creatures who experience it. The familiar inadequacies of utilitarianism derive from this fact.

In contrast, neo-Kantian deontological moral theory interprets treating persons as equals not in terms of lower-order ends persons may pursue (pleasure or pain, or talent, or whatever) but in terms of the capacity of each person self-critically to evaluate and give order and personal integrity to one's system of ends in light of a point of view of how to live one's life. Treating persons as equals in this sense expresses equal respect for the capacities of each person to take ultimate responsibility, as free and rational beings, for adopting and revising a point of view on how to live their lives. It is no accident that this perspective justifies human rights that are not merely nonutilitarian, but antiutilitarian. Thus to express equal respect for personal autonomy is to guarantee, on fair terms to all, the conditions requisite for the exercise of such capacities (e.g., the development and cultivation of critical rationality); ethical principles of obligation and duty insure that this is so, and correlatively define human rights.[67] Without such rights, persons would lack, inter alia, the basic opportunity to develop a secure sense of an independent self, instead being simply the locus of impersonal pleasures which may be manipulated and rearranged in whatever ways would aggregate maximum utility overall, for all individual projects must, in principle, give way before utilitarian aggregates. Rights insure that this not be so, and thus have the characteristic force in our normative vocabulary which Dworkin describes in terms of rights as trumps over countervailing utilitarian calculations.[68]

It is important to see that this deontological moral perspective, while it rejects as an ultimate moral principle the utilitarian maximization of the aggregate of pleasure over pain, is not incompatible with forms of assessment of consequences in thinking about ethical issues.[69] The asumption that the Kantian interpretation of treating persons as equals is incompatible with assessing consequences is a blundering mistake.[70] Certain kinds of consequences (those of utilitarian aggregation) are ruled out, but other forms of consequences, relevant to the assessment of what the autonomy-based interpretation of treating persons as equals requires in certain circumstances, are crucially invoked. Both the neo-Kantian theories of Rawls and Gewirth illustrate this truth. Rawls interprets treating persons as equals in terms of principles of conduct which rational persons would unanimously agree to, while under a veil of ignorance as to who they are, as the general critical standards in terms of which personal relations would be governed;[71] and Gewirth interprets the Kantian moral imperative in terms of the general requirements for rational autonomy that an agent would demand for the self on the condition that the requirement be consistently extended to all other agents alike.[72] Both these theories appeal to consequences in arguing that certain substantive principles would be agreed to (Rawls) or universalized (Gewirth). Rawls imputes to his contractors the maximin strategy of deciding in terms of which alternative possible principles secure the highest lowest prospect of rational goods,[73] and thus assesses different kinds of principles and their formulation in terms of their consequences in securing this aim. Correspondingly, Gewirth argues that the universalizing agent would assess the necessary material conditions for rational autonomy (roughly, what any rational agent would want, whatever his lower-order ends). The consequences of universalization thus determine what would be universalized.

Such autonomy-based interpretations of treating persons as equals analyze the demands of ethics and ethical reflection in a way strikingly different from that called for by utilitarianism. Since the sympathetic benevolence central to utilitarian reasoning focuses only on the greatest net aggregate of pleasure over pain, the utilitarian moralist must, in principle, ignore and disassociate himself from any fundamental frustration of the basic interests of the person (in oneself or others) which may be required in order to realize the utilitarian aggregate. Since the point of view of the person has no basic significance for the utilitarian theory of ethics (which, in its most profound exponents like Sidgwick, looks only to the point of view of the universe),[74] such sacrifices of personal interests may fairly commonly be required by the pursuit of aggregates. In contrast, the burdens of deontological ethics are not the impossible ones of the self-sacrificing alienation of self in the interest of universal benevolence. Rather, since the interests of the person define the basic point of view from which ethical reasoning starts, there is not more basic or elemental unit of moral analysis (e.g., the pleasure of utilitarianism) into which this point of view may be dissolved. The person is the ultimate unit of ethical analysis. Correspondingly, ethical reasoning expresses the moral capacities of moral personality. We start, for example, from higher-order capacities to self-critically evaluate and revise one's ends in terms of arguments and evidence to which one rationally assents; we assess the basic demands of such personal autonomy for the goods which express basic respect for its development, exercise, and realization; and we universalize such demands to other persons who, by definition, share these capacities. Such moral capacities are not the extraordinary demands of utilitarian personal dissolution, for no such sacrifice of the person could, on this analysis, be justified. On the other hand, the exercise of such capacities often will call for critical constraints on one's egoistic pursuits justified in terms of the minimum moral decency that we expect all persons to extend to other persons. Consider a racist who claims incapacity to think of himself as a black, or a sexist man as a woman, or a homophobe as a homosexual. We blame the egoism of such people, not for lack of extraordinary capacities of sympathy or self-sacrifice, but for something much more minimal and inhuman: the moral indecency of perverse willfulness in failing to exercise humane capacities incumbent on moral agents, as such—to think of people as persons and to regulate their conduct by principles persons would accept whether they were on the giving or receiving end. Deontological ethics thus requires the moral decency of people of good will: neither the sacrifice of self for impersonal utilitarian aggregates nor egoism, but the deeper insight into the foundations of one's own demands for personal integrity which one extends to others on fair terms.

An important advantage of this Kantian model is that it illuminates what the utilitarian model obscures: that the kinds of capacities on which ethical deliberation depends do not call for any form of impersonality or radical denial of the personal attitudes of the self, but a kind of impartiality in weighing reasonably moral claims of persons, which is quite a different matter. Moral impartiality, properly understood, must by definition give intense expression to deep emotional and intellectual capacities of one's person for self-knowledge about the demands of one's self for dignity, but they are capacites which are sensitive to and engaged by reasonableness in weighing the equal demands of other persons. Far from requiring impersonal detachment, such impartiality in the articulation of rights requires a person's most responsible engagement in the search within one's self for the foundations of one's integrity as a person which, as a person, one extends to all persons alike.

The urgent, demanding, and intransigent character of human rights is explained by their roots in the basic demands of moral personality—in those rational goods which alone secure to the person rational autonomy, the foundation of living a life with the only thing Kant claimed to be of unconditional worth, personal dignity.[75] Thus, rights are fought for in revolutions, are intransigently demanded, and are not compromised.

I began this discussion on the premise of H. L. A. Hart's critique of the inadequate foundations of recent antiutilitarian theories of rights, theories which, in the end, are too much in thrall to their utilitarian opposition. I have argued that, in order to lay the foundation of a sound deontological paradigm of rights, we must focus on the analysis of the autonomy-based interpretation of treating persons as equals. If we see the depth of these ideas and learn to use them to render moral thinking determinate, we will, I believe, in time achieve the desideratum of a general theory of rights which explicates the complex ways in which rights are invoked and weighed. Correspondingly, we may critically disenthrall ourselves of the fiction that rights are tied to ethnocentrism or capitalist ideology, and afford a critical organon for assessing just demands for personal dignity—political, social, economic. We are, I believe, now in a position to articulate a form of critical casuistry of human rights which may inspirit contemporary moral and legal theory with its ancient origins as practical wisdom. I can think of no philosophical achievement, if we could meet it, of greater importance.

Notes

This essay profited from the essential critical advice of Professor Donald Levy, Department of Philosophy, Brooklyn College.

1. H. L. A. Hart, "Between Utility and Rights," in *The Idea of Freedom*, ed. Alan Ryan (Oxford: Oxford University Press, 1979), 77.

2. For the examination of Nozick, see ibid., pp. 80–86; for the examination of Dworkin, see ibid., pp. 86–97.

3. John Rawls, *A Theory of Justice* (Cambridge, Mass.: Harvard University Press, 1971); see also "Kantian Constructivism in Moral Theory," *Journal of Philosophy* 77 (1980), 515–72.

4. Alan Gewirth, *Reason and Morality* (Chicago: University of Chicago Press, 1978).

5. The political revolutions of the seventeenth and eighteenth centuries witnessed such landmarks as the English Petition of Rights (1627), the Habeas Corpus Act (1679), the American Declaration of Independence (1776), the United States Constitution, (1787), the American Bill of Rights (1791), and the French Declaration of the Rights of Man and Citizen (1789).

6. For a general discussion of the form of these rights in American constitutional law, see David A. J. Richards, *The Moral Criticism of Law* (Encino, Calif.: Dickenson-Wadsworth Publishing Co., 1977); Ronald Dworkin, *Taking Rights Seriously* (Cambridge, Mass.: Harvard University Press, 1977), chs. 5–8.

7. See Thomas Paine, *Rights of Man*, ed. Henry Collins (Harmondsworth, UK: Penguin Books, 1969), pt. 2 ch., 5, pp. 232–95. For commentary, see D. D. Raphael, *Political Theory and the Rights of Man* (Bloomington: Indiana University Press, 1967), 62.

8. For a useful discussion and critique, see Charles R. Beitz, *Political Theory and International Relations* (Princeton, N.J.: Princeton University Press, 1979), 68–123.

9. John Stuart Mill, *Utilitarianism*, ed. Oskar Piest (Indianapolis: Library of Liberal Arts, 1957), ch. 5, pp. 76–79.

10. See, in general, J. S. Mill, *Utilitarianism*, where Mill makes this argument quite clearly.

11. See Hart, "Between, Utility and Rights," 78–80.

12. See Bernard Williams, "A Critique of Utilitarianism," in J. J. C. Smart and Bernard Williams, *Utilitarianism For and Against* (Cambridge: Cambridge University Press, 1973), p. 77.

13. See R. M. Hare, "Ethical Theory and Utilitarianism," in *Contemporary British Philosophy*, ed. H. D. Lewis (London: Allen & Unwin, 1976), 113–31.

14. See David A. J. Richards, *A Theory of Reasons for Action* (Oxford: Clarendon Press, 1971), 65–68.

15. Harry Frankfurt, "Freedom of the Will," ch. 4 above, especially p. 64.

16. On the relation of the person to rational choice, including choices of these kinds, see Richards, *A Theory of Reasons for Action*, ch. 3.

17. Ibid., 65–68.

18. See Stanley I. Benn, "Freedom, Autonomy and the Concept of a Person," *Proceedings of the Aristotelian Society* 66 (1976); 109–30, esp. 112–17.

19. See Margaret S. Mahler et al., *The Psychological Birth of the Human Infant: Symbiosis and Individuation* (New York: Basic Books, 1967). See also Louis J. Kaplan, *Oneness and Separateness: From Infant to Individual* (New York: Simon & Schuster, 1978).

20. Julian Jaynes, *The Origin of Consciousness in the Breakdown of the Bicameral Mind* (Boston: Houghton Mifflin Co., 1976).

21. The crucial figure, who develops a radical theory of free will as the predicate of ideas of inalienable human rights, appears to be William of Ockham. See Paul Edwards, ed., *The Encyclopedia of Philosophy* (New York: Macmillan Co., 1967), vol. 8, 315–17. But see Richard Tuck, *Natural Rights Theories* (Cambridge: Cambridge University Press, 1979).

22. For a remarkable collection of political tracts from this period which invoke these ideas, see A. S. P. Woodhouse, ed., *Puritanism and Liberty: Being the Army Debates (1647–9) from the Clarke Manuscripts* (London: J. M. Dent & Sons, 1974).

23. John Milton, *Areopagitica*, in *The Prose of John Milton*, ed. J. Max Patrick (Garden City, N.Y.: Doubleday Anchor Books, 1967), pp. 265–334.

24. John Locke, *Second Treatise*, in *Locke's Treatises of Government*, ed. Peter Laslett (Cambridge: Cambridge University Press, 1967), 285–446.

25. See Jean Jacques Rousseau, *The Social Contact and Discourses*, trans. G. D. H. Cole (New York: E. P. Dutton & Co. 1950).

26. Immanuel Kant, *Foundations of the Metaphysics of Morals*, trans. L. W. Beck (New York: Liberal Arts Press, 1959), *The Metaphysical Elements of Justice*, trans. John Ladd (Indianapolis: Library of Liberal Arts, 1965), *The Metaphysical Principles of Virtue*, trans. James Ellington (Indianapolis: Library of Liberal Arts, 1964).

27. See A. W. H. Adkins, *From the Many to the One* (Ithaca, N.Y.: Cornell University Press, 1970).

28. See A. W. H. Adkins, *Moral Values and Political Behavior in Ancient Greece* (New York: W. W. Norton & Co., 1972). It is, I believe a distinct point that the ancient Greeks had the idea of legal rights, that the legal system, imposing legal obligations, correlatively defines rights. The claim here made is that they had no idea of moral or human rights of persons, as such. Alan Gewirth has, I believe, failed to give proper emphasis to the important distinction between legal and moral rights. See Gewirth, *Reason and Morality*, 98–102.

29. See Jaynes, *The Origin of Consciousness*, 255–92; see also pp. 67–83.

30. See Adkins, *From the Many to the One*; cf. Jaynes, *The Origin of Consciousness*.

31. See R. D. Laing, *The Divided Self* (Harmondsworth, UK: Penguin Books, 1965)

32. For a summary of the Greek view, see Adkins, *From the Many to the One*, ch. 10.

33. See Plato, *The Republic*; Aristotle, *Politics*.

34. See Ernest Barker, ed., *The Politics of Aristotle* (New York: Oxford University Press, 1962), Bk. 1, chs. 2–7, 12–13.

35. See Rousseau, *Social Contract*; and Kant, *Foundations, Metaphysical Elements,* and *Metaphysical Principles*.

36. See Kant, *Foundations*, pp. 51–52. When Freud developed a therapeutic method intended to deepen our capacities for autonomy (see the discussion of Freud in section 1 above), he naturally insisted, consistent with the moral vision of autonomy,

that the free assent of the patient was the only acceptable or legitimate criterion for the validity of the therapist's analytic efforts. See S. Freud, "Constructions in Analysis" (1937), *Standard Edition* (London: Hogarth Press, 1964), vol. 23, 257–69. Since persons have a unique capacity to understand and change their lives, Freud rules out *ab initio* the Platonic forms of intrusive control, for only the person can have the final say in unraveling the mysteries of the self. Freud, like Rousseau and Kant, thus places the integrity of the self at the core of social theory. Of course, Freud applies his therapeutic methods only to neurotics who were, typically, absent neurotic symptoms, reasonable and mature people. Psychotics raise different kinds of problems in terms of the legitimacy of paternalistic interference. See Richards, *The Moral Criticism of Law*, 216–20.

37. See Kant, *Foundations*, 53.

38. See Ronald Dworkin, "Liberalism," in *Public and Private Morality*, ed. Stuart Hampshire (Cambridge: Cambridge University Press, 1978), 113–43.

39. Freud's conception of the ego was classically formulated in his "The Ego and the Id" (1923), *Standard Edition* vol. 19, 12–66, wherein the ego appears as the passive mediator between id and superego impulses. This passive battleground conception was expressly disapproved by Freud in his important later work, "Inhibitions, Symptoms and Anxiety" (1926), *Standard Edition* vol. 20, 87–172, wherein he seeks to characterize the independent power of the ego to deal with internal and external dangers (both realistic and intrapsychic id and superego impulses) by triggering the protective system of defenses. Freud's theory of the defenses was elaborated in Anna Freud's *The Ego and the Mechanisms of Defence* (1936) (New York: International Universities Press, 1946). Later ego psychology has sought to characterize further the reality functions of the ego in addition to its unconscious defensive mechanisms, on which Freud focused. Heinz Hartmann developed accordingly his conception of ego autonomy, focusing on the capacities of the person to engage in adaptive reality testing in a conflict-free zone, that is, a zone free of the warring id and superego impulses; see Hartmann, *Ego Psychology and the Problem of Adaptation* (1939) (New York: International Universities Press, 1958). In the light of the subsequent works of Piaget, Erikson, and studies of animal and child behavior, these notions of ego functions have been developed into a theory of the competent exercise of the capacities of persons as such with independent desires to exercise these capacities competently. See R. W. White, *Ego and Reality in Psychoanalytic Theory* (New York: International Universities Press, 1963).

40. See S. Freud, "New Introductory Lectures on Psycho-Analysis" (1933), *Standard Edition* vol. 22, 5–182, quote from p. 80.

41. See A. Freud, ch. 4.

42. For an example of a possibly self-destructive identification which might possibly be undone, see the discussion of identification with the aggressor, in ibid., ch. 9.

43. For a plausible defense of this position, see F. Weinstein and G. M. Platt, *The Wish to Be Free* (Berkeley and Los Angeles: University of California Press, 1969), ch. 3.

44. See Kant, *Foundations, Metaphysical Elements,* and *Metaphysical Principles.*

45. See Jean-Paul Sartre, *Being and Nothingness*, trans, H. E. Barnes (New York: Philosophical Library, 1956).

46. For a more extended examination of these issues, see Richards, *A Theory of Reasons for Action*, 54–59.

47. See, e.g., B. F. Skinner, *Beyond Freedom and Dignity* (New York: Alfred A. Knopf Inc., 1971), which appears and certainly intends to deny the capacities we have called autonomy.

48. For a suggestion of how such a consideration may be relevant to the injustice in contemporary America of the death penalty, see David A. J. Richards, "Human Rights

and the Moral Foundations of the Substantive Criminal Law," *Georgia Law Review* 13 (1979), 1395–1446, esp. 1442–45. Cf. ibid., 1432–33.

49. For an example of the scope of investigtion that may be called for, see Charles E. Lindblom, *Politics and Markets* (New York: Basic Books, 1977).

50. See R. M. Hare, *The Language of Morals* (New York: Oxford University Press, 1964), and *Freedom and Reason* (Oxford: Clarendon Press, 1963). For a forceful critique, see G. J. Warnock, *Contemporary Moral Philosophy* (London: Macmillan Co., 1967), 30–47. Cf. Richards, *A Theory of Reasons for Actions* 215–16.

51. See Leslie H. Farber, *The Ways of the Will: Essays toward a Psychology and Psychopathology of Will* (New York: Basic Books, 1966); see esp. pp. 105, 205 for discussions of willfulness; see also Leslie H. Farber, *Lying, Despair, Jealousy, Envy, Sex, Suicide, Drugs, and the Good Life* (New York: Basic Books, 1976).

52. See Farber, *Ways of the Will*, 32.

53. See, in general, Adam Smith, *The Wealth of Nations* (New York: Modern Library, 1937). The deeper normative theory underlying Smith's seminal economic theory appears to be a form of benevolent impartial spectator theory leading to utilitarianism. See Adam Smith, *The Theory of Moral Sentiments* (Indianapolis: Liberty Classics, 1976). The central philosophical statement of this normative theory was made by David Hume. See Hume, *A Treatise of Human Nature*, ed. L. A. Selby-Bigge (Oxford: Clarendon Press, 1964), Bk. 3; see also Hume, *An Enquiry concerning the Principles of Morals,* in *Enquiries*, ed. L. A. Selby-Bigge (Oxford: Clarendon Press, 1902).

54. For an extended development of this kind of analogy, see F. A. Hayek, *The Constituion of Liberty* (Chicago: University of Chicago Press, 1960).

55. See Robert Nozick, *Anarchy, State and Utopia* (New York: Basic Books, 1974). For critical commentary, see a review by D. A. J. Richards in *Detroit College Law Review* 3 (1976), 675–85; T. Nagel, "Libertarianism without Foundations," *Yale Law Journal* 85 (1975), 136–49; Hart, 80–86. See also Ronald Dworkin, *Taking Rights Seriously*, 259, and "LIberty and Liberalism," ch. 11. For an example of a related form of argument in the legal literature, see Richard A. Epstein, "A Theory of Strict Liability," *Journal of Legal Studies* 2 (1973), 151–204, who argues, inter alia, that autonomy as egoism justifies the lack of a good samaritan doctrine in the law of torts (see 189–204). In fact, Epstein, I believe, quite misconstrues and therefore misapplies the Kantian doctrine of autonomy to the problem of the good samaritan. See Richards, *The Moral Criticism of Law*, 221–25, for the suggestion of an alternative view. See also Richards, "Human Rights," 1429–30.

56. See, e.g., Karl Marx, *The Economic and Philosophic Manuscripts of 1844*, ed. Dirk J. Struik (New York: International Publishers, 1964).

57. See R. M. Unger, *Knowledge and Politics* (New York: Free Press, 1975); and my review of Unger's book in *Fordham Law Review* 44 (1976): 873–76. For a recent form of his critique of autonomy in the legal literature, see Duncan Kennedy, "Legal Formality," *Journal of Legal Studies* 2 (1973): 351–98.

58. Indeed, Kant expressly distinguishes the value of autonomy as a form of inestimable dignity from any notion of pricing, market or otherwise; see *Foundations*, p. 53.

59. See the discussion of the acting from moral duty as opposed to benevolent or other motives in ibid., 14–22.

60. Cf. Kant's contrasts of sympathy with the rights of man, ibid., 41, 53, 60.

61. See Bernard Williams, "Persons, Character and Morality," in *The Identities of Persons*, ed. Amélie O. Rorty (Berkeley and Los Angeles: University of California Press,

1976), 197–216. Much more needs to be said in reply to Williams. I would, for example, not now defend everything in my early views on the relations of love and morality that Williams labels "righteous absurdity" (p. 212). But his general argument is, for reasons sketched in the text, wrong. For any more recent reflections on the relations of sex, love, and morality, see David A. J. Richards, "Commercial Sex and the Rights of the Person: A Moral Argument for the Decriminalization of Prostitution," *University of Pennsylvania Law Review* 127 (1979), 1195–1287.

62. Cf., for example, the psychoanalytic distinctions between narcissistic primary love (derived from early parental attachments) and the development of the capacity for the mutualities of reciprocal genital love. For a brilliant set of investigations of these data, see Michael Balint, *Primary Love and Psycho-analytic Technique* (New York: Liveright Publishing Corp., 1965), chs. 5, 6, and 7.

63. See David A. J. Richards, "Unnatural Acts and the Constitutional Right to Privacy: A Moral Theory," *Fordham Law Review* 45 (1977), 1281–1348; "Sexual Autonomy and the Constitutional Right to Privacy: A Case Study in Human Rights and the Unwritten Constitution," *Hastings Law Journal* 30 (1979), 957–1018; "Commercial Sex," see n. 61 above.

64. See Rawls, *A Theory of Justice*, 136–42.

65. See Gewirth, *Reason and Morality*, 48–128.

66. See critical commentaries cited in n. 55, above.

67. For a fuller exploration of the conceptual links among these concepts, see Richards, *A Theory of Reasons for Action*, 92–106.

68. See Dworkin, "Liberalism," 90–94, 188–92.

69. It is crucial to distinguish the ideas of teleological and consequentialist moral theories. Kantian moral theory is deontological, which means that it is nonteleological. Cf. Rawls, *A Theory of Justice*, 30, 40. But both teleological and deonotological moral theories may be consequentialist, in the sense of what conduct conforms to ethical principles crucially turns on the assessment of the consequences of acting on the principle.

70. See, e.g., R. A. Posner, "Utilitarianism, Economics, and Legal Theory," *Journal of Legal Studies* 8 (1979), 103–40, esp. 104, n. 4. See also Bruce A. Ackerman, *Private Property and the Constitution* (New Haven, Conn.: Yale University Press, 1977), pp. 71–72.

71. Rawls, *A Theory of Justice*, ch. 3. See also Richards, *A Theory of Reasons for Actions*, ch. 6.

72. Gewirth, *Reason and Morality*, ch. 2–3.

73. See Rawls, *A Theory of Justice*, pp. 150–61. Of course, Gewirth and Rawls do not agree in all substantive particulars; Gewirth, for example, resists Rawls's thoroughgoing invocation of the maximin strategy. But, their theories share a broad consensus on many substantive moral questions, so that we may, for present purposes, highlight their Kantian common ground.

74. In one striking passage, Sidgwick concludes: "I obtain the self-evident principle that the good of any individual is of no more importance, from the point of view (if I may say so) of the Universe, than the good of any other" (Henry Sidgwick, *The Methods of Ethics*, 7th ed. [London: Macmillan Co., 1963], 382).

75. See Kant, *Foundations,* 53.

14

Lives and Liberty

James Rachels and William Ruddick

The God who gave us life gave us liberty at the same time; the hand of force may destroy but cannot disjoin them.

> Thomas Jefferson,
> *A Summary View of the*
> *Rights of British America* (1774)

Philosophy ought to help us understand matters that previously were mysterious. But it may first have to teach us what is mysterious, for we take some things so much for granted that it requires an effort to see them as problematic. Liberty is a case in point. We value liberty as much as we value anything. Political thinkers from Locke to Rawls treat liberty, after life itself, as the supreme political value; and the major declarations of human rights take the same view. The problem is to explain *why* liberty is so important to us. What is it about liberty, or freedom, that makes it so valuable?

Our problem is not new. Many philosophers have addressed it, and three main types of explanations have been devised. We will begin by reviewing these traditional accounts. Then we will present our own account, which is based on a new idea, but which we think preserves the elements of the traditional views that are worth preserving.

1. Traditional Explanations

Liberty as Intrinsically Good

Some philosophers have argued that liberty is intrinsically good. On this view, freedom is important simply because of what it is in itself. It is a mistake, these philosophers say, to look for the importance of freedom in its consequences.

James Rachels is Professor of Philosophy at the University of Alabama/Birmingham.
William Ruddick is Professor of Philosophy at New York University.

Free choices do not necessarily have better results, nor are people necessarily better off, on the whole, when they are acting freely. But that does not matter, for freedom has its own intrinsic value, that makes it worth having for its own sake.

Gregory Vlastos takes this view in his well-known essay "Justice and Equality."[1] Vlastos relies upon an argument from analogy. His strategy is to compare the value of liberty with the value of enjoyment (which he thinks is clearly intrinsically good) and to suggest that they should be thought of in similar terms. In both cases, he says, it is the nature of the thing and not its uses that makes it good. The value of enjoyment is self-evident; it needs no further explanation. And the value of liberty, he adds, is self-evident in the same way.

We believe that the comparison of liberty with enjoyment is illuminating, but for an entirely different reason than Vlastos suggests. A closer comparison of the two does not support Vlastos's conclusion. On the contrary, it suggests just the opposite. In the case of enjoyment, what Vlastos says is plausible enough. We have little difficulty understanding that enjoyment is good simply because of what it is like. Its goodness is transparent. (It is tempting to think that this is because the goodness of enjoyment is guaranteed by its definition, although this is not an easy thought to make out in detail.) But liberty does not seem to be like that. Its value is not similarly transparent (nor does i,   m plausible to think that it is good "by definition"). To say that enjoyment is good in itself seems right; to say that liberty is good in itself is merely puzzling. Therefore, we would argue this way: we agree that enjoyment is intrinsically good, if anything is, but the goodness of liberty does not seem to be comparable; hence, it is doubtful that the goodness of liberty should be understood as intrinsic goodness.

We should be careful not to confuse the notion that liberty (or anything else) is intrinsically good with the different notion that its goodness is self-evident. They are different notions, the first having to do with the kind of goodness it has, the second having to do with the manner and ease with which we recognize it. Nevertheless, it may be thought that the two notions are related in this way: if something is intrinsically good, then we should be able to apprehend its goodness just by focusing our minds on its nature. I take it that this is what Vlastos has in mind when he says that the value of liberty is self-evident.

But this is a difficult view to defend, for its plausibility depends entirely on how readily others will agree. If one cannot simply "see" that something is valuable, without need of further explanation, then one can hardly be convinced that the value is self-evident. And in fact critics have often objected that they cannot simply "see" the value of liberty.[2] How could defenders of this view respond? They are in a difficult position, because the logic of their view prevents them from offering additional explanations of liberty's value. If, in order to make its value plainer, they explain it in some other terms, they run the risk of abandoning the view they are trying to defend, because intrinsic value is by definition not derived from anything else.

Liberty as Instrumentally Good

Rather than having intrinsic worth, liberty may be thought to have "instrumental value," that is, to be desirable because of the pleasure and other consequences it produces. The classic statement of this view was provided by James Fitzjames Stephen, who suggested that "the question whether liberty is a good or a bad thing appears as irrational as the question of whether fire is a good or a bad thing."[3] If one's house is burning, the fire is a bad thing; if the fire is heating one's food, it is a good thing. The fire has no value, positive or negative, apart from the circumstances. Similarly, Stephen argued, liberty has no value apart from its uses. He contended, for example, that if someone freely chooses to do good, then it is good that he was free to choose; but if he chooses evil, it would have been better for him to have been compelled to have acted differently.

This view is also unsatisfying, for it implies that, when the consequences of liberty and compulsion are the same, there is nothing to choose between them. This does not seem right. Suppose a person would choose good, if left free to choose, but is compelled to the "right" option without being given a choice. On the face of it, there seems something objectionable here; but the objection cannot be to the consequences, for they are identical. How could Stephen, or anyone taking his general approach, account for this?

It might be thought that free choice of the good will always have one major benefit, namely strengthening the agent's character. By contrast, being forced to the right action would have no effects, or would even have deleterious effects, on character. (Compelled too often as children to share, we may become misers in later life.) But surely the moral benefits of choice over compulsion are not so general or so evident. Many choices are not choices of the good, but only of the pleasant, the expedient, or the familiar. Do these choices generally build character? (Perhaps they *manifest* character, but why is that desirable—except for the Recording Angel gathering data for God's Final Judgment?) And even in the case of moral good, is every choice character building or preserving? Only perhaps in the early stages of life or in special conditions—emergencies, novel temptations, and the like.

Liberty as Necessary for Self-Realization

This concern for character suggests a third, more plausible type of explanation for liberty's value. It may be valued as a *necessary condition* for the existence of something else that is generally and undeniably valuable. (This type of explanation is easily confused with the view that liberty is instrumentally good, but they are importantly different.) The standard version of this view is that liberty is necessary for developing not only moral character but a whole range of human capacities—it is necessary for developing one's potential as a human being. Joel Feinberg summarizes the argument like this:

> The highest good for man is neither enjoyment nor passive contentment but rather a dynamic process of growth and self-realization. Self-realization

consists in the actualization of certain uniquely human potentialities, the bringing to full development of certain powers and abilities. This in turn requires constant practice in making difficult choices among alternative hypotheses, policies, and actions.[4]

The point is not that such self-development is a *consequence* of being free; it is that freedom is one of the important *conditions* without which this personal growth cannot take place. Freedom makes such growth possible, although it does not make it inevitable.

Mill's View

We believe that each of these three explanations is flawed. However, each has its own special appeal, and it is tempting to affirm that each of them is *in some sense* correct. John Stuart Mill, who was no fool about these matters, did exactly that.

In *On Liberty* Mill seems, in different places, to endorse all three of these views. In one place, he speaks as though liberty is intrinsically good: "all restraint, *qua* restraint, is an evil . . . [L]eaving people to themselves is always better, *ceteris paribus*, than controlling them."[5] The italicized Latin phrases imply that, even if the consequences of freedom and compulsion are the same, freedom is still to be preferred. One would not expect the author of *Utilitarianism* to say such a thing.

In fact, when Mill turns to the discussion of particular freedoms, such as freedom of speech, he reverts to consequentialist arguments: he assumes, compatibly with his general utilitarian approach, that if free speech is to be defended it must be shown to have desirable consequences. So he argues that without freedom of speech it would be much harder for us to come to know and appreciate the truth.[6]

Finally, in still another place, Mill is at his most eloquent in setting out the self-realization argument:

> He who lets the world, or his own portion of it, choose his plan of life for him has no need of any other faculty than the ape-like one of imitation. He who chooses his plan for himself employs all his faculties. He must use observation to see, reasoning and judgment to foresee, activity to gather materials for decision, discrimination to decide, and when he has decided, firmness and self-control to hold to his deliberate decision. . . . It is possible that he might be guided in some good path, and kept out of harm's way, without any of these things. But what will be his comparative worth as a human being? It really is of importance, not only what men do, but also what manner of men they are that do it. Among the works of man which human life is rightly employed in perfecting and beautifying, the first in importance is surely man himself.[7]

An adequate theory of the value of liberty should provide some understanding of why these three views, even if they are mistaken, are so appealing. At the end of this essay, after we have presented our own view, we will offer an explanation of their attractiveness.

2. From Persons to Lives

Of the three traditional explanations, the self-realization argument, we think, comes closest to the truth: liberty is important because it is a necessary condition for the development of one's human potentialities, or to use a currently fashionable term, one's personhood. This way of putting the matter, however, invites some awkward questions. If one is supposed to develop "as a person," *which* human potentialities are thereby singled out for cultivation? (Which of our many potentialities are associated with personhood, and why?) Why should these potentialities take priority over others, or over indolent self-acceptance of one's undeveloped state? And exactly what kind of folly or confusion do we commit if we do not strive to "perfect and beautify" ourselves through development of these potentialities?

These problems of selection and motivation (Which are the person-making traits and why should I prize them?) may be awkward because ill-formulated. Personhood, we think, is a notion too *formal* to yield determinate answers to these questions. Person-making traits vary with context. In religious settings, persons are those beings whom God has created or endowed with souls. ('Person' and 'soul' are often used as though they were synonymous.) In political discourse, persons are those who possess whatever characteristics are deemed necessary for legal protection and standing. Property, race, gender, and age are the most familiar categories. For Locke, it was personal memory, a prerequisite for legal punishment and reward, that gave one the "forensic" status of personhood. But for most philosophers, it is the more demanding (and self-celebrating) capacity for rationality that makes someone a person.

Despite these contextual variations, there is a common thread, namely, the connection between personhood and equal treatment. By definition, persons are entitled to equal treatment (in context-relevant regards) in virtue of their (context-relative) common features. As besouled children of God, we are equally the objects of divine love, and therefore equally entitled to one another's regard. As legal persons, we are entitled equally to the attention of the courts. However striking our differences, we are equal in the eyes of God, or of the law, or of Kant.

Indeed, the rhetorical and moral point of claiming personhood is to override those striking differences and to challenge the unequal treatment to which they give rise. (Hence, the cry "They are persons, too!" from advocates of women, blacks, fetuses, or handicapped people.) Accordingly, personhood is a prescriptive or normative notion with pointedly little descriptive content. Attempts to list defining properties[8] are, we think, misguided by the assumption that personhood is a discernible condition, secular or metaphysical. Rather, personhood is a status conferred (on secular or metaphysical grounds) in the interests of equal treatment in some respect or other.

Liberty, by contrast, is not invoked to set aside differences, but to protect and foster them. Although seeming abstract, liberty is an umbrella for a wide variety of specific rights and privileges that determine the texture of daily life.

It is the heading under which we strive to bring, with legal aid, our reading, writing, working, childbearing and rearing, social and sexual associations, and so on. Equality is a much more formal, law-theoretical, institutional notion. It is appropriate that immigrants sailed past a Statue of Liberty with a torch to light their way, not a Statue of Equality blindfolded against discriminatory judgments.

In short, personhood is too remote to capture liberty's high value on the third view we are examining. Indeed, the "cultivation and perfection of person-hood" has little sense on our account: one cannot cultivate equality, or the metaphysical properties that confer religious equality, or the secular character-istics that have been deemed to confer political equality (being white, adult, male). What is needed is a notion closer to home and the specific activities liberty protects.

Although closely related to personhood, the familiar notion of *a life* has the right degree of domestic specificity. Only persons have lives, but some persons have several lives, concurrently or serially—and some have none. We'll say more later about persons and lives, but it is the relation between lives and liberty we now wish to foster. The idea we propose is: *Without liberty, a person cannot have a life.* We do not mean that a person without liberty cannot have a good life, or a productive or satisfying life, or anything of that sort. The point is more radical than that. It is that, without liberty, a person cannot have a life *at all.*

If this initially paradoxical claim can be made out, the importance of liberty should be transparent. If liberty is necessary for having a life, then to question the value of liberty is to question the value of having a life. In dire circumstances, we might become indifferent to life itself. But given our usual attachments and projects, we cannot sensibly or seriously ask, Why should I care about my life?

3. Having a Life

To begin to make these claims plausible, we need to distinguish two notions that, in English, are expressed by similar words. We need to distinguish *being alive* from *having a life.*[9] The former is fundamentally a biological notion: To be alive is (roughly) to be a functioning, self-preserving organism. The latter is, by contrast, a notion of biography rather than biology. The lives we have and lead are constituted by certain kinds of actions, attitudes, emotions, and social relations outside the biologist's ken.

The importance of the distinction may be doubted, for two reasons. First, our biographies are shaped in various ways by our biology. Our life-possibili-ties and the actual course of our life (our *bios*) are partly defined by our congenital "equipment," our states of health, by our age and expected life span, and so on. Biological events (such as puberty and menopause) are crucial in determining life's stages. Second, biological existence is a condition for biogra-phy: if you are not alive, you cannot have a life. Stars, nations, concepts, and errors may have histories, but they do not have lives—unless we invest them anthropomorphically with agency and appropriate psychology.

But neither consideration casts real doubt on the distinction. On the contrary, by understanding the *relation* between the two notions, we can explain a number of things—for example, it is precisely this dependence of lives upon life that explains our attitudes in some of the most important areas of morality. Consider the morality of killing. The dependence of lives upon life explains our gradations of attitude about killing. In losing their biological existence, the usual victims of homocide necessarily lose their biographical lives as well. But it is the latter, not the former, that is the morally objectionable loss and is the proper object of moral protection.[10] To the extent that people have ceased to have biographical lives (as, for example, the irreversibly comatose), killing becomes less objectionable. (There may, of course, be other grounds for opposing euthanasia.) And to the degree that animals of other species lack the capacity for lives, to that degree our objections to killing them (painlessly) for food, clothing, and scientific study diminish. (Again, there may be other grounds for opposing these uses of animals.)[11]

It has sometimes been argued (by Tooley, for example) that killing an individual is objectionable if and only if that individual has a self-conception. We think it is better to say that killing is objectionable just in case the victim is the subject of a life. But the two notions are related. An individual who has a self-conception will have a far richer and more complex life than one who does not. A life consisting only of such activities as could be described without self-reference would be skimpy indeed. Moreover, the subjects of such lives would be incapable of attitudes such as pride, shame, embarrassment, fear, and obligation, for those attitudes, and others like them, are irreducibly self-referring. 'Self-referring' here does not mean only or even primarily egocentric or narcissistic frames of mind, but rather merely those in which one figures in the content of one's own thoughts. Such thoughts may be solely self-directed (I am proud of what I have accomplished) or other-directed (How may I be of comfort to him?). Or they may fall in between (I am embarrassed by the conduct of someone with whom I am closely associated).

These self-referring attitudes presuppose a sense of oneself as having an existence spread over past and future time. In having plans, hopes, and regrets, one considers one's present condition as part of a temporally extended existence. This is obviously true of people with careers or with the "life plans" often invoked in philosophical discussion.[12] But so, too, for people who on epicurean principles "take life one day at a time," as well as for people whose dire circumstances reduce them to living for the next meal. Even if keeping oneself alive is one's sole "project," this struggle involves a conception of an existence to be prolonged or an extinction to be postponed.

For this sense of self over time, we need capacities for memory and anticipation. (I must remember not only that a promise was made that someone would attend next week, but I must remember that I promised to be there.) These very capacities are also cited as necessary conditions of personhood.[13] There is a close connection, as we said, between having a life and being a person: only persons have lives. But the concepts are not paired one-to-one: a person may have more than one life or none. On certain metaphysical accounts, a person may have several incarnations and hence several lives. Less debatably, a person may lead a double life or a new life, often marked by different names, projects, and styles of dress.

On analysis, perhaps a double life if not two simultaneous lives, but a single life with two aspects; likewise, an old life and a new life may prove to be best counted as two stages or phases of the same life (as, e.g., in the case of religious or political converts). But these questions of individuation or enumeration need not be decided here. Our concern is not with people who have multiple lives (or life stages) but with persons who have none. This may seem impossible: how could someone without a life continue to qualify as a person? The answer lies in the relative abstractness we have noted. A being might retain the capacity for social responses and yet have none of the intentions, plans, and other features of will and action that define a life. The prime candidates for this lamentable condition are people subject to extreme duress, passivity, or restriction. The most obvious cases are victims of dire poverty, illness, and slavery.

Lifeless poverty is that condition of physical need in which even single-minded foraging and fighting for food and shelter have ceased. One becomes wholly and passively dependent on the charity of others. (Victims of war and drought standing silently in relief camp lines are harrowing examples.) Likewise, the seriously ill may be unable to "fight for life" or to manifest the military and athletic virtues expected of hospital patients.[14] Although still capable of socially appropriate expressions of pain, indignation, and gratitude, they may not be able to participate or cooperate in their own care. Again, passive dependence on the decisions and aid of others is their lifeless condition.

4. Can a Slave Have a Biography?

In our society, poverty is not viewed as a deprivation of liberty, nor is hospitalization.[15] Thus, persons whom poverty or illness deprive of any life of their own may not convincingly illustrate our thesis about lives and liberty. Slavery is a clearer test of our slogan "No Liberty, No Life." Does a slave have a life? It might seem so: witness the wealth of slave biographies, especially from the antebellum southern United States.[16] These narratives, first or secondhand, tell of the slaves' efforts to maintain family ties and community. In one study of American slave communities (significantly entitled *From Sundown to Sunup*) there are scenes such as this: "Cooking was usually done outdoors or in a cooking shed; people sat out in front of the cabins and talked and smoked; children played in front of the huts; young men and women courted wherever they could find privacy; gossip was exchanged while engaging in common chores outdoors."[17] Such scenes were, of course, subject to disruption by rape, whip, forced march, or sale. No slave system, it seems, allows permanent family ties among parents, spouses, and children. This "geneological isolation" has taken various forms: Turkish sultans recruited slaves from Christian parents and castrated them, thereby insuring that they would remain perpetual aliens (and objects of fear among Turkish subjects). Just as they suffer "natal alienation" from parents and a past, so slaves are denied a future, living from day to day solely on the whims and mercy of their masters. As such, slaves are made wholly dependent on their masters' definitions of social possibilities and welfare. Slaves have no social existence apart from their masters; they are, accordingly, "socially dead persons," remaining forever "unborn beings (non-né)."[18]

The disappearances of the slave's own life, and its replacement by that of the master, is remarked upon by Simone Weil in her essay on the *Iliad*. In describing the condition of captives, and their radical dependence upon their captors, she writes that:

> for those upon whom it [sc. slavery] has fallen, so brutal a destiny wipes out damnations, revolts, comparisons, meditations upon the future and the past, almost memory itself. It does not belong to the slave to be faithful to his city or to his dead.
>
> It is when one of those who made him lose all, who sacked his city, massacred his own under his very eyes, when one of those suffers, then the slave weeps. And why not? Only then are tears permitted him. . . . On no occasion has the slave a right to express anything if not that which may please the master. That is why, if in so barren a life, a capacity to love should be born, this love could only be for the master. Every other way is barred to the gift of loving, just as for a horse hitched to a wagon, the reins and the bridle bar all directions but one. And if by miracle there should appear the hope of becoming again someone, to what pitch would not that gratitude and that love soar for those very men who must still, because of the recent past, inspire horror? . . . One cannot lose more than the slave loses, he loses all inner life.[19]

Or, as we would put it, a "barren life" with no "inner life" is no life at all. It is, rather, the condition of a tool, or part of the life of another. Weil argues this is indeed the condition of modern factory work, in which workers are made lifeless parts of the productive machine. Only in their nonworking hours can they recover a life of their own. For Weil, workers, like slaves, have biographies only to the extent that they can escape the subordination of will and loss of self-involvement imposed by their overseers.[20]

Few slaves are, however, completely denied ties with the past or hopes for a future free of a master's caprice or anger.[21] For many slaves, a sense of themselves turned on a hope for eventual release, either before or after death. These hopes, however slight, allowed for an imagined life of one's own, free of a master's desires or threat of punishment. The mere possibility of such a distinct life creates a distinction between the slave's will and the master's, and fosters the self-referring attitudes cited above as life-defining.

In most cases, then, slaves do have lives, at least of a minimum kind. Nevertheless, our hypothesis—that liberty is necessary for having a life—is confirmed by the dependence of a slave's having a life or there being a part of his existence that is under his own control. Suppose this part is eliminated. In imagination, let us call someone for whom *everything* is dictated a *total slave*.

The total slave will make no decisions. Every action, from the time he wakes up until he goes to sleep again, will be dictated. Moreover, let us imagine that the master even decrees what the slave thinks as well, so that there is no area of life over which the slave retains control. *This* individual is not the subject of a life. He is like a robot or a tool; we can describe the part he plays in the master's life, but he has no life of his own. Real slaves may have biographies, but only because they are not total slaves.

5. Conclusion

Patterson claims that slavery is the basic notion from which our very conception of liberty derives.[22] Be that as it may, slavery enables us to see the value of freedom and to understand both the attractions and the deficiencies of the three traditional explanations cited at the outset. Those who argued that liberty is intrinsically good were right to insist that it is better to choose to do something freely than to be compelled to do it, even if the outcome is the same. In general, on our account, freely chosen actions are constitutive elements of one's life, while forced actions are interruptions, limitations, or obstacles in that life. Free actions define and execute our characteristic intentions and projects; coerced actions tend to brook or thwart them. In the rare case in which we are compelled to do what we would otherwise have chosen to do, the action falls outside our life (and within the life of our coercer), and to that extent it is a loss for us.

Consider a young person trying to start or lead the life of a painter. An insensitive teacher might instruct the student to complete the painting in a way she would have hit upon herself, thereby preventing the work from being wholly hers. (It is, in a way, the instructor's painting now, too.) Even if she thereby loses no self-respect, adrenalin, or opportunities, the painting does not have the place in her life it otherwise would have had. From a public, or third-party point of view, that may not be objectionable. But from "inside" the life, such "biographical losses" are undesirable, even if they involve no specific pains, loss of pleasure, or even loss of pride. ("Biographical losses" may even occur through coercion intended to spare us pain. Consider the case of a woman intent on natural childbirth whose labor is terminated by anesthetics and forceps.) Since our intentional lives are in a sense our closest possessions, losses cannot be a matter of indifference to the livers, or leaders, of those lives.

Our concern, however, is not to show that lives have intrinsic worth, or to argue that liberty makes beneficial contributions to lives. Both claims are either obscure or dubious, or both. We have undertaken to explicate a version of the third, "self-realization" argument for liberty. Mill praises freedom because, without it, we would have no occasion for developing our powers of observation, reasoning, and the like. But why is it important to develop these abilities? It is not that these powers are ends-in-themselves, and it is not simply, as Mill put it, "to perfect and beautify man." By exercising these capacities in making choices persons create their lives: liberty makes lives not beautiful, but possible. But this is not to say that liberty is like air, causally necessary for lives. Rather, it is like motion, a component of living. Liberty constitutes our lives through the free choices and actions that embody it.[23]

The quotation from Thomas Jefferson that stands at the beginning of this chapter expresses a conviction common among liberal writers: that freedom is so important that without it life is not worthwhile. But if our thesis is correct, the connection between life and liberty is even closer than that. Jefferson's words can be understood in a stronger sense: the hand of force may destroy, but it cannot (logically cannot) disjoin them.

Notes

1. Gregory Vlastos, "Justice and Equality," in *Social Justice*, ed. Richard B. Brandt (Englewood Cliffs, N.J.: Prentice-Hall, 1962).

2. See, for example, J. D. Mabbott, *The State and the Citizen* (London: Hutchinson, 1967), ch. 7. In any case, there is ample reason for doubting that the value of liberty is self-evident. Sartre found freedom "dreadful" and expounded upon our desperate desire to escape it; evangelists and dictators speak knowingly, if paradoxically, about the "freedom" of obedience to a "higher will," and, unfortunately, there has been no shortage of people eager to respond to such appeals. This is enough by itself to make us doubt that the value of liberty will be found in a phenomenological analysis of the experience of it, no matter how that analysis is refined.

3. James Fitzjames Stephen, *Liberty, Equality, Fraternity* (London, 1873), 48.

4. Joel Feinberg, *Social Philosophy* (Englewood Cliffs, N.J.: Prentice-Hall, 1973), 21.

5. John Stuart Mill, *On Liberty*, David Spitz, ed. (New York: Norton, 1975), 88.

6. *On Liberty*, Ch. 2.

7. *On Liberty, op. cit.*, p. 56.

8. See Michael Tooley's analysis in "Abortion and Infanticide," *Philosophy and Public Affairs* Vol. 2, no. 1 (1972) 37–65 and Joseph Fletcher's longer list of person-making characteristics in *Humanhood* (Buffalo: Prometheus, 1979). Tooley's more detailed account is given in his book *Abortion and Infanticide* (Oxford: Clarendon Press, 1983). Mary Anne Warren's defense of abortion in her article "Abortion and the Concept of a Person," *The Monist* 57 (1973) also proceeds from a list of characteristics that she takes to be definitive of personhood.

9. Ancient Greek distinguishes *zoe*, animal life, from *bios*, the course of life. Similar possible distinctions may be found in German, French, and Hindi. In English we have to resort to grammatical devices: life, for the biological, and *a life* for the biographical.

10. This idea is elaborated in J. Rachels, *The End of Life: Euthanasia and Morality* (New York: Oxford University Press, 1986).

11. See, for example, J. Rachels, "Vegetarianism and 'The Other Weight Problem,'" in *World Hunger and Moral Obligation*, ed. William Aiken and Hugh LaFollette (Englewood Cliffs, N.J.: Prentice-Hall, 1977), 180–93.

12. The notion of a life plan occurs (with increasing, but still sketchy analysis) in the writings of Mill, Sidgwick, Royce, Rawls, Fried, and Nozick. Richard Wollheim has offered a detailed account of what it means to *lead* a life in his *The Thread of Life*

(Cambridge, Mass.: Harvard University Press, 1984). A somewhat different account in a different context is sketched in William Ruddick, "Parents and Life Prospects," in *Having Children*, ed. Onora O'Neill and William Ruddick (New York: Oxford University Press, 1979). Also see Rachels, *The End of Life*, ch. 3.

13. Locke, for example, apparently believed that the connections of memory are what make one the "same person" at different times. The Lockean account of personal identity is familiar: suppose we let X and Y name persons existing at different times, X being the earlier. On this view, X and Y are the same person if and only if Y remembers doing what X did, thinking what X thought, and so on. [John Locke, *An Essay Concerning Human Understanding* (1690), Bk 2, Sec 27.] This account has been criticized on various grounds, but its most basic flaw can be exposed by considering the case of total amnesia. If someone loses his memory, does he thereby become a different person? No, for there are too many other connections that remain intact. So Locke seems to have been wrong.

Nevertheless, there is *something* tempting in the idea that the amnesiac has become a "different person," and this temptation is worth analyzing. How is the amnesiac's plight to be understood? We believe the amnesiac's plight is not that he has become a different person, but that he is alienated from his life. He is (temporarily) without a life, forced to "start over." Even if he takes up the same projects he formerly pursued—the same job, the same family, etc.—he adopts them as one might try to fit oneself into someone else's life. He can feel pride in past accomplishments, or regret over past misdeeds, only by the effort of reminding himself, "they were mine," and not in the natural way provided by unprompted memory. Locke was right to think that the connections of memory are crucial to our existence, but he gave a wrong account of why they are crucial. Memory is important, not so much to our continuing existence as persons, as to our continuing ability to lead our lives.

14. See W. Ruddick, "Patient Morality: Compliance, Perseverence, and Other Athletic Virtues," *Philosophic Exchange* 4 (1983), 87–96.

15. Socialist analyses often employ the notion of "economic liberty" in discussing the poverty that, on those analyses, capitalism allows or requires. There is a similar suggestion in Roosevelt's phrase "freedom from want." Hospitals, as much as prisons and army camps, are examples of what Erving Goffman called "total institutions." *Asylums* (Garden City, N.Y.: Aldine, 1962).

16. See, for example, Arna Bontemps, *Great Slave Narratives* (Boston: Beacon Press, 1969). Also Erleen Stetson, "Studying Slavery: Some Literary and Pedagogical Considerations on the Black Female Slave," in *But Some of Us are Brave*, ed. Gloria T. Hull, et al. (Old Westbury, N.Y.: Feminist Press, 1982).

17. George P. Rawick, *From Sundown to Sunup: The Making of the Black Community* (Westport, Conn.: Greenwood, 1972), 77.

18. Orlando Patterson, *Slavery and Social Death* (Cambridge, Mass.: Harvard University Press, 1983), 38.

19. Simone Weil, "The *Iliad*, Poem of Might," reprinted in *The Simone Weil Reader*, ed. George A. Panichas (Mt. Kisco, N.Y.: McKay, 1977), 158–59. Tolstoy gives a strikingly similar account of the emotions of a young woman in love with an older man in "Happily Ever After." Some feminist critics take such feelings to be the ideal of all traditional marriage.

20. Simone Weil, "Factory Work," *The Simone Weil Reader*, 53–72. For American analogues, see Studs Terkel, *Working* (New York: Pantheon, 1972).

21. R. M. Hare distinguishes prisoners of war from slaves on the grounds that the

former know that their condition is not permanent. "What is Wrong with Slavery," *Philosophy and Public Affairs*, Vol. 8, no. 2 (1979), 120.

22. Orlando Patterson, *Slavery and Social Death*, 341–42.

23. Our remarks may suggest a kind of individualism we do not embrace. A life may be associated with public, social, collective purposes, as well as with the narrower goals of "private" life. A life of one's own need not be a life defined by egoistic or narcissistic projects. But it does require that associations or identifications with the good of others be in some sense chosen or freely and reflectively endorsed by the liver of that more generous life.

15

Autonomy, Science, and Morality

Gerald Dworkin

The concept of autonomy has assumed increasing importance in contemporary moral theory. Appeals to the ideal of an autonomous moral agent play a role in grounding moral argument that appeals to sentiment or self-evidence or intuition played in earlier centuries. In such discussions moral judgments are often contrasted with factual or scientific judgments and claims are made about autonomy (as well as related notions such as authority and objectivity) in the moral context which are sharply distinguished from parallel claims in the scientific context. My aim in this essay is, as they say on prelims, to compare and contrast the nature of autonomy in morality and science.

Elsewhere I have characterized autonomy as the capacity of persons to critically reflect upon, and then attempt to accept or change, their preferences, desires, values, and ideals. The idea of moral autonomy is a particular case of this, and the rough idea is that persons are responsible for, and have the capacity for, determining for themselves the nature of the moral reasons, considerations and principles on which they will act.

When I speak of autonomy I shall take this to be a property of persons and I shall only indirectly be concerned with the discussion that has proceeded under the heading of the autonomy of morality, such as, the connection or lack of connection between facts and values. I am primarily concerned with autonomy as specifying certain features of persons involved in their deliberations upon moral issues. I am concerned with moral autonomy and not the autonomy of morals.

As with the general notion of autonomy, there are a number of different and incompatible specifications of the root idea of self-determination in moral matters, since the idea of moral principles being "one's own" has various interpretations. The following are possible characteristics of what it might mean to be morally autonomous.

1. A person is morally autonomous if and only if she is the author of her moral principles, their originator.

2. A person is morally autonomous if and only if she chooses her moral principles. ·

3. A person is morally autonomous if and only if the ultimate authority or source of her moral principles is her will.

4. A person is morally autonomous if and only if she decides which moral principles to accept as binding upon her.

5. A person is morally autonomous if and only if she accepts moral responsibility for the principles she acts upon.

6. A person is morally autonomous if and only if she refuses to accept others as moral authorities.[1]

These are clearly not equivalent to one another. It is one thing, and surely false, to say that a person originates *ab initio* her moral framework; quite another to say that she finds herself confronted with one but bears the responsibility for accepting and acting in accordance with it. For certain purposes, for example, to combat certain extreme subjectivist doctrines, it would be important to explore the differences among these but I am interested in formulating the doctrine in its most plausible versions and for this purpose the last three views are the ones of most interest.

Stated most broadly, the view is that in the moral sphere it is always, finally, up to us to decide what moral principles are valid and how they apply to particular situations. And this claim is often made as a conceptual thesis about the nature of morality or about the nature of moral agents.

To fail to form one's own moral opinions, solve one's own moral problems, make one's own decisions, is to fail as a moral agent.[2] "A man faced with such a problem [a moral one—GD] knows that it is his problem and that nobody can answer it for him.[3] Hare also formulates the view as one about the freedom of the moral agent: "One of the most important constituents of our freedom as moral agents, is the freedom to form our own opinions about moral questions, even if that involves changing our language."[4] Aiken takes a similar view: "As a moral being he must also, in principle, be free to decide absolutely for himself what the law really is."[5]

The question that all these quotations raise is: In what sense are moral agents free or unfree to decide upon the correctness of moral principles in a way in which they are not free or unfree to decide upon the correctness of any other proposition? Hare puts the contrast in the following strong terms:

It might be objected that moral questions are not peculiar in this respect— that we are free also to form our own opinions about such matters as whether the world is round . . . but we are free to form our own moral opinions in a much stronger sense than this. For, if we say that the world is flat, we can, in principle, be shown certain facts such that, once we have admitted them, we cannot go on saying that the world is flat without being guilty of self-contradiction or misuse of language . . . nothing of the sort can be done in morals.[6]

It is clear why Hare believes this. He has already accepted a thesis about the autonomy of morals, which is that we cannot derive a moral or normative judgment from a non-normative or factual judgment. With respect to factual judgments once one has admitted certain facts, then one has to admit whatever follows from those facts. But there are no facts from which we have to accept the truth of any nonfactual or evaluative judgments. Since we are not compelled to accept the normative judgment, then we are free to accept it or not. Hence, the autonomy of moral agents is a consequence of the autonomy of morals.

As a general view about any moral question or any factual question this view is mistaken. With respect to factual matters, or at least those whose truth depends on some evidence or reasoning as opposed to mere observation, the view is wrong on two grounds. First, there is the point that being shown certain facts does not force us to admit or accept them, and so the hypothetical, even if valid, cannot force us to accept the consequent. It might be that if I accepted the fact that this man is mortal, I must then accept the fact that some men are mortal; but why am I not free to refuse to accept the fact that this man is mortal? If it is objected that it is not rational for me to ignore evidence relevant to the truth of a proposition whose truth-value I am uncertain about, then it may be replied that it is not rational for me to ignore those considerations which provide reasons for or against accepting some moral proposition.

But, more significantly, with facts of any moderate complexity, no set of facts that are not logically equivalent to them forces me to accept their truth. Consider the very example that Hare uses—that of the roundness of the earth. This is a nonobservational fact which must be inferred from a set of observations together with a set of physical laws; the whole package constituting an explanation of the original set of facts. The roundness of the earth does not follow from other facts; it is the best explanation of them. As philosophers from Duhem to Quine have argued, it is always possible to maintain that an alternative explanation gives a better account of the facts. Now it is true that it may require *ad hoc* and silly hypotheses in order to maintain that another explanation is as good, but those who put forward silly and *ad hoc* views are not guilty of the two sins of which Hare accuses them. They are not guilty of contradicting themselves or of misusing language. Perhaps they are violating certain canons of rational practice, but since these are normative in character, by Hare's own views they are not required to abide by them unless they choose to.

Note the other side of this coin. It is at least as plausible that to deny that certain facts commit one to certain moral views is a misuse or abuse of language. To admit that I ran over your child deliberately, without excuse or justification, because I disliked you and your child, and to admit all this while maintaining that what I did is morally right, is either a misunderstanding of what moral rightness is, or we will be able to find other moral judgments I make which are inconsistent with this one.

I

The immediate problem is to give a characterization of moral autonomy which at least, prima facie, does appear to differentiate our acceptance of moral judgments from those of some contrast class—preferably scientific judgments.

The essence of the thesis is a connection between the authority or binding-ness of moral judgments on a person and their acceptance or acknowledgment. A conceptual connection is asserted between the acknowledgment of a moral principle and its being authoritative. A corollary of all this is the denial of moral authority. All these connections are supposed to be different in the case of nonmoral judgments.

> No one can be expected to conform his judgment and his will to certain alleged objective principles which he has not in conscience made absolutely his own . . . [an] authority can make no moral claims upon anyone who does not adopt it as his authority.[7]

> The moral agent may learn from others about his moral obligations, but only in the sense that a mathematician learns from other mathematicians— namely, by hearing from them arguments whose validity he recognizes even though he did not think of them himself. He does not learn in the sense that one learns from an explorer, by accepting as true his accounts of things one cannot see for oneself.[8]

Let us consider each of these points in turn, and, in particular, see if the contrast being drawn with the truth or claims upon our belief of nonmoral judgments is as sharp as these views suggest.

First, it seems to me that the quote from Wolff is not correct, even for the mathematician. Mathematicians often accept results of other mathematicians without going through the proofs themselves. And, if it is replied that at least in principle they could assess the proof, the recent advent of proofs based on computer computations makes that notion of "in principle" very dubious.

More importantly, this view seems to deny an entire tradition of moral philosophy which has Aristotle as its first and most important figure. Accord-ing to Aristotle moral virtue is a disposition to choose which is developed in the process of choosing. We do not do good acts because we are already good (at first, anyway). We do good acts and, in doing so, become good. How do we identify those acts which are good? By aiming at the mean which is determined by the proper rule. How do we identify the proper rule? It is the rule by which a morally virtuous and practically wise person would determine his action. So, to become morally virtuous we must follow the example or precept of one who is practically wise. This does seem to be the picture of learning from an explorer who sees things we cannot see for ourself.

Similarly, when we go to others for moral advice, it is not just to hear arguments whose validity we recognize but could not think of ourselves. We may be presented with reasons or facts to consider which we had not recognized as relevant and about whose validity we are unclear. We may simply trust the judgment of our adviser.

In any case, it is quite clear that much of what we learn about the moral life is not acquired in any conscious and deliberate fashion. We imitate exemplary individuals, follow the reasoning and perceptions of persons who are significant and important to us, and we learn far more than we are taught. This is as true, say, for our acquisition of language as for our moral reasoning. If there is a notion of authority here, it is authority of the deed and not of the word.

So far I have argued that there are certainly cases in which it makes sense to think of one relying upon the advice and judgment of others in moral matters. I now want to point out how a version of the autonomy thesis is plausible as an account of what justifies authority in science. For the notion of scientific authority rests upon the acceptance and acknowledgment of canons of evidence, of ideals of explanation, of norms of theory construction, and of norms of relevance. Nothing forces a scientist to accept one rather than another of these presuppositions for the idea of authority making sense. Thus, one could argue that there is freedom to form our own opinions about factual questions, although the existence of this freedom is concealed by the fact that there is fairly widespread agreement about the preconditions for authoritative judgment in various areas of empirical knowledge. Indeed, one might say that it is the existence of this consensus which demarcates, at least descriptively, science from pseudoscience.

Consider, for example, what a scientific dispute among the following might look like: a quantum mechanic, a Christian Scientist, an astrologer, a psychiatrist, and a phrenologist. In the absence of shared norms about what counts as explanation, of what good science is, of the criteria that are relevant to the acceptance or rejection of theories, of the weight to be attached to competing criteria, of the importance of conflicting observations or thought experiments, it will look very much as if it is up to each person to form his own judgment about the "facts."[9] There will be no notion of authority other than the kind of thing Aiken suggests when he says that authority can make no claim upon those who do not accept it as authoritative. We would have the epistemological equivalent of existentialism.

It should not be thought that such a difference in norms of inquiry only takes place among what might be called epistemological deviants. If one looks, for example, at the type of criteria that Aristotle and Plato used to evaluate theories, one sees that the history of science is, in part, a history of the development of various evaluative schemes. For them scientific knowledge involves knowing the final causes of events, that for the sake of which they exist. Mechanism and efficient causes are a lower form of knowledge. Hence, different sorts of consideration would be relevant in assessing the truth of scientific theories.

As another instance, consider the following passage from Descartes concerning his two laws of motion:

> But even if all that our senses have ever experienced in the actual world would seem manifestly to be contrary to what is contained in these two rules, the reasoning which has led me to them seems so strong that I am quite certain that I would have to make the same supposition in any new world of which I have been given an account.[10]

A dispute between Descartes and a crude empiricist would look very much like a dispute between a Nazi and a Ghandian on the legitimacy of force.

All this is by way of trying to undermine the sharp distinction being drawn between our freedom to choose what to believe or accept in matters moral and in matters factual. It is not to deny that there may be important differences in the range of freedom in the two domains. But exactly what those differences are and their implications for issue of rationality and objectivity in the two realms remains to be clarified.

II

Why has it seemed to so many, and so obviously, that a notion of moral authority is impossible or incoherent? To say that nobody else can make one's moral decisions for one has the form of what Wittgenstein called a "grammatical" remark. It is like nobody else can feel my pain (for then it would be his pain and not mine). Who else could make my decisions? You may, in certain contexts, decide for another, as in the case of a parent who volunteers his child for a medical experiment. But then, quite clearly, the child has made no decision. To decide for somebody is not to make their decision. In this sense nobody else can make my medical or financial or career decisions for me. There is nothing special about moral decisions.

But I might consent to having somebody also make my moral decisions for me. I might simply accept whatever decision they would make and, therefore, let them make my decision. If *X* said that humility is a virtue, I would believe humility is a virtue. If he said I should do this thing, I would do this thing. It seems that something is wrong here in a way in which something comparable would not be wrong in scientific matters. If I am uncertain about the correct statistical test to use, or what the pain in my leg is, or why the thermostat is not working, or the number of words for 'snow' that the Eskimo have, then I consult an authority. As Aiken puts it:

> In the domain of science and logic . . . situations often arise in which we properly defer to the authority of observers whom we recognize to be more competent or qualified than ourselves. And it is because of that, without qualms, we accept certain statements as objectively true even though we ourselves do not fully see why they are so. But in morals such situations can hardly arise.[11]

Again, I want to call attention to the extent to which this picture is not accurate in either morals or science. With respect to morality, it is certainly the case that for much of human history, and for most persons, to determine what was right was to consult authorities—whether priests or the elders or the learned. To say that such a practice is not a morality is either to adopt a stipulative definition of morality or to maintain a substantive thesis about the "correct" or "rational" way in which to think about moral matters.

It is interesting to compare the making of moral judgments with esthetic judgment. Although they are both evaluative, although there is much disagreement about particular cases in both areas, the notion of authority has never drawn the same critical fire in esthetics. And, correspondingly, there has not been the same emphasis on the individual as being free to choose his own esthetic principles or standards. Thus, there has been more acceptance of the role of the expert who guides us in our perception of esthetic objects, who calls attention to the relevant features of the object, who has more experience in such matters.

Certainly someone who made no effort to test the views of experts in her own experience, who made no effort to develop her own taste in esthetic matters, would be thought esthetically shallow. But a mathematics student would be thought mathematically shallow who merely accepted the word of her teacher that such and such a theorem is true without trying to discover, or at least verify the proof of the theorem.

Without making the strong claim that matters are on a par in science and morals, one can argue that authority has some role in both. As Anscombe points out, there is a "sort of authority that can hardly be denied to exist by the most recalcitrant modern philosopher. For it is exercised by people in bringing up their children."[12] And, as Toulmin says:

> When we say "it is known that so-and-so" or "biochemistry tells us that so-and-so" . . . we do not mean that everyone knows, or that every biochemist will tell us that so-and-so. We normally imply rather that this is the "authoritative" view—both in the disciplinary sense, i.e., the view supported by the best accredited body of experience, and also in the professional sense, i.e., the view supported by the influential authorities in the subject.[13]

III

Suppose we consider the following notion of moral autonomy. A person is morally autonomous if he "cannot accept without independent consideration the judgment of others as to what he should do. If he relies on the judgment of others, he must be prepared to advance independent reasons for thinking their judgment likely to be correct."[14] The idea of there being independent reasons for thinking the judgment of an authority correct is ambiguous. There are reasons for thinking his *judgment* likely to be correct, that is, independent reasons for believing the specific content of his judgment. Or, there can be independent reasons for thinking *his* judgment to be correct, in other words, for thinking *him* likely to be right.

It is certainly true that there are many occasions in science where we do not insist that we have independent grounds for supposing the particular content of what an authority says is true. The same is true when we seek practical advice from experts, for example, my doctor's opinion on what medicine I should take. There are obvious reasons why the institution of science, and more generally our factual knowledge, should dispense with the requirement of independent checks on authority. We often lack the time, training, skill, and prior knowledge needed to make such checks. It is efficient for each of us to specialize in a few areas of competence and to draw when needed upon the resources and expertise of others. Knowledge is socially stored and there are evolutionary advantages for a species that does not require each member to acquire and retain all knowledge needed for survival and reproduction. Insofar as moral knowledge is advantageous to the species we should expect a similar division of labor there as well.

My conclusion at this point is that any strong claim about differences concerning autonomy in science and morality must rely not on a conceptual point about the nature of moral reasoning, but on a substantive ideal of the moral agent as a critical and self-conscious actor. One way of evaluating that ideal is by examining its implications for various theoretical ideals. One such ideal is that of objectivity, and I propose to discuss the compatibility of an autonomy-based moral theory with the notion of objectivity.

IV

It is clear that different moral theories will have different conceptions of what is involved in being morally autonomous. Let me just briefly illustrate the range of notions.[15] On the Kantian view autonomy is a property of the will of moral agents which allows them to act on principles and not be determined by empirical causes. We commit ourselves to moral principles by reason alone. On the Sartrean, or Hareian, view moral principles are chosen freely, are self-imposed, and cannot be given a more ultimate justification. On the Rawlsian view the parties making a hypothetical choice of principles are characterized as autonomous in the sense that they "are moved solely by their highest-order interests in their moral powers and by their concern to advance their determinate but unknown final ends."[16] In addition, the actual acceptance of principles of justice in a well-ordered society is via a theoretical argument about the original position, so that their acceptance of the principles of justice expresses their conception of themselves as autonomous and equal citizens.

I take it that the root-idea of all these conceptions is a notion of morality as constructed rather than discovered, as chosen rather than imposed. Rawls puts the view this way:

> Apart from the procedure of constructing the principles of justice, there are no moral facts. Whether certain facts are to be recognized as reasons of right and justice, or how much they are to count, can be ascertained only from within the constructive procedure; that is, from the undertakings of rational agents of construction when suitably represented as free and equal moral persons.[17]

Such autonomy-based theories must abandon the idea of the truth of moral principles, or at the least, claim that their being true is not the source of their validity for the agent. As usual, Rawls is clear about the implications of his metatheory. "Given the various contrasts between Kantian constructivism and rational intuitionism, it seems better to say that in constructivism first principles are reasonable (or unreasonable) than that they were true (or false)."[18] Given that such theories dispense with a claim to truth, what role does the notion of objectivity play within such theories? There is also the further question of an account of objectivity when applied to questions about what to do as opposed to what to believe. Let me begin by considering the question of objectivity as applied to theoretical reasoning.

Ultimately the distinction between appearance and reality lies at the heart of questions concerning objectivity. Issues of objectivity arise when we suppose that there is a difference between how things *seem* to us, and how they *really* are. As the terminology of appearance and reality indicates, metaphors of perception are dominant. We are aware that we confront experience from within a certain perspective and that attempts to gain knowledge are conditioned in various ways by the place from which we start. Once we become aware of the possibility of distortion we seek, by gaining an understanding of distorting factors, to arrive at a perspective which is more likely to bring us closer to the way things are.

There are well-known and deep philosophical difficulties associated with the idea of objectivity. Even if we understand the thought of escaping from an idiosyncratic and partial perspective to a more universal and complete one, there always remains the worry of how we are able to jump out of our own skins. For the effort to transcend our own point of view is always launched from within some point of view of our own. I do not intend to solve those problems here; for one reason because one cannot intend to do what one is not able to do. For my purposes it is sufficient to present the ideal of objectivity as fashioned for theoretical reasoning and to see if there is an analogue for theories of practical reasoning, particularly those which do not appeal to a notion of truth.

As Anscombe once put it, the point of practical reasoning is to make the world fit my thought rather than to match my thought to the world. Still there ought to be reasons to justify making the world one way rather than another. In the case of some branches of practical reasoning, for example, prudence, these reasons will have reference to the ends of the agent and the best ways of securing them. For prudential theorizing objectivity will be tied to certain practical tasks which a theory of prudence enables us to perform better or worse than alternative theories. Once we have an idea of what we want prudential theories for, we will know how to evaluate such theories as better or worse (in an objective sense.)[19]

A similar view has been taken with respect to moral reasoning. It has been characterized as an attempt to contribute to the amelioration of the human condition or to enable many persons to solve coordination problems or to promote the general good or to overcome the limitations of self-interest. I myself think that any attempt to find *a* substantive "point" or "purpose" for moral reasoning is mistaken, not least because paying attention to the historical facts shows how varied such tasks have been.[20]

Still I think that in a given historical and philosophical context one can say something illuminating about how moral discussion and theorizing is viewed at a given time, and what one might want a moral theory for. So that *relative* to a particular set of practical tasks one can have a notion of objectivity that is independent of the idea of truth.

For us, now, moral reasoning takes place in a context of seeking to find and provide reasons which will have general scope and appeal. An important motivation for moral discussion arises from desires to justify what we propose to do, or have done, to others. The importance of this idea of interpersonal justification in contemporary moral philosophy can be seen by noting the common element in various tests that have been proposed by moral philosophers: Hare's test of whether one could prescribe for oneself what one prescribes for others, Rawls's unanimity behind the veil of ignorance, Nagel's view that what one does to another must be capable of being justified to that person, and most recently (and most fully developed) Scanlon's defense of contractualism viewed as the attempt to find agreement among those who are motivated by this very desire.[21] This search for a standpoint from which the existence of other independent, equal moral agents is given full weight is the equivalent of that search for that distance from one's own perspective on the universe which defines objectivity for theoretical reasoning.

This view of objectivity is compatible with, although it does not require, the denial of truth value to moral judgments. The constraints on what is acceptable are practical. On the view being advanced here, one role of moral theory is to secure convergence in judgment, agreement by moral agents as to what should be done in particular situations. Part of the "verification" of a theory is a prediction that, over time, judgments will tend to converge. Convergence, however, is neither necessary nor sufficient for "practical" objectivity. It is not sufficient, for the explanation of the convergence may be in terms of relatively external and superficial features of human psychology, for example, brainwashing or manipulation. It is not necessary, because we have similar kinds of explanations for nonconvergence, for example, structures of exploitation may make it impossible for those in power to reason soundly.

Another set of constraints is connected with what it feels like to live by certain moral codes or to attempt to live by them. One of the values of great literature is being confronted by vivid pictures of what it is like to live by certain codes, or to seek to manifest certain virtues, or to be faced with the moral dilemmas that are raised by accepting certain ideals. Moral codes are connected with ways of living and with ideals of human flourishing. The attempt to live by certain moralities or to rehearse what that would be like is the analogue to observational testing of scientific theories. "Try it, you'll like it" is a reasonable criterion for a moral theory.

Being capable of holding up against various kinds of rational criticism, helping us to avoid moral dilemmas, leading to convergence in judgment, proving satisfying, all of these are tasks which a theory can perform better or worse, objectively considered. And all of these are tasks which may be performed by moral theories which are viewed as created or constructed rather than discovered, and which therefore are grounded in a conception of autonomy.

To the question of whether scientific objects are real, Wilfred Sellars once replied: "The correct answer is that we invent them and discover that they do the work which we require of something that is to count as real."[22] I suggest a parallel view of moral principles. We construct them and then discover that they do the work of something that is to count as a correct moral principle.

Notes

1. Cf. Dworken, *The Theory and Practice of Autonomy*, ch. 3, pp. 34–47.

2. Marcus Singer, "Freedom From Reason," *Philosophical Review* 79 (April 1970), 255.

3. R. M. Hare, *Freedom and Reason* (London: Oxford University Press, 1965), 1.

4. *Freedom and Reason*, 2.

5. H. D. Aiken, *Reason and Conduct* (New York: Alfred A. Knopf, 1962), 142.

6. *Freedom and Reason*, 2.

7. *Reason and Conduct*, 143.

8. R. P. Wolff, *In Defense of Anarchism* (New York, Harper & Row, 1979), p. 13.

9. Cf. A. Gewirth, "Positive 'Ethics' and Normative 'Science,'" *Philosophical Review* 69 (1960), 311–30.

10. Quoted in B. Ellis "Truth as a Mode of Evaluation," *Pacific Philosophical Quarterly* 61 (1980), nos. 1 & 2, 87.

11. *Reason and Conduct*, 143.

12. E. Anscombe "Authority in Morals," in R. E. Flathman, *Concepts in Social and Political Philosophy* (New York: Macmillan, 1973), 157.

13. S. Toulmin, *Human Understanding*, (Princeton: Princeton University Press, 1972), 264.

14. Thomas M. Scanlon, "A Theory of Freedom of Expression," *Philosophy and Public Affairs* 1, (Winter 1972), 216. This is not put forward by Scanlon as a conception of *moral* autonomy.

15. I am relying in part on distinctions made by Thomas Hill, Jr., in "Autonomy and Benevolent Lies," *Journal of Value Inquiry*, 18, no. 4 (1984), 251–67.

16. John Rawls, "Kantian Constructivism in Moral Theory," *Journal of Philosophy* 77, no. 9, (September 1980), 525.

17. "Kantian Constructivism," 519.

18. "Kantian Constructivism," 569.

19. Cf. D. Parfit, *Reasons and Persons* (Oxford: Oxford University Press, 1984) for discussions along these lines.

20. Cf. for example, Schneewind's view that in the seventeenth and eighteenth centuries the role of a moral code was to provide us with adequate instruction about the role that we were to play in God's plans for the cosmos. And the role of the moral theorist was to explain what the laws of morality were and to explain how we receive adequate guidance from them. ("The Divine Corporation and the History of Ethics" in

Philosophy in History, ed. Richard Rorty, J. B. Schneewind and Quentin Skinner [Cambridge: Cambridge University Press, 1984].)

21. Thomas M. Scanlon, "Contractualism and Utilitarianism," in Amartya Sen and Bernard Williams, *Utilitarianism and Beyond* (Cambridge: Cambridge University Press, 1984), pp. 103–28.

22. Wilfred Sellers "Is Scientific Realism Tenable?," ed. Fred Suppe and Peter D. Asquith, *Proceedings of the 1976 Philosophy of Science Association*, 2, (1977), 312.

16

Autonomy in Law

David A. J. Richards

Autonomy is a core value in American public and private law, since it is one of
the constitutive ingredients of the generative idea of background rights of the
person to which interpretive controversy in American law characteristically
appeals. In this essay, I first develop a general theoretical account of how and
why autonomy in American constitutional law connects to a larger moral and
political conception of self-governing agents, and then focus the account on
two concrete interpretive debates in law: the scope of liability in the criminal
law and the constitutional guarantees of the First Amendment. I build accordingly a conception of autonomy in the following stages: the minimally adequate internal capacities of agency required as threshold conditions for criminal responsibility, the external conditions of full criminal responsibility, and
the richer framework of external conditions required by the guarantees of the
First Amendment. The central focus of my argument is on the distinctive force
of these latter guarantees.

Autonomy is, I believe, a constitutive normative ingredient of American
democratic constitutionalism because it specifies the empirical and normative
conditions for the value of self-government essential to the very legitimacy of
this form of government. From its beginning in 1787, American democratic
constitutionalism has, of course, distributed the franchise more broadly than
comparable democracies (e.g., Great Britain);[1] and the progressive historical
elaboration of constitutional principles (including the fifteenth, nineteenth,
and twenty-sixth Amendments) has expanded the scope of the democratic
franchise more broadly and, on the ground of the equal protection clause of
the Fourteenth Amendment, more equitably (e.g., reapportionment of voting
power in accord with one person/one vote[2]). But self-government, in the sense
I am exploring the term, cannot focally be understood in terms of the scope
and level of distribution of voting rights, which is, at best, one aspect of the
deeper moral and political conception of self-government that I am exploring.

From its inception, the American conception of democratic constitutionalism distinguished its republican aspirations from the classical democratic

models of antiquity and the Renaissance,[3] with their Aristotelian[4] and Machiavellian[5] focus on the actively engaged and participating citizen-soldier. Political activity on the classical model was the central activity of civilized social life, preoccupying, as the slave society of ancient Athens permitted, the entire space of a well-lived life with the absorbing tasks of democratic participation.[6] Correlatively, Athens proudly touted its regime of free speech as an aspect of the more ultimate evaluative aim of democratic participation.[7] Quite absent from this conception is any valorization of a legitimately private sphere immune from politics, a point bluntly made by Pericles: "we do not say that a man who takes no interest in politics is a man who minds his own business; we say that he has no business here at all."[8] Family life, for example, is contemptuously remitted to the morally inferior class of women, whose labor is given weight only insofar as it releases men for public life;[9] work was often for slaves, releasing citizens for civil life in the agora;[10] and the political system not only failed to understand Socratic individualism, including the conception of free speech that served its moral conception,[11] it ruthlessly persecuted the uses of free speech expressive of an individualistic moral conception, uses interpreted by the Athenian democracy to be impious and heretical and thus worthy of death.[12]

The classical conception specified a richly elaborated theory and practice of democratically controlled collective political life.[13] But that conception—precisely because of its emphasis on collective mass participation—exhaustively identified the moral aims of democracy with voting and participation, and their constitutive role in the flowering of human excellences like civic generosity, military courage, heroism, patriotism, and the like, that is, the perfectionist virtues of Aristotelian ethics.[14] The moral theory of classical republicanism was thus perfectionist heroism in service of the ultimate unit of value, the polis; democratic participation was valued intrinsically as the matrix for the exercise and display of these perfectionist virtues.

I wish to say of the classical democratic conception that it lacked the ideal of self-government that motivates liberal democratic constitutionalism, and that this difference was self-consciously underscored by the very reasons offered by the Framers of the 1787 Constitution for their rejection of the classical democratic conception.[15] For one thing, mass democratic participation in government itself was decisively rejected in favor of representative principles that designedly filter and channel democratic politics in ways more likely to lead to certain substantive results, including both respect for rights and pursuit of the public good.[16] For another, rights to vote for and participate in government were viewed not as exhaustive of value in living, but as importantly instrumental to the defense and vindication of independent values, including defense of one's basic rights of the person.[17] Indeed, on this characteristically Lockean and liberal conception, voting rights were not the ends of republican politics, but the means to independently specified ends, and may be defined and weighted in whatever ways were more likely to secure these ends (e.g., the property qualifications common in American politics in 1787.)[18] Finally, the Framers deeply distrusted the perfectionist virtues of classical republicanism as the reigning political psychology of a well-functioning polity.[19] A well-designed constitutional democracy should not depend on such motives, but should be so designed (federalism, separation of powers, judicial supremacy) that it might achieve its ultimate ends without requiring the heroic virtues of classical republicanism.

What, for the American Framers, were the ultimate ends of governance? They included, importantly, the spheres of self-government that the Framers associated with inalienable rights of the person, the rights that persons could not surrender to the state, and against which the legitimacy of state power must accordingly be critically tested. The idea of such rights of the person—so foreign to classical political theory—centered, for example, on the inalienable right to conscience, the right of each person as a democratic equal to form, express, and revise personal and ethical theories of value in living as an expression of their practical rationality and reasonableness.[20] But why should these ends of government be so antagonistic to the theory of perfectionist excellence of the polity of classical republicanism?

The point is not the mistaken atomistic reading of liberalism, that is that persons are asocial monads who form their identities out of nothing. To the contrary, Locke, for example, assumed that social institutions like language framed the question of how to live a life and were, of course, presuppositions of the liberal state. Rather, the point of liberalism arose when the traditional power of certain institutions (established churches, for example)—when linked to secular power over questions of conscience—were critically rejected on the ground of the political principle of equal liberty of conscience, namely, that such exercise of secular power for sectarian ends unnaturally imposed an orthodoxy of belief to the exclusion of other equally or more reasonable beliefs, and thus usurped the rational and reasonable freedom of persons to select among such social institutions.[21] Indeed, in a straightforward sense, such an exercise of state power degraded the natural moral competence of each person, as a democratic equal, to make reasonable judgments about the basic personal and ethical values around which they organized a theory and practice of a well lived life. The right to conscience was an inalienable human right precisely because it thus defined our essential powers of self-government.

But self-government, thus understood, defines a sphere of sovereign choice among competing communities of belief, and debars a role for legitimate state power in the sectarian support of such choices; the state, on this Lockean conception, must limit itself to the pursuit of uncontroversially nonsectarian general goods like the protection of life, liberty, and property.[22] The important and radical departure of liberal political theory from classical republicanism is that self-government guarantees this sovereign choice, and thus preserves to persons a critical moral independence itself often critical of the claims of state power in the pursuit of personal and ethical ends to which legitimate state power must be accountable, not conversely. Skeptical distrust of state power over these questions arises, of course, with the breakdown of religious and moral orthodoxy in the Reformation, and the grounds for that skepticism importantly arise from a larger skepticism about traditional conceptions of authority in science, religion, ethics, and politics.

When Locke and Bayle, for example, stated their pathbreaking arguments for universal religious toleration (however cramped by contemporary standards), they focused on an incoherence in the traditional Augustinian argument for religious persecution, namely, that Augustine, on the one hand, defended respect for the integrated exercise of rational capacity, belief, and desire of the human person and then, on the other hand, imputed to any dissenter from religious orthodoxy an irrationally demonic fault in the will that, like insanity, called not for respect but for coercive intervention to protect others from irrational injury and the agent from irrational self-injury.[23] But the inference was not only wrong, but viciously circular. Augustine and his epigones took conventional standards of orthodox belief, to which they were committed, as the exclusive measure of all forms of reasonable belief, and, on this ground, imputed to dissenters lack of rational capacity, indeed raving irrationality of the sort that requires not respect but intervention. In effect, they read issues of rational and reasonable capacity through the prism of committed sectarian belief, and thus failed to accord any fair respect for the exercise of rational and reasonable capacity independent of such sectarian belief.

The analysis, in Locke and Bayle, of this political pathology is piercing, focusing as it does on the elaboration of a familiar claim of seventeenth century moral thought: the ways in which the language of moral virtue was often a rhetorical mask for entrenched self-interest, sectarian bias, the manipulative pride of power.[24] Neither Locke nor Bayle was a moral skeptic on the model of Hobbes[25] or Mandeville,[26] and they therefore did not infer from such a political pathology of self-righteousness that there were no applicable standards of ethical justification independent of self-interest. To the contrary, the argument for universal toleration was precisely in service of the political conditions that might allow the development of an ethics of equal respect uncorrupted by the moral tyrannies of sectarian self-righteousness (including, for Locke, the unconscionable legitimation of the political tyrannies of absolute monarchy.[27])

It is this perspective, I believe, that crucially explains the American Framers' rejection of the political virtues of classical republicanism as the operative political psychology of American constitutionalism. For one thing, classic republicanism's elitist Aristotelian perfectionism was inconsistent with the egalitarian ethics of equal respect that, for Framers like Madison, was the distinctive public morality of American republicanism. That egalitarian ethics, crucially made possible by respect for each person's equal liberty of conscience, was by definition an ethics whose demands could be justified to our common human nature,[28] and which, therefore, could in principle only impose burdens of civil duty that could be reasonably borne by all persons and justified to them as such. The perfectionist elitism of classical republicanism imposed self-sacrificing ideals of heroic excellence well beyond what could thus be reasonably demanded of all persons, indeed often was blatantly inconsistent with the reasonable demands of what Madison and Adams would call "human nature."[29] In effect, the enforcement at large of such controversial perfectionist ideals by the state would impose a factionalized moral view that obfuscates the legitimating responsibility of the state to respect inalienable human rights and to pursue the public good. For example, the civic virtue of the ancients not only *legitimated* slavery and the subjugation of women (in contrast, for example, to Framers' clear unease with the harsh political realities that perpetuated slavery in the new republic,[30]) but a rampant imperialism of military adventure and glory.[31] The civic virtues of classical republicanism thus were, as both Montesquieu[32] and Hume[33] made clear to the Framers, often masks for political manipulation and tyranny, an elitist ideology that self-blinded people to the moral demands of equality.[34]

The Framers' skepticism about classical virtue thus reflected the larger skepticisms of the argument for universal toleration and the egalitarian ethics of equal respect that it made possible. But, consistent with these skepticisms, the Framers believed like Locke and Bayle in ethically valid principles, and they designed their constructivist task in 1787 as mobilizing human nature, as they had skeptically come to understand it, in service of such objective principles of equal justice under law. Their fundamental political theory of legitimacy was, of course, familiarly Lockean.[35] Their innovativeness came in the way they constructed political forms (federalism, the separation of powers, judicial review premised on inalienable rights of the person immune from political bargaining) self-consciously designed to take seriously their skepticism about heroic political virtue. This skepticism took two important forms: first, the fact that many political arguments would be motivated by sectarian commitments to a person, group interest, or idea (Madison's Humean theory of faction)[36] that disabled persons from fairly giving weight to the rights and interests of those outside one's sectarian circle; and second, that aspirations for political power were importantly motivated by a competitive emulativeness for admiration and reputation (John Adams's theory of fame.)[37] Both such facts of political psychology were importantly assumed by the Framers and taken seriously as central political motivations that the constitutional construction institutionally channeled in ways more likely to achieve the objective ends of republican justice (respect for rights and pursuit of the public good). The theory of representation underlying the federal system, for example, was precisely designed, so Madison argued in No. 10 of *The Federalist*, to detoxify faction in service of republican justice;[38] the theory of separation of powers, including an independent and powerful executive, had been framed by John Adams in the Massachusetts constitution—so influential on the Framers[39]— expressly to use emulation among various branches of government as a competitive prod to republican justice.[40]

Both these assumptions of political psychology bespeak a skeptical distrust, consistent with the argument for universal toleration, of the distortions of moral judgment by political power, whether by economic interests, sectarian self-righteousness, or willful pride. The lesson to be learned from a sober reading of political history, including that of classical republicanism, was—so the Framers acutely argued—institutionally to break the easy link between sectarian moral and political judgment and political power. Indeed, from this perspective, the very commercialism of the American polity was a republican virtue, not a vice, because it focused on common economic goods and interests that created common grounds for reasonable cooperation and collaboration for persons of widely differing moral and political backgrounds.[41]

Autonomy, on this view, plays the role that it does in American constitutional law because it specifies the normative value of self-government that is the ultimate aim that the constitutional design, including voting rights, serves. But, autonomy, thus understood, has weaker and stronger normative strands.

The weakest such strand is the conception of minimal standards of criminal responsibility, that is, the capacities of epistemic and practical rationality that are the necessary predicates of criminal liability. The impositions of criminal law under American constitutional principles are, of course, among the most serious deprivations of life, liberty, and property and must accordingly require justification in ways most clearly consistent with basic constitutional values. One important aspect of this scrutiny must be close examination of the substantive grounds for criminalization on the terms of the pursuit of secular interests, for the enforcement of purely sectarian moral or political values degrades the reasonable scope of self-government essential to constitutional legitimacy; I mention this complex requirement only for completeness, and now put it aside.[42] My present concern is with another requirement, namely, that the criminal law may only be applied to persons whose conduct expresses the capacities of epistemic and practical rationality essential to self-government. If the criminal law expresses the minimal standards of action and forbearance that may reasonably be demanded of all persons, it may reasonably make these demands only on the terms that respect the capacities of persons to have known and acted on these demands, and to have planned their lives accordingly. This principle of fairness, which is lexicographically prior to aims of deterrence, protection, and reform, affords the respect for the reasonable liberty of persons in choosing to obey or not obey the law, and insures the scope for that liberty that is to be expected in a constitutional regime that dignifies the capacity of persons for self-government under the rule of law.[43]

Autonomy, thus understood, is a weak normative requirement, covering the requirements of *actus reus* under current criminal law and that form of the insanity defense limited to psychotic incapacities.[44] It requires only capacity to guide conduct by reasons, in this case, the reasons offered clearly and prospectively by the system of criminal law.

In addition, doctrines of full and partial excuse in criminal law suggest stronger normative strands of autonomy as a value in law. For example, the excuse of duress or coercion exculpates from criminal liability when a person subject to a certain coercive threat could not reasonably be expected to resist.[45] The excuse shows that the value of autonomy in law incorporates an undemanding conception of reasonable demands applicable to ordinary human nature, not the supererogatory ideals of saints and heroes. It further shows that autonomy as a normative value assumes normal external background conditions of a fair liberty and opportunity to exercise one's reasonable capacities of choice and deliberation, and that the absence of these external conditions (e.g., when under duress) negate the reasonable liberty essential to self-government. When agents are not reasonably self-governing in the required way, they are not the proper objects of punishment. This requirement of autonomy, while stronger than the minimal conditions for criminal responsibility, still only requires that the fair liberty and opportunity to exercise reasonable judgment be available; it places no further constraint on the nature of that judgment.

Autonomy in a stronger sense, indeed in the sense prefigured by my earlier reflections on American constitutionalism, appears in the respect for persons implicit in the guarantees of the First Amendment of the United States Constitution. Here the background value of autonomy is not merely respect for the capacity, liberty, or opportunity to act on reasons as such, but respect for the capacity to act on reasons that reflect one's own internal judgment of the worth or value of those reasons. We may put the point as follows: whereas autonomy in the criminal context adverts to the capacity, liberty, and opportunity to act on the reasons for action offered by the criminal law, the value of autonomy in the law of religious liberty and free speech protects people's autonomous decisions to form, express, and revise their rational and reasonable standards of value in living often precisely against the conflicting standards of reasonable value held by the state or persons who control the state.[46]

The doctrinal point—pervasive both in the law of religious liberty and free speech[47]—may be put in terms of the argument for universal toleration earlier discussed, an argument that the protections of the First Amendment self-consciously assume. The argument for universal toleration skeptically distrusts the power of the state to make impartial judgments about the scope of reasonable judgment in the formation, expression, and revision of one's religious conscience, and the moral and political judgments of ultimate value in living that are at the core of conscience. In effect, the fallacy of the Augstinian argument for religious persecution (that unreasonable beliefs—from the perspective of sectarian religious commitments—justify the inference of irrationally self-destructive madness) is generalized into a constitutional principle that is a prophylaxis against this fallacy: judgments of the state about the unreasonableness of beliefs of conscience or the irrational worthlessness of speech cannot justify the abridgement of the liberty to form, express, or revise conscience, or to make decisions to communicate or be communicated to. The state may not make repressive judgments predicated on the worth or value of conscience or speech absent some impartially verifiable ground of necessary protection from a clear and present danger of secular harm.

The moral nerve of these constitutional doctrines is protection of autonomy in a stronger sense than any we have so far examined. The point is not merely to insure that an agent has the capacity, liberty, and opportunity to act on the reasons for action offered by the criminal law, but offers protection to the exercise of reasonable judgment independent of the conventional judgments of reasonableness embodied in law and public policy. Autonomy, in this sense, protects not the agent's reasonable capacities to conform to law, but the agent's higher-order reasonableness to reflect on ultimate value in living as an independent person. Autonomy at this juncture is clearly close to the moral nerve of Kantian constructivist legislation in the kingdom of ends, for the value in law here protected is precisely the capacity for moral independence that Kant took to be foundational to the distinctive moral status of persons.[48]

Full autonomy, as a value of the First Amendment, does not, however, require the full Kantian machinery of causal indeterminism, noumenal and phenomenal worlds, and the like. The political point is not that moral persons create themselves *ex nihilo*, or are independent of all causal law or explanation. Rather, the point is that persons have a rational capacity not only to reflect on and order their own desires and appetites over time and the capacity to act on reasons supplied by the state or conventional authority, but also have a higher-order capacity to reflect on the nature and weight of all such reasons and whether they have ultimate normative authority.

The value in law of full autonomy is not a metaphysical one, nor does it arise in a vacuum of atomistically ahistorical self-creation. Contextually, as we have seen, full autonomy arises as an exigently important political issue only when pluralistic moral perspectives become in the Reformation a live issue, and when the traditional role of the state in the enforcement of sectarian value is subject to searching criticism as compromising the range of intelligence and imagination of persons in the exercise of their rationality and reasonableness in constructing conceptions of value in living in a way alternative to sectarian orthodoxy. The point is not that sectarian orthodoxy is irrational or even nonrational, but that it has so defined the scope of debate about value in living that it has deprived many reasonable persons of fair access to that debate and thus compromised the reasonableness of its own internal debates.[49]

The constitutional guarantees of full autonomy, like those of the First Amendment, are thus directed at a concrete historical context and problem, namely, the degree to which the state's enforcement of sectarian values had compromised the practical ethics of equal respect for self-government required for constitutional democracy to be a live political option. The guarantees of the First Amendment protect persons from the enforcement of sectarian conceptions of conscience or speech not because those conceptions are always irrational or without enduring value, but because each person's own exercise of reasonable judgment over the full range of such competing conceptions most fully empowers, on fair terms, the sense of self-government of free people, and thus makes possible the practical ethics of equal respect of constitutional democracy.

Self-government, in this sense, is not, properly understood, autarkic. Persons govern their lives by standards they take and adapt from the available public culture, and often do so as members of subcommunities of the larger culture, cultivating and elaborating a distinctive conception of value in living within their subcommunity in contrast to alternative conceptions available in other subcommunities of the larger society. Full autonomy, as a basic value in self-government, assumes these facts and remits to each person, not the state, the ultimate judgments of choice and deliberation over which standards and associated subcommunities best embody their reasonable conception of permanent value in living.

Persons, under such a constitutional regime of full autonomy, have responsibility for their ends in living; indeed, it is that responsibility, more focally than any other, that makes them self-governing agents. The resulting conception of constitutional government thus importantly views voting rights and participation not as the exhaustive locus of value in living, but as instrumental to a larger conception of self-government that is, of course, not exclusively or even primarily political in nature (for example, self-government in the formation of communities of conscientious belief and ways of life, or in the formation of intimate personal life and the larger ethical values that personal life expresses and promotes).

We may indeed say, or rather now more fully explain than could be done earlier, that liberal constitutional democracy incorporates in its foundational structure a conception of private spheres of self-government quite foreign to classical republicanism in which political life largely exhausts value in living.[50] Such spheres of self-government are private in the sense that they enjoy, within limits, immunity from state power, for example, the immunity of conscience and speech from state censorious judgments that is required by the principles of the First Amendment. Such spheres of self-government enable persons to take responsibility for their ends and their lives, the spheres of activity classically defined by inalienable rights of the person—those that cannot justly be surrendered to any state and against which the legitimacy of state power must accordingly be searchingly tested; for state power that abridges these rights is, by definition, illegitimate.

The constructivist problem of liberal constitutionalism—the problem so brilliantly addressed by the Framers of 1787—was to design a constitutional system that, on the one hand, immunized these spheres of self-government from political bargaining and, on the other hand, democratically mobilized the power of the state reasonably to pursue the public good in the areas justly surrendered to the state. Arguments of principle and arguments of policy roughly capture the distinction that the Framers contemplated, and that the interpretation of the constitutional system clearly contemplates (e.g., the arguments of principle central to the First Amendment and the equal protection clause of the Fourteenth Amendment versus the arguments of policy characteristic of debates over federalism).[51]

It is because the conception of voting rights and participation is in service of this more structurally complex conception of legitimate government that they occupy a different moral space in liberal constitutionalism than they did in classical republicanism. Voting rights, for example, are thought of by the Framers as importantly instrumental, that is, as ways better to secure that the state indeed respects inalienable rights and pursues the public good, and thus they are so structured and distributed, as by Madison's invocation of the representative principle in No. 10 of *The Federalist*, to pursue these ends. It is wholly consistent with the spirit of this constitutional design that, as the maldistribution of voting rights was perceived to frustrate effective respect for equal rights under law and fair pursuit of the public good, the scope and distribution of such voting rights should be more fully and fairly extended in service of these goals.

On the other hand, it is equally consistent with the liberal conception of voting rights that, since these rights do not properly extend to the abridgement of inalienable rights of the person, the scope of democratic political bargaining should not be extended to this sphere. The extraordinary efflorescence and vitality of the American conception of judicial review today depend on these distinctive normative commitments of liberal constitutionalism, for the central role of the judiciary today is largely preoccupied with monitoring the proper scope of political bargaining consistent with the underlying premises of constitutional legitimacy, namely, the inalienable rights of self-government.

Liberal constitutionalism, in contrast to classical republicanism, does not celebrate political life as the locus of value in living, but serves a more complex conception in which persons may themselves generate and pursue attractive and powerful conceptions of value in living that are pointedly apolitical or not primarily political or else sharply critical of dominant conceptions of value in living embodied in law. Indeed, self-government, in the sense central to Lockean constitutionalism, achieves its fullest expression in what I have called full autonomy, which is precisely made possible by a constitutional culture that restrains the power of the state in service of the generation of one's own rational and reasonable powers. Indeed, the distinctive mark of liberal constitutionalism is precisely its insistence on constitutionally guaranteed independent spheres not only of religion, speech, and private life but, within democratic politics, of federalism and separation of powers. Democratic politics has an important place in this conception, for the right to vote and participate is often in service of other rights and of the use of political power for the public good. But liberal culture does not define ultimate value in democratic politics as such, for its most glorious achievements may be precisely its defense on grounds of principle of what classical republicanism made possible but then ruthlessly crushed, the critical and dissenting moral individualism of Socrates.

Notes

1. See, in general, J. R. Pole, *Political Representation in England and the Origins of the American Republic* (London: Macmillan, 1966).

2. See *Baker v. Carr*, 369 U.S. 186 (1962); *Reynolds v. Sims*, 377 U.S. 533 (1964).

3. For elaboration of this theme, see ch. 2, David A. J. Richards, *Foundations of American Constitutionalism* (New York: Oxford University Press, forthcoming).

4. See, e.g., Aristotle, *The Politics of Aristotle*, trans. Ernest Barker (New York: Oxford University Press, 1962), 92–110.

5. See Machiavelli, *The Discourses*, ed. Bernard Crick, trans. Leslie J. Walker (Harmondsworth, UK: Penguin, 1970), 265–90.

6. See, e.g., Paul A. Rahe, "The Primacy of Politics in Ancient Greece," *American Historical Review* 89 (1984), 265; M. I. Finley, *Politics in the Ancient World* (Cambridge: Cambridge University Press, 1983); M. I. Finley, *Democracy Ancient and Modern*, rev. ed. (New Brunswick, N.J.: Rutgers University Press, 1985).

7. See Pericles's Funeral Oration, in Thucydides, *History of the Peloponnesian War*, trans. Rex Warner (Harmondsworth, UK: Penguin, 1954), 147.

8. Thucydides, *Peloponnesian War*, 147.

9. See Aristotle, *Politics*, 8–38.

10. See, e.g., Aristotle, *Politics*, 9–17. For pertinent comparisons of ancient and modern conceptions of work, see Hannah Arendt, *The Human Condition* (Garden City, N.Y.: Doubleday, 1959).

11. For statement of such a conception, see David Richards, *Toleration and the Constitution* (New York: Oxford University Press, 1986), chs. 6–7.

12. Socrates makes precisely this predictive point about his own fate at the hands of his fellow Athenians in Plato, *Gorgias*, trans. Terence Irwin (Oxford: Clarendon Press, 1979), 101–2. For a recent political study of the trial that rather misses the underlying conflicts of philosophical principle, see I. F. Stone, *The Trial of Socrates* (Boston: Little, Brown, 1988).

13. See, e.g., Finley, *Democracy Ancient and Modern*.

14. See, in general, Aristotle, *Nicomachean Ethics*, trans. Martin Ostwald (New York: Bobbs-Merrill, 1962).

15. I examine these reasons at much greater length in ch. 2, *Foundations of American Constitutionalism*.

16. In No. 63 of *The Federalist*, Madison characterizes the rejection of mass participation as the "true distinction" between classical republicanism and American representative government, Jacob E. Cooke, ed., *The Federalist* (Middletown, Conn.: Wesleyan University Press, 1961), 428.

17. Madison so argues in No. 10 of *The Federalist*, 56–65.

18. See, in general, Pole, *Political Representation*.

19. The rejection of such a perfectionist political morality was a prominent aspect of the constitutional thought of John Adams. See, in general, Zoltan Haraszti, *John Adams and the Prophets of Progress* (Cambridge, Mass.: Harvard University Press, 1952). In No. 51 of *The Federalist*, Madison put the same point as follows: "Ambition must be made to counteract ambition. The interest of the man must be connected with the constitutional rights of the place. It may be a reflection on human nature, that such devices should be necessary to control the abuses of government. But what is government itself but the greatest of all reflections on human nature? If men were angels, no government would be necessary", p. 349.

20. For further elaboration of this argument, see Richards, *Toleration and the Constitution*, 67–102.

21. For further discussion of these points, see Richards, *Toleration and the Constitution*, 67–162.

22. For a contemporary restatement of the same intuition, see John Rawls, "Social Unity and Primary Goods," in Amartya Sen and Bernard Williams, eds., *Utilitarianism and Beyond* (Cambridge: Cambridge University Press, 1982), 159–85.

23. For citations to pertinent texts, see Richards, *Toleration and the Constitution*, 85–98.

24. For a good general study, see Arthur O. Lovejoy, *Reflections on Human Nature* (Baltimore: Johns Hopkins Press, 1961).

25. See, in general, Thomas Hobbes, *Leviathan*, ed. Michael Oakeshott (Oxford: Basil Blackwell, 1960). There is some question whether Hobbes actually believed in psychological and ethical egoism as facts of human nature as opposed to truths of political science about life under conditions of radical intellectual and religious heterogeneity in the English Civil War. His actual ethical views may have endorsed aristocratic values far more demanding than the mean picture of *Leviathan*. See Keith Thomas, "The Social Origins of Hobbes's Political Thought," in K. C. Brown, ed. *Hobbes Studies* (Oxford: Basil Blackwell, 1965), 185–236. I am indebted for this reference to John Rawls.

26. See Mandeville, *The Fable of the Bees*, ed. Phillip Harth (Harmondsworth, UK: Penguin, 1970). For useful commentary, see M. M. Goldsmith, *Private Vices, Public Benefits: Bernard Mandeville's Social and Political Thought* (Cambridge: Cambridge University Press, 1985).

27. See, in general, John Locke, *Two Treatises of Government*, ed. Peter Laslett (Cambridge: Cambridge University Press, 1960).

28. Cf. T. M. Scanlon, "Contractualism and Utilitarianism," in Sen and Williams, *Utilitarianism and Beyond*, 103–28.

29. Madison writes: "What is government itself but the greatest of all reflections on human nature?" *The Federalist*, 349; and Adams writes of Sparta: "Human nature perished under this frigid system of national and family pride," John Adams, *A Defence of the Constitutions of Government of the United States of America*, in Charles Francis Adams, ed., *The Works of John Adams*, vol. IV (Boston: Little, Brown, 1851), 554.

30. See, e.g., Herbert J. Storing, "Slavery and the Moral Foundations of the American Republic," in Robert H. Horowitz, ed. *The Moral Foundations of the American Republic*, 3d ed. (Charlottesville: University Press of Virginia, 1986), 313–32; but cf. Paul Finkelman, "Slavery and the Constitutional Convention: Making a Covenant with Death," in Richard Beeman, Stephen Botein, and Edward C. Carter II, eds., *Beyond Confederation: Origins of the Constitution and American National Identity* (Chapel Hill: University of North Carolina Press, 1987), 188–225.

31. See Finley, *Politics in the Ancient World*, 17; and *Democracy Ancient and Modern*, 87.

32. See, e.g., Montesquieu, *The Spirit of the Laws*, trans. Thomas Nugent (New York: Hafner, 1949), vol. 1, 34–39. For pertinent commentary, see Thomas L. Pangle, *Montesquieu's Philosophy of Liberalism* (Chicago: University of Chicago Press, 1973), 48–106; Judith Shklar, *Ordinary Vices* (Cambridge, Mass.: Harvard University Press, 1984), 33, 196–97, 233.

33. See, e.g., James Moore, "Hume's Political Science and the Classical Republican Tradition," *Canadian Journal of Political Science* 10 (1977), 809–39; David Miller, *Philosophy and Ideology in Hume's Political Thought* (Oxford: Clarendon Press, 1981), 121, 150–51.

34. Cf. Martin Diamond, "Ethics and Politics: The American Way," in Horwitz, *Moral Foundations*, 75–108.

35. I develop this theme at greater length in Richards, *Foundations of American Constitutionalism*.

36. See, e.g., No. 10, *The Federalist*, 56–65. For David Hume's development of the idea, see, e.g., "Of Parties in General," in *Essays Moral, Political and Literary* (Oxford: Oxford University Press, 1963), 54–62.

37. John Adams gave his most extended philosophical explication of this theory in his *Discourses on Davila*, in C. F. Adams, ed., *Works of John Adams*, vol. VI, 232–81.

38. See, for useful general commentary, David F. Epstein, *The Political Theory of the Federalist* (Chicago: University of Chicago Press, 1984); Morton White, *Philosophy, The Federalist, and the Constitution* (New York: Oxford University Press, 1987).

39. On the impact of the Massachusetts executive on the thinking of the Framers, see *The Federalist*, 327–28, 464, 499. A reference to "the ablest adepts in political science," *Federalist*, 445, is probably to Adams himself. See also *id.*, 472. Adams had created for Massachusetts the strongest executive among the state constitutions, elected by the people independent of the legislature and with a suspensive veto (Adams had preferred an absolute veto). See R. R. Palmer, *The Age of the Democratic Revolution*,

vol. I (Princeton: Princeton University Press, 1959), 225. Adams's constitutional theory, elaborated at length in his *Defence of the Constitutions of Government*, was that, consistent with the political psychology of fame and a reasonable political science of comparative constitutions, such political independence should recommend itself to Lockean constitutionalists as a reasonable way to give the executive the incentives to perform executive functions justly and to resist the ambitions of political leaders in other branches of government that would otherwise corrupt republicanism into aristocracy. See, e.g., *A Defence*, in C. F. Adams, *Works of John Adams*, vol. IV, 585, and vol. VI, 171–72. On the same grounds, Adams also defended an upper house. See, e.g., *Defence*, vol. VI, 44.

40. Madison echoes this argument in No. 51, *The Federalist*, 347–53.

41. See, e.g., Ralph Lerner, *The Thinking Revolutionary: Principle and Practice in the New Republic* (Ithaca, N.Y.: Cornell University Press, 1987), 195–221.

42. The most important recent philosophical exploration of this idea is Joel Feinberg's multivolume, *The Moral Limits of the Criminal Law*. See Joel Feinberg, *Harm to Others* (New York: Oxford University Press, 1984); *Offense to Others* (New York: Oxford University Press, 1985); and *Harm to Self* (New York: Oxford Univesity Press, 1986). See also David Richards, *Sex, Drugs, Death and the Law: An Essay on Decriminalization and Human Rights* (Totowa, N.J.: Rowman & Littlefield, 1982).

43. For a powerful statement of this view, see H. L. A. Hart, *Punishment and Responsibility: Essays in the Philosophy of Law* (New York: Oxford University Press, 1968), 1–27.

44. See, in general, Hart, *Punishment and Responsibility*, 28–53.

45. See, e.g., commentary on the Model Penal Code's formulation of the defense of duress, in Sanford H. Kadish, Stephen J. Schulhofer, and Monrad G. Paulsen, *Criminal Law and Its Processes*, 4th ed. (Boston: Little, Brown, 1983), 795–96.

46. See, for elaboration of this view, Richards, *Toleration and the Constitution*, 67–227.

47. See *Toleration and the Constitution*, 67–227.

48. See Immanuel Kant, *Foundations of the Metaphysics of Morals*, trans. Lewis White Beck (New York: Macmillan, 1959), 59. For a recent restatement of this moral vision, see John Rawls, "Kantian Constructivism in Moral Theory," *Journal of Philosophy* 77 (1980), 515.

49. Cf. Thomas Nagel, "Moral Conflict and Political Legitimacy," *Philosophy and Public Affairs* 16 (1987), 215.

50. See Richards, *Toleration and the Constitution*, 231–54. Benjamin Constant marked the distinction as that between ancient liberty (that lacked the idea of private spheres) and modern liberty (that distinguishes private and public spheres). See, in general, Stephen Holmes, *Benjamin Constant and the Making of Modern Liberalism* (New Haven: Yale University Press, 1984).

51. I explore these points at greater length in Richards, *Foundations of American Constitutionalism*. The distinction between arguments of principle and policy is a prominent feature of the jurisprudence of Ronald Dworkin. See, in general, Ronald Dworkin, *Taking Rights Seriously* (Cambridge, Mass.: Harvard University Press, 1977); and *Law's Empire* (Cambridge, Mass.: Harvard University Press, 1986).

Bibliography

Allen, R. T. 1982. "Rational Autonomy: The Destruction of Freedom," *Journal of Philosophy of Education* 16: 199–207.

Arneson, Richard. 1980. "Mill Versus Paternalism," *Ethics* 90, no. 4: 470–89.

————— 1985. "Freedom and Desire," *Canadian Journal of Philosophy* 15, no. 3: 425–48.

Arrow, Kenneth. 1977. "Extended Sympathy and the Possibility of Social Choice," *American Economic Review Papers and Proceedings (Feb.)*: 219–25.

Asch, S. 1956. "Studies of Independence and Conformity I. A Minority of One Against a Unanimous Majority," *Psychological Monographs: General and Applied* 70, no. 9.

Beardsley, Elizabeth. 1971. "Privacy: Autonomy and Selective Disclosure," in R. Pennock and J. Chapman, eds., *Nomos Vol. VIII: Privacy*. New York: Atherton Press, 56–70.

Beauchamp, Thomas L., and James Childress. 1979. *Principles of Medical Ethics*. New York: Oxford University Press.

Benn, S. I. 1967. "Freedom and Persuasion," *Australasian Journal of Philosophy* 45: 259–75.

————— 1976. "Freedom, Autonomy and the Concept of a Person," *Proceedings of the Aristotelian Society* 66: 109–130.

————— 1982. "Individuality, Community and Autonomy," in E. Kamenka, ed., *Community*. London: E. Arnold Publishers.

————— and R. S. Peters. 1959. *Social Principles and the Democratic State*. London: Allen and Unwin, Ltd.

————— 1988. *A Theory of Freedom*. Cambridge: Cambridge University Press.

————— and W. L. Weinstein. 1971. "Being Free to Act and Being a Free Man," *Mind* 80: 194–211.

Benson, John. 1983. "Who is the Autonomous Man?" *Philosophy* 58: 5–17.

Benson, Paul. 1987. "Freedom and Value," *Journal of Philosophy* 84, no. 9: 465–87.

Berlin, Isaiah. 1969. "Two Concepts of Liberty," in *Four Essays on Liberty*. Oxford: Oxford University Press.

Bernstein, M. 1983. "Socialization and Autonomy," *Mind* 92: 120–23.

Berofsky, Bernard, ed. 1966. *Freewill and Determinism*. New York: Harper and Row.

Bettelheim, Bruno. 1979. *The Informed Heart*. London: Free Press.

Brandt, Richard. 1979. *A Theory of the Good and the Right*. Oxford: Oxford University Press.

Braybrook, David. 1974. "From Economics to Aesthetics: The Rectification of Prefer-
    ences," *Nous* 8: 13–24.
Brock, Dan. 1983. "Paternalism and Promoting the Good," in Rolf Sartorius, ed.
    Paternalism, Minneapolis, Minn.: University of Minnesota Press, 237–60.
Christman, John. 1987. "Autonomy: A Defense of the Split-Level Self," *Southern
    Journal of Philosophy* 25, no. 3: 281–93.
——— 1988. "Constructing the Inner Citadel: Recent Work on Autonomy," *Ethics* 99,
    no. 1: 109–24.
Connolly, William. 1974. *The Terms of Political Discourse*. Lexington, Mass.: D.C.
    Heath & Co.
Crocker, Lawrence. 1980. *Positive Liberty*. The Hague: Martinus Nijhoff.
Cyert, R. M., and DeGroot, M. H. 1975. "Adaptive Utility," in R. Day and T. Groves,
    eds., *Adaptive Economic Models*. New York: Academic Press.
Day, J. P. 1970. "On Liberty and the Real Will," *Philosophy* 45: 177–92.
Dearden, R. F. 1972. "Autonomy and Education," in R. F. Dearden et al., eds.,
    Education and the Developments of Reason. London: Routledge and Kegan
    Paul, pp. 451–52.
——— 1975. "Autonomy as an Educational Ideal I," in S. C.. Brown, ed., *Philosophers
    Discuss Education*. London: Macmillan.
Dennet, Daniel. 1985. *Elbow Room: The Varieties of Free Will Worth Wanting*.
    Oxford: Clarendon Press.
Downie, R. S., and E. Telfer. 1971. "Autonomy," *Philosophy* 46: 296–301.
Dworkin, Gerald. 1970. "Acting Freely," *Nous* 4, no. 4: 367–83.
——— 1976. "Autonomy and Behavior Control," *Hastings Center Report* 6: 23–28.
——— 1978. "Moral Autonomy," in H. Tristram Englehardt, Jr., and Daniel Callahan,
    eds., *Morals, Science and Sociality*. New York: Hastings Center, 1978.
——— 1982. "Is More Choice Better Than Less?" *Midwest Studies in Philosophy VIII.*
    Minneapolis: University of Minnesota Press, 47–62.
——— 1988. *The Theory and Practice of Autonomy*. Cambridge: Cambridge University
    Press.
Edwards, Rem. 1981. "Mental Health as Rational Autonomy," *Journal of Medicine
    and Philosophy* 6: 309–21.
Elster, Jon. 1976. "A Note on Hysteresis in the Social Sciences," *Synthese* 33: 371–91.
——— 1978a. *Logic and Society*. London: Wiley.
——— 1979. *Ulysses and the Sirens*. Cambridge: Cambridge University Press.
——— 1983. *Sour Grapes*. Cambridge: Cambridge University Press.
——— 1984. "Belief, Bias and Ideology," in M. Hollis and S. Lukes, eds., *Rationality
    and Relativism*. Cambridge, Mass.: MIT Press, pp. 123–48.
Engelhardt, H. Tristram, Jr. 1986. *The Foundations of Bioethics*. New York: Oxford
    University Press.
Engels, F. 1975. *The Condition of the Working Class in England*, in Marx and Engels,
    Collected Works, Vol. 4. London: Lawrence and Wishart.
Engstrom, Stephen. "Conditioned Autonomy," *Philosophy and Phenomenological Re-
    search* 48, no. 3: 435–53.
Farber, L. 1976. *Lying, Despair, Jealousy, Envy, Sex, Suicide, Drugs, and the Good
    Life*. New York: Basic Books.
Feinberg, Joel. 1970. *Doing and Deserving*. Princeton: Princeton University Press.
——— 1973. *Social Philosophy*. Englewood Cliffs, N.J.: Prentice Hall.
——— 1986. *Harm To Self*, vol. 3 of *The Moral Limits of the Criminal Law*. New York:
    Oxford University Press.

Festinger, L. 1957. *A Theory of Cognitive Dissonance*. Stanford, Calif.: Stanford University Press.

—— 1964. *Conflict, Decision, and Dissonance*. Stanford, Calif.: Stanford University Press.

Fischer, John Martin, ed. 1986. *Moral Responsibility*. Ithaca, N.Y.: Cornell University Press.

Flathman, Richard. 1987. *The Philosophy and Politics of Freedom*. Chicago: University of Chicago Press.

Fleming, N. 1981. "Autonomy of the Will," *Mind* 90: 201–23.

Frankfurt, Harry. 1972. "Coercion and Moral Responsibility," in Ted Hondrich, ed., *Essays on Freedom of Action*. London: Routledge and Kegan Paul, pp. 65–86.

—— 1975. "Three Concepts of Free Action: II," *Proceedings of the Aristotelian Society* 49: 113–25.

—— 1987. "Identification and Wholeheartedness," in F. Shoeman, ed., *Responsibility, Character and the Emotions*. Cambridge: Cambridge University Press, 27–45.

Friedman, Marilyn. 1986. "Autonomy and the Split-Level Self," *Southern Journal of Philosophy* 24, no. 1: 19–35.

Garrison, James. 1986. "The Paradox of Indoctrination: A Solution," *Synthese* 68: 261–73.

Gewirth, Alan. 1978. *Reason and Morality*. Chicago: University of Chicago Press.

Goldman, Alvin. 1972. "Toward a Theory of Social Power," *Philosophical Studies* 23: 221–68.

Goodin, Robert. 1981. "The Political Theories of Choice and Dignity," *American Philosophical Quarterly* 18: 91–100.

Gray, John. 1983. *Mill on Liberty: A Defense*. London: Routledge and Kegan Paul.

Gross, H. 1971. "Privacy and Autonomy," in J. W. Chapman and J. R. Pennock, eds., *Nomos VIII: Privacy*. New York: Atherton, 169–81.

Grünbaum, A. 1971. "Free Will and the Laws of Human Behavior," *American Philosophical Quarterly* 8: 299–312.

Gutmann, Amy. 1980. "Children, Paternalism and Education," *Philosophy and Public Affairs* 9: 338–58.

Hampshire, Stuart. 1975. *Freedom and the Individual*. Princeton: Princeton University Press.

Haworth, Lawrence. 1986. *Autonomy: An Essay in Philosophical Psychology and Ethics*. New Haven: Yale University Press.

Hill, Sharon. 1975. "Self Determination and Autonomy," in Richard Wasserstrom, ed., *Today's Moral Problems*. New York: Macmillan: 118–33.

Hill, Thomas. 1984. "Autonomy and Benevolent Lies," *Journal of Value Inquiry* 18, no. 4: 251–67.

—— 1987. "The Importance of Autonomy," in E. Feder Kittay and D. Meyers, eds., *Women and Moral Theory*. Totowa, N.J.: Rowman and Littlefield, 129–38.

Hondrich, Ted, ed. 1973. *Essays on Freedom of Action*. London: Routledge and Kegan Paul.

Hurka, Thomas. 1987. "Why Value Autonomy?" *Social Theory and Practice* 13, no. 3: 361–82.

Husak, Douglas. 1980. "Paternalism and Autonomy," *Philosophy and Public Affairs* 10: 27–46.

Jeffrey, Richard. 1974. "Preference Among Preferences," *Journal of Philosophy* 71 (July): 377–91.

Kant, I. 1969. *Foundations of the Metaphysics of Morals*, translated by Lewis White Beck, with Critical Essays, edited by R. P. Wolff. New York: Bobbs-Merrill.

Katz, Jay. 1984. *The Silent World of Doctor and Patient*. New York: Free Press.

Kenny, A. 1965/6. "Happiness" *Proceedings of the Aristotelian Society*, 66: 93–102.

Kleinig, John. 1983. *Paternalism*. Totowa, N.J.: Rowman and Allenheld.

Kolm, S. C. 1979. "La Philosophie Buddhiste et les 'Hommes Economiques,'" *Social Science Information* 18: 489–588.

Kuflick, Arthur. 1984. "The Inalienability of Autonomy," *Philosophy and Public Affairs* 13: 271–98.

Ladenson, R. F. 1975. "A Theory of Personal Autonomy," *Ethics* 86: 30–48.

Lindley, Richard. 1986. *Autonomy*. London: Macmillan.

Lukes, Steven. 1974. *Individualism*. Oxford: Basil Blackwell.

—— 1974. *Power. A Radical View*. London: Macmillan.

MacCallum, Gerald. 1967. "Negative and Positive Freedom," *Philosophical Review* 76: 312–32.

MacIntyre, Alasdair. 1957. "Determinism," in Bernard Berofsky, ed., *Freedom and Determinism*. New York: Harper and Row, 240–54.

Merton, R. K. 1957. *Social Theory and Social Structure*. Glencoe, Ill.: Free Press.

Meyer, Michael J. 1987. "Stoics, Rights and Autonomy," *American Philosophical Quarterly* 24: no. 3: 267–71.

Meyers, Diana. 1987. "Personal Autonomy and the Paradox of Feminine Socialization," *Journal of Philosophy* 84, no. 11: 619–28.

—— 1987a. "The Socialized Individual and Individual Autonomy: An Intersection Between Philosophy and Psychology," in E. Feder Kittay and D. Meyers, eds., *Women and Moral Theory*. Totowa, N.J.: Rowman and Littlefield, 139–53.

Mill, J. S. 1975. *On Liberty*, David Spitz, ed. New York: Norton.

Miller, Bruce. 1981. "Autonomy and the Refusal of Life-Saving Treatment," *Hastings Center Report* 11, no. 4 (August): 22–28.

Nagel, Thomas. 1986. *The View From Nowhere*. Oxford: Oxford University Press.

Nauta, Lolle. 1985. "Historical Roots of the Concept of Autonomy in Western Philosophy," *Praxis* 4, no. 4: 363–77.

Neely, Wright. 1974. "Freedom and Desire" *Philosophical Review* 83: 32–54.

Nozick, Robert. 1969. "Coercion," in Sidney Morgenbesser et al., eds., *Philosophy, Science and Method: Essays in Honor of Ernest Nagel*. New York: St. Martins Press.

—— 1974. *Anarchy, State and Utopia*. New York: Basic Books.

Parent, W. D. 1974. "Some Recent Work on the Concept of Liberty," *American Philosophical Quarterly* 11: 149–67.

Parfit, Derick. 1984. *Reasons and Persons*. Oxford: Oxford University Press.

Pateman, Carole, and Elizabeth Gross, eds. 1986. *Feminist Challenges*. Boston: Northeastern University Press.

Penhelhum, Terrence. 1976. "Self Identity and Self Regard," in Amelie Rorty, ed., *The Identities of Persons*. Berkeley: University of California Press, 253–80.

—— 1979. "Human Nature and External Desires," *The Monist* 62: 304–19.

Rachels, James. 1975. "Why Privacy is Important," *Philosophy and Public Affairs* 4: 323–33.

—— 1986. *The Ends of Life: Euthanasia and Morality*. Oxford: Oxford University Press.

Rawls, John. 1971. *A Theory of Justice*. Cambridge, Mass.: Harvard University Press.

——— 1980. "Kantian Constructivism in Moral Theory," *Journal of Philosophy* 77: 515–79.

——— 1982. "Social Unity and the Primary Goods," in Amartya Sen and Bernard Williams, *Utilitarianism and Beyond.* Cambridge: Cambridge University Press, 159–86.

Raz, J. 1982. "Liberation, Autonomy and the Politics of Neutral Concern," *Midwest Studies in Philosophy* 7: 89–120.

——— 1986. *The Morality of Freedom.* Oxford: Clarendon Press.

Richards, David. 1977. "Unnatural Acts and the Constitutional Rights to Privacy: A Moral Theory," *Fordham Law Review* 45: 1281–1348.

——— 1979. "Sexual Autonomy and the Constitutional Right to Privacy: A Case Study in Human Rights and the Unwritten Constitution" *Hastings Law Journal* 30: 957–1018.

Rorty, Amelie, ed. 1976. *The Identities of Persons.* Berkeley: University of California Press.

Sartorius, Rolf. 1983. *Paternalism.* Minneapolis: University of Minnesota Press.

Sanders, Steven. 1982. "Autonomy, Authority and Moral Education," *Journal of Social Philosophy* 13 (May): 1824.

Scanlon, Thomas M. 1972. "A Theory of Freedom of Expression," *Philosophy and Public Affairs* 1 (Winter): 204–26.

Schelling, Thomas. 1978. "Economics, or the Art of Self-Management," *American Economic Review* 68: 290–94.

Schrader, George A. 1969. "Autonomy, Heteronomy, and Moral Imperatives," in I. Kant *Foundations of Metaphysics of Morals*, trans. L. W. Beck, with critical essays, ed. by R. P. Wolff. New York: Bobbs-Merrill, 117–33.

Sen, Amartya. 1975. *Employment, Technology, and Development.* Oxford: Oxford University Press.

——— 1977. "Rational Fools: A Critique of the Behavioral Foundations of Economic Theory," *Philosophy and Public Affairs* 6: 317–44.

——— 1979. "Utilitarianism and Welfarism," *Journal of Philosophy* 76, no. 9: 463–89.

——— and Bernard Williams. 1982. *Utilitarianism and Beyond.* Cambridge: Cambridge University Press.

Siegler, Mark. 1977. "Critical Illness: The Limits of Autonomy," *Hastings Center Report* 8:12–15.

Skinner, B. F. 1971. *Beyond Freedom and Dignity.* New York: Alfred Knopf.

Smith, G. W. 1987. "J. S. Mill on Freedom," in Zbigniew Pelcynski and John Gray, eds., *Conceptions of Liberty in Political Philosophy.* New York: St. Martins Press, 182–216.

Stouffer, S., et al. 1949. *The American Soldier.* Princeton: Princeton University Press.

Strachey, J. 1954–75. *Standard Edition of the Complete Psychological Works of Sigmund Freud*, vols. I–XXIV. London: Hogarth Press.

Strawson, Galen. 1986. *Freedom and Belief.* Oxford: Oxford University Press.

Strawson, P. F. 1968. "Freedom and Resentment" in *Studies in the Philosophy of Thought and Action.* Oxford: Oxford University Press.

Taylor, Charles. 1976. "Responsibility for Self," in Amelie Rorty, ed., *The Identities of Persons.* Berkeley: University of California Press, 281–99.

Thalberg, Irving. 1979. "Socialization and Autonomous Behavior," *Tulane Studies in Philosophy* 28: 21–37.

Van de Veer, D. 1979. "Autonomy Respecting Paternalism," *Social Theory and Practice* 6: 187–207.

Veatch, Robert. 1979. *A Theory of Medical Ethics*. New York: Basic Books.

von Weiszacker, C. C. 1971. "Notes on Endogenous Chage of Taste," *Journal of Economic Theory* 3: 345–72.

Watson, Gary, ed. 1982. *Free Will*. Oxford: Oxford University Press.

―― 1987. "Free Action and Free Will," *Mind* 96, no. 384: 145–72.

Watzlawick, P. 1978. *The Language of Change*. New York: Basic Books.

Wikler, Daniel. 1979. "Paternalism and the Mildly Retarded," *Philosophy and Public Affairs* 8: 377–92.

Williams, Bernard. 1976. "Persons, Character, and Morality" in Amelie Rorty, ed., *The Identities of Persons*. Berkeley: University of California Press, 197–216.

Wolf, Susan. "The Importance of Free Will," *Mind* 90 (July): 386–405.

Wolff, Robert Paul. 1979. *In Defense of Anarchism*. New York: Harper and Row.

Yaari, Menahem. 1977. "Endogenous Changes in Tastes: A Philosophical Discussion," *Erkenntnis* 11: 157–96.

Young, Robert. 1979. "Compatibilism and Conditioning," *Nous* 13: 361–78.

―― 1980. "Autonomy and Socialization," *Mind* 89 (October): 565–76.

―― 1986. *Personal Autonomy: Beyond Negative and Positive Liberty*. New York: St. Martin's Press.

Zimmerman, David. 1981. "Hierarchical Motivation and Freedom of the Will," *Pacific Philosophical Quarterly* 62: 354–68.

Index